PERSUASION AND SOCIAL MOVEMENTS

Second Edition

Is Bush's war on drugs an institutionalized movement?

PERSUASION AND SOCIAL MOVEMENTS

Second Edition

Charles J. Stewart

Purdue University

Craig Allen Smith

University of North Carolina at Chapel Hill

Robert E. Denton, Jr.

Virginia Polytechnic Institute and State University

Prospect Heights, Illinois

For information about this book, write or call:
Waveland Press, Inc.
P.O. Box 400
Prospect Heights, Illinois 60070
(312) 634-0081

ISBN 0-88133-451-0

Printed in the United States of America

7 6 5 4 3 2 1

Contents

Preface xi

Part One: The Roles of Persuasion in Social Movements

1 The Social Movement as a Unique Collective Phenomenon 3

An Organized Collectivity 5
An Uninstitutionalized Collectivity 6
Large in Scope 8
Proposes or Opposes Change 9
Moral in Tone 11
Encounters Opposition 12
Persuasion Is Pervasive 13
Conclusions 17

2 The Life Cycle of Social Movements 21

Stage 1: Genesis 22
Stage 2: Social Unrest 24
Stage 3: Enthusiastic Mobilization 25
Stage 4: Maintenance 28
Stage 5: Termination 30
Conclusions 32

3 Leadership in Social Movements 35

The Nature of Leadership in Social Movements 37
How Leadership Is Attained in Social Movements 39
How Leadership Is Maintained in Social Movements 43
Conclusions 48

4 A Typology of Political Argument 53

Rossiter's Political Spectrum 54
Insurgent Argument 57
Innovative Argument 58
Progressive Argument 60
Retentive Argument 61
Reversive Argument 63
Restorative Argument 64
Revolutionary Argument 65
Conclusions 67

5 A Rhetoric of Legitimation 71

The Notion of Legitimacy 71
The Social Movement's Rhetorical Situation 72
Legitimacy Through Coactive Strategies 74
Legitimacy Through Confrontational Strategies 76
Conclusions 78

6 Resistance to Social Movements 83

Establishments and Social Order 83
Democracy and Resistance to Social Movements 85
Administrative Rhetoric 87
The Strategy of Avoidance 88
The Strategy of Suppression 90
The Strategy of Adjustment 92
The Strategy of Capitulation 93
Conclusions 93

Part Two: Approaches to the Study of Social Movement Persuasion

7 A Social Systems Approach to Social Movement Persuasion 99

Systems Theory and Communication 99
Mechanical vs. Social Systems 103
Views of Influence, Conflict, and Relationships 105
Social Systems and Criticism 110
Conclusions 115

8 A Functional Approach to Social Movement Persuasion 119

A Functional Scheme for Studying Persuasion in Social Movements 120
Transforming Perceptions of History 122
Transforming Perceptions of Society 125
Prescribing Courses of Action 127
Mobilizing for Action 129
Sustaining the Movement 131
Conclusions 132

9 A Burkean Approach to Social Movement Persuasion 137

Kenneth Burke's Philosophy of Human Communication 137
Kenneth Burke's Theory of Dramatism 139
Key Concepts in Burkean Theory 143
Burkean Analysis of Social Movements 148
Conclusions 154

Part Three: Studies of Social Movement Persuasion

10 The Authoritarian Character of the John Birch Society 159

The John Birch Society 159
Characteristics of Authoritarianism 161
The Authoritarian Dimension of Birch Society Persuasion 164
The Authoritarian vs. Closed-Mind Theses Compared 169
Conclusions 170

11 A Rhetoric of Transcendence: Pro-Life Responds to Pro-Choice 175

A Rhetoric of Transcendence 175
The Abortion Issue 177
Pro-Choice Confronts Pro-Life 178
Pro-Life Responds to Pro-Choice 179
A Contrasting of Rights 180
In Defense of the Movement 181
Conclusions 187

12 The Panama Canal Treaties and Argument from Narrative Vision 193

Narrative and Rhetorical Vision 193
The Politics of Renegotiation, 1964-1978 196
The Past: America's Claim to the Canal 200
The Present: The Western Hemisphere Today 203
The Future: The Kind of Power We Wish to Be 205
Discussion 206
Conclusions 208

13 The Persuasive Functions of Songs 213
Transforming Perceptions of History 216
Transforming Perceptions of Society 217
Prescribing Courses of Action 222
Mobilizing the Movement 225
Sustaining the Movement 228
Conclusions 230

14 The Persuasive Functions of Slogans 233
The Nature of Slogans 233
Slogans as Tools of Persuasion 235
Types of Slogans 237
Persuasive Functions of Slogans 238
Conclusions 250

15 Obscenity and Social Protest 253
The Act of Swearing 253
Definition and Forms of Swearing 254
Obscenity as Rhetoric 255
Obscenity as Confrontational Rhetoric 256
Rhetorical Characteristics of Obscenity 257
The Persuasive Functions of Obscenity 259
Adverse Effects of Obscenity on Social Protest 267
Conclusions 269

Part Four: Conclusions and Bibliography

16 Summary and Conclusion 277

Selected Bibliography 281
Articles 281
Book Chapters 295
Books 296
Sources of the Persuasive Efforts of Social Movements 301

Index 303

Preface

Why a book about persuasion and social movements? Ever since neanderthals thought their tribe's "system" needed alterations, social movements have directly or indirectly provided the impetus for almost all important socio-political changes. In just over a century in our country alone, social movements have contributed to the freeing of the slaves, the end of child labor, the suffrage of blacks, women, and 18-20 year olds, the eight-hour workday and the forty-hour week, direct election of U.S. Senators, the graduated income tax, social security, collective bargaining, prohibition, the end of prohibition, and desegregation of public facilities and schools.

Nevertheless, only recently have people begun to regard social movements as more than nuisances to be harshly corrected. Studies of social movements were encouraged in the field of speech-communication as early as 1923, and they received periodic attention from such writers as Donald C. Bryant, Dallas Dickey, and Bower Aly. But the first serious discussion of *how* one should study the persuasive efforts of social movements did not appear until 1947 when S. Judson Crandell discussed social movement patterns developed by social psychologists and offered suggestions to the prospective rhetorical critic. Five years later, Leland Griffin's "The Rhetoric of Historical Movements" presented a rudimentary "rhetorical" pattern for movement studies and a workable approach to the criticism of social movements. The 1950s and 1960s witnessed an increased interest in the persuasive dimensions of social movements, but the intellectual advances were modest. Many studies fell into the ruts left by generations of rhetorical critics. For example, some authors spent most of their time trying to demonstrate that the "public speaking" in a movement was all important—at the expense of other kinds of communication. Other authors could not avoid pursuing the worst sort of "neo-Aristotelian" criticism. A 1964 master's thesis about the woman's suffrage movement, for example, asked whether the speakers were formally trained and whether their speeches were consistent with the classical teachings of invention, disposition, memory, style, and delivery. These early studies investigated few topics with the thoroughness needed either for theory building or for the understanding of complex historical events.

This state of affairs began to change rapidly with the dawn of the 1970s, undoubtedly in part because social movements had become commonplace on most college campuses. Three publications more than any others helped us turn an intellectual corner. Herbert Simons' "Requirements, Problems, and Strategies: A Theory of Persuasion for Social Movements," published in 1970, was the first methodological statement since Griffin's 1952 article. Simons synthesized the notions of social-psychological resources, situational tasks, and rhetorical adaptation into an emphasis upon the social movement's management of its persuasive resources—a leader-centered approach to social movements. *The Rhetoric of Agitation and Control* by John Bowers and Donovan Ochs appeared the next year. It was the first book about persuasion and social movements that was not primarily a collection of speeches and the first to focus on the methods used by institutions to counter the persuasive efforts of social movements. Then in 1972 Simons wrote "Persuasion in Social Conflicts: A Critique of Prevailing Conceptions and a Framework for Future Research," arguing that most previous research had reflected an establishment bias by focusing on persuasive tactics more appropriate for the drawingroom than for the streets.

The contributions of these three works are evident in both the quantity and quality of social movement studies since the early 1970s. Most issues of speech-communication journals have included at least one "movement" study, and in 1980 an entire issue of the *Central States Speech Journal* was devoted to the study of persuasion and social movements. Literally hundreds of articles and book chapters have generated thought-provoking results, research approaches, and controversies. Many students of persuasion and social movements—whether undergraduates, graduates, or professors—have experienced difficulties in understanding and using the results and approaches and in resolving the controversies that have often appeared in brief and highly sophisticated journal articles. We conceived this book, in part, as a solution to this state of affairs. Our purpose was threefold: to synthesize, to extend, and to apply many of the findings, theories, and approaches generated since the late 1960s.

This book is divided into four parts. Part One focuses on the role of persuasion in social movements and includes chapters that explore the characteristics of social movements, their typical life cycle, the sources of leadership, a typology of political argument, a rhetoric of legitimacy, and the nature of resistance. Part Two contains chapters that outline three symbolic interactionist frameworks for studying social movement persuasion—a social systems model, a functional scheme, and a Burkean or dramatistic approach. Part Three presents six studies of social movement persuasion. Three critical analyses examine the interdependence of personality and message appeal, the role of transcendent moral argument, and the role of narrative rationality in the mobilization of discontent, while three empirical studies consider the persuasive functions of protest songs, slogans, and obscenities. Part Four contains conclusions and a comprehensive bibliography.

We have approached this book with five fundamental assumptions. The first assumption is that since persuasion is inherently practical, we can study it most profitably by examining the functions of persuasive acts. Second, we presume that even apparently irrational acts make sense to the actor—the trick is discovering the reasoning behind the act. Third, people create and comprehend their world through symbols, and it is people who create, use, ignore, or act upon these symbolic creations. Fourth, public speeches are an important form of social movement persuasion, but they are neither the most prevalent nor necessarily the most effective form. And fifth, we can rarely explain social movements as mere instances of orneriness, perversion, or ignorance. Someone once wryly observed that a rebel who loses is a traitor, while a rebel who wins is a founding father. These assumptions, as well as many of the first edition's arguments, struck some readers as heresy and still others as "old-hat." We hope this revised and expanded edition strikes a similar balance.

This book truly represents a joint undertaking by the three of us who have spent long hours in graduate seminars, at conventions, and during visits to one another's campuses discussing the persuasive efforts of social movements and, in particular, the topics included in this book. It may be of interest to note the primary contributions of each author. Charles Stewart was primarily responsible for chapters on the social movement as a unique collective phenomenon, the life cycle of social movements, the nature of leadership in social movements, a rhetoric of legitimation, a functional approach to movement persuasion, the rhetoric of transcendence, the persuasive functions of protest songs, and the selected bibliography. Craig Smith was primarily responsible for the preface and conclusions, the typology of political argument, the social systems approach to movements, and the studies of the John Birch Society and the Panama Canal controversy. Robert Denton was primarily responsible for the chapters on resistance, a Burkean approach to movement persuasion, and the analyses of the persuasive functions of slogans and obscenity.

Charles J. Stewart
Craig Allen Smith
Robert E. Denton, Jr.

Part One

The Roles of Persuasion in Social Movements

Chapter 1

The Social Movement as a Unique Collective Phenomenon

The second half of the 20th century may well be called "the age of the social movement" in America. Blacks, students, women, the aged, gays, hispanic peoples, native Americans, prison inmates, and workers of all varieties from the vineyard to the university campus have demanded rights, equality, identity, and a fair share of the American dream. Others have organized to protest the American way of dying, involvement in unjustified wars, pollution and destruction of the environment, nuclear power, forced busing of public school students, violence and sex on television, legalized abortion, marijuana laws, centralized power in corporate, governmental, and educational bureaucracies, and changes in the American social structure and values. But this is not to say that social movements are new to the American scene. The American Revolution began as a social movement, and the 19th century witnessed great struggles to free the slaves, to improve working conditions and compensation, to reduce (and later to prohibit) the selling of alcoholic beverages, to gain equal rights for women, and to return religion to the fundamentals of the Bible.

In our efforts to understand and to explain the bewildering variety of protests and demands that have affected our lives during the past quarter-century and the lives of our predecessors during the past two centuries of American history, we have attached a forest of labels to "social movement" phenomena such as political, historical, rhetorical, reform, revisionary, nationalistic, resistance, conservative, and individualistic. This plethora of labels, coupled with the tendency to select labels that denigrate social movements (radical, reactionary, revolutionary, repressive) and the tendency to attach the name "movement" to virtually all collective phenomena (internal change within groups, social movement organizations, campaigns, violent revolutions, civil wars, trends, fads, manias, and panics), have confused our efforts to understand the social movement as a unique collective phenomenon.

Attempts to define the term "social movement" have added to rather than lessened the confusion and disagreement. For instance, some writers have developed "collective action" definitions. William Bruce Cameron says "a social movement occurs when a fairly large number of people band together in order to alter or to supplant some portion of the existing culture or social order."[1] And Malcolm Sillars, in an attempt to "cast the widest net," defines social movements as "collective actions which are perceived by a critic."[2] These definitions appear to encompass all collective actions and do not distinguish the social movement from collective actions such as political campaigns, civil wars, or efforts by members of Congress to reform their procedures.

Other writers have developed more precise "social psychological" definitions. For example, John Wilson writes that a social movement is "a conscious, collective, organized attempt to bring about or to resist large scale change in the social order by noninstitutionalized means."[3] And Herbert Simons defines a social movement as an "uninstitutionalized collectivity that mobilizes for action to implement a program for the reconstitution of social norms or values."[4] Social psychological definitions address more precisely *what* a social movement *is* and *is not*, but they do not address *how* this collective phenomenon achieves its goals.

A third group of writers have developed "rhetorical" definitions of social movements. Charles Wilkinson, for instance, defines social movements as "languaging strategies by which a significantly vocal part of an established society, experiencing together a sustained dialectical tension growing out of moral (ethical) conflict, agitate to induce cooperation in others, either directly or indirectly, and thereby affecting the status quo."[5] Wilkinson's definition addresses precisely *how* a social movement achieves its goals but not precisely *what* a social movement is and is not. Robert Cathcart's definition comes closer to identifying both how and what: "A social movement can be said to emerge when the languaging strategies of a change-seeking collective clash with the languaging strategies of the establishment and thereby produce the perception of a group's operating outside the established social hierarchy."[6]

If we are to comprehend the social movement as a unique collective action in which persuasion is pervasive, then we must be able to determine if the phenomenon under investigation is in fact a "social movement." Each current definition, whether collective action, social psychological, or rhetorical, makes important but partial contributions to this comprehension. In this chapter, we attempt, first, to identify the essential characteristics of social movements and, second, to develop a complete definition that distinguishes social movements from other collective actions and identifies the functions of persuasion.

An Organized Collectivity

A social movement has at least minimal organization. If we cannot identify leaders (or spokespersons), membership (or followers or believers), and one or more organizations, the phenomenon we are studying is a trend, fad, or social unrest, not a social movement.[7] The degree of organization and visibility varies considerably from one movement to another. For instance, Martin Luther King, Jr., leader of the Southern Christian Leadership Conference, was an internationally known leader of the black civil rights movement, but it would be difficult for most people to name a single leader or organization of the gay rights or native American rights movements. Leaders, members, and organizations of social movements that employ frequent public demonstrations are more visible than ones that choose to operate through the press, courts, in small groups, or primarily within the social movement community.

The mass media, as Chesebro and Howe have noted, may create the illusion of a social movement by treating "relatively isolated, but similar, rhetorical situations throughout the nation....as a single, dynamic and interrelated phenomenon."[8] For example, the "death of God theology" attracted a great deal of media coverage and appeared to be a booming social movement when, in fact, no leaders, membership, or organization existed.[9] The death of God theology was a fascinating phenomenon but not a social movement.

Social movements and campaigns are often confused even though they have significant differences.[10] Unlike social movements, campaigns tend to be organized from the top down. Some person or group designates a campaign manager who in turn selects a staff and then organizes and runs the campaign. A social movement leader (or more typically leaders) is usually selected from the protest group as it develops and discovers the need for such a person. Campaigns have managers with assigned roles, organizational charts, chiefs of staff, schedules of operations, a specific goal, and a known end-point such as election day or the date a fund drive or membership drive is to "go over the top." A social movement may last for decades or months, must be flexible as circumstances change, can rarely obtain or maintain tight control over unpaid volunteers, and often alters and adds to its goals as it proceeds.

Social movement organizations are often confused with social movements. The National Organization for Reform of Marijuana Laws (N.O.R.M.L.), the National Organization for Women (N.O.W.), the American Indian Movement (A.I.M.), and the John Birch Society are social movement organizations, not social movements. Each is *one* organization of *several* striving to change the image of marijuana and laws governing its use, working for women's rights, trying to regain rights for native

Americans, or attempting to prevent or to reverse changes in American norms and values.

In our efforts to comprehend complex social movements, we have too often tried to simplify them and to compare them with collective actions we know best: political campaigns, political parties, and governmental or corporate bodies. Efforts have been frustrating because social movements rarely proceed in an orderly step-by-step manner, contain one supreme leader who controls *the* organization, appeal to a single target audience, have a carefully defined and identifiable membership, or strive to attain a single, well-defined goal through the employment of one persuasive strategy. *Minimal* organization is both necessity and reality for most social movements.

An Uninstitutionalized Collectivity

A social movement is an uninstitutionalized collectivity. A social movement is not part of an established order that governs and changes social, political, religious, or economic norms and values.[11] Thus, moves by the Roman Catholic hierarchy to alter its liturgy, or by members of Congress to reform committee membership, or by the United Auto Workers Union to gain a better contract are not social movements.[12] These are establishments changing themselves and achieving goals through institutionalized means and procedures. A social movement may try to persuade members of the established order (legislators, governors, judges) to change or to aid its program for change, but it ceases to be a social movement if it becomes part of the established order.

Herbert Simons has maintained that the uninstitutionalized nature of social movements presents leaders with "extraordinary rhetorical dilemmas" in requirements they must fulfill, problems they face, and strategies they may adopt to meet these requirements.[13] David Zarefsky counters Simons' position by arguing that "establishment" movements such as Lyndon Johnson's "War on Poverty" have rhetorical careers "identical to that of a social movement" and that the major dilemmas Simons cites "are not unique to persuasive campaigns mounted by uninstitutionalized collectivities."[14] After discussing three "establishment movements," Zarefsky concludes that "officially sanctioned organizations do not always have controls to assure effectiveness."

Although success is never assured for any collective endeavor, a comparison of the situations uninstitutionalized and institutionalized groups confront suggest that social movements do indeed encounter unique persuasive problems and handicaps. The social movement is always an "out-group" and thus tends to be viewed by society as illegitimate. It is criticized for not handling the controversy through normal, proper channels and procedures—even when the channels and procedures are denied to the movement. The movement has virtually no powers of reward and punishment beyond personal recognition or expulsion, and expulsion often leads to competing organizations created by the exiled. Social movements have neither legislative nor enforcement powers and no assured means of financial support. Monetary funds are a fraction of those readily available to establishment groups and leaders. Uninstitutionalized leaders survive only as long as they perform the needed tasks exceedingly well. When new tasks or abilities are demanded, the leader may be unceremoniously discarded. A leader usually has minimal control over one faction of a movement and of the established order. The mass media are rarely favorable toward social movements (unless success appears to be near), are rarely controlled in any manner by social movements, and provide exposure at great monetary expense or when a social movement does something spectacular or stupid. Persuasion is the sole means available to most social movements for accomplishing such functions as transforming perceptions of society, prescribing courses of action, and mobilizing the movement.

The institutionalized group, on the other hand, is always an "in-group" and thus tends to be viewed by society as legitimate. It strives to maintain at least the appearance of dealing with the controversy through normal, proper channels and procedures. It has immense powers of reward and punishment since it may control law enforcement agencies, investigative groups, regulatory agencies, legislative bodies, political parties, tax authorities, courts, prisons, lucrative positions, and a bureaucracy. Leaders may serve guaranteed terms of two years to life, enjoy the support of organized and well-financed groups, and have opportunities to advance in the hierarchy. Institutionalized groups and leaders are newsworthy and demand attention of the media. They may command multiple network or front page coverage of speeches, press conferences, conventions, and important announcements or ceremonies. At the same time, leaders may stifle uncooperative or unfriendly media through threats of unleashing regulatory agencies or creating new regulations and restrictions. A President may gain international attention merely by strolling through the rose garden at the White House or by visiting a "typical" American family. All major networks and newspapers are owned by institutionalized groups and exist to make a profit and to maintain societal norms and values. Finally, institutionalized groups often have access to nearly unlimited funds.

Zarefsky may be correct in arguing that "establishment movements" follow rhetorical careers nearly identical to social movements. However, we find it difficult to believe that the President of the United States, even when following a similar rhetorical career, has no advantages over the uninstitutionalized social movement and, indeed, faces identical persuasive dilemmas. Social movements often try to use institutions such as courts and legislatures to further their goals, but the rate of success—seen in the efforts of blacks and women—is fragmentary and slow.

Large in Scope

A social movement must be significantly large in scope. The word "significant" means large enough—in geographical area, time, events, and participants—to carry out the program of the movement.[15] Few movements in America can afford to be characterized as "small" because small ventures in this country tend to be ignored, ridiculed, or suppressed. The native American movement, small in numbers and isolated in scattered, remote regions of the country, has had difficulty attracting attention, maintaining interest, and persuading audiences to take it seriously. Institutions and supporters went to great length in the 1960s to characterize the anti-war, student, and black power movements as small groups of radicals, sex perverts, traitors, cowards, racists, and degenerates clearly not representative of the great "silent majority" of good citizens, students, and blacks. The *Wall Street Journal* described the Indian occupation of the Bureau of Indian Affairs building in Washington as "an exercise in play-acting—an effort by a relative handful of militants, claiming to speak for the broader Indian community."[16] Forces countering the pro-life movement have portrayed it as a "vocal minority" and a "handful of people."[17]

The established order has time on its side. It can wait until social, economic, and political crises pass, until a war ends, until establishment leadership changes occur through normal processes, until the public becomes disenchanted with protest and disorder, until the mass media and their audiences become bored with the issue, until movement leadership changes through graduation, military discharge, power struggles, death, assassination, or until movement leaders and followers tire of the struggle or become disillusioned by lack of real progress toward a goal. If social movement leaders and followers do not tire, they may become desperate and make mistakes, mistakes the establishment can use to discredit or to suppress the movement.

A few major victories do not guarantee success. Even spectacular events, such as the 1963 civil rights march on Washington that drew over 300,000 persons and ended with Martin Luther King's famous "I Have a Dream" speech, are soon forgotten. "What's next?" is asked by friend and foe. Social movements and the media have insatiable appetites for "rhetorical happenings," but few social movements have adequate leaders, members, energy, and funds to satisfy wisely these appetites over long periods of time while fending off counter efforts by other movements and the established order. Unlike campaigns, social movements must sustain efforts for years. They do not select a single leader, conduct one membership drive, create one organization, set one goal, and pick one strategy; they select many leaders, conduct many membership drives, set and alter many goals, create several organizations, and employ many strategies. The longevity of social movements requires frequent changes, and each change may prove fatal.

Proposes or Opposes Change

A social movement proposes or opposes a program for change in societal norms, values, or both. We can identify three general types of social movements by the nature of the change they advocate. An *innovative* social movement may seek a limited replacement (reform) or a total replacement (revolutionary) of existing norms or values with *new* norms or values.[18] Examples of innovative social movements are women's liberation, black civil rights, socialism, and gay liberation. A *revivalistic* social movement may seek a limited replacement (reform) or total replacement (revolutionary) of existing norms or values with ones from a *venerable, idealized past.*[19] Examples of revivalistic movements are the native American movement, the Disciples of Christ Movement, and the Back to Africa movement. A *resistance* social movement seeks to block changes in norms or values because it perceives nothing to be wrong with the status quo—at least nothing that cannot or will not be resolved by established institutions. Examples of resistance movements are the anti-women's liberation, anti-black civil rights, pro-choice, and pro-Vietnam war movements.[20]

Efforts to identify social movements as valuistic or normative are often frustrating because changes in values alter norms and changes in norms alter values. For instance, guaranteeing women equal employment opportunities or busing children to integrate schools, basically normative changes, have affected values.

Efforts to identify social movements as either reform or revolutionary have proven equally frustrating. For example, the student, black, and women's rights movements have had both reform-oriented and revolutionary-oriented leaders, members and organizations. Movements may change over time. Student protest began as a reform movement and ended as a revolutionary movement. Our perceptions may determine where we place a movement along the reform to revolution continuum. One person may view women's liberation as merely a reform movement aimed at achieving constitutional rights, while a second may view the movement as a revolutionary effort aimed at total transformation of American society, including destruction of the family and marriage.

Classifications of social movements as "radical" or "moderate" have failed for several reasons. First, what one person perceives to be "radical" another person may perceive to be "moderate." Second, many social movements contain both radical and moderate elements: the anarchists vs. the Knights of Labor in the 19th century labor movement, Women's International Terrorist Conspiracy from Hell vs. the National Organization for Women in the women's liberation movement, and the Weathermen vs. Students for a Democratic Society in the counter culture movement of the 1960s and 1970s. And third, the terms moderate and radical describe types of persuasive strategies or argument better than types of social movements, a point we will develop in Chapter 4. Too often we have confused movement type with a type of strategy used at a given time in the movement's life cycle.

Precise identification of each social movement, regardless of the typological system employed, is difficult because of the nature of social movement ideologies. They tend to be strange mixtures of vagueness and precision, to borrow from old systems while espousing the new, to be both flexible and inflexible, to be static and ever-changing, and to be consistent and contradictory. Some social movements have one ideology for true believers and another for the public. In addition, as Hans Toch states, "Each person joins a somewhat different social movement," often "for reasons far removed from the central concerns of the movement."[21] Each person perceives the movement's enemies, goals, strategies, and membership from his or her unique perspective. One person may join a group protesting the proliferation of nuclear power plants to save the environment, a second to fight giant corporations, and a third for the fellowship of the group. In general, individuals come together because of what they perceive to be shared interests, often as a result of interpersonal contacts.

Regardless of the difficulties encountered in typing social movements, the effort is important because the nature of the change a movement advocates may determine the situational variables that mold and constrain its persuasive efforts, persuasive dilemmas encountered, availability and appropriateness of persuasive strategies and tactics, and the openness of communication channels. A reform-oriented innovative social movement such as pro-life, for example, is aided by the Roman Catholic and Baptist Churches, encounters relatively few obstacles in gaining media coverage and access to establishment leaders, raises funds rather easily, and uses a variety of persuasive strategies because it is not seen as a threat to the American way of life. On the other hand, a revolutionary-oriented innovative movement such as communism is perceived to threaten everything that is American. It faces major limitations on persuasive strategies, communication channels, and its legal existence. The resistance or counter movement, the polar opposite of innovative and revivalistic movements, may serve as a surrogate for an established order that wishes to maintain real or apparent neutrality. For example, local southern governments that opposed integration claimed impartiality while aiding the counter efforts of white citizens councils. A great many state legislators welcomed the anti-ERA efforts of Phyllis Schlafly and other anti-women's liberation forces. The John Birch Society has received considerable support from conservative elements among established religious, economic, political, educational, military, and social groups because the Society seems to be supporting their interests.

Moral in Tone

A social movement's rhetoric is moral in tone. Whether a social movement's leaders and members are striving to bring about or to resist change in societal norms and values, they see themselves as having the power to distinguish right from wrong, good from evil, and ethical from unethical in choices, actions, behavior, and character. Each movement believes that it alone constitutes an ethical, virtuous, principled, and righteous force with a "moral obligation" to raise the consciousness of "the people" and thus to reveal the "moral, intellectual, and coercive bankruptcy of the opposition."[22] Kenneth Burke and Leland Griffin conclude that "all movements are essentially moral—striving for salvation, perfection, the 'good.'"[23]

The moral stance or tone of a movement's rhetoric is critical to its claim of legitimacy. Anthony Oberschall writes that a movement's legitimacy rests upon an "elaboration of systems of belief and moral ideas," while Herbert Simons notes that a movement establishes "its legitimacy by representing its cause as one that any virtuous individual must endorse."[24] As with most individuals or collectives who place themselves upon a moral pedestal—particularly ones striving for the mantle of legitimacy—social movement rhetoric often magnifies its righteousness. Herbert Simons, Elizabeth Mechling, and Howard Schreier claim that "Most ideological messages" of social movements "tend to exaggerate the strength, unity, and intellectual and moral legitimacy of the movement."[25]

Encounters Opposition

A social movement is countered by an established order. As a social movement develops or resists a program for change from a moral perspective and lays claim to legitimacy, its members become frustrated to the point of disaffection with the established order and institutionalized means of change and control. They are willing to devote their lives—on occasion to sacrifice their lives—to attain victory in the moral struggle between good and evil. Innovative and revivalistic social movements perceive the establishment to be unaware of, disinterested in, or openly resistant to necessary change. Resistance movements may perceive the established order to be unwilling or unable to meet the threat to social norms and values and, perhaps, to be actively compromising norms and values.

Sooner or later the social movement becomes a threat that the established order can no longer ignore. Robert Cathcart contends that the social movement must create a "drama or agonistic ritual which forces response from the establishment commensurate with the moral evil perceived by movement members."[26] The perceived threat of the social movement and its confrontational strategies eventually produces, according to Robert Cathcart, a "dialectical tension growing out of moral conflict" and provokes a clash between the social movement and the threatened established order.[27] The struggle between institutional and uninstitutional forces becomes a "true moral battle for power and for the legitimate right to define the true order."[28]

"Social conflict," Herbert Simons writes, is "a clash over incompatible interests in which one party's relative gain is another's relative loss."[29] Established orders, often portraying themselves as goaded into action by a dangerous, fanatical, irresponsible, unreasonable threat to legitimate social order, counter social movements directly and indirectly through a combination of the following:

1. *Agencies:* legislative bodies, executive and administrative groups, courts, police, armed forces, tribunals, councils, committees, regulatory bodies, tax authorities, communication media, investigative groups, and so on.
2. *Agents:* legislators, presidents, governors, bishops, judges, police officers, soldiers, owners of communication media, editors, reporters, commentators, committee or council chairpersons, investigators, and so on.
3. *Beneficiaries:* many of the above plus corporations, business owners and operators (including farmers), colleges and universities, churches, patriotic and civic groups, the "silent majority," and so on.

Ralph Smith and Russell Windes, in their effort to develop a rhetorical theory for the "innovative movement," have challenged the notion that social movements are always countered by established orders.[30] An innovative movement, according to Smith and Windes, tries to prevent dialectical tension by stressing common ground between itself and the established order and by avoiding confrontational strategies and tactics. During their analysis of the Sunday school movement as an innovational movement, however, they remark:

> Sunday schools were described as an "entering wedge to a union of church and state." This threat became especially salient when Ezra Styles Ely, a leading Presbyterian minister, urged from the pulpit a "Christian Party in Politics" which could "govern every public election in our country." Throughout the nation came charges that Sunday schools would train the young to abandon the religion of their sectarian fathers in favor of an established evangelical church.

The Sunday school movement, intentionally or unintentionally, had created a dialectical tension and was being countered by an established order—sectarian religious leaders and followers. Confrontation was not the essence of this reform-oriented innovative movement, but neither was it absent as Smith and Windes seem to contend. John Wilson writes:

> Such is the hold of custom and tradition on men and women and such is the power of those already in authority positions to perpetuate their privileges, that a great deal of the impetus for change must be looked for in the noninstitutionalized sector of society.[31]

Establishments, however, are tolerant only of minor challenges to norms and values and cannot sustain a "relative loss" to the noninstitutionalized sector and, at the same time, maintain their credibility and control over constituencies.

Persuasion Is Pervasive

Persuasion is the essence of social movements. The extensive literature on social movements posits that movements must satisfy a number of major requirements or functions if they are to *become* and to *remain* significant forces for change in societal norms and values. Social movements must transform perceptions of history and society, prescribe courses of action, mobilize forces for action, and sustain the movement. Chapter 8 delves into each of these persuasive functions.

Theoretically, social movements may attempt to satisfy these functions through a combination of three strategies: coercion, bargaining, and persuasion. Coercion is the "manipulation of the target group's situation in such fashion that the pursuit of any course of action other than that sought by the movement will be met by considerable cost or punishment." Bargaining may occur when the "movement has control of some exchangeable value that the target group wants and offers some of that value in return for compliance with demands."[32] Persuasion is a communication process by which a social movement seeks through the use of verbal and nonverbal symbols to affect the perceptions of audiences and thus to bring about desired changes in ways of thinking, feeling, and/or acting. In reality social movements discover that inherent constraints deny them free selection and use of these interrelated strategies.

The typical uninstitutional, minimally organized social movement enjoys few means of reward or punishment necessary either to coerce people to join or to remain loyal to a cause or to coerce the established order to capitulate to all or some of its demands. Established orders, with little to gain and much to lose, resist "bargaining" with social movements whose followers they have stigmatized as dangerous social degenerates. "People in power do not like to sit down with rogues." Mere association with a social movement's leaders may grant a degree of legitimacy to the social movement, an outcome institutions wish to avoid. In addition, as Michael Lipsky has noted, established orders doubt the capability of social movements to bargain effectively: "Protest oriented groups, whose primary talents are in dramatizing issues, cannot credibly attempt to present data considered 'objective' or suggestions considered 'responsible' by public officials. Few can be convincing as both advocate and arbitrator at the same time."[33] Social movements often have little or nothing to exchange in bargaining sessions. Ralph Turner and Lewis Killian comment, for instance, that "the difficulty that constantly besets black movements is that they have nothing to offer whites in a bargaining exchange to match their disruptive potential.[34] Social movements are equally loathe to bargain with the devil—the established order—when they are morally correct in their demands for change and have often suffered mental and physical abuse for their protest. Talking to, let alone compromising with, an established order may be deemed a moral outrage. Thus, the invited party and the constituencies of both parties are likely to perceive an offer to bargain as a sign of weakness, desperation, deception, or "selling out."[35]

Social movements can satisfy only a few major requirements through bargaining and coercive strategies. For example, bargaining may help to mobilize for action by uniting disparate elements and it might place mild pressure on the opposition to grant a degree of legitimacy to a collectivity willing to discuss potential compromises. However, bargaining cannot transform perceptions of history, prescribe courses of action, or justify setbacks. Coercion is limited mainly to pressuring the opposition or to transforming perceptions of society by goading the established order into excessive repression. Although a social movement may "unmask" an established order and gain sympathy by provoking violent suppression, the public may just as easily perceive the suppression to be an "unfortunate but inevitable result" of dangerous radicalism.[36] Many social movements have splintered into factions over the issue of employing coercion (particularly violent coercion) to achieve their ends. Thus, because of numerous constraints under which social movements must operate, *persuasion* is the primary strategy or agency available for satisfying major requirements.

Persuasion is pervasive when a movement attempts to bargain. For instance, a social movement that decides to bargain must convince both supporters and opposition that it is serious, that it is operating from a position of strength, and that it has something of value to exchange for concessions. Persuasion is center stage if bargaining sessions take place. On the other hand, persuasion may preclude bargaining as a strategy. Michael Lipsky notes that "admission to policymaking councils is frequently barred because of the angry, militant rhetorical style adopted by protest leaders."[37]

Persuasion and coercion are often inseparable. Turner and Killian observe that "nonviolence always couples persuasive strategy to coercion."[38] Herbert Simons uses the phrase "coercive persuasion" and notes that "all acts of influence are rhetorical in at least some respects." He writes:

> The trouble with the persuasion-coercion dichotomy is that it cannot be applied reliably to the real world, and *especially to most conflict situations.* Although the criteria used to distinguish persuasion and coercion enable us to identify different elements within a given act, and although there are a great many cases of "pure" persuasion which are free of coercive elements, by these same criteria, acts conventionally labelled as "coercive" are almost never free of persuasive elements.[39]

When is an act devoid of "symbolic" value and thus an instance of pure coercion? The Supreme Court has ruled that many "coercive" acts such as marches, sit-ins, boycotts, and demonstrations constitute "symbolic speech" and are entitled to First Amendment protection. The Berrigans' seizure and destruction with napalm of draft records from the Selective Service office in Catonsville, Maryland was a coercive and yet highly symbolic act during the Vietnam War.[40] When do two parties sit down to bargain and make no efforts to *convince* one another that they are sincere, have something of value to offer, are operating from a position of strength, and can and will break off negotiations (and resort to force) if all does not proceed as desired? When is an act pure persuasion and, thus, devoid of any hint of the carrot or the stick? Malcolm X's famous speech, "The Ballot or the Bullet," is by definition persuasive, yet the opening attempts to appease orthodox Muslims and Christian elements in the audience (persuasive bargaining) and the body contains veiled threats to resort to the bullet if the ballot is unavailable or ineffective (persuasive coercion). Robert Doolittle reveals that some people perceived the riots of the 1960s as inherently symbolic, others conceded that the riots were potentially symbolic, and some viewed them as lawless and totally lacking in symbolism.[41]

Persuasion plays key roles when social movements threaten to employ coercive tactics. Parke Burgess writes that:

> the victim must be convinced that dire consequences are likely, not to say certain, *before* he can feel coerced to comply, just as he must become convinced of the coercer's probable capacity and intent to commit the act of violence *before* he can conclude that the act is likely to follow non-compliance.[42]

James Andrews suggests that persuasion may be most effective when established orders "accept the harsh reality that they may be coerced."[43]

Clearly, persuasion permeates social movements and is the primary agency available to social movements for satisfying major requirements or functions. The role of persuasion distinguishes social movements from civil wars and revolutions. *In social movements, persuasion is pervasive while violence is incidental and often employed for symbolic purposes. In civil wars and revolutions, violence is pervasive while persuasion is incidental.*

To say that persuasion is pervasive in social movements and that it is the primary means for satisfying major requirements is *not* to suggest that persuasion *alone* can bring ultimate success to social movements. Social movements must have skilled leaders, dedicated followers, satisfactory organizations, a social system that tolerates protest, and a climate conducive to change. Events such as Three Mile Island, Kent State, and Brown v. Board of Education are essential for the progress of social movements. However, such events would disappear quickly into the pages of history if social movements did not employ persuasion to interpret them, to focus attention upon them through the mass media, and to bring them back to audiences in ceremonies, songs, and anniversary celebrations. But persuasion alone grows stale without the urgency that events inject into protest.

Conclusions

A social movement, then, is an organized, uninstitutionalized, and significantly large collectivity that emerges to bring about or to resist a program for change in societal norms and values, operates primarily through persuasive strategies, and encounters opposition in what becomes a moral struggle. This definition addresses both *what* a social movement is and *how* it attempts to achieve its program for change. Persuasion is a pervasive element and is not restricted to a particular audience, purpose, requirement, strategy, or stage in a movement's life cycle.

Our attempt to describe the *social* movement as a unique collective phenomenon is designed to provide a clear focus for the chapters that follow and to inform readers of the underlying premises upon which this book is based. Our definition is not designed to place rigid limitations on "movement" studies. We recognize that "movements" occur within established institutions, describe changes in academic fields of study and voting trends, and determine our personal habits and tastes. The debate over whether or not social movements are unique or exist beyond our imaginations seems analogous to the study of campaigns.[44] Researchers analyze political, sales, advertising, recruiting, and military campaigns, and they recognize that campaigns share many common characteristics. They do not, however, claim that each is totally unique or that because they share some characteristics they should all be called "political campaigns" or "sales campaigns." The same is true of movements. As David Zarefsky has pointed out, establishment or institutional movements share many characteristics with social movements. These shared characteristics, however, do not make them identical twins. Thus, we are using the word "social" to identify a particular type of movement and see such words as "institutional," "political," and "historical" as identifying similar but different movement phenomena.

In Chapter 2, we will describe the life cycle of social movements to explain further the ever-changing persuasive requirements, problems, and functions of social movements and the interaction of social, political, philosophical, and rhetorical forces. A delineation of the stages that movements pass through will also help us to understand the nature, changes, and apparent paradoxes in political argument.

Endnotes

[1] William Bruce Cameron, *Modern Social Movements: A Sociological Outline* (New York: Random House, 1966), 7.

[2] Malcolm O. Sillars, "Defining Movements Rhetorically: Casting the Widest Net," *Southern Speech Communication Journal*, 46 (Fall, 1980), 30.

[3] John Wilson, *Introduction to Social Movements* (New York: Basic Books, 1973), 8.

[4] Herbert W. Simons, "Requirements, Problems, and Strategies: A Theory of Persuasion for Social Movements, *Quarterly Journal of Speech*, 56 (February, 1970), 3.

[5] Charles A. Wilkinson, "A Rhetorical Definition of Movements," *Central States Speech Journal*, 27 (Summer, 1976), 91.

[6] Robert S. Cathcart, "Defining Social Movements by Their Rhetorical Form," *Central States Speech Journal*, 31 (Winter, 1980), 269.

[7] See for example, Simons, 1-11 and Wilson, 156-166.

[8] James W. Chesebro, "Cultures in Conflict—A Generic and Axiological View," *Today's Speech*, 21 (Spring, 1973), 12.

[9] Roger W. Howe, "The Rhetoric of the Death of God Theology," *Southern Speech Communication Journal*, 37 (Winter, 1971), 150.

[10] Herbert W. Simons, James W. Chesebro, and C. Jack Orr, "A Movement Perspective on the 1972 Presidential Campaign," *Quarterly Journal of Speech*, 59 (April, 1973), 168-179.

[11] Simons, 3; and Neil J. Smelser, *Theory of Collective Behavior* (New York: Free Press, 1962), 110 and 129-130.

[12] At one time labor groups such as the United Auto Workers, Teamsters, and AFL-CIO were clearly social movement organizations. Today, however, they are parts of the established order that control workers and production. The Teamsters, for example, have openly opposed non-established labor groups such as the Cesar Chavez led United Farm Workers.

[13] Simons, 11.

[14] David Zarefsky, "President Johnson's War on Poverty: The Rhetoric of Three 'Establishment' Movements," *Communication Monographs*, 44 (November, 1977), 352-373.

[15] Wilkinson, 92-93.

[16] *Wall Street Journal*, 16 November 1972, 26, col. 1.

[17] "Five Ways to Prevent Abortion (And One Way That Won't)," Lafayette, Indiana *Journal and Courier*, 8 September 1985, A-15; "In 1982, If You Have a Miscarriage You Could Be Charged for Murder," Lafayette, Indiana *Journal and Courier*, 26 May 1981, B-4.

[18] Other common titles for innovative movements are revisionary, alternative, redemptive, and transformative.

[19] Other names for revivalistic movements are reactionary, regressive, and nationalistic.

[20] Other names for resistance movements are conservative and counter.

[21] Hans Toch, *The Social Psychology of Social Movements* (Indianapolis: Bobbs-Merrill, 1965) 21-26.

[22] R.R. McGuire, "Speech Acts, Communicative Competence and the Paradox of Authority," *Philosophy and Rhetoric*, 10 (Winter, 1977), 33; Herbert W. Simons, "Persuasion in Social Conflicts: A Critique of Prevailing Conceptions and a Framework for Future Research," *Speech Monographs*, 39 (November, 1972), 233.

[23] Leland M. Griffin, "A Dramatistic Theory of the Rhetoric of Movements," *Critical Responses to Kenneth Burke*, William Rueckert, ed. (Minneapolis: University of Minnesota Press, 1969), 456.

[24] Anthony Oberschall, *Social Conflict and Social Movements* (Englewood Cliffs, NJ: Prentice-Hall, 1973), 188; Simons, *Persuasion*, 235.

[25] Herbert W. Simons, Elizabeth W. Mechling, and Howard N. Schreier, "The Functions of Human Communication in Mobilizing from the Bottom Up: The Rhetoric of Social Movements," *Handbook of Rhetorical and Communication Theory*, Carroll C. Arnold and John W. Bowers, eds. (Boston: Allyn and Bacon, 1984), 797.

[26] Robert S. Cathcart, "Movements: Confrontation as Rhetorical Form," *Southern Speech Communication Journal*, 43 (Spring, 1978), 242.

[27] Cathcart, "Movements," 242; Robert S. Cathcart, "New Approaches to the Study of Movements: Defining Movements Rhetorically," *Western Speech*, 36 (Spring, 1972), 87.

[28] Cathcart, "Movements," 246.

[29] Herbert W. Simons, *Persuasion: Understanding, Practice and Analysis* (Reading, MA: Addison-Wesley, 1976), 18.

[30] Ralph R. Smith and Russell R. Windes, "The Innovational Movement: A Rhetorical Theory," *Quarterly Journal of Speech*, 61 (April, 1975), 140-143.

[31] Wilson, 4.

[32] These definitions of coercion and bargaining appear in Ralph H. Turner and Lewis M. Killian, *Collective Behavior* (Englewood Cliffs, NJ: Prentice-Hall, 1972), 291.

[33] Michael Lipsky, "Protest as Political Resource," *The American Political Science Review*, 52 (December, 1968), 1154.

[34] Turner and Killian, 421.

[35] James R. Andrews, "Reflections of the National Character in American Rhetoric," *Quarterly Journal of Speech*, 57 (October, 1971), 316-324; and Lipsky, 1153-1157.

[36] Kurt W. Ritter, "Confrontation as Moral Drama: The Boston Massacre in Rhetorical Perspective," *Southern Speech Communication Journal*, 42 (Winter, 1977), 114-136.

[37] Lipsky, 1154.

[38] Turner and Killian, 298.

[39] Simons, *Persuasion*, 43-44; and "Persuasion in Social Conflict," 232.

[40] John H. Patton, "Rhetoric at Catonsville: Daniel Berrigan, Conscience, and Image Attraction," *Today's Speech*, 23 (Winter, 1975), 3-12.

[41] Robert J. Doolittle, "Riots as Symbolic: A Criticism and Approach," *Central States Speech Journal*, 27 (Winter, 1976), 310-317.

[42] Parke G. Burgess, "Crisis Rhetoric: Coercion vs. Force," *Quarterly Journal of Speech*, 59 (February, 1973), 69.

[43] James R. Andrews, "The Rhetoric of Coercion and Persuasion: The Reform Bill of 1812," *Quarterly Journal of Speech*, 56 (April, 1970), 195.

[44] Michael C. McGee, "'Social Movement': Phenomenon or Meaning," *Central States Speech Journal*, 31 (Winter, 1980), 233-244; and David Zarefsky, "A Skeptical View of Movement Studies," *Central States Speech Journal*, 31 (Winter, 1980), 245-254.

Chapter 2

The Life Cycle of Social Movements

To study a social movement is to study an intricate and ever-changing social drama.[1] Like dramas, social movements involve multiple acts, scenes, agents, agencies, and purposes. William Bruce Cameron writes that each "social movement is determined by so many variables that its success or failure, the speed of its growth or decline, the consistency or inconsistency of its operations will not fit any *a priori* formula."[2] Social movements such as women's rights and social movement organizations such as the Ku Klux Klan disappear and then reappear with altered purposes, ideologies, leaders, structures, and persuasive strategies.

Any effort to prescribe a life cycle suitable to all social movements, then, is fraught with dangers. The effort can be productive, however, if the life cycle is constructed with the full realization that social movements differ, change, and develop to varying degrees of sophistication and at varying speeds—stalling at times, rushing forward at others, retrenching to earlier stages, or dying premature deaths before all stages are completed.

Recent attempts to detect cycles and phases of human interactions are helping us to understand complex communicative events, collectives, and exchanges. A study by Donald Ellis and Aubry Fisher, for example, revealed three phases of conflict in small group development: interpersonal conflict, confrontation, and substantive conflict.[3] Julia Wood has focused on human relationships and "how communication functions at each stage to contribute to the building or dissolution of a relational culture.[4] Among the stages or states Wood presents are individuals, invitational communication, explorational communication, intensifying communication, revising communication, bonding communication, and navigating communication. Mark Knapp has developed a model of interaction stages within relationships.[5] The process of *coming together,* according to Knapp, includes the stages of initiating, experimenting, intensifying, integrating, and bonding; and the stage of *coming apart* includes differentiating, circumscribing, stagnating, avoiding, and terminating. Like these models or phases of relationships and conflict within small groups, a portrayal of each stage in the life cycle of "typical" social movements can help us to understand the ever-changing persuasive requirements, problems, and functions of social movements and the interaction of social-psychological, political-institutional, philosophical-ideological, and rhetorical forces.[6] The life cycle presented in this chapter consists of five stages: genesis, social unrest, enthusiastic mobilization, maintenance, and termination.[7]

Stage 1: Genesis

A social movement usually begins during relatively quiet times, quiet at least with respect to the issue that the new movement will address. The "people" and established institutions are unaware of the problem or perceive it to be insignificant or of low priority.[8] Other concerns dominate the attention of the people, their leaders and institutions, and the mass media. Individuals, often scattered geographically and unknown to one another at first, perceive an "imperfection" in the existing order. The imperfection may be institutional or individual corruption, abuse of power, inequality (in rights, status, power, income, opportunities, possessions), an identity crisis, unfulfillment of "legitimate" expectations, or a threat to the social order or environment. Restless individuals view the imperfection as a serious problem that is likely to grow more severe unless appropriate institutions address it quickly and in earnest.

These early leaders—sometimes called intellectuals, prophets, or men of words—strive for salvation, perfection, or the "good" in society.[9] Although they "see through" an institution and strive to expose the institution's leaders, they meet little opposition in the genesis stage because few people take them seriously. As "prophets" they produce essays, editorials, songs, poems, pamphlets, books, and lectures designed to transform perceptions of the past, the present, and the future. They define and they visualize. Revivalistic movements address a venerable, idealized past to which society must return; innovative movements address an intolerable present and prescribe a means to reach a glorious future; and resistance movements address a terrible future that is certain to result if current trends or movements are not stifled. Above all, the movement's initial leaders believe, often with remarkable naivete, that appropriate institutions will act if the movement can make institutional leaders and followers aware of the urgent problem and its solution. The intellectual or prophet or man of words is more of an educator than a "rabble rouser" or fanatic. "Thus," by intention or by accident, Eric Hoffer writes, "imperceptibly the man of words undermines established institutions, discredits those in power, weakens prevailing beliefs and loyalties, and sets the stage for the rise of the mass movement."[10]

In Lloyd Bitzer's words, the prophet not only apprehends an exigence ("an imperfection marked by some degree of urgency. . . a problem or defect, something other than it should be") but attempts to create interest within an audience for perceiving and solving the exigence. The prophet, however, often differs little from Bitzer's "man alone in a boat and adrift at sea" who "shouts for help although he knows his words will be unheard." But the prophet persists because of the belief that "interest will increase insofar as the factual condition" becomes "known directly and sensibly, or through vivid representation."[11]

The genesis stage may last for months, years, or decades. Harold Mixon claims, for instance, that artillery election sermons sowed the seeds of independence in colonial America decades before the Declaration of Independence in 1776.[12] Folk songs by Dylan and others addressed war and peace barely a year before the Gulf of Tonkin incident thrust the United States into the Vietnam conflict. If comparable social movements are active, a fledgling social movement may take shape rapidly. For example, students involved in the black civil rights movement created the student free speech movement and then the peace movement that opposed the war in Vietnam. Female members of these movements who awakened to their second class status in both the movements and in society while fighting for the rights of others were instrumental in establishing the women's liberation movement.

The genesis stage, what Leland Griffin calls the "period of inception," is "a time when the roots of a pre-existing sentiment, nourished by interested rhetoricians, begins to flower into public notice."[13] A triggering event is usually required to move the generally unorganized and invisible social movement from the genesis stage to the social unrest stage. The trigger may be a Supreme Court decision, a nuclear accident, an insensitive reaction or statement by an institutional agent, a new law, an economic downturn, a military action, or the appearance of a movement-oriented book on the best seller list. For instance, the comment by a North Dakota legislator to a farm delegation in 1915, "Go home and slop your hogs," infuriated farmers and gave rise to the Nonpartisan League in the midwest.[14] Betty Freidan's *The Feminine Mystique* helped to launch the women's liberation movement, and Rachel Carson's *The Silent Spring* served as the impetus for the ecology movement. The initial result of triggering events may be the first signs of organization with titles that begin: "Citizens for. . .," "Concerned Parents Against. . .," or "Workers United to. . ."

The most important contributions of the genesis stage, Lloyd Bitzer would agree, are the apprehension of an exigence—something other than it should be—and the cultivating of interest in the exigence within an audience. Without a genesis stage, there will be no movement.

Stage 2: Social Unrest

As growing numbers of people rise up and express their concern and frustration over the issue, the movement passes from the genesis to the social unrest stage. Spokespersons for institutions may openly deny the severity or the existence of the problem (exigence) and, often for the first time, take official notice of the fledgling social movement. They may stigmatize the "movement" as naive, ill-informed, or outside the mainstream of society. Their strategy is to stall the movement by ignoring or discrediting it in hopes that it will succumb to ridicule or inattention. The mass media may note with interest, amusement, or mild foreboding the infant social movement and its pathetic claims or overtures.

The prophets turn into, or join, "agitators"—literally ones who stir things up. Together they begin to organize the disparate elements of the movement and to take it beyond the drawing room and the lecture hall. An initial act is often the calling of a convention or conference of like-minded people for the purpose of framing a manifesto, proclamation, or declaration. The manifesto sets forth the movement's ideology, an "elaboration of rationalizations and stereotypes into a consistent pattern."[15] The manifesto serves three important functions: (1) to describe the problem, (2) to identify the devils, scapegoats, and faulty principles that have caused and maintained the problem, and (3) to prescribe the solution and the gods, principles, and procedures that will bring it about. The ideology tends to identify the movement with "the people" and with established norms and values. For example, both the Declaration of Sentiments issued by the First Woman's Rights Convention in 1848 and the Constitution drawn up by the National Labor Union in 1868 were modifications of the Declaration of Independence.

The movement's ideology contains a set of common devil terms such as liberalism, wage slavery, conformity, and welfare state and a set of common "god" terms such as conservatism, cooperation, individualism, and free enterprise.[16] An overarching principle or slogan unifies the movement: "An injury to one is an injury to all (Knights of Labor), "Failure is impossible" (Susan B. Anthony and woman's rights), and "Never to laugh or love" (pro-life movement). For the first time, there is a feeling of "standing together" and "movement" as the concerned individuals are now members of the Knights of Labor, the National Association for the Advancement of Colored People, the National Organization for Women, or the United Farm Workers Organizing Committee. The act of organization sets members apart from non-members and established institutions and fosters a "we-they" division that becomes more pronounced as the movement enters succeeding stages. Members increasingly see themselves as an "elect" with a "mission" and a strategy for fulfilling the mission. Movement persuaders attempt to instill a new self-respect and feeling of power within members.

Although the social movement pays increasing attention to transforming perceptions of society (creating we-they distinctions) and to prescribing courses of action (citing demands, proposing solutions, and identifying who must bring about change and through which strategies), the major persuasive effort is aimed at transforming perceptions of the past, the present, and the future. Persuaders still believe that if they can raise the consciousness of institutional leaders and followers—make them aware of the facts—the institutions will take appropriate actions. Faith in success through the social chain-of-command remains strong. Thus, the movement expends most of its rhetorical energies in "petitioning" courts, councils, legislatures, boards of trustees, synods, and hierarchies.[17]

The duration of the social unrest stage depends upon the numbers of people who are attracted to the movement, reactions of institutional agents, and new triggering events that may greatly exacerbate the social situation or problem—the exigence. For example, the nuclear accident at Three Mile Island and the arrest of Rosa Parks in Montgomery, Alabama because she would not surrender her seat on a city bus to a white male passenger boosted the anti-nuclear and black civil rights movements from the social unrest stage to the enthusiastic mobilization stage. Such events cause significant numbers of people to lose faith in institutions and the normal means of solving problems and addressing issues. Movement members and sympathizers may begin to see the institution as *the* problem or as part of a conspiracy to maintain power and to defeat all legitimate and reasonable efforts to bring about urgently needed change. When *frustration* leads to *disaffection* with institutions and their ability to change, the social movement enters the stage of enthusiastic mobilization. The growth of social unrest, Bitzer's Stage 1 in the rhetorical situation, culminates in the development of a dominant exigence, an audience, and constraints.[18]

Stage 3: Enthusiastic Mobilization

The social movement in this phase is populated with true believers who have experienced conversion to the cause. They have grown "tired of being sick and tired.''[19] The converted see the social movement as the *only* way to bring about urgently needed change, and they are imbued with the belief that the movement's time has come. Optimism is rampant. Important legitimizers—actors, senators, clergy, physicians, labor leaders, educators—lend an air of excitement and inevitability to the cause.

Institutions and resistance movements are keenly aware of the movement's growth, change in attitude, altered rhetorical strategies, perceived legitimation, and potential for success. They, too, mobilize during this stage. The greater the threat from a social movement, particularly if it is perceived to seek revolutionary changes rather than reforms, the greater are the counter efforts by institutional agents, agencies, and surrogates. Institutions may encourage the creation of counter movements and provide them with resources, freedom of action, and an aura of legitimacy. The plan is to stifle the social movement through actions of ''the people'' or the ''silent majority''—the persons the movement claims it is fighting for—and thus to avoid the appearance of institutional involvement. If these actions fail and the establishment comes to view the movement as a radical revolutionary force, it may unleash police forces to suppress the perceived threat to society.

As social movements expand, evolve, and confront serious opposition from institutional forces, they generally abandon judicial and legislative chambers for the streets, marketplaces, and hallways. They lose faith in both institutions and institutional means to bring about change. Mass meetings, marches, demonstrations, and symbolic actions replace sedate conventions and conferences. The highly visible movement makes news and captures media coverage. New organizations such as Martin Luther King's Southern Christian Leadership Conference and Samuel Gompers' American Federation of Labor arise and compete with or overshadow earlier organizations such as the N.A.A.C.P. and the Knights of Labor. Charismatic agitators—adept at countering growing opposition to the movement—replace moderate men of words or prophets. They control the movement and must be able to stage symbolic acts and to confront institutions and resistance movements. Leaders and members may experience martyrdom for the cause by suffering injury, imprisonment, banishment, or death. They may readily accept and even seek suffering; the ''cause'' has become the true believer's reason for being. The persuasive goal is to raise the consciousness level of the people so that the majority will adopt and pressure the establishment to adopt the movement's highly simplified ''if-only'' images of social processes, problems, and solutions. The people must come to see themselves as the oppressed who have both right and power on their side.

Leaders during this stage of the social movement's life cycle face severe persuasive crises both inside and outside the movement. Externally, movement persuaders must employ harsh rhetoric and stage symbolic acts designed to pressure institutions into capitulation or compromise, to polarize the movement from its opposition (all who are not active supporters of the movement), and to provide acts that reveal the true ugliness of institutions and counter efforts. Movement persuasion during this stage is replete with invective against the devils and conspirators who have perpetrated and prolonged the evil that the social movement alone has the will and the strength to fight. If movement leaders are inept at adapting and changing persuasive strategies and in judging how far to push for positive results and images, they may provoke institutional and public outrage and eventual suppression of the movement. At the very least, the movement may lose essential support from the public, the media, and sympathetic legitimizers within the establishment. A few violent acts may doom years of protest, even if the acts are by a fanatical, splinter group. The public and institutions do not make fine distinctions: an act *in the name* of the social movement is *an act by the movement.*

Internally, the movement's persuaders must deal with competing organizations, each with its own leaders, followers, ideological quirks, and pet persuasive strategies. Coalitions, even fragile ones, are essential for the appearance and effect of a united front against the opposition. Persuasive feats of magic are required to keep coalitions intact for extended periods. Further splintering of the movement and the rise of radical elements that propose violence instead of symbolism and demands unacceptable either to the movement as a whole or to institutions drain persuasive resources from the cause. The movement's major spokespersons may decide that alterations in ideology or persuasive strategies are necessary to keep the movement fresh, to counter specific resistance strategies, or to meet changing circumstances. They must sell each change to the movement's membership or face charges of "revisionism" and fracturing of the movement. A movement's ideology often expands with its membership and diversity. For example, the pro-life movement came into existence to make abortion illegal. As it has progressed, however, it has come to champion the cause of all human life—the aged, the infirm, the mentally retarded, and minorities as well as the unborn.

When confrontations between the movement and institutional forces become severe, the movement stresses "we-they" distinctions more sharply and bitterly. Persons who do not join and former members become hated traitors, "scabs," and "Uncle Toms." The social movement may look within and decide that some members (whites, males, non-skilled workers) are incapable of true understanding or involvement in the cause. These members are purged to purify the movement in time of decision. Leaders must explain and justify the new elite internally and externally.

The movement often achieves some notable goals and victories during the enthusiastic mobilization stage, but the earlier visions of sweeping and meaningful changes remain unfulfilled. Instant success eludes the movement. Leaders are unable to satisfy the insatiable appetites of members and the mass media for new and more spectacular events and achievements. What were viewed as imaginative and potent persuasive strategies or "revolutionary" victories a few years before are ridiculed by new leaders and members. "It is easier for the disgruntled to agree on what is wrong with the old than on what is right with the new."[20] Leaders devote increasing amounts of persuasion to explaining and justifying setbacks, delays, lack of meaningful gains, and failures of old successes to fulfill exaggerated expectations. The extravagant hopes that have energized the movement begin to fade and with them the enthusiasm of the movement. Many people join social movements because they are impatient with the gradualism that institutions espouse, and they have little tolerance for leaders or movements that begin to preach a noninstitutional brand of gradualism. Neither the social movement nor society can sustain a harsh rhetoric for long. Fatigue and boredom inevitably set in.[21] The maturing social movement needs new leadership and a less impassioned and strident rhetoric as it enters the maintenance stage. The loss of a charismatic leader such as Martin Luther King, Jr. or Nazi leader George Lincoln Rockwell may hasten the movement into the next stage because no one else is capable of maintaining mobilization or reenergizing the movement. The remnants of the old enthusiasm often die with the movement's martyr.

Stage 4: Maintenance

The onset of the maintenance stage is a critical time for the social movement because it is a turning point. One direction is toward ultimate victory of some sort; the other is toward oblivion. Unfortunately, the odds are against victory, for "frustration is the fate of all social movements."[22] The movement is undergoing change that is inevitable for all organisms and, as Lloyd Bitzer writes, "a situation deteriorates when any constituent or relation changes in ways that make modification of the exigence significantly more difficult."[23]

The social movement returns to more quiet times during the maintenance stage as the media and the public turn to other, more pressing concerns. Movement persuasion once again emanates from the legislative or judicial chamber and the conference room or convention hall. It is time to hold onto what the movement has gained and to consolidate movement organization for the duration. Radical organizations such as WITCH (Women's International Terrorist Conspiracy from Hell) and SCUM (Society for Cutting Up Men) are gone, and original, more conservative groups such as NOW (National Organization for Women) remain to carry the movement forward.

The agitator must change or leave because the social movement during this stage requires a statesman or administrator who can appeal to disparate elements of the movement, maintain organizations, and deal with institutional leaders. "Many a stirring evangelist," William Bruce Cameron writes, "makes a poor pastor."[24] The statesman, a pastor of sorts, must perfect the social movement and sustain its forward progress as it emerges from its "trial by fire." The agitator's harsh and uncompromising rhetoric of polarization and confrontation has created too many enemies within and outside of the movement and is unsuited for diplomatic and administrative roles. The agitator is a superb street fighter but a poor bureaucrat.

While leaders expend some persuasion trying to transform perceptions of history and society, to prescribe courses of action, and to mobilize for action, their primary persuasive function is to sustain the movement. Both membership and commitment decline during the maintenance stage, so leaders must recruit new members and reinforce beliefs in the movement's ideology and potential for ultimate success. They must sustain or resuscitate hope and optimism in the membership. Unfortunately, leaders become more distant from members during the maintenance stage. There are fewer opportunities to see, hear, and talk with leaders. Dominant communication channels during this stage are newsletters, journals, and movement newspapers. Interpersonal exchanges, once the most frequent channel, decline precipitously.

Incessant fund raising is required to support organizations, property, and publications. Any of these tasks—fund raising, recruiting, publications—may become ends in themselves, and the leader becomes an entrepreneur rather than a reformer. Routinization of dues, meetings, leadership, decision-making, and rituals seems essential for a highly structured and disciplined movement that will survive and carry the cause forward. These bureaucratic necessities, however, siphon off much of the old spontaneity, excitement, and *esprit de corps* that made the movement vibrant and attractive. What was improvised during an emergency or passionate moment in an earlier, exciting stage now becomes a "sacred precedent and wisdom of the past" that cannot be altered.[25]

Lack of visibility is a major preoccupation. The movement is rarely newsworthy during this stage, and the mass media begin to address the social movement and its leaders in editorials and columns that begin with phrases such as "What ever happened to" and "Where is ... now?" The adage "out of sight, out of mind" haunts movement persuaders, but their persuasive options are few. Paradoxically, neither movement members nor the public will support the mass demonstrations of old, but quiet seems to indicate satisfaction. Institutions may not tolerate or may have learned how to deal with old persuasive tactics. Worst of all, institutions might simply ignore an outdated symbolic act. Leaders resort to ceremonies, rituals, annual meetings, and anniversary celebrations during which martyrs, tragedies, events, and victories are recounted and memorialized. The rhetoric of the movement is increasingly internal toward maintenance functions rather than external toward pressuring the opposition.

The social movement looks for a triggering event that would give birth to a new phase of enthusiastic mobilization, make the cause fun again, and counteract the gradual hardening of the arteries that elderly social movements experience. The hoped-for rebirth eludes most social movements, or it arrives too late. For example, when the ideals of the woman's rights and industrial union movements were taken up by the women's liberation and C.I.O. (Congress of Industrial Organizations) movements, the original leaders and organizations were history.

As the movement shrinks or faces a long stalemate, it may select a single issue or solution upon which to focus its persuasive energies. The refrain is appealing: "All will be well if only we can get" the right to vote, or a prohibition amendment, or the eight-hour day, or equal rights legislation, or integration of public schools and accomodations. The single goal is simple and more attainable than a panacea of hopes and dreams and is often highly attractive to the movement and institutions that have grown weary of confrontation. Elements of the social movement can unite behind a single, less divisive goal. Institutional agents are more likely to support a non-radical goal that is proposed through normal means and channels.

The social movement is on the threshold of the final stage: termination. The movement as a movement will come to an end. The only question is whether it will die or become another form of collectivity.

Stage 5: Termination

The social movement ceases to be a social movement during the termination stage. If it is successful, the movement may celebrate its victory and disband, as the anti-slavery movement did in 1865 after passage of the Thirteenth Amendment to the Constitution. Total disbandment is unlikely, however, because elements of every movement have made the cause their livelihood, and they will trust no one with its principles or their jobs. Also, the movement's ideology is usually so broad that *all* of its tasks are rarely fulfilled. Thus, if the social movement maintains an effective organization and its principles come to match current mores, it is more likely to become the new order, as the communist and nazi movements did in Russia and Germany, or to become a new institution as Methodism and the American Federation of Labor did in America.

Leaders of social movements transformed into new orders or new institutions face new persuasive challenges. They must strive for obedience among the membership and the people, bring an end to tensions, and establish a perfecting myth. Leaders must purge elements who will not accept the transformation of the social movement or who pose threats to the leadership's attempts to achieve peace and harmony among the classes. The reformers of movement days become the priests of the new order or institution and must be capable of performing pastoral functions. Inevitably, the movement-turned-institution will face a new generation of reformers.

Few social movements are totally successful, however. Some shrink into pressure groups, philanthropic associations, political parties, or social watchdog roles. Others are absorbed or coopted by established institutions. Many of the principles that the populists, progressives, and socialists espoused, for instance, have been adopted into the system with no recognition of the social movements that championed them for years. Occasionally, an institution will crush a social movement or a movement organization such as the Black Panther Party, Weathermen, and Communist Party because the institution and the people come to view the movement or organization as a grave danger to society. A great many movements merely fade away.

Social movements shrink and die for many reasons. Leaders and members may despair of ever changing anything or of achieving permanent and meaningful gains equal to the sacrifices they have made. They may become overwhelmed by the magnitude or multiplicity of the problems that must be solved, or they lose faith in society's capacity for reform. For others, the social movement becomes merely a job, or the new lifestyle becomes boring and meaningless as years pass. Both leaders and followers experience fatigue because they cannot continue to endure the dangers, thrills, and privations that social movements demand.[26] Violent actions by radical groups may frighten movements, institutions, and the people into seeking "normalcy."

During the termination stage, then, leaders and followers may become as disaffected with social movements as they once were with established institutions. They may opt for military rather than symbolic warfare and wage a civil war or revolution to force change. More likely, however, movement members and sympathizers drop back into the institutions from which they came.[27] Some leaders like Eldridge Cleaver, a founder of the Black Panther

Party, have "conversion" experiences and become "born again" Christians, capitalists, or government bureaucrats and may or may not continue to work for change. Sam Riddle, a former Michigan State University rebel, has become an oil company lawyer and remarks: "I can do a lot more with a base of capital than with a pocketful of rhetoric. I'm no longer interested in standing on my soapbox and shouting into the wind. Now I'm more interested in producing the soapboxes."[28] Other social movement disciples turn inward—toward "privatism"—in an effort to protect or to change themselves or their inner circles of family and friends.[29]

Conclusions

Social movements are intricate and ever-changing social dramas, and each of their stages requires both subtle and blunt changes in acts, scenes, agents, agencies, and purposes. Sometimes they resemble oldtime melodramas with their ever-present villains lurking about and waiting for the leaders and members of the movement—the do-gooders—to make foolish mistakes or to fail in their gallant efforts to perfect the world. Villains know that time is on their side and that perfection is always elusive.

Each stage—genesis, social unrest, enthusiastic mobilization, maintenance, and termination—requires specific persuasive skills and personalities. Genesis, for example, demands an intellectual or prophet who excels at defining and visualizing, at using words. Enthusiastic mobilization requires an agitator who can confront and polarize, excite and insult, unite and fragment. Maintenance requires a diplomat who is capable of healing, sustaining, administering, and bargaining.

Each stage also poses unique persuasive dilemmas for social movement persuaders and requires persuasion to serve one or more major functions. For example, transforming perceptions of history—past, present, and future—dominates the first stage. Transforming perceptions of history and society and prescribing courses of action dominate the persuasive efforts of the second stage. Transforming perceptions of society and mobilization for action dominate the third stage. Sustaining dominates the fourth stage.

For social movements that survive to the final stage—termination—the results are usually disappointing and disillusioning. Early goals, even when partially reached, never bring about the perfection envisioned by the creators of the movement. Some movement members condemn society, institutions, or human beings as incapable of reform, unable to attain perfection. Others see the means—social movements, persuasion, violence—as impotent tools for achieving lasting and meaningful change. Ultimately, all social movements come to an end and experience some degree of frustration, but this does not mean that social movements have no influence or that their causes die with them. As Leland Griffin writes:

> And if the wheel forever turns, it is man who does the turning—forever striving, in an "imperfect world," for a world of perfection. And hence man, the rhetorical animal, is saved: for salvation lies in the striving, the struggle itself.[30]

Chapter 3 will examine the nature of leadership in social movements and how leadership is attained and maintained in social movements.

Endnotes

1 Leland M. Griffin, "A Dramatistic Theory of the Rhetoric of Movements," *Critical Responses to Kenneth Burke*, William Rueckert, ed. (Minneapolis: University of Minnesota Press, 1969), 456-478; Kenneth Burke, *A Grammar of Motives* (Englewood Cliffs, NJ: Prentice-Hall, 1950).

2 William Bruce Cameron, *Modern Social Movements* (New York: Random House, 1966), 27-29.

3 Donald G. Ellis and B. Aubrey Fisher, "Phases of Conflict in Small Group Development: A Markov Analysis," *Human Communication Research*, 1 (Spring, 1975), 195-212.

4 Julia T. Wood, "Communication and Relational Culture: Bases for the Study of Human Relationships," *Communication Quarterly*, 30 (Spring, 1982), 75-84.

5 Mark L. Knapp, *Interpersonal Communication and Human Relationships* (Boston: Allyn and Bacon, 1984), 32-54.

6 Bruce E. Gronbeck, "The Rhetoric of Social-Institutional Change: Black Action at Michigan," *Explorations in Rhetorical Criticism*, Gerald Mohrmann, Charles Stewart, Donovan Ochs, eds. (University Park, PA: Pennsylvania State University Press, 1973), 98-101.

7 This life cycle is based on ones developed by Carl A. Dawson and Warner E. Gettys, *An Introduction to Sociology* (New York: Ronald, 1935); John Wilson, *An Introduction to Social Movements* (New York: Basic Books, 1973); and Griffin, 462-472.

8 For a theoretical discussion of the concept of "the people," see Michael McGee, "In Search of 'The People': A Rhetorical Alternative," *Quarterly Journal of Speech*, 61 (October, 1975), 235-249.

9 Griffin, 457-462; Eric Hoffer, *The True Believer* (New York: Harper and Row, 1951), 120-121.

10 Hoffer, 20.

11 Lloyd F. Bitzer, "Functional Communication: A Situational Perspective," *Rhetoric in Transition: Studies in the Nature and Uses of Rhetoric*, Eugene E. White, ed. (University Park, PA: Pennsylvania State University Press, 1980), 23, 26, 27, 28-29, and 32.

12 Harold D. Mixon, "Boston's Artillery Election Sermons and the American Revolution," *Speech Monographs*, 34 (March, 1967), 43-50.

13 Leland M. Griffin, "The Rhetoric of Historical Movements," *Quarterly Journal of Speech*, 38 (April, 1952), 186.

[14] Leslie G. Rude, "The Rhetoric of Farmer-Labor Agitators," *Central States Speech Journal*, 20 (Winter, 1969), 281.

[15] S. Judson Crandell, "The Beginnings of a Methodology for Social Control Studies," *Quarterly Journal of Speech*, 33 (February, 1947), 37; Griffin (1969), 462-463.

[16] Leland M. Griffin, "The Rhetorical Structure of the 'New Left' Movement: Part I," *Quarterly Journal of Speech*, 50 (April, 1964), 115.

[17] John W. Bowers and Donovan J. Ochs, *The Rhetoric of Agitation and Control* (Reading, MA: Addison-Wesley, 1971), 17.

[18] Bitzer, 34.

[19] Wilson, 89-90.

[20] Wilson, 109-110.

[21] Saul D. Alinsky, *Rules for Radicals: A Pragmatic Primer for Realistic Radicals* (New York: Vintage Books, 1972), 159-161.

[22] Wilson, 360.

[23] Bitzer, 35.

[24] Cameron, 93.

[25] Cameron, 87.

[26] Jerry Rubin "Growing Up Again," *Human Behavior*, March, 1976, 17-23.

[27] Peter Goldman and Gerald Lubenow, "Where the Flowers Have Gone," *Newsweek*, September 5, 1977, 24-30; Margie Casady, "Where Have the Radicals Gone?" *Psychology Today*, October, 1975, 63-64, 92; "Yesterday's Activists: Still Marching to a Different Drummer?" *Notre Dame Magazine*, October, 1975, 10-21.

[28] "Yesterday's Radicals Put on Gray Flannel," *U.S. News and World Report*, January 19, 1981, 41.

[29] Jerry LeBlanc, "Unplug the World, We Want to Get Off," *Indianapolis Star Magazine*, July 28, 1974, 7-8.

[30] Griffin (1969), 472.

Chapter 3

Leadership in Social Movements

The American public's view of leadership in social movements is heavily influenced by its faith in *individualism* and in American *institutions* and the ability of individuals and institutions to cope with "real" social problems. Roberta Ash writes that "Only in America is the belief that individualism and collectivism are necessarily in conflict so widely held."[1] After decades of persuasive efforts to organize factory workers, farmers and farm workers, women, blacks, chicanos, and gays, only small percentages of each were ever active members of organizations created to resolve their plights.[2] John Wilson writes that during the farm income decline of the 1950s, "Most farmers had come to feel that the American public was paying too little for its food or else the middle man was taking too large a slice of the cake, and hence believed there was something drastically wrong with the marketing system." Despite this widespread belief, only six percent of farmers actually joined the National Farmers Organization (NFO).[3]

American institutions are able to sustain themselves even in times of massive economic breakdowns.[4] During the depression of the 1930s, voters turned to Franklin Roosevelt and the Democratic Party to return the nation to economic prosperity rather than to the Socialist or Communist Parties. Public opinion polls reveal a persistent confidence in American institutions even when that confidence is allegedly shaken, as during the final year of President Carter's administration. A Gallup Poll conducted in early May, 1980 asked this question: "How much confidence do you, yourself, have in these American institutions to serve the public needs—a great deal of confidence, a fair amount, or very little?" The answers which follow combine the percentages for "a great deal" and "a fair amount."[1]

Churches	82%	Federal Government	61%
Public Schools	74%	Labor Unions	55%
State Government	69%	Big Business	55%
Courts	64%		

A clear majority of respondents maintained their faith in American institutions in spite of the oil crisis, high inflation, and the hostage situation in Iran. However, the remainder percentages representing "little or no confidence" (ranging from 18% to 45%) are significant enough to show that the legitimacy of institutions is vulnerable to rhetorical assaults by social movements. Institutions cannot take public support for granted or ignore the challenges social movements pose.

People who choose to *organize* and to operate *outside of American institutions* and to claim that there is an urgent problem being ignored, hidden, or promoted by the very persons or institutions Americans revere or cherish are likely to be branded as losers, misfits, outcasts, extremists, or rabble-rousers.[6] If these un-American "trouble-makers" persist and organize protests, the public (often with the aid of the mass media and institutional agents and agencies) may attach new labels suitable for social destroyers: communists, fascists, terrorists, anarchists, or fanatics.

American institutions such as government agencies and agents, schools and teachers, churches and clergy, labor unions and officers, corporations and executives, and social theorists reinforce the public's attitudes toward social movement leaders. Former governor of Alabama George C. Wallace was not the first institutional leader, and certainly will not be the last, to characterize social movement leaders and members as anarchists, social schemers, sex perverts, pinkos, communists, and pointy-headed liberals.[7] Eric Hoffer, the self-made social philosopher, claims in his book *The True Believer* that social movement leaders desire to divest themselves of an "unwanted self." "The revulsion from an unwanted self, and the impulse to forget it, mask it, slough it off, and lose it," Hoffer writes, "produce both a readiness to sacrifice the self and a willingness to dissolve it by losing one's individual distinctness in a compact collective whole."[8] Comments such as these led Herbert Simons to write in 1972 that "rhetoricians and other scholars have tended to assume that methods of influence appropriate for drawing room controversies are also effective for social conflicts, including struggles against established authorities."[9] He concludes that scholars "have failed to suggest viable strategies for those engaged in rough and tumble conflicts, and some of them have dismissed militant protestors as pathological."

The mass media, institutional authorities, and the public too often assume that any person who appears to act in behalf of a social movement or cause is a movement "leader." In his study of the Watts Riot that occurred in Los Angeles in 1965, Anthony Oberschall notes that those who assaulted police, threw rocks, set fire to buildings, and harangued crowds "were neither leaders prior to these incidents nor do they subsequently play a leader role in other incidents."[10] A number of studies by Crane Brinton (the American, French, English, and Russian revolutions), Ming T. Lee (the Communist revolution in China), and Seymour Lipset (the socialist movement in Saskatchewan) provide substantial evidence that *social movement leaders do not come from the marginal areas or "lunatic fringe" of society* but from the higher strata of groups and subcultures: teachers, editors, farmers, civil servants, businessmen, clergy, and lawyers.[11] Writing about the leaders of the French and American revolutions, Brinton notes that they "were not in general afflicted with anything the psychiatrist could be called about. They were certainly not riffraff, scoundrels, scum of the earth."[12]

Anthony Oberschall and Herbert Simons recommend that researchers and students of social movements look at the rhetorical-social situation leaders face rather than pathological traits or early childhood experiences. The typical leader of a typical social movement has no sanctioned position, no sanctioned authority to implement decisions, no regular salary, no orderly personal or family life, and no job security. At the same time, the leader often encounters threats, harassment, denial of access to the mass media, persecution, arrest, jail terms, exile, or the necessity of going into hiding. Simons observes that "unless it is understood that the leader is subjected to incompatible demands, a great many of his rhetorical acts must seem counterproductive."[13] "Put any ordinary, stable individual into a similar position," Oberschall concludes, "and he, too, would probably exhibit what some observers consider confused or arbitrary behavior as a result of the pressures and dilemmas that one is continually faced with as a leader in an uninstitutionalized and emergent organizational setting."[14]

The purpose of this chapter is to go beyond the public and institutional view of social movement leadership and the simplistic typologies many social theorists have developed during the past half-century to examine the *nature* of leadership in social movements and how it is *attained* and *maintained*. Implications for the persuasive efforts of social movements will become obvious.

The Nature of Leadership in Social Movements

Theorists generally agree with John Wilson that "the typical pattern of domination in the typical social movement is subsumed under neither the concept of power nor that of authority."[15] Leadership in social movements, Wilson notes, tends to be more structured than a naked power relationship and less structured than an authority relationship associated with an organizational position. Simons claims the leader, at best, "controls an organized core of the movement (frequently mistaken for the movement itself) but exerts relatively little influence over a relatively larger number of sympathizers on its periphery."[16] Essentially, the leader gains the right (the legitimacy) to exercise specific skills within a specific social movement organization or coalition, and these skills are often learned through costly trial and error as the movement unfolds.[17]

Leaders as Decision Makers

The social movement leader is a "decision maker," but rarely has the powers of reward and punishment or the claim to legitimacy of an established authority.

Joseph Gusfield notes that although the leader is the head of a decision-making hierarchy within a social movement organization, the leader operates in an environment of clients, enemies, adherents, and potential recruits in which he or she has no authority but merely represents the movement.[18] This environment is fraught with repressive uncertainty, complex conditions, conflicting demands, pressures from inside and outside the movement, power struggles among movement elements and organizations, disagreements over philosophies and strategies, financial crises, and competition among aspiring leaders.[19] Herbert Simons perceptively summarizes the plight of social movement leaders:

> Shorn of the controls that characterize formal organizations, yet required to perform the same internal functions, harassed from without, yet obligated to adapt to the external system, the leader of a social movement must constantly balance inherently conflicting demands on his position and on the movement he represents.[20]

The difficulties social movement leaders encounter and the limitations placed upon them were evident during the civil rights movement. The most common images Americans have of Martin Luther King, Jr. come from memories and pictures of King delivering his famous "I Have A Dream" speech on the steps of the Lincoln Memorial, walking arm-in-arm with other civil rights leaders through southern towns, or meeting with the press. These were mere highlights of a social movement leader in action.[21] Most of King's time was spent trying to keep or make peace among fellow clergymen with giant-sized egos or among competing civil rights organizations such as the National Association for the Advancement of Colored People (NAACP), Congress of Racial Equality (CORE), Student Nonviolent Coordinating Committee (SNCC), and his own Southern Christian Leadership Conference (SCLC). He preferred to be on the front lines of the movement, particularly during such major campaigns as Selma, Montgomery, and Birmingham. More frequently he was in New York or Washington trying to raise the funds necessary to keep the campaign alive. Bail for hundreds of protestors arrested during demonstrations and fines levied for breaking local and state ordinances represented a mere fraction of the expense incurred in the operation of the enormous organization. Only Martin Luther King could perform these essential fund-raising activities effectively, but friends of the movement often grumbled about his absence at critical moments in the streets of the South. Enemies accused him of cowardice, of running away when things got rough, of accepting bail while others remained in jail.

Leaders as Symbols

Although social movement leaders typically do not have the powers and legitimacy of institutional authorities, *they are able to lead because their skills enable them to function as the symbols of their movements.*[22] Leaders tend to become totally *identified* with the cause and its followers and thus are often able to instill absolute devotion, love, trust, and dependence in members.[23] Eugene V. Debs provides an illustrative example. In April 1894, he led his American Railway Union in a victorious strike against the powerful James J. Hill and the Great Northern Railroad, a remarkable victory for a union that was barely two years old. As Debs left by train from St. Paul, Minnesota to return to his home in Terre Haute, Indiana, railroad workers lined both sides of the tracks with their hats in their hands in homage to their leader.[24] Some social movements actually take on their leaders' names: Martin Luther (the Lutheran Church), John Wesley (the Wesleyan movement among British and American protestants), Francis Townsend (the Townsend movement of the 1930s for old age pensions), Joseph McCarthy (the McCarthyite movement of the 1950s to fight alleged communist influences in American government and society), and Karl Marx (the Marxist-communist movement that began in Europe and spread around the world), to name a few.[25]

The leader is the "face" of the social movement for members, the public, and the mass media. "It is with leadership that the public identifies in describing and judging a movement," Joseph Gusfield writes, "the leader personifies the movement in cartoon, picture, story, and legend. For much of the public, the leader becomes synonymous with the movement and its adherents."[26] For instance, more than one generation of Americans viewed the labor movement among coal miners as synonymous with John L. Lewis. The fiery, bushy eyebrowed leader of the United Mine Workers was seen frequently during newsreels in theatres, on front pages of newspapers and magazines, and in numberless cartoons on editorial pages.

Herbert Simons concludes that "The primary rhetorical test of the leader—and, indirectly, of the strategies he employs—is his capacity to fulfill the requirements of his movement by resolving or reducing rhetorical problems."[27] In a very real sense, then, the social movement leader is a *rhetorical* leader of a *social* movement.

How Leadership is Attained in Social Movements

A leadership position is attained in a social movement when members perceive a person to possess one or more of three attributes: charisma, prophecy, or pragmatism.[28]

Charisma

The charismatic leader's source of legitimacy lies in his or her apparent access to a higher source or divine inspiration.[29] An "awe-inspiring personality," William Cameron writes, leads social movement members to see "truth" in the charismatic leader's utterances.[30] The charismatic leader tends to be a showperson with a sense of timing and the rhetorical skills necessary to articulate what "others can as yet only feel, strive towards, and imagine but cannot put into words or translate explicitly into action."[31] This person leads followers in direct actions that stir things up.[32] A Martin Luther King (leader of the civil rights movement of the 1950s and 1960s), Samuel Gompers (a founder and leader of the American Federation of Labor from 1886 to 1924), Susan B. Anthony (a leader of the women's rights and women's suffrage movements from 1848 to 1906), or Frederick Douglass (an escaped slave who became an internationally known leader of the anti-slavery movement) supply vigor to the social movement and make people believe in the impossible.[33] Susan B. Anthony coined the slogan "failure is impossible" for the women's rights movement. The charismatic leader feels a duty, not merely an obligation or opportunity, to lead the movement and often exhibits exceptional heroism, bravery, and endurance to the point of martyrdom for the cause.[34] The intense, unwavering support of followers (even when the charismatic leader blunders in selecting targets, strategies, and times to act) maintains unity within the movement and prevents a shifting of the power structure so common within minimally organized social movement organizations.[35]

Perhaps there is no better example of a charismatic leader than Mahatma Gandhi who for over thirty years led India's fight for independence from Great Britain.[36] He developed a philosophy and program called *satyagraha* (literally "truth-force") that embodied a method of persuasion that used moral means to achieve moral ends. Gandhi understood the need for showmanship when leading a mass movement and refined actions that gained international attention, identified himself with the Indian people, and required few resources. He dressed in simple sandals and a loincloth that represented the daily attire of male laborers in India. As a protest against British textile laws, Gandhi learned to weave his own simple clothing and made the spinning wheel a major symbol of independence from British rule and influence. He underwent fifteen fasts, his "fiery weapon," to protest low wages and working conditions, to restore peace after riots had erupted during a visit by British royalty, to end violence (particularly among Hindus and Muslims), to protest his own imprisonment, and to pressure several British Prime Ministers into altering actions and decisions.

Gandhi spent nearly a third of his life as a social movement leader conducting propaganda tours that often covered hundreds of miles and lasted for months. Each walk took him among the people most sympathetic with the movement and gained attention and followers. As "sacred pilgrimages," these walks identified Gandhi and the movement with the religious traditions of India. He literally became a "holy man" for millions of Indians. Allen Merriam writes that "The primacy of symbolic behavior in extending Gandhi's influence corresponded to the traditional pattern of Indian gurus, who are identified more by their life-style than by their pronouncements."[37] Gandhi was assassinated shortly after the movement culminated in an independent but strife-torn India.

Prophecy

The prophet's source of legitimacy lies in his or her apparent proximity to the writings of the social movement, its ideology.[38] The person may have written all or important segments of the movement's doctrine, may be considered the most knowledgeable authority on the doctrine, or may be seen as nearest in spirit to the doctrine. As a spokesperson for the movement's "god"—capitalism, socialism, freedom, equality—the leader with the gift of prophecy elaborates, justifies, and explains the movement's values, myths, and beliefs.[39] The prophet knows the "truth" and sets a moral tone for the social movement.[40] Because the "prophet" is a person of vision, has a psychological commitment to principles, and perceives the writings of the movement to be sacred, he or she is unlikely to be a reconcilor between movement factions or between movement and the established order.[41] The legitimacy of decisions is judged by reference to ideology, not by ends achieved.

When Robert Welch called eleven men together for a two-day meeting in Indianapolis on December 8 and 9, 1958 to found the John Birch Society, he launched his effort to become the undisputed "prophet" for the anti-communist movement in the United States. He opened his two-day speech to these eleven like-minded businessmen by establishing his qualifications to lead the movement:

> I personally have been studying the problem increasingly for about nine years, and practically full time for the past three years. And entirely without pride, but in simple thankfulness, let me point out that a lifetime of business experience should have made it easier for me to see the falsity of the economic theories upon which Communism is supposedly based, more readily, than might some scholar coming into that study from the academic cloisters; while a lifetime of interest in things academic, especially world history, should have given me an advantage over many businessmen, in more readily seeing the sophistries in dialectical materialism.[42]

Welch's two-day speech became *The Blue Book of the John Birch Society*, the organization's bible. It not only exposed the imminent dangers of the world communist conspiracy but outlined in detail how the Society would be led, organized, and proceed in its "battles" in the "war" against communism. Sunday supplements in major conservative newspapers such as *The Chicago Tribune* and *The Arizona Republic* introduced the John Birch Society to millions of Americans in the fall of 1964. An item entitled "He Has Stirred the Slumbering Spirit" presented Robert Welch as a person of vision and commitment in the struggle against the communist menace, a person whose words were gaining converts:

> Mr. Welch's writings have created widespread comment—some critical. Few were ready to believe him when he warned of the impending Communist takeovers by Castro in Cuba, Ben Bella in Algeria, and Sukarno in Indonesia. But with events proving him correct again and again, his writings are now closely scrutinized by all serious students of anti-Communism.[43]

Welch created a monthly periodical for the movement entitled *American Opinion* and remained its editor and frequent contributor until his death in 1986. In an open letter to readers in the October 1978 issue, Welch wrote of the periodical's reason for being:

> You were to read *American Opinion* in order to learn the truth; the plain unmistakable truth about what was really happening. We set out twenty-two years ago to make this monthly compendium the most accurate, most penetrating, and most widely accepted authority in the world on the nature and the menace of the revolutionary cabal that was steadily undermining our whole civilization.[44]

Welch was never a reconciler in the struggle between good and evil that was a matter of life and death for the American way of life. As a prophet for the movement, his Society's purpose was to build "rededication to God, to family, to country, and to strong moral principles."[45]

Pragmatism

The pragmatist's source of legitimacy lies in his or her apparent organizational expertise, efficiency, and tact.[46] As a person who believes that the social movement must have a secure and stable foundation for growth, the pragmatic leader brings commonsense and a healthy skepticism to the movement, seeks to reconcile diverse interests, desires "communication" rather than "excommunication," and replaces unattainable goals with diffuse goals and a broader range of targets.[47] The pragmatist believes that ideals and principles are useless without organization and implementation. This type of leader seeks to make the social movement inclusive rather than exclusive by making it more acceptable to outsiders, including important legitimizers from the established order, and devotes energies to fundraising, recruitment, and organization.[48] The pragmatist is more likely to compromise the "sacredness" of the movement's writings than the "integrity" of the organization, and may come to see the organization as an end in itself.[49]

Samuel Gompers, who led (with the exception of one year) the American Federation of Labor from its founding in 1886 to his death in 1924, was above all a pragmatist. He was keenly aware of the labor movement's history, of organizations that had blossomed and wilted, of American opposition to labor "radicals," and of the needs and desires of workers, particularly among the skilled trades. Above all, he understood the need for a strong organization with a central focus (trade unionism) and a sound financial base.[50] Although Gompers was sympathetic with all elements of the labor movement, he refused, for example, to aid the Knights of Labor when it became embroiled in the aftermath of the Haymarket Riot and the trials of the accused anarchists. The A.F. of L. was too young, could not afford to become identified with the Knights or the anarchists and was, after all, in competition with the "industrial unionism" espoused by the

Knights. Gompers saw the "trade union" as "the historic and natural form of working class organization" and shed no tears when the Knights of Labor declined rapidly after the Haymarket affair.[51] Speaking to the Machinists' Convention in 1901, he remarked:

> Those of us who have gone through the movement of the Knights of Labor, which is now happily removed from the path of progress; those who have studied the previous effervescent movements of that character, know the danger with which such movements are always confronted.

Gompers understood the American value system and the inherent conservatism of most workers and industrialists in his struggle to make the A.F. of L. the accepted umbrella organization for all trade unions.

While trying to avoid unnecessary confrontations, Gompers was not reluctant to attack elements that posed dangers to his beloved organization. At the A.F. of L. Convention in 1903, Gompers attacked socialist members head on:

> And I want to say that I am entirely at variance with your philosophy. I declare it to you, I am not only at variance with your doctrines, but with your philosophy. Economically, you are unsound; socially, you are wrong; industrially, you are an impossibility.[52]

Gompers succeeded in building and maintaining a social movement organization that would withstand the onslaught of industrialists, competing labor organizations, depressions, and wars to become an institutionalized force in American society.

How Leadership is Maintained in Social Movements

Social movement leaders tend to maintain their positions as long as they hold the confidence of followers, seem to have obvious solutions to problems, meet the exigencies of new and often unexpected situations, and perform the rhetorical functions necessary for the stage the movement is in.[53] William Cameron writes that all leaders "do something exceedingly well" and "when they stop doing it well, they often cease to lead."[54]

A Mix of Leadership Attributes

Theorists agree that every successful social movement leader must display two or more of the three essential leadership attributes—charisma, prophecy, or pragmatism—though not necessarily in the same context. Joseph Gusfield, for example, argues that "leadership can be conceived as a set of simultaneous roles." As mobilizer, the leader must "breathe the fire and brimstone of enthusiastic mission," and as articulator, the leader "pours the oil of bargaining, compromise, and common culture."[55] John Wilson claims that leaders gain the esteem of fellow movement members because of the peculiar mix of their rhetorical abilities.[56] And

Anthony Oberschall concludes: "Leaders, in sum, are the architects of organization, ideology, and mobilization for the movement."[57]

Unfortunately, a great many social movement leaders tend to be one-dimensional. Few spokesmen for black rights during the 1960s were more charismatic, particularly among young blacks who were growing disillusioned with the "civil rights" movement, than Stokely Carmichael, Chairman of SNCC (Student Nonviolent Coordinating Committee) during the famous Meredith March in Mississippi in June 1966. He was attractive, intelligent, articulate, and understood the importance of timing and showmanship. During the Meredith March, Carmichael cooperated with the leaders of the NAACP and SCLC until the march reached Greenwood, SNCC territory, and Martin Luther King had left for meetings in Chicago. The sheriff arrested Carmichael and others briefly on June 16 for pitching tents in a schoolyard, and Carmichael used the occasion to escalate his confrontational rhetoric at an evening rally: "This is the 27th time I've been arrested. I ain't gonna be arrested no more. . . . Every courthouse in Mississippi should be burnt down tomorrow so we can get rid of the dirt."[58] The next evening Stokeley Carmichael delivered more of the same confrontational message and then, on cue, Willie Ricks shouted: "What do you want?" Carmichael responded: "Black power!" and the crowd was soon echoing this new slogan enthusiastically. He had seized the moment beautifully. During the next several months, he traveled throughout the country both explaining and extolling "Black Power." But while Carmichael became a hero among the growing numbers of young "black nationalists" within the movement, his slogan and rhetoric of confrontation shattered the fragile coalition of black rights organizations and polarized white liberals and blacks.[59] He lacked the attributes of both the prophet in failing to develop a clear doctrine of "black power" and the pragmatist by attacking "leaders" in his speeches to black audiences. In Detroit on July 30, 1966, Carmichael remarked:

> I'm very concerned, because you see we have a lot of Negro leaders, and I want to make it clear I'm no leader. I represent the Student Nonviolent Coordinating Committee. That's the sole source of my power, and that's Black Power. I'm no Negro leader, but I think that we have to speak out about the war in Vietnam.[60]

By 1968 Carmichael had left SNCC, reestablished his relationship with Martin Luther King, and formed a new organization called the Black United Front, an organization that experienced a short lifespan.[61] He remained an eloquent spokesperson for black power, pride, and independence, but he failed as a "leader." William Cameron undoubtedly had one-dimensional movement leaders such as Stokely Carmichael in mind when he wrote, "many a stirring evangelist makes a poor pastor."[62]

Handling Diverse, Conflicting Roles

Few social movement leaders, even multi-dimensional ones, are capable of handling the diverse and often conflicting roles thrust upon them and the rhetorical dilemmas encountered daily by social movements.[63] The leader must adapt to different audiences at once but not appear to be a political chameleon, produce short-run successes but not preclude long-run successes, use militant tactics to gain visibility for the movement but use moderate tactics to gain entry into decision-making centers, and grasp at opportunities to deal with the established order on its own turf but not appear to be "selling out" or "going soft." The difficulty of meeting and adapting to role demands that require different rhetorical skills and tactics typically results in a proliferation of leaders that cause conflict within and among movement organizations and results in fragmentation of structure and persuasive efforts.[64]

The civil rights movement during the 1950s and 1960s produced a variety of leaders who performed *specific* roles skillfully but could not meet all rhetorical demands of the movement.[65] Roy Wilkins of the NAACP, for instance, believed in working through the system (particularly the courts) to bring about change and feared both the tactics and results of direct actions such as sit-ins, marches, and demonstrations. Andrew Young was highly effective as a conciliator and diplomat within SCLC, particularly among its younger members and elements, but his soft-spoken style and devotion to Martin Luther King prevented him from speaking out on his views and becoming visible beyond the SCLC. Ralph Abernathy was highly visible and usually silent during the movement (seemingly always at King's side in marches, jails, meetings, and press conferences), but his loyalty, dedication, and bravery prepared him in no way to succeed King as leader of the SCLC in 1968. Fred Shuttlesworth founded the Alabama Christian Movement for Human Rights in 1956 and later allied this group with the SCLC. He was highly respected within the movement and feared by the southern establishment for his reckless courage and ability to organize and lead demonstrations, but his efforts to become a major leader of the movement were plagued by autocratic, egocentric, and tactless personality traits.

Changing as the Movement Changes

Perhaps the greatest obstacle for leadership tenure in social movements is the necessity for movements to change and, as movements change, leaders and followers must change. As Joseph Gusfield notes, "The disjuncture between ideology and the adaptive problems of the movement constantly raises the issue of too much or too little accommodation; of renunciation of the mission or overrighteous inflexibility."[66]

Jerry Rubin, for example, was an archetypal leader of the student, anti-Vietnam War, and counter culture movements of the 1960s and early 1970s.[67] He was intelligent, articulate, imaginative, brave and, above all, outrageous in manner, actions, and dress. He was an effective organizer of civil disobedience at Berkeley, troop-train demonstrations, the October 1967 march on the Pentagon, and of the "Yippies" that created chaos at the Chicago convention of the Democratic Party in 1968. He was brilliant at manipulating the media and creating "put-ons" that led to both humorous and violent reactions from the establishment, especially police agencies who confronted the Yippies in the trenches. He helped to polarize society along age lines with the slogan, "Don't trust anyone over thirty." As one of the famous "Chicago Seven," he stood trial for five-and-a-half months charged with "conspiracy" for actions during the Democratic convention. By the early 1970s, Jerry Rubin knew "the movement" was rapidly dwindling in numbers and fervor, that society was changing, that old methods would no longer be effective, and that ironically most leaders (including himself) were nearing or had passed their thirtieth birthdays. Many members of the movement, particularly younger ones, did not want to change and both loved and hated Rubin as a symbol of the 60s. They longed for another 1968 style confrontation during the 1972 Republican and Democratic conventions in Miami Beach and called Rubin a sellout because he stayed in a hotel instead of a park. On July 14, Rubin's 34th birthday, a group calling themselves "Zippies" ("put the zip back into yip") marched on his hotel in Miami armed with a cake to throw in his face to celebrate his retirement from the movement. Later in the year, a band of Zippies "trashed" Rubin's car in New York to demonstrate their independence from older yippies. Rubin came to realize that "changes cannot be made on the political level alone, or that society we are changing will be repeated. We must examine our own process."[68] These were not words the movement and its younger members wanted to hear. Several leaders of the anti-war and counter culture movements committed suicide because either they could not accept or could not adapt to the new social situation.

Adapting to Events

Events may thrust the movement and its leader in new directions, and the leader may appear to be merely a puppet controlled by events and the whims of some members.[69] Leaders must appear to be in the forefront of necessary change and wise adaptation, while not appearing to abandon major norms, beliefs, attitudes, and values of their movements in order to meet situational exigencies.[70]

Terrence Powderly became General Master Workman (president) of the Order of the Knights of Labor in 1880 and helped make it the largest and most powerful labor union in the history of the United States, reaching over one million members in 1886.[71] But 1886 was to be a fateful year for the Knights. The government, newspapers, and the public identified the Knights of Labor with the anarchists and blamed it for the bloody Haymarket Riot in Chicago. Membership and influence plummeted year after year in spite of Powderly's charisma, rhetorical skills, and considerable organizational abilities. In 1893 he decided that only the most drastic of actions could save the Knights, and he approached Samuel Gompers with the notion of merging with the A.F. of L. Other Knights were incensed at Powderly's willingness, regardless of his honorable intentions, to compromise the Order's "fundamental and vital" principle of industrial unionism open to the "laboring masses" by merging with a "trade union" limited to a few skilled workers and headed by archenemy Samuel Gompers. Powderly and his lieutenants were "retired from office," and new General Master Workman, James R. Sovereign, declared to the assembled Knights at the 1894 convention that "any action by members of this Order inimical to or in contravention to this principle [industrial unionism] and this policy is *treason* to the Order and the best interests of labor."[72] Powderly was expelled from the Order and never forgiven for his treachery.

Leading by Not Getting Too Far Ahead or Behind

Bruce Cameron observes that "The leader must seem to lead. In order to lead, he must be a little ahead of his followers, a little wiser, a little more informed. But if he gets out too far ahead, contact is broken, and he may be a 'leader' without followers."[73]

In a study of Malcolm X's autobiography, Thomas Benson focuses on the final year of Malcolm X's life in which he broke with Elijah Muhammad (founder of the Black Muslims), shifted positions on integration and participation in civil rights demonstrations, and no longer saw "uncle Toms" and whites as devils.[74] Many of Malcolm X's supporters and enemies viewed these changes as signs of weakness, inconsistency, softening of commitment, or evidence of the "hustler" element resurfacing. But Benson argues that a careful reading of *The Autobiography of Malcolm X*, published a few months after his assassination, reveals that Malcolm X "contained the principle of change within himself," that his changes can be "seen as consistent steps forward rather than as random and untrustworthy conversions by faith," and that his growing "sense of brotherhood with all men is not the weakening of militancy or a softening of commitment, but an extension of potency."[75] In the months before his assassination when he was facing growing opposition and harassment, Malcolm X opposed "strait-jacketed thinking, and strait-jacketed societies."[76]

While some leaders streak ahead of their movements and lose contact, others lag behind or are unwilling or incapable of adapting to new circumstances or new stages in their social movements' life cycles. A person with strong attributes of charisma and prophecy, for instance, may be unable to abandon unattainable goals or to reconcile diverse elements for the harmony of the larger movement.[77] Or events may revitalize a social movement that has settled into a comfortable bureaucratic state with a pragmatist who is task oriented, has administrative skills, and thrives on the routine and mundane. This skilled bureaucrat, unable to instill vigor, set a moral tone, and make followers believe in the impossible, is likely to be thrust aside by a charismatic leader with the strong traits of the prophet who can put into words and actions what others can only feel or imagine.[78]

Joseph Gusfield's study of the Women's Christian Temperance Union (WCTU) leadership following repeal of prohibition in 1933 illustrates a leader who refused to move with the movement.[79] The president of the WCTU was determined to uphold the centrality of total abstinence even though the American public, Protestant churches, many members of the movement, and other movement organizations such as Alcoholics Anonymous (AA) argued for lesser restrictions on drinking. In her annual report to the WCTU in 1952, Mrs. Z. declared:

> In order not to be considered narrow or unable to see both sides some of the Drys have allowed themselves to be maneuvered into accepting the idea that [total abstinence and Prohibition] is an old-fashioned approach. . . . Between right and wrong there is only one ground and that is a battleground.[80]

Mrs. Z's refusal to modify her stance on principle brought ridicule upon the organization and herself. Movement members and the press described her as being "too rigid" and as a "one-woman drought," a "fire-eating leader," and a "die-hard." When Mrs. A. assumed the presidency of the WCTU in the 1960s, she emphasized the necessity of finding common ground and common goals within the WCTU and between the WCTU and other temperance organizations. Mrs. A. was chosen because she was astride of the movement instead of lagging behind in defense of a principle no longer accepted by much of society and the temperance movement.

Conclusions

Contrary to the impressions of the American public and members of American institutions, social movement leaders tend to be much like the rest of us rather than fire-breathing misfits, fanatics, or perverts. Like all collectives, however, social movements do attract their share of losers, extremists, and the pathological. The public, established orders, and media too often assume that every person involved in a social movement's activities, regardless of the person's involvement, commitment, or position in the movement, is a "leader."

This chapter has focused on the nature of leadership in social movements and how it is attained and maintained. Typical leaders of typical social movements are decision-makers with limited legitimacy and powers to reward and punish while constantly facing conflicting demands on their positions and movements. Leaders are able to lead because they possess one or more of three critical attributes—charisma, prophecy, and pragmatism. They become the symbols and faces of their movements for members, the public, and the media. Attaining leadership positions within social movements is easier than maintaining positions because leaders must sustain an appropriate blend of the three critical attributes, handle diverse and conflicting roles, change as the movement changes, adapt to events, and lead without getting too far ahead or behind their movements.

Chapter 4 develops a typology of political argument and continues our efforts to distinguish types of collective efforts and argumentative stances.

Endnotes

[1] Roberta Ash, *Social Movements in America* (Chicago: Markham, 1972), 40.

[2] John Wilson, *Introduction to Social Movements* (New York: Basic Books, 1973), 124.

[3] Wilson, 78.

[4] Ash, 230.

[5] George H. Gallup, *The Gallup Poll: Public Opinion 1980* (Wilmington, DE: Scholarly Resources, 1981), 178-179.

[6] Eric Hoffer, *The True Believer* (New York: Mentor, 1951), 119-138.

[7] Richard D. Raum and James S. Measell, "Wallace and His Ways: A Study of the Rhetorical Genre of Polarization," *Central States Speech Journal*, 25 (Spring, 1974), 28-35.

[8] Hoffer, 58.

[9] Herbert W. Simons, "Persuasion in Social Conflicts: A Critique of Prevailing Conceptions and a Framework for Future Research," *Speech Monographs*, 39 (November, 1972), 236.

[10] Anthony Oberschall, "The Los Angeles Riot," *Social Problems*, 15 (Winter, 1965) 324-326.

[11] Crane Brinton, *The Anatomy of Revolution* (New York: Vintage Books, 1952), 107; Ming T. Lee, "The Founders of the Chinese Communist Party," *Civilisations* 18 (1968), 115; Seymour Lipset, "Leadership and New Social Movements," in *Studies in Leadership*, Alvin Gouldner, ed. (New York: Harper and Row, 1950), 360.

[12] Brinton, 127.

[13] Herbert W. Simons, "Requirements, Problems, and Strategies: A Theory of Persuasion for Social Movements," *Quarterly Journal of Speech*, 56 (February, 1970), 4.

[14] Anthony Oberschall, *Social Conflict and Social Movements* (Englewood Cliffs, NJ: Prentice-Hall, 1973), 148-149.

[15] Wilson, 198.

[16] Simons (1970), 4.

[17] Oberschall (1973), 158.

[18] Joseph R. Gusfield, "Functional Areas of Leadership in Social Movements," *Sociological Quarterly* 7 (1966), 137.

[19] Oberschall (1973), 158.

[20] Simons (1970), 4.

[21] Adam Fairclough, *To Redeem the Soul of America: The Southern Christian Leadership Conference and Martin Luther King, Jr.* (Athens, GA: University of Georgia Press, 1987).

[22] Yonina Talmon, "Pursuit of the Millennium: The Relation Between Religious and Social Change,: *The European Journal of Sociology*, 2 (1952), 140-141; Ralph Turner and Lewis M. Killian, *Collective Behavior* (Englewood Cliffs, NJ: Prentice-Hall, 1972). 391.

[23] Hadley Cantril, *The Psychology of Social Movements* (New York: John Wiley and Sons, 1963), 132.

[24] Ray Ginger, *The Bending Cross* (New Brunswick, NJ: Rutgers University Press, 1949), 106.

[25] Joseph R. Gusfield, *Protest, Reform, and Revolt: A Reader in Social Movements* (New York: John Wiley and Sons, 1970), 454.

[26] Gusfield (1966), 141.

[27] Simons (1970), 2-3.

[28] Max Weber, *The Theory of Social and Economic Organizations*, trans. by A.M. Henderson and Talcott Parsons (New York: Free Press, 1964), 328-329; Wilson, 201.

[29] Turner and Killian, 390-392; Neil S. Smelser, *Theory of Collective Behavior* (London: Routledge and Kegan Paul, 1962), 355; Wilson, 203; Kenelm Burridge, *New Heaven New Earth: A Study of Millenarian Activities* (Oxford: Basil Blackwell, 1969), 155-156.

[30] William Bruce Cameron, *Modern Social Movements* (New York: Random House, 1966), 73.

[31] Burridge, 155.

[32] Rex D. Hopper, "The Revolutionary Process: A Frame of Reference for the Study of Revolutionary Movements," *Social Forces*, 28 (March, 1950), 272; Smelser, 297.

[33] J.P. Roche and S. Sachs, "The Bureaucrat and the Enthusiast: An Exploration of the Leadership of Social Movements," *Western Political Quarterly*, 8 (1955), 257.

[34] Theodore Abel, "The Pattern of a Successful Social Movement," *American Sociological Review*, 2 (1937), 352.

[35] Turner and Killian, 389-393; Abel, 352.

[36] Allen H. Merriam, "Symbolic Action in India; Gandhi's Nonverbal Persuasion," *Quarterly Journal of Speech*, 61 (October, 1975), 290-306.

[37] Merriam, 305.

[38] Wilson, 201.

[39] Hooper, 275; Turner and Killian, 394.

[40] Roche and Sachs, 258.

[41] Roche and Sachs, 250-251.

[42] *The Blue Book of the John Birch Society* (Belmont, MA: Western Islands, 1961), xiv-xv.

[43] "The John Birch Society: A Report," *The Arizona Republic*, October 25, 1964; advertising supplement, 6.

[44] *American Opinion*, October, 1978, 56.

[45] "The John Birch Society: A Report," *Chicago Tribune*, November 15, 1964, advertising supplement, 16.

[46] Wilson, 201.

[47] Roche and Sachs, 249 and 259; Mayer Zald and Roberta Ash, "Social Movement Organizations: Growth, Decay, Change," *Social Forces*, 44 (1966), 327-340.

[48] Turner and Killian, 394; Roche and Sachs, 250 and 253.

[49] Roche and Sachs, 253.

[50] Walter B. Emery, "Samuel Gompers," in *A History and Criticism of American Public Address*, Vol. II, William Norwood Brigance, ed. (New York: Russell and Russell, 1960), 557-579.

[51] Samuel Gompers, "President's Report," December 13, 1887, *Report of the Proceedings: American Federation of Labor*, 1888, 8; Samuel Gompers, "Address to the Machinists' Convention," *American Federationist*, 8 (July, 1901), 251.

[52] Samuel Gompers, *American Federation of Labor Proceedings*, 1903, 198.

[53] Cantril, 235; R.L. Hamblin, "Leadership and Crisis," *Sociometry*, 21 (1958), 322-335.

[54] Cameron, 164.

[55] Gusfield (1966), 139 and 141.

[56] Wilson, 198 and 201.

[57] Oberschall, 146.

58 Fairclough, 316.

59 Robert L. Scott and Wayne Brockriede, *The Rhetoric of Black Power* (New York: Harper and Row, 1969), 1-9.

60 From a recording and a copy in Scott and Brockriede, 88-89.

61 Fairclough, 364-366.

62 Cameron, 93.

63 Simons (1970), 1-11.

64 Smelser, 297.

65 See Fairclough for discussions of the leadership strengths and weaknesses of civil rights leaders.

66 Gusfield (1966), 152.

67 Jerry Rubin, "Growing Up Again," *Human Behavior*, March, 1976, 17-23.

68 Rubin, 22.

69 Turner and Killian, 396.

70 Muzafer Sherif, *An Outline of Social Psychology* (New York: Harper and Row, 1948), 171.

71 Charles J. Stewart, "Labor Agitation in America: 1865-1915," in *America in Controversy: History of American Public Address*, DeWitte T. Holland, ed. (Dubuque, IA: W.C. Brown, 1973), 153-169.

72 James R. Sovereign, "Annual Address of the General Master Workman," *Proceedings of the General Assembly: Knights of Labor* (1894), 71.

73 Cameron, 107.

74 Thomas W. Benson, "Rhetoric and Autobiography: The Case of Malcolm X," *Quarterly Journal of Speech*, 60 (February, 1974), 1-13.

75 Benson, 7, 9, 10.

76 Benson, 12.

77 Zald and Ash (1966), 533-535; Roche and Sachs, 248-261.

78 Burridge, 155.

79 Gusfield (1966), 142-145.

80 *Annual Report of the National Women's Christian Temperance Union* (1952), 85.

Chapter 4

A Typology of Political Argument

Previous chapters have discussed social movements as unique collective phenomena and suggested that we can profitably study their persuasive efforts. This chapter explores social movement persuasion by developing a typology of political argument that will enable us to compare the persuasive efforts of different movements over time.

Studies of social movements as collectivities have typically focused on the general strategies characteristic of all social movement persuasion,[1] on the strategies unique to a particular type of movement (innovational, revivalistic, resistance),[2] or upon the unique strategies of a specific movement.[3] Much of this research has been productive and illuminating, but integration and synthesis of the findings into a coherent theory are exceedingly difficult. Furthermore, as we discussed in Chapter 1, it is both theoretically and politically naive to presume either that different types of movements obediently follow strategic guidelines (the right sees conspiracies, the left is non-violent) or that persuasive strategies and types of *movements* can be neatly compartmentalized. But a typology of political *argument* can enable us to study types of argument, both as they occur in various movements and as they occur in ordinary (or systemic) political rhetoric. *The distinctive flavor of any social movement's persuasion therefore derives from its blend of available arguments.* A typology should help us to understand the kinds of ingredients from which the movement's persuasion is distilled.

Previous authors have discussed the rhetoric of "historical movements," "social movements," "rhetorical movements," and "political movements."[4] We do not wish simply to add another word to the growing list. Our focus is upon movement over time, which is historical. Since we see that history as the result of human activity in various noninstitutionalized situations, this movement is social. And since we believe that any social act involves the rhetorical function of "adjusting ideas to people and people to ideas,"[5] we see this movement to be fundamentally rhetorical or persuasive. Thus, history is social, and social phenomena have rhetorical dimensions. We do not believe that historical events can, or should, be divorced from the people who participated in them; nor should those people be divorced from their rhetorical characterizations of dreams, fears, enemies, or heroes. All of those arguments are "political" in the sense that they involve discussion of the public good and in the sense that candidates, parties, and Political Action Committees adopt or oppose the arguments raised by the movement.

Rossiter's Political Spectrum

Clinton Rossiter needed a typology of political philosophies within which to discuss *Conservatism in America*.[6] He created a circle marked by seven roughly equidistant points. The first of the seven, *Revolutionary Radicalism*, sees societal institutions as "diseased and oppressive, traditional values dissembling and dishonest; and it therefore proposes to supplant them with an infinitely more benign way of life." *Radicalism* is "dissatisfied with the existing order, committed to a blueprint for thoroughgoing change, and thus willing to initiate reform, but its patience and peacefulness set it off sharply from the revolutionary brand." *Liberalism* is generally satisfied with the existing order and believes that this way of life can be improved "substantially without betraying its ideals or wrecking its institutions." *Conservatism*, like Liberalism, is satisfied with the existing order and sees change as necessary and inevitable. But unlike Liberalism, Conservatism is suspicious of change. "The Conservative," says Rossiter, "knows that change is the rule of life..., but insists that it be sure-footed and respectful of the past.... [The Conservative's] natural preferences are for stability over change, continuity over experiment, the past over the future." *Standpattism*, however, prefers today over either past or future. Rossiter's Standpattism opposes any change, no matter how respectful of the past. "Despite all evidence to the contrary," Standpattism believes that "society can be made static." If Standpattism prefers today over yesterday and tomorrow, and Conservatism prefers tomorrow over yesterday, *Reaction* "sighs for the past and feels that a retreat back into it, piecemeal or largescale, is worth trying." Reaction is unlike Standpattism in two ways: it is unwilling to accept the present, and it is amenable to changing the present state of society. Reaction, like Radicalism, limits the means it will employ to effect that change. But *Revolutionary Reaction* is willing and anxious to use subversion and violence to overthrow established values and institutions and to restore the era it views as the "Golden Age."

Rossiter's spectrum emphasizes philosophy over people. It is developed through the study of history, philosophy, and political theory. It is a parsimonious typology with several rhetorical implications which merit scrutiny.

The first rhetorical implication is that "revolutionaries" have much in common, whether they seek a New Age or a Golden Age. They are willing to subvert and to kill, and they disdain discussion and compromise.

A second rhetorical implication is that adjacent philosophies share fundamental assumptions. Consequently, their disagreements are couched in roughly compatible worldviews. The believers in adjacent philosophies appear reasonable (if a bit misguided) to one another. Each finds the other potentially persuasible, so they concur enough to converse but disagree enough to argue.

The third rhetorical implication is that philosophies opposite one another on the circle share no common assumptions. Thus, believers in opposite philosophies make little sense to one another. These partisans have great difficulty persuading one another because their fundamental differences preclude compromise and constrain their ability to adjust to the other's assumptions. Indeed, they are more likely to talk *about* one another rather than *with* one another.

This leads to a fourth rhetorical implication that is consistent with the social judgment approach to attitude change: we tend to distort our comparative judgments, especially when we are ego-involved in the subject.[7] Thus, when a Liberal who is accustomed to arguing with Conservatives encounters a Standpatter, he or she may too quickly dismiss the Standpatter as a Reactionary. On the other hand, a Standpatter may regard a Liberal as Radical or even Revolutionary because of their disagreement about the desirability of change. Such *contrast effects,* exaggerate differences between positions and complicate persuasion. The counterpart to contrast effects, *assimilation effects* exaggerate agreement in the face of disagreement. The familiar phenomenon of two quarrelling brothers banding together when a neighbor joins the fray has its counterpart in the alliance of Liberals, Conservatives, and Standpatters when Revolutionaries threaten their established order. In short, when we are ego-involved in a political topic, we distance ourselves from those with whom we disagree, and we lump them perceptually into one group. We presume that, since they disagree with us, they must agree with one another. But this is rarely the case. At the same time, we find people and positions *relatively* close to our own and exaggerate the similarity.

Nevertheless, Rossiter's spectrum has several shortcomings. The points on Rossiter's circular model (e.g., Radicalism, Liberalism) are too narrow to depict most political arguments. Second, an argument involves at least two positions seen by the arguers as conflicting (while Rossiter discusses them individually).[8] Third, Rossiter skirts the subject of apathy, ambivalence, and indecision in political theory and argument, thus omitting intensity and fervor from the model.

We can overcome the disadvantages of Rossiter's spectrum while retaining its advantages by considering the *area* of the circle as well as the perimeter. Secondly, let us regard the center of the circle as apathy, ambivalence, and/or indecision.

The alterations allow us to conceive of Rossiter's seven philosophical types as spokes on a wheel rather than points on a circle. The pure philosophical stance is located on the rim with apathy at the hub. We can thus conceptualize and compare various degrees of particular positions with one another. The person who takes a radical stance in speeches or pamphlets is located toward the rim; the person who reads, listens, and responds to those messages is along the spoke; and the person who does not respond (through apathy, indecision, or ignorance) is at the hub.

Just as the revised model permits us to study two points along the continuum from perimeter to hub, it also enables us to study the area between the spokes. *These seven areas between the spokes provide us with our typology of political argument*. As we proceed, let us remember that the spokes represent discrete philosophical positions argued with varying degrees of intensity of conviction.

Argument *along* these spokes (Revolutionary Radical, Radical, Liberal, Conservative, Standpat, Reaction, and Revolutionary Reaction) attempts to reinforce, sustain, intensify, or energize that philosophy. It is "in-group" argument. In-group argument is important for social movements because it is the process through which, for example, Radicals decide just how radical they wish to be. The arguers agree about the nature of change but disagree about the intensity of their beliefs or about the need for action.

Argument *between* the spokes (i.e., between Radical and Liberal, Liberal and Conservative) reflects differences in the arguers' philosophical assumptions, not their degree of conviction.

The seven types of political argument delineated by Rossiter's philosophical stances are: Insurgent, Innovative, Progressive, Retentive, Reversive, Restorative, and Revolutionary (see Figure 1). Let us examine each in turn.

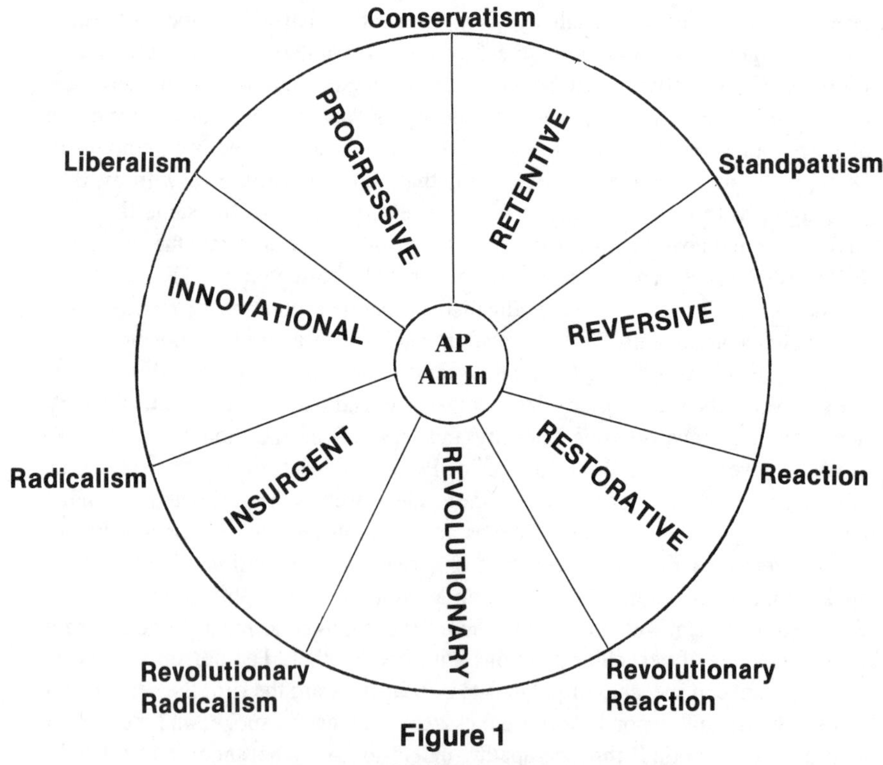

Figure 1

Typology of Political Argument

Insurgent Argument

Insurgent Argument falls between the Revolutionary Radical and Radical spokes of the model. It is typified by agreement on the corrupt, mendacious, and exploitative nature of societal norms, values and institutions. The established order is villified and particular individuals, institutions, and groups are held directly accountable for problems. Seldom is heard an encouraging word.

The Industrial Workers of the World (I.W.W.) blamed employers, as a group, for social conditions in America. The preamble to their Constitution of 1908 declared that:

> The working class and the employing class have nothing in common. There can be no peace so long as hunger and want are found among the millions of working people and the few, who make up the employing class, have all the good things in life. Between these two classes a struggle must go on until the workers of the world organize as a class, take possession of the earth and the machinery of production, and abolish the wage system.[9]

Labor leader John Swinton was more specific in his denunciation of President Grover Cleveland for breaking the Pullman Strike of 1894:

> [President Cleveland] has this year stood out as a servile, mercenary and pusillanimous politician, the ally of money against manhood, fully ready to exercise his power, real and assumed, for the enslavement of the laborious masses who elected him to office.[10]

Roughly fifty years later, Black Muslim leader Malcolm X blamed the American government in its totality for the condition of Black America. In "The Ballot or the Bullet" he argued that:

> You and I in America are faced not with a segregationist conspiracy, we're faced with a government conspiracy. Everyone who's filibustering is a senator—that's the government. Everyone who's finagling in Washington, D.C. is a congressman—that's the government. You don't have anyone putting blocks in your path but people who are part of the government. The same government that you go abroad to fight and die for is the government that is in a conspiracy to deprive you of your voting rights, deprive you of your economic opportunities, deprive you of decent education.[11]

The I.W.W., John Swinton, and Malcolm X all attributed blame for undesirable social conditions to a group or class of people, an important individual, or institution. Presumably social ills could be cured simply by destroying the perpetrator. If insurgent argument blames institutions and people for societal ills, it advocates diverse medicines.

The more revolutionary strains of insurgent argument at least implicitly condone subversion and violence. Socialist Eugene V. Debs, who ran five times for President of the United States, proclaimed that:

> The working class must get rid of the whole brood of masters and exploiters, and put themselves in possession and control of the means of production.... It is therefore a question not of reform, the mask of fraud, but of revolution.[12]

Clifford Odets concludes his 1934 proletariat play, "Waiting for Lefty," with the following speech by a tough insurgent cab driver:

> AGATE: Christ, we're dyin' by inches! for what? For the debutant—ees to have their comin' out parties at the Ritz!... It's slow death or fight. It's war!... **Hello America! We're stormbirds of the working class. Workers of the world... our bones and our blood!** And when we die they'll know what we did to make a new world![13]

Urgency need not necessarily call for violent change. Indeed, much insurgent argument is anti-violent. While these advocates are not willing to let the new order arrive slowly and naturally, neither are they prepared to shed blood. Abolitionist William Lloyd Garrison in 1844 exhorted his followers:

> Up, then, with the banner of revolution! Not to shed blood—not to injure the person or estate of an oppressor—not by force of arms to resist any law—not to countenance a servile insurrection—not to wield any carnal weapons! No, ours must be a bloodless strife, excepting our blood be shed... to overcome evil with good.... Secede, then, from the government. Submit to its exactions, but pay it no allegiance, and give it no voluntary aid.[14]

Even in "Waiting for Lefty," Odets has a disillusioned wife tell her cab-driver husband how to fight the "bosses:"

> JOE: One man can't...
> EDNA: I don't say one man! I say a hundred, a thousand, a whole million, I say. But start in your own union. Get those hack boys together! Sweep out those racketeers like a pile of dirt! Stand up like men and fight for the crying kids and wives... Get brass toes on your shoes and know where to kick![15]

Insurgent argument, then, is confrontational. It focuses upon one or more social ills, and blames those ills on persons, institutions, or values which are integral parts of the established order. Strategically, insurgent argument calls for strong action which may, or may not, be violent.

Innovative Argument

Innovative argument falls between the Radical and Liberal spokes of the model. It is characterized by a nagging dissatisfaction with the existing order and a preference for experimental change. There is an almost equal aversion to violence and the status quo. Fundamental questions include: is the political system part of the problem or part of the solution? can the normal channels produce sufficient change? can actual practice be made to conform with traditional values? Smith and Windes suggest that it is advisable for movement persuaders to (1) identify discrepancies between traditional values and current practice, and (2) argue that their innovation is, in fact, more traditional than the status quo.[16]

American Federation of Labor founder Samuel Gompers, for example, tied the goals and tactics of labor to "Americanism." In a 1908 article he explained that:

> We American trade unionists want to work out our problems in the spirit of true Americanism—a spirit that embodies our broadest and highest ideals. If we do not succeed, it will be due to no fault of ours. We have been building the A.F. of L. in conformity with what we believe to be the original intent and purpose of America.[17]

Similarly, Martin Luther King's "I Have a Dream" speech grounded his call for integration in both Americanism and Christianity:

> I still have a dream. It is a dream deeply rooted in the American dream. It is a dream that one day this nation will rise up and live out the true meaning of its creed: "We hold these truths to be self-evident; that all men are created equal." . . . I have a dream that one day every valley shall be exalted, every hill and mountain shall be made low, the rough places will be made plane and crooked places will be made straight, and the glory of the Lord shall be revealed, and all flesh shall see it together.[18]

Of course, innovative argument will frequently elicit charges that the innovation is unwise or impractical. Such argument should therefore pave the way for implementation by differentiating the situation in question from similar situations in the past. In a familiar, but often misquoted, passage, industrialist Henry Ford dismissed history as a standard by which to assess proposed innovation:

> What do we care what they did 500 or 1000 years ago? It means nothing to me. History is more or less bunk. It's tradition. We don't want tradition. We want to live in the present and the only history that is worth a tinker's damn is the history we make today.[19]

Innovative argument, then, seeks substantial changes in the norms, values, or institutions of society without violent action. It characteristically grounds its proposals in the society's dominant creeds or values, and rejects as irrelevant any suggestion that the innovation cannot or will not work.

It is not difficult to see that innovative argument is safer for the speaker than is insurgent argument. Innovators embrace rather than scorn the principles upon which the society is founded, and hence claim a moral advantage over their adversaries. This enables Innovators to confront the immediate but transient manifestations of the social order (e.g., a corrupt official, a discriminatory law, an unfair labor practice) without confronting the social order itself.

The danger of innovative argument is that, by the nature of contrast effects, the more moderate elements of society often mistake innovative argument for insurgency because it seeks major change through the use of "unpleasant" tactics. Just as Gompers' message contrasts with that of Debs, and as King's dream contrasts with Malcolm X's indictment; so any innovative argument should be advanced as a reasonable alternative to insurgency. It argues that major changes are necessary *in order for the established order to fulfill its own destiny.* When it fails to present such a clear contrast, it is vulnerable to characterization as "subversive" or "revolutionary."

Progressive Argument

Progressive argument is a clearly "systemic" approach to political argument. By this we mean that unlike either insurgents (who want to replace the established means for reconciling differences) or innovators (who believe in the underlying creed but object to the ways that the society practices that creed), progressive argument takes established procedures as givens. Put differently, Liberalism and Conservatism both agree that change of some sort is inevitable and that the established system for resolving disagreements should be used. Neither Liberalism nor Conservatism pursues change through "extra-systemic" or proscribed means (e.g., subversion, violence, or illegal strikes). Progressive argument is therefore conducted within the "rules of the game." Cathcart has described this as "managerial" rather than "confrontational" rhetoric.[20]

Lyndon Johnson's answer to critics who charged that "The System" was responsible for poverty, discrimination, and other social ills was a "War on Poverty." In his first State of the Union address, Johnson told Congress and the nation that:

> We have in 1964 a unique opportunity and obligation—to prove the success of our system; to disprove those cynics at home and abroad who question our purpose and our competence. If we fail, if we fritter and fumble away our opportunity in needless, senseless quarrels between Democrats and Republicans, or between the House and the Senate, or between the South and North, or between the Congress and the administration, then history will rightfully judge us harshly.[21]

Johnson offered his audience an implicit choice: keep pride in your established system of government by making serious efforts to change socio-economic conditions or, alternatively, keep socio-economic conditions roughly as they are at the expense of proving the insurgents accurate and the innovators too charitable and naive. Of course, the logical extension of the latter choice is insurgency or revolution. Thus progressive argument often attempts to stress the feasibility of patience and compromise with "The System," as Johnson did in his 1968 State of the Union address:

> A moment ago I spoke of despair and frustrated hopes in the cities where the fires of disorder burned last summer. We can—and in time we will—change that despair into confidence, and change those frustrations into achievements. But violence will never bring progress.[22]

In her stirring keynote address to the 1976 Democratic National Convention, black Congresswoman Barbara Jordan made it clear that she believed in the political system (specifically the Democratic Party) and distanced herself from the insurgent argument of Malcolm X and, subtly, from the innovative argument of Martin Luther King: "We cannot improve on the system of government handed down to us by the founders of the Republic, there is no way to improve upon that. But what we can do is to find new ways to implement that system and realize our destiny."[23] But the rules of the game supported by Johnson and Jordan are illusive: the system praised by Jordan in 1976 was not the same system as that faced by Malcolm X in 1965 or Dr. King in 1963. Labor unions today are often able to resolve grievances through collective bargaining—the system for which they struggled prior to the New Deal. Thus, yesterday's insurgency and innovation can become today's Standpattism.

The rules of the game supported by progressive argument pose a serious dilemma for Insurgent and Revolutionary persuaders: refusal to follow the rules or procedures leaves them vulnerable to both prosecution and villification. Yet following the established rules renders them subservient to the guardians of the established order and minimizes their own demands for change. A general consensus in support of the system is necessary at all times, and progressive argument often refers to the Insurgent threat in order to press for moderate change.

Retentive Argument

Retentive argument revolves around Conservative and Standpat efforts to preserve important elements of the status quo. The Standpatter would retain it in its entirety, while the Conservative regards this as impossible, infeasible, and hopeless. But the Conservative prefers the present to the proposed future, and attempts to insure that only necessary and practical changes are instituted. Retentive argument concerns cautious, minimal change, and it will therefore often seem trivial or stubborn to Radicals and Reactionaries, both of whom want substantial changes.

Since retentive argument seeks to retain important procedures or qualities that are under attack, it often exhibits an ominous tone. In his memoirs, Senator Barry Goldwater reveals his hope that, "If what I have to say strikes a response in the hearts and minds of other Americans, perhaps they will enlist in the cause to keep our country strong and to restrain those who seek to diminish the importance and significance of the individual."[24] Segregationists argued for retention of the old ways by wearing buttons that said simply, "**NEVER!**" and (as we will see in Chapter 12) the New Right Movement coalesced around arguments to retain control over the Panama Canal.

Retentive argument is heard in presidential campaigns when we are warned about opponents. Gary Allen (who frequently writes for the John Birch Society) warned in 1976 that:

> If even half of the Carter program is adopted, the average worker in America will face crippling new taxes, horrendous new regulations, and a spiraling rate of inflation that could wipe out any savings he hopes to have. It is a program for Big Government and "efficient Socialism." It is enough to make any sensible person wring his hands in horror.[25]

Carter Democrats in 1980 and Mondale Democrats in 1984 said comparable things about the anticipated effects of the Reagan programs on the poor, the elderly, and delicate foreign relations. All three campaigns lost, a sign that threatening apocalyptic visions often reflect more fear than they generate.

Not all retentive argument is threatening. While still governor, Ronald Reagan ridiculed those critical of socio-economic conditions in America by dwarfing social ills in comparison to material accomplishments:

> I think if you put your minds to it you could match the Soviet Union's achievements. You would only have to cut all the paychecks 75 percent, send 60 million people back to the farm, tear down almost three-fourths of the houses in America, destroy 60 percent of the steel-making capacity, rip up fourteen of every fifteen miles of road, two-thirds of the railroad track, junk 85 percent of the autos, and tear out nine out of ten telephones.[26]

In short, retentive argument seeks to save or to preserve as much of the present as possible. It may range from Allen's alarm to Reagan's ridicule. In either case, retentive argument usually presents an unattractive picture of its adversaries, impugns their motives, and (exhibiting contrast effects) reduces progressive, innovative, and insurgent argument into one pattern which it characterizes as insane, ill-conceived, evil, and/or dangerous.

Reversive Argument

Reversive argument concerns efforts to return to a previous societal or political condition. Rather than urge retention of "today" in the face of tomorrow, it uses the proposed "tomorrow" to argue that society has gone too far and that the tide must be reversed. Reaction wants change; Standpattism does not. Thus, the true Standpatter struggles against the Reactionary's call for change just as he or she struggles against the Conservative's call for careful, respectful change.

One Right to Life pamphlet asks its audience to oppose abortion essentially because of the precendent it sets:

> The U.S. Supreme Court has excluded an entire group of humans from legal personhood and with it their right to life.... How long will it be before other groups of humans will be defined out of legal existence when it has been decided that they too have become socially burdensom? Senior Citizens beware! Minority races beware! Crippled children beware! It did happen once before in this century you know. Remember Germany? **Are you going to stand for this?**[27]

William Rusher, publisher of the conservative *National Review*, paints a bleak picture of America's future:

> if we succeed, we will have accomplished a mighty thing. We will have reversed... the whole downward-spiraling tide of the 20th century. There is no reason why this country's great experiment with freedom *must* end in failure. It was men and women who created the opportunity, and they who have botched it; and they can rescue it, even now, if they only will.[28]

In a similar vein, Senator Jesse Helms laments that:

> For forty years an unending barrage of "deals"... have regimented our people and our economy and federalized almost every human enterprise. This onslaught has installed a gigantic scheme for redistributing the wealth that rewards the indolent and penalizes the hard-working.[29]

However, this onslaught can be reversed: "I believe we can halt the long decline. There is nothing inevitable about it. There is a way back."[30]

But let us not presume from the foregoing examples that reversive arguments are heard only on the American Right. Ironically, several powerful pieces of reversive argument attack the Right itself. Liberal Republican

Nelson Rockefeller, then a candidate for president, addressed the 1964 Republican Convention to propose that the platform condemn extremism:

> There is no place in the Republican Party for such hawkers of hate, such purveyors of prejudice, such fabricators of fear, whether Communist, Ku Klux Klan, or Bircher.... These people have nothing in common with Republicanism. These people have nothing in common with Americanism. The Republican Party must repudiate these people.[31]

Although reversive argument is near the middle of the typology, it is hardly moderate in tone. Indeed, it is frequently quite vehement as befits its function of reversing societal direction (analogous in some respects to shifting into reverse at 55 mph).

Reversive argument, then, must direct its audience to (1) see the current direction of society as dangerous, (2) see an alternative direction as desirable, and (3) provide some vehicle for facilitating the necessary change in direction. It cannot rely upon foot-dragging, stubbornness, or apathy. Instead, the willingness of the people simply to "go along" with trends is part of the problem. Reversive argument seeks action, and it can fail either because it sounds too "radical" to Standpatters and Conservatives, or because it is insufficiently inspiring to accomplish its three objectives.

Restorative Argument

Restorative argument urges a full-scale return to a previous state of affairs. The relative merits of that Golden Age are no longer debated: it is clearly preferable to the existing order. Restorative argument centers upon questions of when and why society went astray and how restoration can be accomplished. Reactionaries typically propose legislative or electoral solutions, a change in funding or enforcement of existing means, or a reconstitution of values to conform more closely to an earlier ideology. Revolutionary Reactionaries urge more abrupt tactics for the overthrow of the existing order and restoration of the Ancient Regime.

Believing that our national problems stemmed from the intrusion of the federal government into unnecessary ventures, a campaign was advanced during the 1960's on behalf of "The Liberty Amendment" to the U.S. Constitution. Briefly, this amendment would have prohibited government engagement in "any business, professional, commercial, financial, or industrial enterprise except as specified in the Constitution." All such enterprises would be sold to private entrepreneurs, and the federal government's right to tax would be repealed.[32] Supporters of the Amendment argued that:

> We can renew the effectiveness of our Constitution.... We can restore the efficiency of our capitalist economy. The Liberty Amendment will accomplish both these purposes, by reducing the functions and powers of the Federal Government, and by restoring the abilities of people to take care of themselves,...and by curtailing destructive intervention in our free enterprise economy.[33]

For Jesse Helms, the critical turning point in our demise seems to have been the ban on prayer in public schools. He explains that:

> It is hardly coincidence that the banishment of the Lord from the public schools has resulted in their being taken over by a totally secularist philosophy. Christianity has been driven out. In its place has been enshrined a permissiveness in which the drug culture has flourished, as have pornography, crime, and fornication.... I think there is no more pressing duty facing the Congress than to restore the true spirit of the First Amendment.

Robert Welch of the John Birch Society encouraged his followers to work toward restoration of the nature of America in the latter half of the 19th century. He prescribed that America:

> Push the Communists back, get out of the bed of a Europe that is dying with the cancer of collectivism, and breathe our own healthy air of opportunity, enterprise, and freedom.... And despite the bad scars and the loss of some muscles, this young, strong, great new nation, restored to vigor, courage, ambition, and self-confidence, can still go ahead to fulfill its great destiny, and to become an even more glorious example for all the earth than it ever was before.[36]

Restorative argument, therefore, alludes to an era or condition which was preferable to the present in one or more respects. Like reversive argument it is characteristically immoderate; unlike reversive argument, it often presents a goal to be pursued.

Revolutionary Argument

Revolutionary argument urges total overthrow of the existing order but disagrees as to the form and/or nature of the new regime. While Revolutionary Radical and Revolutionary Reactionary groups frequently terrorize one another, they agree that the existing order is intolerable, corrupt, and burdensome. They also agree that its despicable nature justifies violent overthrow. Thus, some reactionaries migrate from radical to reactionary variants of revolutionary argument, and back again. It is possible to become a Revolutionary Radical from either direction: a frustrated Radical or a disenchanted Revolutionary Reactionary. Revolutionary argument is clearly the most confrontational form of political argument. Here, the confrontation is more than symbolic (as in insurgent and progressive argument). Instead, revolutionary argument relies heavily upon brute force to destroy the persons and established institutions which it holds responsible for the problems of society.

Nevertheless, revolutionary argument depends upon dramatic rhetorical depictions of its violent acts for its effect. This is why several terrorist groups (often rivals) may claim responsibility for the same bombing—the destruction of property is generally less important than the symbolic mileage gained from it.

Perhaps the most prominent advocate of revolutionary argument was the anarchist Johann Most. While others simply blew buildings to pieces, Most savored violent acts through language. In a pamphlet on dynamite, he wrote:

> Dynamite! Of all the good stuff, that is the stuff!...Place this in the immediate vicinity of a lot of rich loafers who live by the sweat of other people's brows, and light the fuse. A most cheerful and gratifying result will follow. In giving dynamite to the downtrodden millions...science has done its best work....A pound of this stuff beats a bushel of ballots all hollow—and don't you forget it.[37]

On another occasion, Most proclaimed in his famous speech, "The Beast of Property," that:

> If the people do not crush them, they will crush the people, drown the revolution in the blood of the best, and rivet the chains of slavery more firmly than ever. Kill or be killed is the alternative. Therefore massacres of the people's enemies must be instituted.[38]

Dennis Kearney, a California labor leader during the 1870s, sought to rid California of Orientals who constituted a source of cheap labor. But his violence was directed not only at the Orientals, but also at his own union:

> The first time you find a man in the ranks who is not true to the core take him by the nape of the neck and chuck him into the street and then take the bloody shrimps by the throat and tell them you will put big stones around their necks and throw them in the bay.[39]

Of course, exhorting people to violence entails risks—to both the speaker and the audience. Anarchist Albert Parsons, who was hanged in connection with the 1886 Haymarket bombing in Chicago, was a master of revolutionary argument. He told his audience that:

> If we would achieve our liberation from economic bondage and acquire our natural right to life and liberty, every man must lay by a part of his wages, buy a Colt's navy revolver, a Winchester rifle, and learn how to make and use dynamite. Then raise the flag of rebellion, the scarlet banner of liberty, fraternity, equality and strike down to the earth every tyrant that lives upon this globe.[40]

Lest his audience hesitate, Parsons reminds hearers that, "Until this is done you will continue to be robbed, to be plundered, to be at the mercy of the privileged few."[41]

Revolutionary argument recommends violent actions against the established order. It is possible for such terrorist rhetoric to be largely devoid of social or political ideology. While the threat of violence may pave the way for less extreme advocates, actual violence more often polarizes negotiations and renders reasoned, moderate argument exceedingly difficult. Of course, this is rarely important to the revolutionary, who sees moderation as part of the problem.

Conclusions

Seven types of argument—Insurgent, Innovative, Progressive, Retentive, Reversive, Restorative, and Revolutionary—are found throughout political controversy. Various social movements have engaged in revolutionary terrorism, insurgency, and progressive arguments, while others have sought to preserve the status quo, reverse trends, or restore various Golden Ages. Each type of argument serves a different purpose, and prudence dictates that we judge a political proposal neither on the basis of its source, nor on the basis of arguments advanced by other persuaders. Instead, we need to consider carefully the argument facing us. Having done so, we need to compare it with other arguments for, and against, the same measure. In this fashion we can understand more clearly (1) what is being advocated, (2) the basis on which we are asked to support it, and (3) its place in the universe of political talk.

Two notes of caution are in order. First, notice that we are not describing seven types of *movements*—all seven types of argument can be found (at various points) in the rhetoric of almost any social movement, as our examples have demonstrated. The important question is which types of argument appear between which people at what points in the movement's development? We should be able to classify movements more accurately on the basis of their persuasion *after* we have assessed their clusters of argument.

Endnotes

[1] See for example John W. Bowers and Donovan J. Ochs, *The Rhetoric of Agitation and Control* (Reading, MA: Addison-Wesley, 1971).

[2] See for example Barbara Warnick, "The Rhetoric of Conservative Resistance," *Southern Speech Communication Journal*, 42 (Spring, 1977), 256-273.

[3] See for example Martha Solomon, "The 'Positive Woman's' Journey: A Mythic Analysis of the Rhetoric of STOP ERA," *Quarterly Journal of Speech*, 65 (October, 1979), 262-274.

[4] See for example Leland M. Griffin, "The Rhetoric of Historical Movements," *Quarterly Journal of Speech*, 38 (April, 1952), 184-188; and Stephen E. Lucas, "Coming to Terms with Movement Studies," *Central States Speech Journal*, 31 (Winter, 1981), 259-262.

[5] Donald C. Bryant, "Rhetoric: It's Function and Its Scope," *Quarterly Journal of Speech*, 39 (December, 1953), 413.

[6] Unless otherwise noted, all references to Rossiter's typology refer to Clinton Rossiter, *Conservatism in America*, 2nd rev. ed. (New York: Vintage Books, 1962), 11-14.

[7] The Social Judgment Ego-involvement theory of attitude change incorporates perception and ego-involvement into the study of persuasion. It posits a latitude of acceptable positions, a latitude of rejected positions, and a latitude of non-commitment. Thus, rather than conceiving of one's attitude as a point, it is thought of as a range of acceptable positions around a *most* acceptable position or "anchor." The theory further suggests that each of us judges the discrepancy between an advocated position and our anchor first, before judging the substance of that position. When this discrepancy appears smaller than expected (e.g., "Premier Andropov is a Dallas Cowboys fan.") we perceptually enhance its acceptability ("assimilation effect"). Conversely, when the discrepancy is greater than expected (e.g., "Mickey Mouse is an alcoholic wife-beater.") disagreement is perceptually enhanced ("contrast effect"). Both assimilation and contrast effects are heightened when the individual is ego-involved in the subject. See Muzafer Sherif and Carl Hovland, *Social Judgment: Assimilation and Contrast Effects in Communication and Attitude Change* (New Haven: Yale University Press, 1961).

[8] However, this is not to say that both (or all) points in the controversy are clearly stated. Indeed, most political argument *anticipates* a discrepancy between the arguer and some other, distant spokesperson. Whether explicit or implicit, political argument concerns differences between the arguer's set of beliefs and his conception of one or more others' set of beliefs.

[9] "Preamble of the I.W.W. Constitution as amended in 1908," *The American Labor Movement*, ed. Leon Litwack (Englewood Cliffs, NJ: Prentice-Hall, 1962), 42.

[10] John Swinton, *Striking for Life: Labor's Side of the Question* (Westport, CT: Greenwood Press, 1970), 104-110.

[11] Malcolm X, "The Ballot or the Bullet?" *Malcolm X Speaks*, George Breitman, ed. (New York: Ballantine Books, 1965), 31.

[12] Eugene V. Debs, "Outlook for Socialism in the United States," *Debs*, Ronald Radosh, ed. (Englewood Cliffs, NJ: Prentice-Hall, 1971), 21.

[13] Clifford Odets, "Waiting for Lefty," *Modern American Plays*, Frederick Cassidy, ed. (Freeport, NY: Books for Libraries Press, 1949), 192.

[14] William Lloyd Garrison, "No Union with Slaveholders," *William Lloyd Garrison*, George M. Frederickson ed. (Englewood Cliffs, NJ: Prentice-Hall, 1968), 54.

[15] Odets, 195.

[16] Ralph Smith and Russell Windes, "The Innovational Movement: A Rhetorical Theory," *Quarterly Journal of Speech*, 61 (April, 1975), 143. Although we disagree with their conception of innovational *movement*, we find their characteristics of such movements useful for understanding innovational *argument*.

[17] Samuel Gompers, *Seventy Years of Life and Labor,* quoted in *Samuel Gompers Credo* (New York: American Federation of Labor Samuel Gompers Centennial Committee, 1950), 37.

[18] Martin Luther King, "I Have a Dream," *American Rhetoric from Roosevelt to Reagan*, Halford R. Ryan, ed. (Prospect Heights, IL: Waveland Press, Inc., 1983), 171-172.

[19] Henry Ford, "History Is More or Less Bunk," *Henry Ford*, John B. Rae, ed. (Englewood Cliffs, NJ: Prentice-Hall, 1969), 53.

[20] Robert S. Cathcart, "Movements: Confrontation as Rhetorical Form," *Southern Speech Communication Journal*, 43 (Spring, 1978), 237-238.

[21] Lyndon B. Johnson, "Annual Message to the Congress on the State of the Union," *Public Papers of the Presidents of the United States: Lyndon B. Johnson, 1963-1964*, Book 1 (Washington, DC: U.S. Government Printing Office, 1965), 113.

[22] Lyndon B. Johnson, "Annual Message to the Congress on the State of the Union," *Public Papers of the Presidents of the United States: Lyndon B. Johnson*, Book 1 (Washington, DC: U.S. Government Printing Office, 1970), 31.

[23] Barbara C. Jordan, "Democratic Convention Keynote Address," reprinted in Ryan, 230-231.

[24] Barry M. Goldwater, *With No Apologies* (New York: William Morrow, 1979), 14.

[25] Gary Allen, *Jimmy Carter, Jimmy Carter* (Seal Beach, CA: 76 Press, 1976), 68.

[26] Ronald Reagan, "Free Enterprise," in Ryan, 273.

[27] Dr. and Mrs. J.C. Wilke, "The U.S. Supreme Court Has Ruled It's Legal to Kill a Baby. . . . " (Cincinnati: Hayes Publishing, n.d.), 4.

[28] William A Rusher, *The Making of the New Majority Party* (Ottawa, IL: Green Hill, 1975), 161-162.

[29] Jesse Helms, *When Free Men Shall Stand* (Grand Rapids, MI: Zondervan, 1976), 11.

[30] Helms, 12.

[31] Nelson A. Rockefeller, "Address to the Third Session of the 1964 Republican National Convention in Moving Adoption of the Amendment to the Report of the Committee on Resolutions on the Subject of Extremism," Cow Palace, San Francisco, California, July 14, 1964," *Public Papers of Governor Nelson A. Rockefeller, 1964*, 1330.

[32] Lloyd G. Herbstreith and Gordan van B. King, *Action for Americans: The Liberty Amendment* (Los Angeles: Operation America, 1963), inside cover.

[33] Herbstreith and King, 105.

[34] Helms, 108.

[35] Robert H.W. Welch, *The Blue Book of the John Birch Society* (Boston: Western Islands, 1961), 39.

[36] Welch, 46.

[37] Quoted in Louis Adamic, *Dynamite; The Story of Class Violence in America* (New York: Chelsea House, 1958), 47.

[38] Johann Most, "The Beast of Property," reprinted in Charles W. Lomas, *The Agitator in American Society* (Englewood Cliffs, NJ: Prentice-Hall, 1968), 39.

[39] Dennis Kearney, "The Chinese Must Go!" reprinted in Lomas, 29.

[40] Albert Parsons, "The Board of Trade: Legalized Theft," reprinted in Lomas, 44.

[41] Parsons, in Lomas, 44.

Chapter 5

A Rhetoric of Legitimation

The word "legitimacy" or "legitimation" appears with nagging persistence in writings on the rhetoric and sociology of social movements. Theorists have presented it as the principal goal or demand of social movements, the primal challenge of movements to established institutions, and the most critical obstacle leaders of movements must overcome.[1] Gaston Rimlinger and Joseph Gusfield, for example, argue that for a social movement to be successful, its demands and methods must somehow *become legitimate* in the eyes of institutions, government, the public, and potential members.[2]

The uninstitutionalized nature of social movements relegates them to near-zero legitimacy when they come into existence. They have in their favor only the somewhat mythical American tradition of tolerance of dissent, a tolerance most evident when dissent is nonthreatening or ineffective. Moreover, social movements may lose even this grudging level of legitimacy as they challenge social institutions, norms, and values. As Robert Cathcart writes, "The leadership of the movement is not recognized, for it has no legitimacy, and to confer with it would be tantamount to doing business with the devil."[3]

The Notion of Legitimacy

The notion of "legitimacy" contains two inherently rhetorical elements. The first element is the act of conferring, by one person or group to another person or group, the "right to exercise authoritative influence in a given area or to issue binding directives."[4] Tradition, laws, rules, charisma, assumed power, performance of mythic feats, and the dictates of a "higher authority" (perhaps a divine source) are the bases upon which legitimacy is conferred most often.[5] The second element is the act of retaining legitimacy once it is conferred. Robert Francesconi, for example, sees legitimation as "an on-going process of reason-giving, actual and potential, which forms the basis of the right to exercise authority as well as the willingness to defer to authority."[6] "Rhetoric," Francesconi writes, "bridges the gap between legitimacy "as *claimed* and legitimacy as *believed*."[7] Herbert Simons characterizes legitimacy "as the perception by receivers that the source has a right to exact obedience from" them.[8] It is not surprising then that legitimacy almost always accrues to established institutions that in turn strive to "engender and maintain the belief that the existing . . . institutions are the most appropriate ones for the society."[9]

Although the elements of legitimacy are well-known and the importance of legitimacy to the rise and success of social movements is widely recognized, Herbert Simons' assessment in 1972 that "The legitimacy variable is among the most neglected and most important variables in credibility research" remains accurate today.[10] The purpose of this chapter is to explicate a rhetoric of legitimacy for social movements. The ingredients of a rhetoric of legitimacy can be comprehended, however, only by first reviewing the elements of the rhetorical situation that make the attainment of legitimacy a major obstacle for social movements.

The Social Movement's Rhetorical Situation

Social movements usually emerge during relatively quiet times when the people and established institutions are going about business as usual. If either people or institutions are aware of a problem (whether it be social, political, religious, economic, educational, or environmental) they typically view it as insignificant, of low priority, or unresolvable—"the poor will always be with us." If a serious problem is recognized, the usual stance is that it can and will be resolved in due time by legitimate institutions through legitimate channels and means.

Societies and their institutions have prevalent ideologies (symbolic systems of norms and values) that explicitly and implicitly support and are supported by the prevailing social structure.[11] Educational systems, for instance, help to legitimize and preserve the social order by disseminating approved norms and values.[12] Thomas Farrell claims that the fundamental function of political communication is to legitimize the political system, and Herbert Simons has argued on several occasions that persuasion theorists have identified with the maintenance of existing social systems and have deemed social movements to be unnecessary, irrational, dysfunctional, and potentially dangerous.[13]

When a people or social order confers legitimacy upon a person or institution, it also confers powers of retention. This bestowal of power has led Robert Cathcart to identify the struggle between institutional and noninstitutional forces as "a true moral battle for power and the legitimate right to define the true order."[14] Specifically, legitimacy confers five powers which, in combination, perpetuate the original grant.

The *power to reward* is perhaps the most important retentive power because it allows legitimate institutions to reward those who conform and obey and to coerce or to punish those who strive to be different or challenge approved norms, values, or institutional arrangements.[15] Institutional leaders urge protestors and reformers to consider the positive and negative consequences of their actions, typically the granting or denial of tangible benefits and rewards such as jobs, official positions, advancements, incomes, recognition, land, research and development grants, and tax exemptions. If the disaffected refuse to take the carrot, an institution may resort to the stick to gain compliance and to justify its use of coercive persuasion (perhaps even violence) in the name of God, the founding fathers, the people, the Constitution, the law, social harmony, progress, the common good, or national security.[16] Philip Zimbardo and Herbert Simons have noted that people who modify their behaviors as a result of coercive persuasion by legitimate authorities "are more likely to make the attribution error of overestimating the extent to which they have had choice in the matter."[17] This attribution error is understandable because institutions *define* rewards and reward systems and thus are able to meet or to withhold expectations, to distribute finite resources, and to alienate groups and individuals when it is to an institution's advantage.

The *power of control* allows legitimate institutions and leaders to regulate the flow of information and persuasion to members of organizations and the populace. Thus, they are able to determine if, how, when, where, under what circumstances, and with whom communication will occur. Control power helps institutions maintain perceptions that the established order is in compliance with accepted values and standards, is meeting the legitimate expectations of persons and groups (particularly those of protestors), and is on the side of good in its struggle with evil.[18] In a sense, then, institutions act interdependently with audiences in rewarding those who hear, agree, and acquiesce.

The *power of identification* accrues to established orders because they are the keepers, protectors, and proselytizers of the sacred symbols, emblems, places, offices, documents, codes, values, and myths of the institution or order.[19] They are typically seen as the legitimate heirs or successors of the order's founding fathers, patriots, revered leaders, prophets, martyrs, or high priests. Identification with the sacred is easy and frequent. As Anthony Oberschall writes, their positions allow institutional leaders to provide "elaborate systems of beliefs and moral ideas upon which legitimacy rests."[20]

The *power of terministic control* allows social orders to control language and thereby the "legitimated meanings for such politically sensitive terms as order, violence, repression, deviance, protest, persuasion, coercion, and symbolic speech."[21] Thus, violence by established orders is the legitimate maintenance of law and order, never "terrorism."[22] Over-zealous supporters of the order are patriots, never fanatics. "National security" justifies withholding or distortion of information pertaining to everything from infiltration of protest groups and spying on citizens to results of studies by presidential commissions and secret files on social movement leaders and members.

The *power of moral suasion* allows institutions to exert control by operating in the realms of affectual attitudes and emotional attachments.[23] R.R. McGuire claims that people often come to see obedience or deference to legitimate authority as a moral obligation.[24] Thus, institutions are able to persuade people that they have a *duty* to honor institutional decisions even when these decisions have "unpleasant consequences."[25] Herbert Simons writes that "one important means by which influence agents may persuade us to *want* to do what we would not otherwise *choose* to do is first convince us that they have legitimate authority over us and hence that we are duty bound to obey them."[26] The potential emotional consequences of disobeying legitimate authority keeps many people under control. Louis Kriesberg, for example, contends that "people learn rules and if they accept them they may become so internalized that violation would be shunned in order to avoid the feelings of guilt or shame which would follow violation."[27]

Thus, when uninstitutional forces collide, the rhetorical deck is heavily stacked in favor of "legitimate" institutions and leaders. People tend to "maintain the faith" even in the face of massive economic breakdowns in society.[28] What strategies, then, should comprise a rhetoric of legitimation that would enable social movements to meet situational exigencies and counter the powers granted to legitimate authorities?

A rhetoric of legitimation must be a combination of coactive and confrontational strategies.[29] *Coactive strategies* emphasize similarities, shared experiences, and a common cause. The social movement is projected as respectful of societal norms, values, and institutions and hence deserving, by worth and right, of legitimate status.[30] *Confrontational strategies* emphasize dissimilarities, diverse experiences, and conflict. Such strategies are essential to deprive institutions and leaders of all or part of the legitimacy they enjoy and thus to elevate the social movement to a transcendent position in the societal hierarchy.[31]

Legitimacy Through Coactive Strategies

If, as Robert Francesconi claims, "an implicit requirement" of legitimacy is a "rationality of good reasons," then social movements must identify with the fundamental norms and values of social orders if they are to transport themselves from the margins of society to the centers where legitimacy resides.[32] They must access the very sources that social orders claim as their rightful domains.

First, social movements may identify with what Max Weber refers to as the "sanctity of immemorial traditions."[33] Arthur Smith (Molefi Asante) and John Wilson note that social movements usually link themselves with the traditional rights and values of equality, justice, and dignity, while Irving Zaretsky and Mark Leone claim that non-legitimacy of religious social movements is a function of appearing to threaten deeply held secular values.[34] Movements would be wise to identify with the moral symbols, sacred emblems, heroes, founding fathers, and revered documents of society rather than attack them as many movements of the 1960s and 1970s were prone to do.[35] To avoid being stigmatized as a mere fad or craze or an evil force in society, movements might emphasize the hallowed tradition of protest in American history.[36] For example, the "Women's Declaration of Independence" adopted by the Seneca Falls convention in 1848 was modeled closely after the Declaration of Independence with such modifications as "We hold these truths to be self-evident: that all men and women are created equal." The National Labor Union used the same strategy when it adopted its "Platform of Principles" in 1868. Thus, social movements may rework the pieces of tradition into new stories that befit their ideologies.[37]

Second, social movements may strive to establish their actions as those of legitimate organizations.[38] They can achieve this in part by identifying with the legal status of protest in America, by conforming to rules and accepted procedures perceived to be formally correct by the populace and social orders, and by avoiding direct attacks on basic institutions and authorities.[39] Endorsements of those with legitimacy may produce a "rub-off" effect. Social movements, like individuals in society, are frequently judged by their affiliations, so they work hard to attract "legitimizers"—organizations, members, speakers, writers, senators, clergy, entertainers, scientists, military leaders, war veterans, ex-presidents, and medical professionals—who are respectable, safe, and beyond reproach.[40] Movements often link themselves with other social movements that are active at the time and who have gained a degree of respect.[41]

And third, social movements may employ a strategy of transcendence by identifying themselves with what is large, good, important, and of the highest order in society. Movements typically claim to speak in the name of the people, for the will of the people, and in the "soul and spirit" of the people.[42] They are the true heirs of societal norms, values, and traditions. Size itself becomes a sign of acceptance and thus of legitimacy. Thus, a movement may portray itself as a "majority movement," a "great people's movement," or the "largest grassroots citizen's movement in recent history."[43] Anthony Oberschall notes that visible signs of large-scale dissaffection may shake confidence in established orders and thus undermine the legitimacy of their leaders.[44] Many social movements, particularly religious ones, stress a sense of mission and claim to operate in accordance with a predetermined divine plan.[45] They identify with the American belief that divine plans transcend the temporal ones of social orders, argue that "expressive" values rather than "instrumental" values are the truly universal ones, and try to locate the movement within what Irving Zaretsky and Mark Leone call a "sacred cosmos."[46] Thus, moral obligations to the state are limited by moral obligations to a higher authority.[47]

A coactive rhetoric is essential, then, for a social movement in its struggle for legitimacy because it chips away at three powers enjoyed by the social order: identification, terministic control, and moral suasion. Coactive rhetoric obviously serves more than the "managerial" or "reinforcement" functions Robert Cathcart and Herbert Simons ascribe to it, for it demonstrates that a social movement deserves legitimacy by both worth and right.[48] With worth and right established, institutions can no longer call into question the fundamental legitimacy of a social movement but, as Rhodri Jeffreys-Jones explains, must attack its tactics instead.[49] John Bowers and Donovan Ochs address the importance of a coactive rhetorical approach in establishing legitimacy when they argue that the early employment of a strategy of "petition" is crucial because "an establishment, by showing that petition has not occurred, can discredit the agitators as irresponsible firebrands who disdain normal decision-making processes in favor of disturbance and disruption."[50]

A coactive rhetoric by itself, however, cannot attain legitimacy for a social movement because it merely establishes the movement as "similar" to the social order in important ways—legal, law-abiding, supporter of traditions, moral—and therefore worthy of legitimacy.[51] Thus, a coactive rhetoric is likely to produce, at best, a rhetorical stalemate between institutional and uninstitutional forces that leaves institutions with their powers possibly diminished or shared but intact. A confrontational rhetoric is required to break the rhetorical stalemate and to allow the social movement to transcend the social order in perceived legitimacy.

Legitimacy Through Confrontational Strategies

If a confrontational rhetoric is to raise the social movement to a transcendent position in society, it must make the people see the social order as illegitimate or at least less legitimate than the social movement.[52] Carol Jablonski argues that a "rhetoric of discontinuity" is necessary to "establish the legitimacy of the collective's grievances as well as the need to induce changes from the outside."[53] Movements employ a variety of confrontational strategies to show that establishment leaders, organizations, rules, and norms systematically distort communication, create barriers to will formation, and constrain and distort an alleged "reciprocal accountability." Thus, as R.R. McGuire writes, movements hope to demonstrate that the order is "irrational and hence illegitimate—involving no moral obligation."[54]

Institutions must "maintain a perceived consistency between values and actions" and appear to follow approved patterns of operation.[55] Movements exploit this societal restriction on institutional actions. The civil rights, labor, Chicano, gay rights, and anti-war movements, for example, employed strategies of nonviolent resistance and civil disobedience—strikes, boycotts, sit-ins, demonstrations, symbolic acts, and violations of ordinances and laws—to reveal the inconsistency, and therefore the illegitimacy, of values and establishment procedures, customs, and laws.[56] Social movements take advantage of outdated laws or quasi-legal practices of authorities by demanding that authorities stick to the letter of the law, actions that might make authorities look ridiculous, unfair, or heavyhanded.[57] Saul Alinsky, in his book *Rules for Radicals*, urges would-be-radicals to "Make the enemy live up to their book of rules. You can kill them with this, for they can no more obey their own rules than the Christian church can live up to Christianity."[58] If an institution represses peaceful, nonviolent dissent or refuses to enforce or obey the laws, it may seriously undermine its legitimacy in the eyes of the people and other institutions.[59]

Militant confrontational strategies (such as disruptions, verbal violence, and assaults on property, symbols, and police) may provoke the establishment into overreactions and violent suppression, for, as Robert Cathcart claims, "The establishment, when confronted, must respond not to the particular enactment but to the challenge to its legitimacy."[60] If the establishment "responds with full fury and might to crush the confronters, it violates the mystery and reveals the secret that it maintains power, not through moral righteousness but through its power to kill."[61] The result may be outrage among the institution's constituency and thus counter productive to control efforts.[62] Protestors charge that the "civility and decorum" of authorities "serve as masks for the preservation of injustice" and constitute a thin veneer that hides a vicious, repressive—and thus illegitimate—social order.[63] Robert Scott and Donald Smith write that social movements prod the established order to "show us how ugly you really are."[64] And Robert Cathcart claims that "Confrontational rhetoric shouts 'Stop!' at the system, saying, 'You cannot go on assuming you are the true and correct order; you must see yourself as the evil thing you are.'"[65] Authorities often discredit and humiliate themselves when they lose control and thereby become collaborators with protestors bent on stripping them of legitimacy. Violent acts on behalf of established institutions in Selma, Birmingham, Chicago, and My Lai were shown on television in millions of American homes and aided the efforts of the civil rights and anti-Vietnam War movements by revealing an ugly side of institutions rarely witnessed by the American populace.[66]

There may be two significant byproducts of ugly and sometimes violent confrontations between protestors and social orders. First, violent suppression by an institution allows the social movement to claim that it acted in self-defense—a noble and legal act—to institutional force and violence.[67] And second, verbal and nonverbal violence by institutions and militant elements of a movement may confer legitimacy upon *moderate* movement leaders and organizations.[68]

A confrontational rhetoric is essential, then, for a movement to gain legitimacy because it chips away at four powers enjoyed by the establishment: reward, control, identification, and moral suasion. First, a confrontational rhetoric breaks the rhetorical stalemate between institutional and noninstitutional forces by demonstrating that the institution deserves neither its claim of legitimacy nor its high place in the social hierarchy. And second, a confrontational rhetoric reveals the ugliness of a situation and a social order that needs urgent remedy. Relying on Burkean principles, Robert Cathcart argues that:

> Hierarchy includes what is *not* proper, *not* useful, *not* valuable; thus, 'the negative.' Man, the seeker after perfection, recognizes the negative and becomes aware of his own guilt. And to remove guilt he must seek redemption either through striving to perfect the hierarchy (i.e., established order) or by recognizing the evil of the erroneous system, confession to his own victimage (mortification) and confronting the evil system with a new, more perfect order (redemption).[69]

Although a confrontational rhetoric is essential for a social movement in its struggle for legitimacy, it cannot by itself attain legitimacy for the movement. Destruction or reduction of Order A's legitimacy does not automatically bestow legitimacy on Order B, even when Order B was instrumental in revealing the evilness and unworthiness of Order A. The Yippies, for example, artfully unveiled the ugliness of Chicago police and officials during the 1968 Democratic convention, but the Yippies and other movements involved gained little if any legitimacy for having done so. Frank Sullivan, the press officer for the Chicago police, charged that the demonstrations were perpetrated by a "pitiful handful" of "communist revolutionaries," and polls indicated that a great many Americans agreed with this assessment.[70] A social movement can assume its rightful place in society only if it can also establish *its* worth and right to assume the mantle of legitimacy.

Conclusions

Theorists agree that perhaps the greatest challenge social movements encounter is the necessity of *becoming perceived* as *legitimate* in the eyes of the people, institutions, and other social movements. Legitimacy, and the powers that accompany it, traditionally and legally accrues to societal institutions, so the rhetorical deck is heavily stacked against uninstitutional forces. In this chapter, we have attempted to describe the rhetorical situation social movements face in their efforts to bring about or to stifle change and we have offered an explication of a rhetoric of legitimacy for meeting situational exigencies.

Societies create institutions that legitimize and preserve the social order and its attendant systems of norms and values. Various powers allow institutions to carry out these tasks. The power to reward allows institutions to compensate those who conform and obey and to punish those who do not. The power of control enables institutions to regulate the flow of information and persuasion. The power of identification makes institutions the protectors of society's sacred symbols, places, documents, codes, and values. The power of terministic control permits institutions to control language and thus to define good and evil. And the power of moral suasion allows institutions to exert control in the realms of affectual attitudes and emotional attachments to establish a moral obligation to obey legitimate authority.

The rhetorical situation requires social movements to develop a rhetoric of legitimation that is a blend of coactive and confrontational strategies. A coactive or common ground approach allows the social movement to establish itself as respectful of societal norms, values, and institutions—deserving of legitimacy by worth and right. A confrontative or conflict approach allows the movement to provoke the institution into actions that reveal the institution as a violator of societal norms and values and thus undeserving of all or part of the legitimacy it enjoys. Neither approach by itself is sufficient. A coactive approach may produce a rhetorical stalemate in which both movement and institution enjoy degrees of legitimacy but in which the institution remains in control. Or the social movement may appear to become so similar to the institutions it opposes that it disappears as a noninstitutional force for change or resistance. This was the fate, for instance, of the National Labor Union when it became best known as the National Labor Party and the socialist movement when it became little more than the Socialist Party. A confrontational rhetoric may strip legitimacy from an institution, but this success contains no guarantee that the lost legitimacy will be transferred to the movement. Indeed, a confrontational rhetoric may boomerang as the people come to see the movement as an outrageous violator of norms and values—if not a grave threat to the whole social order—and urge institutions to repress the irrational, dangerous threat to all that is sacred. Militant groups such as the Industrial Workers of the World, the Black Panthers, and the Weathermen suffered this fate.[71] Only a rhetoric of legitimation that includes both coactive and confrontational strategies permits social movements to establish their worthiness and institutions' unworthiness of legitimacy and to neutralize, or transfer, those powers that attend legitimacy.

Endnotes

[1] Joseph R. Gusfield, *Protest, Reform, and Revolt: A Reader in Social Movements* (New York: John Wiley & Sons, 1970), 310; Arthur L. Smith (Molefi Asante), *Rhetoric of Black Revolution* (Boston: Allyn and Bacon, 1969), 1; John W. Bowers and Donovan J. Ochs, *The Rhetoric of Agitation and Control* (Reading, MA: Addison-Wesley, 1971), 13.

[2] Gaston V. Rimlinger, "The Legitimation of Protest: A Comparative Study in Labor History," In Gusfield, 363.

[3] Robert S. Cathcart, "Movements: Confrontation as Rhetorical Form," *Southern Speech Communication Journal*, 43 (Spring, 1978), 246.

[4] Herbert W. Simons, *Persuasion: Understanding, Practice, and Analysis* (Reading, MA: Addison-Wesley, 1976), 234.

[5] Max Weber, *The Theory of Social and Economic Organization*, trans. by A.M. Henderson and Talcott Parsons (New York: The Free Press, 1964), 130-132; Simons (1976), 234-236; Gerald S. Mathisen, "Evangelical Social Concern: A Case Study in the Rhetoric of Legitimization," unpublished doctoral dissertation, Purdue University, 1982, 3-6; Anthony Oberschall, *Social Conflict and Social Movements* (Englewood Cliffs, NJ: Prentice-Hall, 1973), 120.

[6] Robert A. Francesconi, "James Hunt, The Wilmington 10, and Institutional Legitimacy," *Quarterly Journal of Speech*, 68 (February, 1982), 49.

[7] Francesconi, 50.

[8] Herbert W. Simons, "Persuasion in Social Conflicts: A Critique of Prevailing Conceptions and a Framework for Future Research," *Speech Monographs*, 39 (November, 1972), 244.

[9] Oberschall, 188.

[10] Simons (1972), 244.

[11] Roberta Ash, *Social Movements in America* (Chicago: Markham, 1972), 3; William B. Cameron, *Modern Social Movements* (New York: Random House, 1966), 72; Weber, 130.

[12] Simons (1972), 241.

[13] Thomas B. Farrell, "Political Communication: Its Investigation and Praxis," *Western Speech Communication*, 50 (Spring, 1976), 96; Herbert W. Simons, Elizabeth W. Mechling, and Howard N. Schreier, "The Functions of Human Communication in Mobilizing for Action from the Bottom Up: The Rhetoric of Social Movements," *Handbook of Rhetorical and Communication Theory*, Carroll C. Arnold and John W. Bowers, eds. (Boston: Allyn and Bacon, 1984), 800.

[14] Cathcart (1978), 246.

[15] Herbert W. Simons, "The Carrot and the Stick as Handmaidens of Persuasion in Conflict Situations," *Perspectives on Communication in Social Conflict*, Gerald R. Miller and Herbert W. Simons, eds., (Englewood Cliffs, NJ: Prentice-Hall, 1974), 196; Simons, Mechling, and Schreier, 820).

[16] Simons (1974), 193; Francesconi, 56; Weber, 131 and 328; Simons (1976), 235.

[17] Simons (1974), 192.

[18] Mathisen, 6; James L. Wood and Maurice Jackson, *Social Movements: Development, Participation, and Dynamics* (Belmont, CA: Wadsworth, 1982), 126; Cameron, 72; Robert L. Scott and Donald K. Smith, "The Rhetoric of Confrontation," *Quarterly Journal of Speech*, 55 (February, 1969), 3; John Wilson, *Introduction to Social Movements* (New York: Basic Books, 1973), 69; Oberschall, 61.

[19] Cameron, 72.

[20] Oberschall, 188.

[21] Simons, Mechling, and Schreier, 810.

[22] Michael Stohl, "Demystifying Terrorism: The Myths and Realities of Contemporary Political Terrorism," in *Politics of Terrorism*, Michael Stohl, ed., (New York: Marcel-Dekker, 1988), 1-28; R.D. Duvall and Michael Stohl, "Government by Terror," in Stohl (1988), 231-271.

[23] *The Oxford Universal Dictionary* (Oxford: Clarendon Press, 1955), 2054; Weber, 130.
[24] R.R. McGuire, "Speech Acts, Communicative Competence and the Paradox of Authority," *Philosophy and Rhetoric*, 10 (Winter, 1977), 31 and 33.
[25] William A. Gamson, *Power and Discontent* (Homewood, IL: Dorsey Press, 1968), 127.
[26] Simons (1974), 191.
[27] Louis Kriesberg, *The Sociology of Social Conflicts* (Englewood Cliffs, NJ: Prentice-Hall, 1973), 111.
[28] Ash, 230.
[29] Simons (1972), 239-247.
[30] Herbert Simons coined the term "co-active" persuasion to refer to all persuasive efforts that reach "out to persuadees both physically and psychologically" and emphasize "similarities between persuader and persuadee." See Simons (1972), 236; and Herbert W. Simons, *Persuasion: Understanding, Practice, and Analysis* (New York: Random House, 1986), 121-122.
[31] Robert Cathcart describes rhetorical confrontation as a "ritual enactment that dramatizes the symbolic separation of the individual from the existing order (Cathcart, 1978, 236); Robert Scott and Donald Smith emphasize the "sense of division" in confrontational strategies (Scott and Smith, 1969, 2).
[32] Francesconi, 50; Simons, Mechling, and Schreier, 792.
[33] Weber, 328.
[34] Smith, 1; Irving I. Zaretsky and Mark P. Leone, *Religious Movements in Contemporary America* (Princeton, NJ: University of Princeton, 1974), 10 and 26.
[35] Cameron, 72.
[36] Gusfield, 310; Zaretsky and Leone, 500; Wilson, 125; Richard L. Johannesen, "The Jeremiad and Jenkin Lloyd Jones," *Communication Monographs*, 52 (June, 1985), 156-172.
[37] See, for example, David Carr, *Time, Narrative, and History* (Bloomington, IN: Indiana University Press, 1986); and Walter R. Fisher, *Human Communication as Narration: Toward a Philosophy of Reason, Value, and Action* (Columbia, SC: University of South Carolina Press, 1987.)
[38] Rhodri Jeffreys-Jones, *Violence and Reform in American History* (New York: New Viewpoints, 1978), 12, 16, 38; Ash, 2-3, 9.
[39] Weber, 125; Gusfield, 310.
[40] Simons (1976), 235; Simons, Mechling, and Schreier, 810; Cameron, 55; Bowers and Ochs, 19.
[41] Gusfield, 366.
[42] Michael C. McGee, "In Search of 'The People': A Rhetorical Alternative," *Quarterly Journal of Speech*, 61 (October, 1975), 235-249; Cameron, 72; Wilson, 125.
[43] Wilson, 171-172.
[44] Oberschall, 308.
[45] Wilson, 126; Zaretsky and Leone, 509.
[46] Zaretsky and Leone, 500 and 510.
[47] McGuire, 33.
[48] Cathcart, 237; Simons (1972), 236.
[49] Jeffreys-Jones, 16, 30, and 38.

[50] Bowers and Ochs, 17.

[51] Cathcart, 238; Robert S. Cathcart, "New Approaches to the Study of Movements: Defining Movements Rhetorically," *Western Speech*, 36 (Spring, 1972), 87.

[52] Wood and Jackson, 126.

[53] Carol J. Jablonski, "Promoting Radical Change in the Roman Catholic Church: Rhetorical Requirements, Problems, and Strategies of the American Bishops," *Central States Speech Journal*, 31 (Winter, 1980), 289.

[54] McGuire, 44.

[55] Francesconi, 51; Farrell, 96.

[56] Bowers and Ochs, 26-37; Gusfield, 310.

[57] Ash, 2.

[58] Saul Alinsky, *Rules for Radicals: A Pragmatic Primer for Realistic Radicals* (New York: Vintage Books, 1971), 128.

[59] Simons, Mechling, and Schreier, 835.

[60] Cathcart (1978), 246.

[61] Cathcart (1978), 246.

[62] Kriesberg, 176.

[63] Simons (1972), 243; Scott and Smith, 8.

[64] Scott and Smith, 8.

[65] Cathcart (1978), 243.

[66] Selma and Birmingham, Alabama were scenes of police brutality and bombings of black churches during the civil rights movement; a study commission called police actions during the 1968 Democratic National Convention a "police riot;" and My Lai, South Vietnam was the scene of a massacre of men, women, and children by American troops during the Vietnam War.

[67] Wilson, 244; Simons, Mechling, and Schreier, 829.

[68] Simons, Mechling, and Schreier, 829; Theodore Otto Windt, "The Diatribe: Last Resort for Protest," *Quarterly Journal of Speech*, 58 (February, 1972), 14.

[69] Cathcart (1978), 242-243.

[70] Daniel Walker, *Rights in Conflict: The Violent Confrontation of Demonstrators and Police in the Parks and Streets of Chicago During the Weeks of the Democratic National Convention* (New York: Bantam Books, 1968), 327.

[71] The Industrial Workers of the World (IWW) was active in the labor movement during the early 1900s; the Black Panthers was active in the black power movement of the late 1960s; and the Weathermen was active in the anti-Vietnam War and counter culture movements of the late 1960s and early 1970s.

Chapter 6

Resistance to Social Movements

An essential characteristic of social movements, as argued in Chapter 1, is that they encounter resistance. Any program for change threatens an established order (government, religious denomination, corporate industry, agricultural class, or educational system), but the specific source, form, and types of response to social movements are varied and complex. Rather than identifying specific agents, agencies, or beneficiaries of confrontation, this chapter investigates the nature of resistance to social movements by focusing on the philosophical bases of response as well as specific strategies and tactics utilized by establishments and their surrogates.

Establishments and Social Order

Goal orientation is a characteristic of all social organizations. Every organization has a set of explicit or implicit purposes that include self-preservation, perpetuation, value-maintenance, policy-making, and enforcement to name a few.[1] All societies are protective of territorial boundaries and cultural norms. Enemies exist from within as well as from without, and leaders and rulers must concern themselves with authority, legitimacy, and power. Rituals and emblems of authority are easily recognized; uniforms, legislation, and arrests are direct expressions of authority.

Power is a concept relevant to both individuals and groups. In Chapter 5, we noted that when society confers legitimacy upon institutions, it confers upon such institutions five powers to perpetuate this grant: reward, control, identification, terministic control, and moral suasion. John Bowers and Donovan Ochs discuss how French and Raven's five "social powers" (legitimate, coercive, reward, referent, and expert) are distributed between institutions and social movements.[2] They maintain that the establishment always controls legitimate power (is perceived to have a charter, social contract, or assigned position through which it can exert influence) and normally is capable of exerting coercive power (is perceived as

able to influence by threat of punishment). Both establishments and social movements, according to Bowers and Ochs, share reward power because each is capable of conferring some rewards. While both establishments and social movements share referent power (ability to identify with groups and individuals) and expert power (the image of having superior knowledge or skill in a particular area), social movements "depend almost completely on referent power and expert power."[3]

Andrew King argues, from a group perspective, that power is derived from three bases: material resource base, psycho-social base, and organizational/syntactic base.[4] In feudal times, the material resource base was primarily land, but today the material resource tends to be money. The psycho-social base provides a sense of identity for group members who are bound together by common interests, habits, culture, and values. Organizational/syntactic bases of power are legislative rules, regulations, and norms of behavior. Power, then, is a multidimensional offensive and defensive weapon of establishments. How established orders and their surrogates use the forms of power will be discussed later.

The element of legitimacy, as discussed in Chapter 5, provides an entree of attack for social movements. Regimes must actively demonstrate that they are competent, fair, just, and reasonable in order to maintain public support. Social control is usually viewed as the result of institutional influences such as laws or the police, but social order is not totally dependent upon agencies of control. No institution can long survive solely on the threat of force. The power to create and control images that legitimize authority lies within public communication. According to Hugh Duncan, social order is always expressed in some kind of hierarchy.[5] Hierarchy differentiates people into ranks based on variables such as age, sex, race, skills, and wealth. For Duncan, "all hierarchies function through a 'perfection' of their principles in final moments of social mystification which are reached by mountings from lower to higher principles of social order."[6] Forms of social drama help to create national symbols that unify and transcend local, isolated concerns. Drama, as enacted within situations that provide legitimacy and continuation of regimes, ultimately results in social order and control.

Situations are never neutral. They are created and manipulated throughout society. Consequently, the "definitions of situations" are a commodity that leaders of establishments and social movements compete to control and "own." Public cognitions and impressions are influenced by the investment and utilization of "significant symbols" that are emotional, intense, and cultural in nature such as freedom, justice, and equality. Society, therefore, is a dynamic, interacting entity consisting of many levels acting simultaneously. The fight for legitimacy is a fight for public cognitions and symbols.

Thus, from an organizational perspective, it is naive to think that an established order would not respond to challenging definitions of situations ("the police provoked the confrontation"), symbols ("our legal system is prejudiced and unjust"), or violence ("the pigs hit me because of my long hair"). Our form and philosophy of democratic government makes establishment response to social movement challenges and activities problematic.

Democracy and Resistance to Social Movements

There is probably no concept more important to the theory of democratic government than free speech. Freedom of expression is a First Amendment right guaranteed in our Constitution. Historically, however, local, state, and national governments have made many attempts to limit, control, or suppress freedom of expression by the press and individuals. For instance, the Sedition Law of 1798 attempted to suppress newspapers that attacked the American government for remaining neutral when the Republic of France declared war upon England. This law forbade the publication of matter intended to defame the government or to bring its officers into disrepute. The Espionage Acts of 1917 forbade anyone to cause or to attempt to cause insubordination, disloyalty, mutiny, or refusal of duty in the armed forces. These acts made it unlawful to write or speak against American involvement in World War I. Eugene V. Debs, longtime leader of the socialist movement, was arrested in Canton, Ohio in 1918 shortly after he gave a speech opposing America's involvement in a "European war." He was tried under the Sedition Acts and received a ten-year sentence, entering a federal prison four months after the war had ended. During World War II, Congress established the U.S. Office of Censorship to monitor all actions and written material that challenged the wisdom of America's presence in Europe.

During the mid-1960s, demonstrators brought numerous challenges to laws restricting free expression. The civil rights, students' rights, and anti-Vietnam War movements stimulated the consideration of free speech issues such as limits of expression, limits of criticism of public officials, citizen surveillance, the right to privacy, and the right to wear emblems such as peace symbols, flags, and black armbands.[7] In response to the broadening of civil rights and rights of expression, institutions sought to control access and dissemination of information as the principal means of shaping and guiding public understanding of social policy. The "war" over the freedom of expression became the war over the freedom of information.[8] Beginning with President Lyndon Johnson, the press had less access to government leaders and information. Official information from many government agencies became "secret," "classified," and "selective," so it became increasingly difficult to distinguish fact from fiction, truth from propaganda. "Good" reporters got interviews and important news leaks while others got little of either. President Nixon viewed the press as an enemy rather than a partner in the democratic process and, through Vice President Spiro Agnew, led the charge against the "liberal" and "biased" press.

The problem of free expression for those who resist social movements is in determining how much free expression to tolerate. Should there be limits? Are all opinions equal? Is there a difference, and hence limits, between the form and content of expression? These are difficult and important questions, especially for a democracy, and a balance is difficult to maintain. For example, communication scholars generally agree that speakers who appeal only to the emotions of audiences impede logical and critical thinking. Thus, many scholars have concluded, such appeals are unethical and undemocratic because they undermine the free, full, and rational discussion of issues. Wayne Flynt argues that during the 1963 civil rights disturbances in Birmingham, Alabama, prominent leaders took undemocratic stances, employed faulty logic, and appealed to white fear, frustration, and anger.[9] A former mayor of Birmingham publicly charged that he was "kicked out of the city hall by niggers" and that the new mayor would probably make the African violet the city's official flower.[10] Is such rhetoric more unethical, however, than protestors shouting obscenities and making obscene gestures to public officials and police officers?

Another problematic area for established orders is the level of response. The national government may be most concerned with issues, policy, and movement leaders, while the local government may focus primarily on property, events, maintenance of order, and citizens' rights. Local police, for example, believe they are charged with maintaining law and order. A "good" officer is one who strictly enforces the law. A "bad" officer is one who uses discretion and overlooks certain offenses. Police have often viewed protestors as disruptors of peace and users of tactics that would lead ultimately to anarchy. And, of course, protestors have viewed police as brutish "pigs" and mindless enforcers of suppression.[11] Law enforcement officers have often been more reactors to rather than initiators of either protest or institutional counter-actions. Police, for example, have responded to individual demonstrators and their actions (long hair, tattered clothing, unlawful activity, and obscene gestures) rather than to or from an ideological view of civil rights or the Vietnam War. Protestor's actions tended to be contrary to the basic values and upbringing of police officers. While local responses to social movements have often been more "in-the-flesh" direct, and sometimes counter to national policy, some of these responses were symbolic of national attitudes and responses.

This discussion suggests problems inherent in institutional bureaucracies. First, there is little agreement on whether negotiations with social movements should rest with executive, legislative, judicial, or enforcement bodies. Second, institutions are comprised of individuals with their own beliefs, attitudes, and values. Third, consensus and policy implementation are not merely matters of issuing directives because there are differences between theory and practice, issues and policy implementation. And fourth, democracy is not an entity but a process of regulating human behavior. This process is often slow and insensitive with contradictory principles. How does an established order balance the rights of society against individuals, the majority against the minority, or the popular against the unpopular?

For most social movements, the *cause* is supreme, the resources are *few*, and the time for action is *now*. The *expression* of these *cause* and *now* sentiments runs counter to the expectations nurtured by the *rhetoric* of democratic government, which attributes to the majority those sentiments it enacts and attributes those it rejects to a *small* minority.

Thus, the philosophical principles as well as the operational structure of a democracy dictate not only the strategies and tactics of social movements but also the forms and types of institutional responses. Democracy makes resistance to social movements varied and complex.

Administrative Rhetoric

According to Theodore Windt, administrative rhetoric is characterized by a defensive posture that views all questions of policy as attacks on the authority and credibility of the institution.[12] In the same vein, John Bowers and Donovan Ochs write that the principle that governs the rhetorical stance of decision-makers is the assumption that the worst will happen in any instance of outside agitation.[13] Institutional leaders, to maintain their power and credibility within the hierarchy, must continually provide evidence of superiority, control, and the willingness to respond quickly and decisively to all threats or attacks upon the institution. It is mandatory, then, for institutional leaders to confront the opposition to maintain support among establishment members and sympathizers. Windt presents five principles of administrative rhetoric:[14]

1. Specific issues are transformed into general ones of authority.
2. Establishment leaders must act in the interests of the majority.
3. Protestors are linked to illegitimate political categories such as outsiders, anarchists, and communists.
4. Establishment leaders portray themselves as defenders of law and order.
5. Establishment leaders predict dire consequences and a bleak future if the problem is not dealt with quickly and efficiently.

In summary, institutions seem to maintain a universal perspective toward outside threats and attacks. All challenges are viewed as questioning established authority. For most protestors, however, their challenges are questions of legitimacy, such as "How good are certain policies or actions?" Obviously, these divergent views toward challenges influence the nature and types of establishment responses to social movements. Bowers and Ochs identify four major rhetorical strategies establishments employ in response to outside challenges: avoidance, suppression, adjustment, and capitulation.[15]

The Strategy of Avoidance

When using a strategy of avoidance, the establishment attempts to counter challenges with persuasion that discredits a social movement's goals and leaders. Direct counter-persuasion is often the first and most prevalent tactic utilized. The secret to success is for the establishment not to overreact but to characterize the social movement, its leaders, and its ideas as ill advised and lacking merit. By manipulating the social context, an institution can expand, narrow, or selectively alter arguments and definitions of the situation.[16] For example, an institution may justify a "get tough" attitude or armed resistance to "preserve law and order," "protect the demonstrators," or "prevent anarchy." Thus, the establishment is not merely meeting a challenge to its authority but is protecting American values, citizen's lives, and property.

Counter persuasion often becomes most pronounced at the local or community level. Reverend George Fisher, pastor in 1963 of the Edgewater Baptist Church in Birmingham, Alabama, obtained 75,000 signatures on petitions endorsing the closing of schools rather than face integration, and he presented those petitions publicly to city officials.[17] Henry Gonzalez, elected to Congress in 1961 from Texas, led an aggressive counterattack against militant Chicanos. His charges followed three themes: (1) militants practiced reverse racism and preached hate based upon race; (2) militants displayed bad qualities and harmed the Mexican-American community; and (3) militant attacks on him were personal and unfair. Gonzalez's perspective was that the militants "have adopted the same positions, the same attitudes, the same tactics as those who have so long offended them."[18] In another case, the Reverend Ferrell Griswold encouraged parents from his pulpit in Birmingham, Alabama to keep their children out of public schools and to enroll them in private facilities. A thirteen-year-old black youth was shot to death following one of Griswold's rallies, and the sheriff's report accused Griswold of inspiring the two white boys who committed the murder.[19] Citizens and counter-group supporters usually deplore violence, but when respected political, social, and religious leaders of a community oppose compliance with laws, followers may resort to violence as a means of coping with frustration.

Moral outrage and righteous indignation provide justification for counterattack upon social movements, and a good counterattack nearly always employs labelling and name-calling. Lawrence Rosenfeld defines coercive semantics as attempts "to discourage real discussion of alternatives, and to render counter arguments meaningless by labelling the opponents as evil."[20] S.I. Hayakawa, President of San Francisco State University in 1968, claimed that rebellious students were attempting to overthrow the government and were all drug addicts. He referred to students as "cowards who resort to violence, lies, and deceit."[21]

Negative labelling and name-calling ridicule social movements, leaders, and members. Martha Solomon, in examining the rhetorical strategies of the Stop ERA

Movement, found that opponents of the women's movement labelled members as unattractive and lesbian. She concluded that "with sharp satire the group paints an unappealing picture of the feminists' physical appearance and nature, emphasizing their disregard for traditional standards of feminine attractiveness and sexuality."[22] Men were not alone in stereotyping pro-ERA women; Phyllis Schlafly (leader of the Eagle Forum) proclaimed "if man is targeted as the enemy, and the ultimate goal of women's liberation is independence from men and the avoidance of pregnancy and its consequences, then lesbianism is the highest form in the ritual of women's liberation."[23] Ridicule may weaken the self-confidence and self-esteem of protestors and challenge their efforts to attain legitimacy among potential sympathizers and members.

Another tactic of avoidance is to generate fear. Cries of anarchy help to unite the "silent majority" by labelling protestors as dangerous criminals. Institutions throughout American history have found it rather easy to generate feelings of suspicion toward those who are "different" or "foreign" and to create fears about social movement motives, goals, and objectives. Hesitation among the public and those who might sympathize with a social movement slows the process of change and forces movement leaders to spend a great amount of rhetoric and time explaining and justifying actions as well as ideology. Local officials during the racial confrontation in Birmingham in 1963 identified integration with despised external movements and threats such as communism.[24] Thus, integration became a tool of the communist conspiracy that was a grave threat to Christian and democratic principles and values.

Other avoidance tactics include evasion, postponement, and denial of means. Forms of evasion include "passing-the-buck," "unavailable for comment," and "getting the run-around." Postponement involves actions that slow or delay the decision process regarding social movement charges and demands. Institutions maintain the appearance of addressing an issue by referring it to a committee, special commission, or task force. In contrast, denial of means includes denying movements access to public facilities for meetings, parks or streets for demonstrations, and communication channels. For example, in 1968 during the Democratic National Convention, Mayor Richard Daly of Chicago denied permits for the Yippies to use Soldier's Field and members of the National Mobilization Committee to use Lincoln Park after curfew hours.[25]

Avoidance tactics deal with social movement leaders and members rather than the movement's issues and demands in two ways. First, name-calling, labelling, and ridicule attack a movement's active leaders and members directly. Perhaps the easiest way to discredit a movement is to discredit its leaders and most fervent followers. If the leaders and "true believers" are evil, then the motives, goals, and objectives of the movement must be evil. Second, bureaucratic procedures allow the established order to "take the high road" that often delays official response to a movement or denies movement access to public facilities, property, and communication channels. In either case, the establishment "buys time" and avoids direct confrontation with the social movement.

The Strategy of Suppression

The strategy of suppression involves tactics ranging from general harassment to purgation of social movement leaders and members. Suppression tactics tend to evolve when avoidance tactics fail to stifle a social movement and an institution commits itself to direct action and sustained conflict. Jerome Skolnick claims that many protestors have been attacked by counter-demonstrators with the knowledge and tacit approval of administrative and civil authorities. For example, the Ku Klux Klan and White Citizens' Councils served as surrogates for southern state and community authorities during the civil rights struggles. Skolnick writes that "by far the greater portion of physical harm has been done *to* demonstrators and movement workers, in the form of bombings of homes and offices, crowd-control measures used by police, physical attacks on demonstrators by American Nazi Party members, Hell's Angels and others, and random harassment such as the Port Chicago Vigil has endured."[26]

Harassment tactics may be covert as well as overt. During the Nixon Administration, agencies of the federal government such as the FBI, the CIA, and the Treasury Department investigated anti-war demonstrators and student leaders for communist connections or sympathies upon which the government might base administrative actions. Students were secretly photographed, files and lists of "suspected communist sympathizers" were created, letters (many allegedly from parents and concerned citizens) were sent to boards of trustees and school boards suggesting that certain teachers be fired, and some college officials reported activities of students to parents. Government agents and sympathizers infiltrated protest groups during the 1960s and 1970s with the purpose of instigating militant and violent acts. Michael Stohl reports that "regimes and their 'agent provocateurs' (both official and self-identified) have both encouraged insurgent groups to plan and execute terrorist actions not only to provide grounds for arrest but also to alienate potential supporters within the population."[27]

In an overt form of harassment, the head of the Selective Service System ordered the reclassification of leading student protestors as draftable.[28] For example, Peter Wolff and Richard Shortt had II-S student classifications as full-time students at the University of Michigan. When they participated in a demonstration protesting American involvement in Vietnam, the local Selective Service Board reclassified both as I-A, eligible for the draft. The Board argued that by participating in the anti-war demonstration, Wolff and Shortt became "delinquents" and thus were in violation of Section 12(a) of the Universal Military Training and Service Act. They further argued that a student deferment was not a "right" but a "legislative grace."[29] Direct forms of harassment are often used to intimidate. National

Guardsmen were called out to "protect students" in a two-day march on the Pentagon in 1967. The large number of heavily armed troops restricted the movement of and access to the student marchers. It soon became clear that the troops were present to control rather than to protect the protestors; this establishment show of force cost the taxpayers more than one million dollars.[30]

The easiest method of suppression is the passage and implementation of restrictive legislation and policies. For example, the University of California at Berkeley in 1964 established a policy prohibiting individuals from the solicitation of funds and advocacy of political causes on campus. The administration had several students arrested for violating this policy.[31] This undemocratic and unconstitutional policy suppressed student actions until protest organizations challenged it in court. Legal challenges of restrictive policies and legislation takes time and money, assets that favor established orders rather than social movements.

Some suppression is indirect and opportunistic. For instance, a student at the University of California at Berkeley was arrested for public obscenity because he carried a sign that read "Freedom Under Clark Kerr" (Kerr was president of the University). The first letter of each word was highlighted.[32] This arrest was obviously aimed more at the protestor than the "offending" obscenity. The establishment's arsenal of laws, rules, and regulations is a vast and powerful tool of suppression. Arrest is perhaps the most common form of suppression, and multiple charges can tie-up movement leaders for years with court appearances, bad publicity, and drains on a movement's precarious financial state. Bowers and Ochs write that the Black Panthers were involved in more than sixty criminal prosecutions requiring $300,000 in bail money in the first six months of 1967.[33]

The most severe forms of suppression—expulsion and assassinations—are often acts of individuals rather than institutions and institutional policies. Nevertheless, many movement leaders and followers have been killed in the United States. Students at Jackson State, Kent State, and individuals Medgar Evers, Malcolm X, and Martin Luther King, Jr. are merely the best known. Michael Stohl writes that "disappearance" of leaders and followers "is one of the quiet terrors employed by many governments in the modern world."[34]

The strategy of suppression has several advantages for the establishment. First, suppression tactics generate fear among a social movement's leaders, followers, and sympathizers. Michael Stohl notes that "The violence of the terrorist act is not intended simply to destroy but also to be heard." "For regimes," he continues, "the terror is a message of strength, a warning designed to intimidate, to ensure compliance without the need to physically touch each citizen."[35] Thus, leaders may become hesitant to act; followers may become hesitant to take part in demonstrations; and sympathizers may withdraw moral and financial support. Second, suppression isolates leaders from followers. And third, suppression enables institutions to portray social movement leaders as common criminals and dangerous social deviants.

The Strategy of Adjustment

The strategy of adjustment involves making some concessions to a social movement while not accepting the movement's demands or goals. Adjustment tactics give the appearance of being responsive to movement concerns. Accommodation, according to Andrew King, is usually a short-term solution that, for the establishment, buys time, saves face, and appears gracious.[36] This strategy, by design, addresses only superficial elements of conflict and seldom results in permanent solutions to social unrest and movement demands.

Adjustment tactics range from symbolic gestures to concrete acts of concession. Symbolic tactics include issuing press releases that promise investigation of problems or the naming of special committees and commissions to study the issues raised by the social movement. Such gestures provide a visible response and show of concern while reducing the sense of urgency of social movement demands which buys time for the establishment.

Sacrificing personnel is a common tactic of institutional leaders. University deans and presidents, police chiefs and officers, and mid-level executives often are dismissed from their positions when they become targets of social movements, are portrayed as unresponsive to citizen or group needs, or become convenient and expendable symbols of establishment "responsiveness." This tactic may be particularly effective when a social movement focuses its agitation and hatred upon a single individual or unit. Elimination of the individual or unit leaves the movement without a target. Public sympathy for an established order may increase when sacrificed individuals are seen as tragic victims of radical protestors.

A subtle adjustment tactic is cooperation with protestors and movement organizations by providing protection, access to facilities, or material support. Open and publicized cooperation frustrates social movements by making institutions less of an obvious enemy and target of outrage. Cooperation may defuse a movement's energy, momentum, and recruiting efforts, buy time for counter-efforts, encourage attitudes of neutrality among citizens, and generate favorable press.

Incorporation of movement leaders and sympathizers within institutional bodies is another common adjustment tactic. During the 1960s and 1970s, students, blacks, and women became appointees, often as "tokens," to committees, boards, and study commissions. Governmental agencies, schools, religious groups, and corporations began to hire a few minorities and to appoint them to serve in a variety of non-threatening positions. For example, American colleges and universities appointed one or two students to serve on boards of trustees, grievance committees, grade appeal committees, and curriculum committees. "Representation," however, did not mean power to influence policy decisions.

The strategy of adjustment can be tricky for institutions because they must not appear to be deceptive, cynical, weak, or tyrannical. Nearly any concession may rejuvenate a social movement by renewing hope of immediate or ultimate victory. Adjustments are most often mere tokens to appease public questioning and social movement demands.

The Strategy of Capitulation

Capitulation is the total acceptance of a social movement's ideology: beliefs, goals, objectives, and solutions, This has rarely happened in American history because (1) institutions control rewards, channels of communication, and regulatory agencies, and (2) as noted in previous chapters, Americans cherish the institutions they have created, adapted, and borrowed from other societies and are not inclined toward social-political instability or revolutionary change. Indeed, as Raymond Duvall and Michael Stohl write, Americans can hardly imagine their governments being evil.

> Particularly in the American political culture, the concept of the state as neutral conflict manager or arbiter of social conflict within society is so ingrained that many have difficulty emotionally accepting the idea of state terrorism. Terrorism is felt to be something done by revolutionaries *against* the state. How could a government—at least a *legitimate* government like that in the United States—be thought to engage in terrorism? Surely such talk must be revolutionary rhetoric![37]

Conclusions

Established orders must confront challenges and threats to their beings even though complete annihilation of existing institutions seldom occurs in today's world. For an institution, any concession to dissenters may be costly. Even negotiations create strains within an order by creating an atmosphere of tension and risk in a win-lose situation. Thus, established orders and their surrogates tend to employ a combination of four strategies in meeting the threats posed by social movements: avoidance, suppression, adjustment, and capitulation.

Over time, bits and pieces of social movement ideologies find their way into institutional policies. Social security, farm supports, unemployment benefits, the eight-hour day, civil rights, equal opportunity, voting rights, collective bargaining, and fair housing were social movement demands long before established political parties enacted them into law. The task for the establishment is to allow, perhaps even to encourage, dissent without threatening social, political, economic, or religious orders. Institutions and their surrogates have many more resources than social movements, and responses may emanate from individuals, organized resistance groups, local leaders, state-wide organizations, and national authorities that may include the whole federal government. The trick for an institution is to use the best strategy for the situation and to avoid the appearance of overreacting or abusing the powers granted to it by "the people."

Endnotes

[1] See John W. Bowers and Donovan J. Ochs, *The Rhetoric of Agitation and Control* (Reading, MA: Addison-Wesley, 1971), 9.

[2] Bowers and Ochs, 10-11.

[3] Bowers and Ochs, 12.

[4] Andrew King, *Power and Communication* (Prospect Heights, IL:Waveland Press, 1987), 48-53.

[5] Hugh Duncan, *Symbols in Reality.* (New York: Oxford University Press, 1968), 78-92.

[6] Duncan, 78.

[7] For specifics of such issues, see Robert O'Neil, *Free Speech* (Indianapolis: Bobbs-Merrill, 1972).

[8] Dale Minor, *The Information War* (New York: Hawthorn Books, 1970).

[9] Wayne Flynt, "The Ethics of Democratic Persuasion and the Birmingham Crisis," *Southern Speech Communication Journal*, 35 (Fall, 1969), 44.

[10] Flynt, 44-45.

[11] For a discussion of police response to protestors, see Irving Horowitz, *The Struggle Is the Message* (Berkeley, CA: The Glendessary Press, 1970), 48-58.

[12] Theodore Windt, "Administrative Rhetoric: An Undemocratic Response to Protest," *Communication Quarterly*, 30 (Summer, 1982), 247.

[13] Bowers and Ochs, 39-40.

[14] Windt, 247-248.

[15] Bowers and Ochs, 41-56.

[16] King, 27.

[17] Flynt, 45-46.

[18] John Hammerback, Richard Jensen, and Jose Gutierrer, *A War of Words* (Westport, CT: Greenwood Press, 1985), 104.

[19] Flynt, 47.

[20] Lawrence Rosenfeld, "The Confrontation Policies of S.I. Hayakawa: A Case Study in Coercive Semantics," *Today's Speech*, 18 (Spring, 1970), 18.

[21] Rosenfeld, 20.

[22] Martha Solomon, "The Rhetoric of Stop ERA: Fatalistic Reaffirmation," *Southern Speech Communication Journal*, 44 (Fall, 1978), 47.

[23] Solomon, 47.

[24] Flynt, 49.

[25] Bowers and Ochs, 43 and 45.

[26] Jerome Skolnick, "The Politics of Protest," *Dissent: Symbolic Behavior and Rhetorical Strategies*, Haig Bosmajian, ed. (Boston: Allyn and Bacon, 1972), 156.

[27] Michael Stohl, ed., *The Politics of Terrorism* (New York: Dekker, 1983), 5.

[28] Horowitz, 56.

[29] Harold Medina, "Students Have Rights Too," *Free Speech and Political Protest*, Marvin Summers, ed. (Lexington, MA: D.C. Heath, 1967), 102.
[30] Horowitz, 58.
[31] Windt, 245.
[32] Windt, 246.
[33] Bowers and Ochs, 47-48.
[34] Stohl, 3.
[35] Stohl, 3.
[36] King, 27-38.
[37] Raymond Duvall and Michael Stohl, "Governance by Terror," in Stohl, *The Politics of Terrorism*, 181.

Part Two

Approaches to the Study of Social Movement Persuasion

Chapter 7

A Social Systems Approach to Social Movement Persuasion

We said in Chapter 4 that history is social and that all social acts have implicit rhetorical or persuasive dimensions. This chapter and the two that follow describe three approaches to the study of social movements which focus upon their persuasive activities. While these are by no means the only approaches to studying social movement persuasion, they represent three fruitful paths to understanding the persuasive dimensions of social movements. This chapter presents a "social systems" model for studying social movement persuasion, contrasts it with other systems models of persuasion, and suggests a framework for criticism.

Systems Theory and Communication

Over the years, students of human communication have found it useful to create models or paradigms which metaphorically compare communication to other familiar phenomena. The most popular of these models has been the "systems model." B. Aubrey Fisher has suggested four tenets of system theory: the principle of nonsummativity; the role of structure, function, and evolution; the principle of openness; and hierarchical organization.[1] Let us review each of these tenets and its relevance to persuasion and social movements.

Characteristic 1: Nonsummativity

A system is comprised of *interdependent* components, and the "principle of nonsummativity" holds that this interdependence makes the whole something other than merely the sum of its parts. Individual items in a pile, heap, or aggregation do not noticeably affect one another; usually, one piece can be removed from the pile without directly altering other individual pieces. But the interdependence among system components means that a change in any one component can produce changes in other components as well as changes in the overall system. Because of the effects of this interaction, you may enjoy family gatherings more (or less) than you enjoy the company of individual family members. The interdependent relationships among components of a system serve as a catalyst that fosters the creation of a whole which behaves differently from its individual components. As these individual components interact they become a group, usually with its own identity. Thus, just as auto parts can be put together to form a Mercedes, a Chevette, or a Model T, similar people interacting differently can create noticeably different human groups—each with its own identity, behavioral tendencies (syntality), needs, and energy for survival (synergy). *It is communication that transforms a ''heap of individuals'' into a group.* The principle of nonsummativity is important to the study of social movements because a movement collectivity is something more (or less) than the sum of its parts. In fact, Fisher illustrates nonsummativity by contrasting labor unions with "all left-handed people:"

> There is simply little or no consistent effect of one left-handed person on another because of their left-handedness. But the labor union does function as a whole in many significant ways. Its members go on strike as a whole. They all go to work, perform assigned jobs, and in other ways honor the labor contract as a whole. In short, the actions of one affect the actions of others.[2]

The interaction between individuals—their communication—serves as a catalyst for the creation of something other than an "aggregate" or "heap" of individuals.

It should be apparent by now that students of social movement persuasion should pay close attention to the communication opportunities and activities which transform individuals into groups. Fisher's "left-handed people" constitute a heap only because they have yet to interact on the basis of their shared concerns with left-handedness. Conversely, the labor union is a system only because individual workers interacted over the years and developed a sense of "usness." In his autobiography, American Federation of Labor founder Samuel Gompers reflected upon the opportunities for interaction among the cigarmakers:

> It gave education in such a way as to develop personality, for in no other place were we so wholly natural. The nature of our work developed a camaraderie of the shop such as few workers enjoy. It was a world in itself—a cosmopolitan world. Shopmates came from everywhere—some had been nearly everywhere. When they told us of strange lands and peoples, we listened eagerly.[3]

More recently these interactions have developed into the "consciousness-raising" sessions of the women's liberation and gay rights movements. In each of these cases, individuals discover common experiences, aspirations, problems, and solutions through communication. Identification with a cause or social movement can emerge from the development of a communication system, in this case a movement.

Characteristic 2: Function-Structure-Evolution

The second axiom of systems theory is that interdependent relationships can be explained in terms of function, structure, and evolution. Behavior and action are purposeful (a point elaborated on in Chapters 8 and 9) because they fulfill needs or "functions" for individuals and collectivities. When a function regularly recurs (such as seasonal greetings, monthly bill payments, and the selection of government representatives), we develop behavioral "structures" that assure their performance (Christmas cards, household budgets, and elections). Most of these structures perform the function imperfectly, and we continue to quibble and tinker along the same lines to enhance the performance of the function. Sometimes we create a structure that performs the function so nicely that new needs and functions that had been obscured from view become apparent. At this point, we "evolve" into a phase guided by the new functional necessities and the search for fresh behavioral structures. Thus, the interplay of functional behaviors leads to evolutionary change as the system moves from the performance of one hierarchy of functions to another.

The structure of a social movement can refer to its membership profile, its organizational structure, or its strategic efforts. The anti-Vietnam War movement needed dedicated workers during its early phases, but it needed a plurality of voters in 1968 and 1972. The A.F. of L. organized skilled tradesmen and excluded unskilled industrial workers, a tactic that worked until the increasing industrialization of American led to the formation of the Industrial Workers of the World and, later, the Congress of Industrial Organizations. David Duke's branch of the Ku Klux Klan has moved from the old Klan's cross-burnings and lynchings to recruitment of Catholic and women members and the use of television and radio talk shows. Chapter 8 explains a "functional approach" to the study of persuasion and social movements which emphasizes the ways in which persuasive communication fulfills the movement's needs, and Chapters 13, 14, and 15 explore the persuasive functions performed by songs, slogans, and obscenity in social movements. *The point here is that social movements evolve structures to perform functions, thereby altering the pattern of functions remaining to be performed.* This process is continuous—every aspect of a system has evolved from, and will evolve to, something else; hence beginnings and endings are purely relative.

Characteristic 3: Hierarchical Organization

The third axiom is that all systems have hierarchical organization. It is possible to locate each system (e.g., a social movement) within an encompassing "supra-system" (the society) and to ascertain "sub-systems" (individual organizations and, ultimately, individual persons) within each system. All systems are therefore influenced both by their sub-systems and by their supra-systems. However, the precise distinction between sub-system, system, and supra-system is generally a matter of the observer's perspective (one could reasonably consider the movement as the supra-system, an organization as the system, and the individual as the subsystem). Once one has identified the hierarchical structure of systems, the level of analysis is largely a matter of choice.

The "nesting" of systems in other systems is important for understanding social movements. It is not uncommon for social movements led by major figures, or having widespread support, to fail. Eugene V. Debs' American Railway Union won several major victories in 1893 leading to vast increases in membership which created an uncontrollable, undisciplined organization that was promptly and permanently demolished only months later in the Pullman Strike.

An energetic movement can change the behavior of the supra-system by changing the larger system's functional needs. The civil rights movement raised American society's concerns about discrimination, poverty, and voting rights by demonstrating that all was not well in America. The War on Poverty, the Civil Rights Act of 1964, the Voting Rights Act of 1965, and other changes were responses to a restructured set of American functional priorities which derived from black Americans' demands for justice and white Americans' discomfort over those demands. In 1964 the Democratic Party had little need for black support to defeat Barry Goldwater and the Republicans. But by 1988, the Democrats sorely needed Jesse Jackson and his multitude of new voters to contest the presidential election. As the institution's functional needs changed, so did the party structure. With the Dukakis-Jackson-Carter convention meeting and Jackson's historic convention address, the civil rights movement took its rhetorical place alongside the labor and women's movements as institutionalized pillars of the Democratic Party, not challengers at the convention gate.

Characteristic 4: The Degree of Openness

Fisher's fourth axiom of systems theory is that any system can be described on the basis of its "openness"—the permeability of its boundaries. A system can be assessed with respect to the freedom of exchange between the system and its environment and thereby classified as either "open" or "closed." Open systems have boundaries which permit the interaction of system and environment, whereas closed systems are entirely self-contained. Openness is important because open and closed systems are governed by different principles.

Closed systems, according to Fisher, are governed by the principle of "equilibrium"—"the final state of the closed system is determined by the initial state" because a self-contained system must balance without any help from the outside. Thus, a closed system will *always* return to its initial starting point.

Conversely, open systems are governed by the principle of "equifinality" which states that "the same final state may be reached from different initial conditions and in different ways . . . [and] different open systems with the same initial condition could well achieve different final states."[4] Put differently, you can get anywhere in an open system from anywhere else, and you can get there by a variety of paths.

The difference between the equilibrium of closed systems and the equifinality of open systems derives from the principle of "entropy"—an irreversible process of disintegration. Closed systems can only respond to entropy by exerting a counter-force (negentropy) to slow that disintegration. But once slowed, the disintegration is not reversed. As Fisher observes, "The balanced state of homeostasis . . . does not suggest an increase in order or structure, only a slowing down or stoppage of the disintegrative process."[5]

Open systems, capable of exchange with their environment, can combat entropy either by adding new information from the environment or by generating their own original or novel information. In this sense, open systems take stock of their environment and adjust to it. The net result is that open systems can actually *increase* order over the original state.

Even in the natural sciences there are few truly closed systems, and human or social systems are considered open. Nevertheless, many theorists have found it useful to draw upon the similarities between persons and machines to explain the process of human communication. Let us note, therefore, that all systems models of communication emphasize that the whole is more than the sum of its parts because of the interaction of persons, that communication systems evolve as structures perform functions, that each system is comprised of sub-systems while itself constituting part of a supra-system both of which influence it and both of which it influences, and that each system is to some degree capable of exchange with its environment. Having said that much, let us consider the differences between "mechanical" and "social" systems as models of human communication.

Mechanical vs. Social Systems

We employ a mechanical systems model to describe communication every time we mention transmission, reception, feedback, noise, barriers, breakdowns, leverage, being pushed around, or being on the same wavelength. We have taught ourselves that communication is a process of mechanical adjustment. That thesis pervades the works of Norbert Wiener and the team of Shannon and Weaver, all of whom observed parallels between human communication and mechanical systems.[6]

Indeed, it is possible for a closed-system to measure its environment and adjust to it. Wiener's study of "cybernetics" suggests that people can be profitably compared to self-regulating machines like thermostats. Yet even a thermostat has only one pattern of reaction—when it detects too low a temperature, it begins to heat, only to stop when a satisfactory temperature is reached. The thermostat, unlike a person, cannot *decide* whether to offer you a sweater, close the windows, or build a fire—it simply and directly performs its specified function for the system.

The thermostat cannot choose; it can only execute. Even the most sophisticated computer can only execute programs provided for it by a programmer.

This mechanical view of human communication was challenged as long ago as 1970 when Dennis Smith noted that our study of speech-communication was too heavily influenced by the engineering sciences. He argued that the differences between human communication and mechanical systems were more important than the similarities. Smith specifically challenged the concept of "communication breakdown" on the grounds that it teaches four fallacies about communication:

1. *The Fallacy of Linearity* presumes that communication is a straight line of actions from one person to another, rather than an *interdependent* process in which people anticipate and build upon one another's (and even outsiders') behaviors to create meaning.
2. *The Fallacy of Mechanism* mistakenly treats persons as machines rather than humans, thereby omitting consideration of biological, psychological, and sociological influences.
3. *The Fallacy of Noncommunication* presumes that communication involves purely what is said or written, and overlooks the communicative significance of *interpretation*.
4. *The Fallacy of Reification* presumes that unsatisfactory communication results from a "thing" (breakdown) which can be removed or fixed, rather than from interpretive behavior.[7]

We would add a fifth fallacy to Smith's list. *The Fallacy of Success* presumes that communication will be effective and satisfactory unless something goes wrong (i.e., the breakdown). Much communication is fairly difficult (e.g., asking for a first date, complimenting a friend's unattractive hairdo, interviewing for a job), and effective or satisfying communication is more often the exception than the rule. It seems more productive to approach communication as a constructive, adaptive process at which people sometimes succeed and often fail. All of our conflicts are *not* due to a "failure to communicate;" many derive from deep-seated, irreconcilable differences between subsystems. Too often references to "ineffective communication" or a "breakdown in communication" distract us from more important issues.

Smith's critique of communication breakdowns illustrates the implications of choosing inappropriate metaphoric models for explaining human communication. Like Smith and Fisher, we find mechanical models inappropriate for the explanation of human communication because of their omission of human choice and creativity from the process of communication. However, the concept of system need not be discarded simply because mechanical systems are inappropriate.

Social Systems

One alternative to mechanical systems is a "social systems model" of communication that differs markedly from the "mechanical systems model." Brent D. Ruben sumarized the four propositions of a social or "living" systems approach as follows:

1. People, like other animals, are instances of living systems.
2. Living systems are structural and functional units (individual and social) which maintain themselves (and grow, change, and deteriorate) *only* through interactions with their environment.
3. Environmental interaction[s] are of two types: (a) transactions which involve the transformation of matter-energy, which may be termed *bio-physical metabolism*; and (b) transactions which involve the transformation of data-information, which may be termed *informational-metabolism* or *communication*.
4. The functional goal [of the behavior] of all living systems is adaptation with the environment.[8]

First, Ruben differentiates living systems which grow and change *only* through interaction with their environments from both mechanical systems (which only deteriorate) and from closed systems (which cannot interact with their environments). Elaborating upon the characteristics of living systems, Ruben concurs with Smith that "communication is both continual and inevitable. There are no 'breakdowns in communication'; there is no option to be in communication with the environment so long as the system is alive." Indeed, silence itself is a means of adapting to the environment.

Second, Ruben observes that an organism *adapts to its environment, and adapts its environment to it*. Thus, one should be encouraged neither to ask with Lloyd Bitzer how a persuader responds to a rhetorical situation, nor to ask with Richard Vatz how the persuader created the rhetorical situation through language.[9] Instead, we should search for both in the mutual adaptation of system *with* environment.

Third, adaptation occurs as "discrepancies between the needs and capacities of the system and those of the environment emerge, and the system, acting on the discrepancy, strives to close the gap." From a social systems perspective, the natural, healthy state of affairs involves people actively adapting to their environment by creating alternatives and choosing among them. This creative choosing leads us into new eras of human progress.

Views of Influence, Conflict, and Relationships

The choice between social and mechanical systems models of communication rests upon one's preferred conceptions of human influence, human conflict, and human relationships.

Conceptions of Human Influence

Influence in mechanical systems is highly manipulative. A persuader examines the persuasive landscape and ascertains (1) the auditor's susceptibility to influence and (2) the persuader's resources for influence, so that (3) the persuader can construct or apply a formula or equation which creates the *necessary and sufficient stimuli* for the auditor to respond in accordance with the persuader's intent. Mechanical conceptions of influence are therefore analogous to an automobile engine. If we know (1) the automobile's susceptibility to misfire, and (2) that such misfiring is influenced by sparkplugs, timing, and fuel mixture, then we can (3) manipulate sparkplugs, timing, and fuel mixture to produce a necessary and sufficient change in the system to cause the engine's proper operation. The parallel assumption in persuasion is that we can structure message variables to produce consistently the desired auditor behavior. The key to mechanistic persuasion is knowing the right set of equations for a particular "target" audience.

Influence in social systems is adaptive behavior. An organism will adapt to its environment in diverse ways (the principle of equifinality): by attempting to change its environment, by attempting to change itself, or by attempting to escape from the environment through selective attention, selective perception, and selective retention. The metaphor here is not the car on the garage rack, but the driven automobile. The driver *chooses* to ignore speed limits or road conditions, drive faster or slower, take dubious creative shortcuts, or devote adequate attention to maintenance of the car's mechanical operation. No matter how many speed limit signs the driver sees, he or she can always *choose* to ignore them. Sometimes, as when the driver chooses to pay the cost of a CB radio or a radar detector for the benefit of an additional 5-10 miles per hour, the adaptive choice is not purely rational.

Adaptive humans have often confounded mechanical systems theorists. Sensing that someone has concocted a formula to influence them, auditors can feel that their essential human ability to choose is endangered. These concerned humans may refuse to comply by imposing new conditions, misunderstanding the message, and/or reconstructing the relationship and its groundrules. While mechanistic theorists revise their equation to account for this erratic behavior, the social systems theorists recognize it as the kind of adaptive behavior that is central to communication studies.

Mechanical systems models are particularly ill-suited to the study of persuasion and social movements because movements need to be creative and unusual. Any social movement that responds predictably to the establishment will not long survive, since the establishment creates and enforces all of the rules. Organizer Saul Alinsky succinctly recommended that:

> Radicals must be resilient, adaptable to shifting political circumstances, and sensitive enough to the process of action and reaction to avoid being trapped by their own tactics and forced to travel a road not of their own choosing. In short, radicals must have a degree of control over the flow of events.

A social movement needs to adapt in a manner that retains its freedom and independence from the established order, which seems to render equations for influence almost useless.

Additionally, it is very difficult to predict the effectiveness of a tactic. An assassination may end a movement or perpetuate it by creating a needed martyr (perhaps even removing an unpopular leader). Non-violence worked well for Gandhi in India and Martin Luther King, Jr. in America, but it failed horribly for Jews in Nazi Germany (whether from their lack of organization or the society's lack of moral sensitivity is arguable). Human influence in movements, then, is highly adaptive and does not conform to manipulative mechanical laws.

Conception of Human Conflict

Mechanistic systems view conflict as imbalances (barriers or breakdowns) that should be either prevented or repaired. At best, imbalance is prevented and the system hums along, quietly disintegrating under the law of entropy. When imbalance does occur, balance can only be restored after considerable upheaval (negentropy). When a car breaks down, it is out of commission until Mr. Goodwrench pronounces it "as good as new" (the principle of equilibrium). The return to normal is attained only through financial setback, children waiting at school, the cat stranded at the vet's, and a strong sense of frustration. In systems terminology, negentropy has been introduced to restore equilibrium. *Nothing is ever gained in mechanical systems*. Thus, we should strive for preventive maintenance of our mechanical systems lest they "breakdown."

Social systems conflict creates the opportunity for growth and progress. Discrepancies between the needs and capacities of the system and the needs and capacities of the environment challenge the organism. If the organism fails to resolve the discrepancy, it dies; if it meets the challenge adequately, it survives and grows or evolves into a new phase of life. As Alinsky observed:

> In the politics of human life, consistency is not a virtue. To be consistent means, according to the Oxford Universal Dictionary, 'standing still or not moving.' Men must change with the times or die.[11]

Of course, this discrepancy simultaneously creates an opportunity for destruction—that is the nature of equifinality. The important fact is that unlike the mechanical systems model, the social systems model views conflict and controversy as potentially constructive or creative, if somewhat troublesome. The difference is that upheaval can lead to an enhanced state of order rather than simply slowed disintegration and temporarily restored order. Let us return to our example of the automobile.

Whereas an automobile with a broken fan belt can only be restored to its antecedent state, the drivers who adapt to the environment by fixing it can improve themselves. Conceivably, they are proud to become self-reliant, able fixers of fan belts. Each person has "grown" as a result of the conflict and will never again be quite as awed by the prospect of car troubles (of course, equifinality also dictates that it can lead to long hours on the side of the road and intense exasperation). Thus, while mechanical conflict is purely disruptive, social systems conflict can lead to evolutionary growth.

Now, if human conflict mirrors mechanical conflict, it should be avoided on the grounds that it is purely wasteful. Since the establishment functions to maintain systemic order, no study rooted in mechanical premises should ever sanction the creation of conflict. Indeed, rhetorical studies of agitation reflected just this kind of establishment bias until Herbert Simons attacked it and suggested a "dual perspective" (establishment and movement). In so doing, Simons revealed this weakness in our mechanistic assumptions. Unfortunately, Simons perpetuated the mechanical systems model instead of reconceptualizing our view of social conflict.[12]

If human conflict is more nearly organic than mechanical, then controversy and conflict are our only means for progress. If this is the case, then we should employ models which encourage consideration of multiple conflicting viewpoints and which focus on the process of on-going adaptation. Simons' works on social movements broke important theoretical ground in the early 1970s. Our objection, from the perspective of the next decade, is that he did not go far enough. *No model based upon mechanical assumptions can admit the equivalence of both agitator and movement perspectives since mechanical systems models assume that (1) no good can come from imbalance, (2) the establishment is empowered to maintain balance, and (3) agitators and social movements function to create imbalance.*

The various sub-systems of a social system attempt to close the discrepancy in different ways. The establishment usually minimizes the discrepancy in favor of the prior state of affairs (in which it was elected), while one or more parts of the system strive to resolve it in other directions. After the U.S. Supreme Court's *Brown v. Board of Education* decision ruled segregation unconstitutional, for example, civil rights activists highlighted for us the discrepancy between the law and our practices; southern politicians such as Ross Barnett raised the possibility that states could ignore the federal law; and the federal government wrestled with the problem of satisfying all of its constituent subsystems. *The important point is that all parts work in their own ways to adjust their system with the environment. Therefore, all of their efforts deserve comparable attention*. Conversely, it would be counterproductive to favor the establishment's effort to maintain balance, since that effort could or would restrain the system's adaptive capabilities.

Conception of Human Relationships

The third issue is systemic maturation. Mechanical systems are at their prime when new or almost new (some require a brief "break-in" period). All mechanical systems experience friction, deterioration, and general wear. With proper maintenance, this process of deterioration (entropy) can be slowed, but it can never be reversed—even if the price of a Rolls-Royce appreciates with age, its mechanical system nevertheless deteriorates. Such an approach to human communication is depressing at best and frightening at worst. It implies that relationships begin at or near their zenith and can only be slowed in their deterioration.

But a social systems approach presumes that relationships develop from initial encounters. Whether we choose to nurture or to ignore them, past experiences influence future conversations. From this perspective, experience and practice become important. Having fixed one broken fan belt is no guarantee that you can fix another, but you expect that experience to prove useful. Similarly, a first date may be the best, or it may simply be the start of a growing relationship—that depends upon the parties' willingness and abilities to build upon their encounter for the process of mutual accommodation. The social systems view suggests that one is likely to find the more successful relationships among the longer ones, while admitting that some may have developed quickly and yet others may have persisted unhappily.

When studying social movement persuasion, the mechanical systems theorist is concerned with stability, while the social systems theorist is concerned with change. And since social systems (governed by equifinality) can develop from any state into any other through any means, *the study of social systems emphasizes the process by which subsystems emerge and adapt by creating alternatives and choosing among them*. Our country is very different today from what it was in the 18th century. While not all of these changes have been improvements, neither have they all been disintegrative. Most, if not all, of these changes have been adaptive efforts by humans not yet born in 1776 to adapt to environments not yet existing in 1776. In this light, the American Revolution, the Civil War, women's suffrage, agrarianism, and the labor and civil rights movements have led us into new eras of life in America which could not be satisfactorily explained as a return to equilibrium, because each of these movements created novel alternatives. Just as we study American history developmentally, a social systems approach to social movement persuasion views the relationship between the movement and the society developmentally. The frequent intransigence of some labor unions today, for example, can be better understood in terms of management's parental behavior during labor's infancy and adolescence.

Summary

While people will probably continue to use the jargon of mechanical systems to describe human communication, we can hope that they will at least become aware of the implications of their metaphors. To conceptualize communication mechanically is to conceive of conflict and change as disruptive, influence as manipulative, and relationships as disintegrative. We believe that it is more accurate, realistic, and therefore productive to conceive of conflict as adjustive and evolutionary, influence as accommodative, and relationships as integrative. Toward this end, we need to formulate approaches to communication that embody these assumptions so that we can ascertain the relative explanatory powers of the mechanical and social systems approaches.

Ruben, Fisher, and Leonard Hawes have moved toward research techniques for the study of interpersonal and small group communication which are consonant with social systems assumptions. Their methods seek changes in the patterns of interaction which indicate new phases of communication.[13] The immediate problem is that we have no social systems framework that is directly applicable to the study of social movement persuasion. Let us turn, then, to the presentation of such a framework.

Social Systems and Criticism

Rhetorical critics can embrace the nature of social systems by pursuing the question, "Which individuals, conceiving themselves to be what 'people' in what environment, use what relational patterns and what adaptive strategies with what evolutionary results?" Let us examine each part of this question.[14]

Which Individuals?

Since persuasion is a human activity, we must ascertain precisely which people create the system's adaptive effort. This means locating prominent individuals, their demographic traits, and their personality or character traits. We must devote more attention to the discovery of similarities and differences among the people who come to share particular rhetorical visions or self-conceptions. Discovering that a particular social movement is largely comprised of people with a low tolerance of ambiguity, a familiarity with crime and violence, and/or a common regional, racial, or religious experience may help us to understand better their susceptibility to one characterization of their environment and their aversion to others. Thus, biological, sociological, and psychological information can help us to understand the movement, the hierarchy, and their interdependence.

Information about leaders is easily found in biographies, autobiographies, movement studies, journalistic accounts, histories, and single-speaker rhetorical studies. The social systems approach does not equate a leader's background or behavior with the movement, but instead seeks to understand the leadership subsystem as a means of understanding the movement system. It helps, for example, to study the theological development of Martin Luther King, Jr. and Malcolm X before studying their persuasion. It is also helpful to know that John Birch Society founder Robert Welch wrote a primer on salesmanship, that socialist labor leader Eugene V. Debs originally opposed strikes, and that neighborhood organizer Saul

Alinsky held a Ph.D. in psychology. Much helpful information about major movement figures and their rhetoric can be found in two recently published reference books on *American Orators* by Bernard Duffy and Halford Ross Ryan.[15]

If studying the leadership subsystem requires biographical materials, studying the membership subsystem requires social-psychological data. This kind of scientific research is rare in speech communication literature. One exception is Michael J. Hogan's study of the people participating in rallies for George Wallace.[16] Consequently, the social systems critic will often need to draw upon surveys and studies from other disciplines, such as political scientist Fred Grupp's survey of John Birch Society members in 1964. His data suggested that Birchers were unrepresentative of the American population in several respects, and he was able to identify four types of Birch Society members based upon their reasons for joining: "informed" who joined for educational benefits, "like-minded" who wanted to associate with people who "thought like them," "politically committed" who wanted an outlet for their political activities, and "ideological" who wanted something in which to believe.[17] Chapter 10 will explore further the role of personality in the adaptive behavior of the John Birch Society members. For the present, it should be apparent that Grupp's study provides valuable information about Birch members' needs, motives, and preferences which can help the critic to explain their enthusiasm for an otherwise unpopular set of beliefs. Our first task, then, is to identify the influential leaders and their followers: who are they? what are their demographic, experiential, sociological, psychological, and political traits? This first step tells us something about the people from whom the movement develops. With this information we can better predict and explain the leaders' and members' adaptive choices. But unfortunately, it is not enough to identify individuals' traits or tendencies since systems theory is based on the principle of nonsummativity.

Conceiving Themselves to Be What 'People'

In an old joke the "faithful Indian companion Tonto" exemplifies our ability to adapt self-conception to environmental discrepancy:

> Lone Ranger: Well, Tonto, the Indians have us surrounded. It looks like we're done for.
>
> Tonto: What do you mean "We," Paleface?

Having ascertained who people are and what they are like, it remains for us to discover who they think they are. Michael C. McGee, Aaron Gresson, and others have described the processes by which "peoples" arise through their shared myths and pasts.[18] In the final analysis, real people, not rhetorical creations, take action. In this sense, then, we need to be concerned with the movement's and the hierarchy's self-conceptions. The critic should ascertain who they think they are, the degree to which this self-image corresponds with the critics' appraisal of who they really are, and the psychological/sociological reasons for their rhetorical susceptibility to these particular characterizations.

When "you" and "I" create an "us," we begin to see something beyond our individuality (which we call "usness"). This "us" is the relational system which is created as you and I each adapt to our environments (including each other's). Tonto adapted to his environment by transforming his relational bonds—his Indian heritage became more salient for him than his friendship with the Lone Ranger. Tonto did not physically become "more Indian," but his perceptions changed significantly. He conceived himself as Indian rather than kimosabe. When the labor movement song asks "Which Side Are You On?" the listener faces a choice much like Tonto's.

The self-conceptions of movement leaders and members are not always consistent with demographic or experiential profiles. Well-heeled labor leaders are often seen on television complaining about inadequate wages as they prepare to be chauffeured back to labor headquarters. Religious groups believe they serve God by throwing bombs in Lebanon or Belfast or by enacting a mass suicide in Guyana. The social systems critic wants to know how these people see themselves and how they develop that self-conception (in light of their objective characteristics) through communication.

In What Environment

"In what environment" draws our attention to the world in which the organism must survive. Just as the organism develops, so does the environment—partly in response to the organism's adaptive behavior. But the environment contains other social and mechanical systems as well as the movement—all of which mitigate one organism's ability to adapt effectively to its environment. The social systems critic needs to pursue factual materials about, for example, labor conditions or discriminatory practices against which to compare labor and civil rights complaints.

We are not solely interested in the objective environment because humans *interpret* their environment. Our experiences (direct and vicarious) and our relationships help us to construct vocabularies and logical frameworks which we use to "make sense" of the world. We interpret people and events through these frameworks whenever possible and renovate them whenever they prove dysfunctional (the interpretive roles of authoritarian and democratic personalities are discussed further in Chapter 10). We therefore must consider characterizations or depictions of the environment. For example, the discrepancies which concern people most are instances of "relative deprivation:" they are denied something to which they feel entitled. These deprivations may be as blatant and specific as a wage cut, denial of the right to vote, or imprisonment. The perceived deprivation can also be more subtle. The important point, as sociologist John Wilson notes, is that "the individuals involved come to feel that their expectations are reasonable."[19] A frequent complaint of protestors is that they are *losing* their status or self-respect. In testimony before the Senate in 1883, a machinist emphasized dehumanization and limited horizons:

> Well, the trade has been subdivided . . . so that a man never learns the machinist's trade now. . . . It has a very demoralizing effect upon the mind. . . . When I first went to learn the trade a machinist considered himself more than the average workingman; in fact he did not like to be called a workingman. Today he recognizes that he is simply a laborer the same as the others.[20]

Persuasion is important to the development of a sense of relative deprivation because people must realize that they have been short-changed. The social systems critic should develop pictures of the environment as it appears to both movement and hierarchy. Real things do happen to real people which constitute an objective reality (a bloodied nose, a picket line, and a wage cut are more than perceptual "tricks of the mind"). But these "real" events are perceived, experienced, and understood in diverse ways, leading to diverse realities. Thus, we should focus on the competing characterizations of the environment and the discrepancies among them.

Use What Relational Patterns

"Use what relational patterns" reminds us that not all social movement persuasion is the product of an orator on a soapbox. The critic of social movement persuasion should examine who establishes and maintains communicative systems with whom. Such relationships are important for several reasons. First, they indicate the audiences whom persuaders consider to be capable of resolving the problem. Second, relational patterns suggest the persuader's conception of the auditor's importance to both the movement (system) and the larger society (suprasystem). Third, these relational choices suggest the persuader's working assumption that the auditors either are, or should be, involved in the process of systemic adaptation.

Attention to relationships, then, may help us to distinguish functional differences between antiwar demonstrations at the local draft board (which seek to influence local implementation), on the steps of the Capitol (which seek to influence national legislation by drawing national attention), and on Main Street (which enhance solidarity and recruiting while polarizing the demonstrators from their opposition). Similarly, it should focus our attention on the hierarchy's response to acts of protest, particularly to the differences between meetings with demonstrators, meetings with the parents of demonstrators, arrests of demonstrators, and press conferences which reassure public and press that the demonstrators are "simply a handful of troublemakers."

In "The Rhetorical Situation," Lloyd Bitzer explained an audience as one or more people capable of resolving an exigence or problem. But we too rarely take the time to ascertain the relationships between persuader and audience, or audience and exigence. Thus, relational systems and their evolution are important elements of a social systems approach to social movement persuasion that deserve careful study. The important point is not that movements use different "channels" (the mechanistic theorist's conveyor belts for meaning). The channel used for transmission may matter, or it may not. Rather, the important point is *how relational patterns include and exclude potential supporters and critics, foster or preclude the sense of transformation from individuals to group, and reinforce or contradict adaptive efforts.*

And What Adaptive Strategies

"And what adaptive strategies" directs our attention to the on-going, thoughtful process of adjustment as individuals and groups, perceiving a discrepancy between their experienced and preferred environments, create instrumental techniques to minimize that discrepancy. Again, we should look for links between individual characteristics, self-conceptions, relationships, and environment. Immigrant workers at the turn of the century who shared no common language marched rather than spoke; reactionary groups with a fundamentalist strain preached; while culturally passive blacks, expecting to be brutalized by white authorities, opted for a Gandhian approach to dramatize the system's inhumanity.

Unlike Bowers and Ochs' dichotomy between a "rhetoric of agitation" and a "rhetoric of control," the critic should search for adaptive, evolutionary patterns in which choices reflect the attempts of individuals to adapt to the system as they try to help their system adapt to its environment.[21] As discussed in Chapter 4, this should produce a richer understanding of movements and their strategies.

"What adaptive strategies" leads us to the classic Aristotelian focus of "discovering the available means of persuasion." Rather than simply cataloguing strategies, critics must view these strategies from the larger perspective of unfolding adaptations—what others have done and what they may be expected to do in response to one's own adaptive efforts.

With What Evolutionary Results

"With what evolutionary results" is our measure of movement growth. The social systems approach is developmental and disdains the notion that adaptations are permanent (since the environment and other organisms are themselves constantly adapting). We can therefore look for evolutionary phases in this developmental process like the typical life cycle presented in Chapter 2. These may be changes in the movement's people or their self-conception, changes in the environment or their characterizations of it, changes in their relational patterns or their adaptive strategies. In any case, the critic wants to know how the change facilitated the organism's adaptation with its environment. Did the system adapt effectively? Did it adapt too late to a discrepancy which was otherwise resolved? Did attempted adaptation exacerbate the initial discrepancy? Did the organism appear to enter a new evolutionary phase? Critics can compare any social movement to the normative life-cycle.

The answers to such questions should enable us to understand more fully the rhetorical (i.e., adaptive, accommodative) functions of movements in society.

Emphasizing evolutionary results requires an examination of the system-environment fit at a minimum of two points in the adaptive process. These points are a matter of critical judgment and may be chosen in either of two ways. The more traditional method historically ascertains transitions in the social movement's life-cycle and studies the role of persuasion in that transition. Although this is a reasonable historical approach, it raises the possibility that persuasive evolution and historical evolution may be "out of synch." The second approach is closer to Fisher and Hawes' interpersonal approach. It involves the careful (usually quantitative) analysis of persuasion over time for the purpose of ascertaining shifts in recurrent patterns. This is an effective method for finding shifts in argument (segregationists' shift from white supremacy to states' rights), audience (the Communist Party's shift from workers to intellectuals), relational patterns (the John Birch Society's shift from study sessions to the Goldwater campaign and back again), self-conceptions (the emergence of the notion of Black Power and Black Is Beautiful), or exigence (pro-life's shift from opposing the legalization of abortion to supporting an anti-abortion amendment to the Constitution).

Regardless of the method employed, the critic should be watchful for signs that the movement and its environment are entering a qualitatively different evolutionary phase. *Since change is unavoidable, the critic is looking for empirically discernible changes in the system-environment fit*, not mere changes in the movement, the hierarchy, the environment, or in rhetorical strategy. To the disappointment of many Americans, Richard Nixon's succession of Lyndon Johnson only marginally changed the system-environment fit; despite the change in personnel, both the movement's argument and the government's response remained essentially the same.

Summary

Social systems critics may wish to ask: *Which individuals, conceiving themselves to be what "people" in what environment, use what relational patterns and what adaptive strategies with what evolutionary results*. Many parts of this question are frequently asked in similar ways. But the social systems critic deemphasizes the parts in favor of their inter-relationship. It is sufficient neither to know which people were active in a movement, nor which symbols pervaded the movement's rhetoric. The critic wants to know why certain symbolic behaviors proved useful (or futile) for certain people in a particular environment.

Conclusions

We have approached communication as a quasi-mechanical system for too long. Stemming from Aristotle's attention to speaker, audience, message, and occasion, we forgot that it is the *interdependence* of these variables, not their separation, that shapes communication. In recent years, we have increasingly noticed that an understanding of the pieces fails to explain the whole of human communication. At the same time, we have seen a growth in organic or social systems models of interpersonal communication that suggest an approach to communication as the efforts of parties in a relationship adapting to one another and their environment.

This chapter has proposed a social systems approach to the persuasive activities of social movements that provides a framework for bringing our analysis of societal communication into line with our knowledge of interpersonal communication. In so doing, we should minimize our recurrent urges to quibble over equally legitimate levels of analysis. At the same time, this approach not only permits but encourages us to examine people and events not always classified as "movement," to incorporate insights from interpersonal and organizational communication, and to turn back to the individual orator and event studies we have so long ignored as unprofitable.

Perhaps the best reason for considering new approaches to the study of social movement persuasion is the abysmal failure of socio-political communication in our lifetimes. In the past thirty-five years, we have witnessed hearings in which reactionaries and conservatives accused liberals of being radicals and revolutionaries, thereby creating an atmosphere in which dissent was decried. In that environment, a new generation of liberals radicalized in response to a hierarchy which refused to hear them. As their liberalism escalated to radicalism and revolution, the central issue was transformed from political to moral, rendering discussion and compromise still more difficult and promoting the politics of self-righteous, single-interest organizations.

Those of us who study persuasion must find and share better ways of understanding and handling systemic adaptation. We must understand that conflict is not simply to be avoided; it is unavoidable. Conflict is a sign of system-environment adaptation. The problem is not, as so many of our public officials have believed, eradicating symptomatic protest. We have all too often seen how such eradication only intensifies the original discrepancy. Instead we must come to grips with the fact that agitation, exhortations and threats of violence are signs that the system is not adapting satisfactorily with its environment. We must recognize that the system-environment relationship is not a thing but a process and that restraining or retarding that process often increases the trauma of adaptation when it ultimately comes. In the final analysis, we must remember that *persuasion* is not something that one does to another or has done to oneself. It is *a process of mutual adjustment in which people and societies engage.*

The mechanical systems approach to social movement persuasion implicitly requires that we adopt a movement-establishment stance. The critic proceeding from that base learns only about inter-connected components. The social systems model presented here seeks to discover and to explain the interdependent, adaptive, growing nature of the social organism. The model is predicated on the notion that all of us—Black Panthers, Gray Panthers, Nazis, Klansmen, radical feminists, populists, Democrats, Republicans, presidents, congressmen, and the Great Silent Majority—are part of the same socio-political-rhetorical system. A full understanding of who we are, why we are as we are, and how we got this way requires that we take a holistic, developmental perspective.

Endnotes

[1] Unless otherwise noted, all references to the axioms of systems theory are taken from B. Aubrey Fisher, *Perspectives on Human Communication* (New York: Macmillan, 1978), 196-204.

[2] Fisher, 197-198.

[3] Samuel Gompers, *Seventy Years of Life and Labor*, vol. I (New York: Augustus M. Kelly, 1967), 69-70.

[4] Ludwig von Bertalanffy, *General Systems Theory: Foundations, Development, Applications* (New York: George Braziller, 1968), 40 cited by Fisher 201.

[5] Fisher, 201.

[6] Norbert Wiener, *The Human Use of Human Beings: Cybernetics and Society* (Boston: Houghton Mifflin, 1954); and Claude Shannon and Warren Weaver, *The Mathematical Theory of Communication* (Urbana, IL: University of Illinois Press, 1949).

[7] Dennis R. Smith, "The Fallacy of the Communication Breakdown," *Quarterly Journal of Speech*, 56 (December, 1970), 343-346.

[8] Brent D. Ruben, "Communication and Conflict: A Systems-Theoretic Perspective," *Quarterly Journal of Speech*, 64 (April, 1978), 205.

[9] Bitzer argues that rhetorical acts are responses to the situation, while Vatz argues that the persuader defines that situation through language. See Lloyd Bitzer, "The Rhetorical Situation," *Philosophy and Rhetoric*, 1 (Winter, 1968), 1-14; and Richard E. Vatz, "The Myth of the Rhetorical Situation," *Philosophy and Rhetoric*, 6 (Summer, 1973), 154-161.

[10] Saul D. Alinsky, *Rules for Radicals: A Practical Primer for Realistic Radicals* (New York: Vintage, 1971), 6-7.

[11] Alinsky, 21-32.

[12] Herbert W. Simons, "Persuasion in Social Conflicts: A Critique of Prevailing Conceptions and a Framework for Future Research," *Speech Monographs*, 39 (November, 1972), 239. Simons did this, first, by implying that "social conflict" is between a government or establishment and a movement, thereby ignoring the influence of competing movements and their arguments (see Chapter 2). Second, Simons assumed an adversarial relationship as a condition of social conflict, thus shedding no additional light on the conditions contributing to the creation or development of that adversarial relationship. And third, he suggested that the system's ability to "deliver the goods" can be improved through conflict, thereby introducing an organic wolf in the mechanistic sheep's clothing and obscuring the inability of mechanical systems to account for improvement through conflict.

[13] See for example B. Aubrey Fisher, "Decision Emergence: Phases in Group Decision-Making," *Communication Monographs*, 37 (March, 1970), 53-66; and Fisher and Leonard Hawes, "An Interact System Model: Generating a Grounded Theory of Small Groups," *Quarterly Journal of Speech*, 57 (December, 1971), 444-453.

[14] For an example of social systems criticism see Craig Allen Smith, "An Organic Systems Analysis of John Birch Society Discourse, 1958-1966," *Southern Speech Communication Journal*, 50 (Winter, 1984), 155-176.

[15] Bernard K. Duffy and Halford Ryan Ross, (eds.) *American Orators of the Twentieth Century* (Westport, CT: Greenwood, 1987).

[16] J. Michael Hogan, "Wallace and the Wallaceites: A Reexamination," *Southern Speech Communication Journal*, 50 (Fall, 1984), 24-48.

[17] Birchers responding to the survey were younger, better educated, and better off financially than the American norm of that period. Most were white-collar Republicans whose education was disproportionately in the natural sciences and engineering, who became politically aware during or after World War II, and lived in states with rapidly fluctuating populations. Fred W. Grupp, Jr., "The Political Perspectives of John Birch Society Members," *The American Right Wing*, Robert A. Schoenberger, ed., (Atlantic: Holt, Rinehart, and Winston, 1969), 83-118.

[18] Michael C. McGee, "In Search of 'The People': A Rhetorical Alternative," *Quarterly Journal of Speech*, 61 (October, 1975), 235-249; and Aaron D. Gresson, III, "Phenomenology and the Rhetoric of Identification—A Neglected Dimension of Communication Inquiry," *Communication Quarterly*, 26 (Fall, 1978), 14-23.

[19] John Wilson, *Introduction to Social Movements* (New York: Basic Books, 1973), 70.

[20] Testimony of John Morrison (excerpted), Leon Litwack, ed., *The American Labor Movement* (Englewood Cliffs, NJ: Prentice-Hall, 1962), 10-12.

[21] John Waite Bowers and Donovan J. Ochs, *The Rhetoric of Agitation and Control* (Reading, MA: Addison-Wesley, 1971), 17 and 41.

Chapter 8

A Functional Approach to Social Movement Persuasion

Leland M. Griffin concluded his pioneering essay, "The Rhetoric of Historical Movements," by envisioning a time when "from the identification of a number of rhetorical patterns, we may discover the various configurations of public discussion, whether rhetorical patterns repeat themselves when like movements occur in the intervals of time, whether a consistent set of forms may be said to exist."[1] Although many studies have appeared since Griffin's essay, we have made little progress toward the goals of understanding the nature of social movement persuasion and of constructing generalizations that apply to different movements in different periods. We have been preoccupied with explicating the events, the people, and the strategies that have captured headlines and intruded upon our world.[2]

An approach that promises significant strides toward Griffin's vision is one that views persuasion as the primary *agency* through which social movements perform necessary *functions* that enable them to come into existence, to meet opposition, and, perhaps, to succeed in bringing about (or resisting) change. Functions are indispensable processes that contribute to the furtherance or maintenance of social movements.[3] This approach is macroscopic in application, treating persuasive efforts with broad brushstrokes, and is thus more capable than traditional microscopic approaches of contributing to our understanding of the immense persuasive canvasses produced by a bewildering array of social movements.

The notion of a *functional* approach to the study of social movement persuasion has appeared in several essays. For example, Richard B. Gregg explored the ego-function of protest rhetoric.[4] Dale G. Leathers observed that the rhetorical strategy of the John Birch Society "was highly functional for the maintenance of in-group solidarity."[5] And Michael McGee concluded his essay, "In Search of 'The People': A Rhetorical Alternative," by suggesting that the "analysis of rhetorical documents should not turn inward, to an application of persuasive, manipulative techniques, but outward to *functions* of rhetoric."[6]

Herbert W. Simons and Bruce E. Gronbeck have provided both theoretical bases for a functional approach and lists of functions that might serve as guides for the study of persuasion in social movements. In his 1970 effort to provide a "leader-centered conception of persuasion in social movements," Simons writes that social movements "must fulfill the same rhetorical requirements as more formal collectives. These imperatives constitute *rhetorical requirements* for the leadership of a movement."[7] He discusses these functions or requirements under three broad headings:

1. They must attract, maintain, and mold workers (i.e., followers) into an efficiently organized unit.
2. They must secure adoption of their product by the larger structure (i.e., the external system, the established order).
3. They must react to resistance generated by the larger structure.

In "The Rhetoric of Social-Institutional Change: Black Action at Michigan," Bruce E. Gronbeck, noted in 1973 that "Rhetorical forces function as a set of skills able to create, sustain, and terminate movements by uniting the other forces."[8] The rhetorical analyst, according to Gronbeck, should ask three questions: (1) What functions are fulfilled by rhetorical discourse? (2) With what substance are these functions fulfilled? And (3) In what form does that substance appear? Gronbeck lists six rhetorical functions and applies them to the Black Action Movement at the University of Michigan in the spring of 1970:

1. Defining: Somebody or some group takes the first step. A problem is defined and a solution is urged.
2. Legitimizing: Legitimizers can lend positive authority, a regional or national presence to a budding movement.
3. In-gathering: The movement builds a power-base, a group of adherents ready to talk, march, and fight for the cause.
4. Pressuring: The movement also mounts a campaign urging reform or revolution.
5. Compromising: After direct confrontation, usually some sort of compromise must be worked out.
6. Satisfying: Leaders must be able to return to the masses of their movement, proclaiming victory, even if only partial gains have been made.

Gronbeck's list of functions is more inclusive than Simons' three rhetorical requirements, but it appears best suited for studying specific social movement campaigns or "actions" rather than the life-cycle of a movement or a stage within this cycle.

A Functional Scheme for Studying Persuasion in Social Movements

Previous writers have tended to delineate very general functions, to omit important functions, or to disregard the importance of altering perceptions in social movement persuasion. Building upon the foundations laid by these writers, we have developed the following more inclusive scheme of interrelated general and specific functions that emphasize the importance of perceptions.

1. Transforming perceptions of history
   a. Altering perceptions of the past
   b. Altering perceptions of the present
   c. Altering perceptions of the future
2. Altering perceptions of society
   a. Altering perceptions of the opposition
   b. Altering self-perceptions
3. Prescribing courses of action
   a. Prescribing what must be done
   b. Prescribing who must accomplish the task
   c. Prescribing how the task must be accomplished
4. Mobilizing for action
   a. Organizing and uniting the discontented
   b. Pressuring the opposition
   c. Gaining sympathy and support from opinion leaders or legitimizers
5. Sustaining the social movement
   a. Justifying setbacks and delays
   b. Maintaining viability of the movement
   c. Maintaining visibility of the movement

Several caveats are in order before we present details of the model and potential research questions.[9]

First, although the functions listed in this scheme are essential to the existence and furtherance of social movements, we do not claim that these functions are unique to social movements. Social movements (as we noted in Chapter 1) differ from institutionalized collectivities, not so much in terms of the functions their persuasive efforts must perform, as in terms of the constraints placed upon their fulfillment of these functions. The uninstitutionalized nature of social movements greatly limits their powers and hence their strategic options.[10] Movements have virtually no reward, punishment, legislative, or enforcement powers. They have no assured means of financial support. And they gain access to the mass media only when they become "newsworthy," which usually requires some sort of public or confrontational action.

Second, while all social movements need to perform the functions in our scheme, their fundamental programs for change (innovative, revivalistic, or resistance), the degree of change desired (reform or revolutionary), the stage a movement is in, and the rhetorical situation may determine that some functions will assume greater prominence than others.

Third, this functional scheme is not intended to be chronological or related to a specific series of progressive stages such as the one presented in Chapter 2. No social movement is likely to perform any function once and then proceed to another task. Although some functions may dominate the persuasion of a social movement at a given time (transforming perceptions of history during the genesis stage or pressuring the opposition and gaining support of legitimizers during the enthusiastic mobilization stage), most functions demand attention on a continual basis.

Fourth, although the functional perspective encourages comparative studies and studies of entire social movements, it is applicable to the persuasive efforts of a single movement or portion of a movement. We may, for example, focus on one or more *general functions* such as transforming perceptions of history or prescribing courses of action. Or we may choose to focus on a *specific function* such as altering perceptions of the opposition or uniting the discontented. Or we may focus on a *specific means* of performing functions such as the use of devil appeals or conspiracy appeals to transform perceptions of the opposition.

And fifth, we may use any persuasion theory, critical approach, or research method that promises to produce insights into how persuasion *functions* for social movements. The task of the analyst, however, is not a mere cataloguing of techniques used to perform various functions.

Transforming Perceptions of History

Target audiences, especially when a social movement is in its infancy, may be unaware of the problem or refuse to believe that it exists, may believe that the problem is not severe or does not require drastic action, may believe that the problem does not affect them, or may believe that the problem should be and will be handled by appropriate institutions through normal procedures. A variety of institutions (schools, governments, courts, labor unions, social and professional groups, religious organizations, political parties, and the mass media) foster and reinforce these perceptions. For example, when the anti-slavery movement emerged in the 1830s and 1840s, American institutions did not see slavery as a degradation of the slave but as the slave's birth and salvation as a civilized, Christianized human being. Slavery was characterized as God's wonderful and mysterious way to save the black savage. When the women's liberation movement emerged during the 1960s, institutions maintained the status of women as housewives and mothers who raised children and supported husbands in their careers. A woman was not to compete in a man's world (not the place for ladies and girls), and a man was not to compete in the woman's world (not the place for a real man). Thus, a major persuasive function of social movements is to alter ways audiences perceive history—the past, the present, and the future—to convince them that an intolerable situation exists and that it warrants urgent action by "the people."[11]

The Past

We know that social movements use a variety of persuasive techniques to transform perceptions of history. Social movements attempt to alter perceptions of the past, for example, by presenting positive or negative versions of events, situations, heroes, villains, and effects by comparing and contrasting the past with the present, by correcting historical accounts, and by producing revelations about the past. The American Nazi Party, for instance, has produced "facts" to prove that the "alleged" Nazi holocaust in Europe was a clever creation of Jews (through untruths, fantastic exaggerations, twisted words, confessions extracted under torture, falsified evidence, a best-seller hoax, and fake photographs) to spread the world communist conspiracy.[12] The Reverend Billy James Hargis, founder and leader of the Christian Crusade against communism, often made startling revelations in his radio addresses about President Roosevelt's deals with Joseph Stalin and how the United Nations was a creation of and for communist Russia.[13]

The Present

Social movements often attempt to alter perceptions of the present by redefining actions, events, and situations through *renaming* them. For example, the Black Power Movement of the 1960s referred to ghettos as colonies and America as the "white mother country" to transform "blacks from a national minority to an international majority," to align the "movement with newly emerging African nations," and to validate "expectations and desires as universal ones."[14] The anti-Vietnam War movement referred to the alleged war of aggression by North Vietnam and China as a civil war or revolution, and thus one in which the United States should not be involved. Gary Woodward writes that "We commit ourselves to different realities through the act of naming because words are devices for telling others *how they should see the world*."[15] Social movements often enhance efforts to "rename" situations, events, and actions by providing graphic, and sometimes gruesome, portrayals through imagery and pictures. The pro-life movement, for example, is famous for its color photographs of aborted fetuses that reveal tiny arms, heads, bodies, and feet, and most recently for its video entitled "The Silent Scream" that purportedly shows a fetus undergoing the agony of abortion.[16]

The Future

Social movements try to transform perceptions of the future by showing it as bright and full of hope or dark and full of despair. The rhetoric of hope relies upon two appeals. Utopian appeals present a perfect space, often a promised land, while millennium appeals present a perfect time, an era when peace, love, and happiness will abound. Eugene V. Debs, a socialist leader and five-time presidential candidate during the first quarter of this century, often spoke of a future in which all workers would have healthy and happy families, nice homes, and free time to enjoy parks and music.[17] On the other hand, a rhetoric of dread or despair warns that the current state of affairs can only get worse unless "the people" act immediately. The "domino theory" (in which one right, power, possession, or place falls after another) abounds, and "apocalyptic" rhetoric predicts ultimate destiny and imminent doom. For example, Robert Welch, founder of the John Birch Society, warned in his speech that launched the Society on December 9, 1958 that:

> Unless we can reverse the forces which now seem inexorable in their movement, you have only a few more years before the country in which you live will become four separate provinces in a worldwide Communist dominion. . . . We are living, in American today, in such a fool's paradise as the people of China lived in twenty years ago, as the people of Czechoslovakia lived in a dozen years ago, as the people of North Vietnam lived in five years ago, and as the people of Iraq lived in only yesterday.[18]

Although we are aware of some of the major persuasive techniques social movements use in efforts to transform perceptions of history, we know relatively little about how and when these techniques are used, how they change over time, or how different types of social movements attempt to transform history. For example, we have hypothesized in previous chapters that a movement's type may determine how it views history. A revivalistic movement may view the past as a paradise lost worth resurrecting at any cost and may portray the future return to an idealized past as a perfect point in time or a perfect place.[19] A resistance movement may contend that society has progressed to a high state and see efforts by social movements and the established order as threatening to return society to a primitive past or to transport it into a future devoid of all that is sacred.[20] An innovative movement may portray the present as the result of or a continuation of an intolerable past and argue that the future will be bright only if the movement is successful[21]

We do not know if these hypotheses hold true for every movement of a specific type or how the lifecycle or traumatic events may affect the amount and nature of persuasion aimed at the past, the present, or the future. For instance, at what point do resistance movements, such as the American Nazi organizations, feel they must correct established versions of the past? And how, for instance, do the clearing of Hitler's name and denials of the "holocaust" help such movements to resist change? Some movements attempt to make dramatic revelations about the past. What functions do such revelations serve; when are they most likely to enter into a movement's persuasion; and which movements are prone to using them? How do social movements revise their versions of history as they age, confront opposition, meet with successes and failures, produce their own heroes, martyrs, and clowns, and adapt to changing situations?[22] For example, do they select different "names" for situations or conditions, rely more or less on graphic portrayals of conditions or events, or devote more of their persuasive efforts to shocking people into

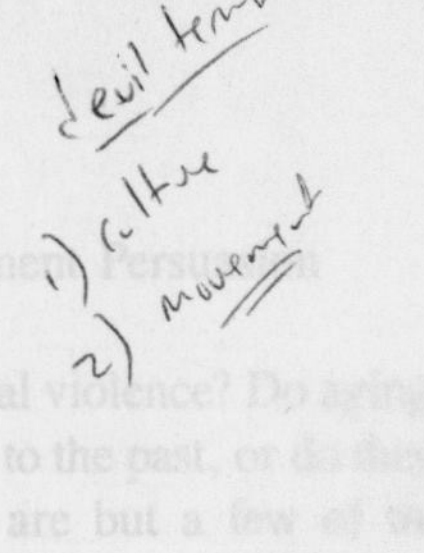

consciousness through verbal and nonverbal violence? Do aging social movements like aging soldiers pay increasing attention to the past, or do they look more toward a future paradise, like prophets? These are but a few of the questions about transforming perceptions of history that we need to answer before we can understand persuasion and social movements.

Transforming Perceptions of Society

Social movements must transform audiences' perceptions of the *opposition* and *self* and, in doing so, create a clear we-they distinction. The opposition includes all individuals and groups who do not openly support the movement and thus are responsible for allowing intolerable conditions to exist or develop. "They" often include established institutions, counter movements, the "silent majority," the mass media, other social movements, factions within the movement, and those for whom the movement is fighting who have not joined in the struggle. Social movements hold firmly to the adage, "If you are not with us, you are against us." The "we" or self include all the righteous, moral, self-sacrificing individuals and groups who are willing to stand up and say "**No!**" to an evil condition, force, or trend. The persuasive task is to gain legitimacy for the movement while stripping the opposition of its legitimacy.

The Opposition

Every social movement identifies one or more devils and then heaps abuse upon them in the form of name-calling, ridicule, negative associations, and metaphors. Special invective is heaped upon individuals who refuse to support the movement that is fighting for them. For nearly two centuries, the labor movement has called nonunion workers (especially strike-breakers) scabs. The black rights movement used the epithets Uncle Tom and oreo (black on the outside and white on the inside). The native American movement copied the black rights movement with the disparaging epithets Uncle Tomahawk and apple (red on the outside and white on the inside). A common strategy, particularly during the enthusiastic mobilization stage, is to provoke the opposition into violent reactions, suppression, or arrests to reveal its true ugliness.[23] Devils may be *mysterious*, *somewhat nebulous forces* (the rich, capitalists, men, secular humanists), *individuals* (Henry Ford during the labor struggles of the 1920s and 1930s, President Johnson during the Vietnam War, and Ralph Nader for the right wing and anti-consumerism movements), or *things* (demon rum, nuclear power plants, or cruise missiles).

Some social movements perceive their devils to be organized plots between two or more evil forces to commit "crimes" against the people. Movements detect ruthless, devious, perverse, ever-scheming, and highly clever *conspiracies* as the causes of all sorts of social, economic, political, and moral problems.[24] Examples are numerous. The populists at the turn of the century blamed international bankers, the political-religious right since World War II targeted communists, H. Rapp Brown and the black power movement resisted white, genocidal conspiracy, and the evangelical Protestant movement combats secular humanism. Portrayals of the opposition may range from powerful, demonic, conspiratorial forces to pathetic, disorganized, impotent obstructions within the persuasion of a movement at a given point in time.

Although conspiracy and devil appeals appear to be prominent in the persuasive efforts of many movements, we know little about them and how they are related. Are these appeals, particularly conspiracy appeals, more common and vitriolic in specific types of social movements? How do they change as movements encounter varying situations and proceed through their life-cycles? Do some social movements come into existence because a group of people perceives a dangerous conspiracy while others come to see conspiracies only after they are confronted by opposing forces or are unsuccessful in capturing the support of legitimizers and "the people"? Are conspiracy appeals more or less common in twentieth century movements compared to eighteenth and nineteenth century movements? How are devil and conspiracy appeals similar and different? Do they serve somewhat different persuasive functions for social movements?

The Self

Social movements must attempt to alter self-perceptions of supporters and potential supporters so they will believe in their self-worth and their ability to bring about urgent change. The "oppressed" are portrayed as innocent victims of circumstances and forces beyond their control. As Richard Gregg writes, "If one feels oppressed, he implies that there is an oppressor—someone responsible for the oppression."[25] Thus, the labor movement has referred to workers as "wage slaves," and the women's liberation movement has referred to women as "slaves of the slaves." Some social movements compare the plight of the oppressed to the most disadvantaged social group. For example, persuasive efforts during the 1960s, 1970s, and 1980s have portrayed students, women, Catholics in Northern Ireland, and French-speaking Canadians as "niggers."[26]

Oppressed people need not remain so, according to social movement persuasion. Persuaders emphasize a heritage to be proud of, important contributions to society in the past and the present, morality, generosity with others rather than self-seeking aggrandizement, power and bravery. Efforts to replace old labels attached to groups by oppressors with newly emphasized traits help to instill feelings of pride and power. Audiences are then free to discover themselves as substantial human beings and to question social relationships and coalitions. When, for instance, black Americans began to object to the label "negro" and to refer to themselves as Afro-Americans, they redefined themselves and began to take symbolic control of their lives and fate. As Karlyn Campbell writes, blacks chose the term "black" to replace "negro" because it was their word, not one chosen by whites; it traced them to descendants of abused field hands, not "house negroes;" it scared whites; it became a badge of pride and strength; it reminded them of their African heritage; and it allowed them to confront whites as equals.[27] Wayne Brockriede and Robert Scott argue that "black power" was not merely a new, catchy slogan for the black rights movement but was, as Stokely Carmichael stated, a "black declaration of independence. It is a turn inward, a rallying cry for a people in the sudden labor of self-discovery, self-naming, and self-legitimation."[28] Social movements often hope that self-discovery may result in a new "personal identity" and in the realization of "a people."[28] Self-discovery is an important means of creating "we-they" distinctions and a basis of group identification through a sense of shared fate.[30] "We," the "people," may come to represent all that is good while "they," the "oppressors," represent all that is evil.

We know that the women's liberation movement has used consciousness-raising groups to enhance self-concept and to heighten each member's awareness of her oppressed state and potential for being more than someone's mother or wife.[31] We do not know if such efforts are unique to the women's liberation movement or are common to social movements that strive for the rights of such groups as blacks, native Americans, and Chicanos. Do movements devote more attention to self-perception during the early stages (genesis and social unrest) than in later stages (enthusiastic mobilization and maintenance) of their life-cycles? How does degree of change desired (reform to revolutionary) affect consciousness-raising? Do confrontations with institutions and resistance groups seem to increase persuasive efforts aimed at maintaining and reinforcing a favorable self-concept? How are these efforts similar to and different from efforts prior to confrontations?

Prescribing Courses of Action

Prescribing courses of action constitutes the ideology of the social movement, what John Wilson defines as "a set of beliefs about the social world and how it operates, containing statements about the rightness of certain social arrangements and what action would be taken in the light of those statements."[32] As a set of beliefs, the ideology addresses what must be done, who must do it, and how it should be done.

The What

Social movements must explain *what* should be done.[33] This function comprises the social movement's list of demands and solutions that will alleviate a condition, prevent undesired changes, or bring on the utopia or millennium.[34] Each movement must explain, defend, and sell its program for change. Problems develop when a number of organizations within a movement prescribe different and perhaps conflicting demands and solutions. Changing social situations, efforts by established orders to negate or to co-opt a movement's demands and solutions, and the necessity to address a variety of target audiences also will require alterations in explanations and content of demands and solutions. As John Wilson notes, "When new sensitivities are created by social events and collectives, ideologies, to be accepted, must cater to these new sensitivities."[35] Efforts to adapt to new sensitivities, however, always expose social movement leaders and groups to charges of revisionism by movement purists. And, as Hans Toch observes, illusions are often offered as solutions to *solve* problems by predicting a rapid transition to a better world. The person, "faced with an intolerable situation, searches for and finds a miracle."[36]

The Who

Social movements must prescribe *who* ought to do the job. For one thing, in order to establish legitimacy, each social movement must convince audiences that only an uninstitutionalized collectivity is willing and able to bring about or to resist change. For another, social movement persuasion must espouse specific types of organization and leadership or specific organizations and leaders best suited to solving urgent problems. Some social movements establish membership limitations to create elites capable of dealing with "unsolvable" conditions and the omnipotent forces that have produced them. "We-they" distinctions may be as prevalent within a social movement as they are between the social movement and its opposition. One movement faction may declare open warfare against another faction it deems ideologically deviant or inferior in membership. Samuel Gompers did not conceal his pleasure over the demise of the Knights of Labor, a union of unskilled workers, that he considered to be an "unnatural" form of labor organization.[37] He viewed his own American Federation of Labor, an organization of skilled tradesmen, to be the natural form of labor organization and the only form that should exist.

The How

Social movements must propose and defend *how* the job is to be done, that is, which strategies, tactics, and communication channels are most appropriate and potentially most effective.[38] A revolutionary resistance movement may have a wide range of tactical choices but a narrow range of channels. A reform movement may have access to many channels but be limited to moderate, socially acceptable tactics. No movement can rely upon the same means of change for long. Followers of the movement and the mass media become bored with them, and established orders learn how to deal with strategies and tactics rather quickly. A social movement may splinter into factions over differing views on how the job must be done, and some movement members may be more committed to means than to ends. Tactics such as strikes and boycotts often affect "innocent people" and may provoke "backlashes" that are fostered by established orders and resistance movements.[39] Thus, social movements must defend their actions and changes in actions to both members and non-members.

Much has been written about the nature of ideology, but little has been written about how social movement persuaders try to sell its ingredients (what, who, and how) or alterations of its ingredients to friend, neutral observer, and foe. We need answers to questions such as the following: How do social movement ideologies define or obscure, stabilize or upset, strengthen or weaken, relieve or exacerbate situations? How do ideologies rationalize group interests, beliefs, and methods? How do ideologies enhance consciousness-raising efforts? How can ideologies combat routinization and creeping bureaucratization of social movements? And how are ideologies stated, developed, and adjusted to attract new members, to sustain members, to bring about coalitions, to appease opposition inside and outside of the movement, to meet the demands of each new stage in the movement's life cycle, to communicate with various publics, to suit a variety of leaders within the movement, and to meet changing situations?

Mobilizing for Action

It is not enough for a social movement to present its views on history, society, and courses of action. Leaders must persuade persons to join in the cause, to organize into effective groups, and to unify through coalitions to carry the message to target audiences and to confront institutions and resistance forces.

Organizing and Uniting the Discontented

Social movements expend great amounts of persuasive efforts (through mailings, leaflets, interpersonal contacts, and speeches) to educate audiences about the "cause" and why it is urgent to bring about or to resist change. Audiences are urged not to sit by and let disaster strike but to "stand up and be counted." Fund raising is an integral part of most persuasive efforts because social movements have few other means to finance full-time leaders, organizational headquarters, publications, demonstrations, lobbies in congress and state legislatures, challenges in the courts, and mailings. But the emphasis is not only on joining and contributing but on organizing and uniting, for social movements contend that only *collective* action can successfully bring about or resist change.

Pressuring the Opposition

Although all social movements are to a greater or lesser degree self-change oriented and believe that followers must purify themselves before they can change others, all movements engage the opposition in symbolic combat. The weapons may be verbal such as ridicule, obscenity, and threats or nonverbal such as demonstrations, sit-ins, walk-outs, boycotts, strikes, and disruptions. The aim may be to gain control of agencies of influence by voting officials in or out of office, purchasing or creating mass media, or gaining control of corporations through stock proxies.[40] Or the aim may be to pressure the opposition to gain recognition, concessions, compromises, or capitulations.

Gaining Sympathy and Support of Legitimizers

Social movement "membership" has a range of commitment and support for the movement and its cause. John Wilson, for example, illustrates this commitment as an onion ring.[41] At the nucleus are full-time, paid professionals (never a very large group); the first ring around this nucleus consists of full-time, non-paid professionals; the second ring consists of the rank and file where total commitment is rare; and the third ring consists of sympathizers who are neither fully inside nor fully outside the movement (always the largest of the four groups). For a social movement to achieve a degree of success, the leaders in the nucleus must gain the attention, sympathy, and support not only of active members (the first and second rings) but of "sympathizers" who make the movement large in scope and are often opinion leaders (politicians, judges, business executives, sports figures, entertainers) who can help to legitimize the movement in the eyes of the public. Movements often attempt to provoke institutions into excessive or repressive acts that reveal the ugliness of the established order and gain sympathy for the "victims" and their demands.

Social movements would seem wise to confine their persuasive efforts to symbols and symbolic acts that are either lawful or are protected by the Constitution. As Donovan Ochs and John Bowers write, violent acts that are devoid of symbolism—or appear to be so—are likely to cost the movement the support of sympathizers and legitimizers and invite outright suppression under the rubrics of law and order, public safety, and national security.[42] Thus, violent acts by the movement (or persons associated with it in the public's or institution's eyes) may negate all that has been gained through the mobilization process.

Whatever their goals, movements need years of untiring efforts by large numbers of people to gain or to prevent change. They must convince followers that victory is near, or at least inevitable, if all is done correctly, if followers remain steadfast in their commitment, and if unity is maintained. Movements must create and maintain within the membership what Eric Hoffer refers to as an "extravagant hope."[43] We know little about how social movements mobilize for action or use persuasion to meet obstacles to effective mobilization.

The social movement's ability to mobilize it forces to action is hindered, for example, by its relationship to established institutions. A movement may be partially equal to (equal on some grounds and not on others), dependent upon (for communication channels, legitimacy, legal protection), or subjugated (completely dominated and controlled) by the establishment. We do not know how social movements adapt persuasive efforts to each of these relationships. Mobilization is also hindered by limited access to communication channels. Movements must attract and employ the mass media, but they have little or no control over what the media report or how the media report confrontations, speeches, and symbolic acts. We need to study how social movements employ the media and how the media report social movements. Most movements produce their own newspapers and magazines, but we know little about how these self-produced publications are designed to mobilize their respective movements or to fulfill other persuasive functions. Mobilization is also hindered by the movement's lack of control over the activities of members and splinter groups. Each movement attempts to instill strong convictions in goals, to establish we-they distinctions, and to preach or to imply that its ends justify any means. Inevitably these convictions, distinctions, and ends lead (1) to impatience with "moderate" leadership, strategies, and slow progress toward goals and (2) to "radical" strategies and actions. How do movement leaders use persuasion to maintain order and discipline and to respond to actions that embarrass the movement and threaten its support among "the people" and legitimizers?

Sustaining the Movement

Since social movements usually last for years and experience changing social circumstances, they must perform functions that sustain them.

Justifying Setbacks and Delays

Social movements may have to explain and justify apparent setbacks, why they appear to be making few meaningful gains, why agreements with established orders have not been implemented or have been ineffective, and why they have not reached a goal by a target date. The variety of audiences social movements address may perceive progress, victories, agreements, and priority of goals differently. Internal and external opponents capitalize on delays and setbacks to proclaim superiority over a movement or its organizations.

Maintaining Viability of the Movement

Social movements must wage a continual battle to remain viable. More rhetorical energy may be expended on fund raising, membership drives, acquisition of materials and property, and maintenance of movement communication media than on selling ideologies to target audiences and pressuring the opposition. Reinforcing commitment of members and satisfying membership gratifications limit a movement's ability to perform other functions. Ironically, a movement may become too successful or too successful too soon. Growth in membership and geographical sphere of influence and creeping institutionalization may seriously reduce the informality of structure and the feeling of urgency that attracted people to the movement.[44] Thus, a serious decline in membership and commitment may occur when success seems near. To counteract declines in membership and commitment, some movements turn to memories to keep the movement alive, while others create new heroes to breathe life into the aging movement. Leaflets, mailings, speeches, and songs may contain personal statements of commitment, often commitment like the persuader's parents had to the movement. Audiences are assured that victory is near or inevitable if strength and unity are maintained.

Maintaining Visibility of the Movement

Social movements must remain visible. "Out of sight, out of mind" is an appropriate adage. Social movements, the media, and target audiences have insatiable appetites for persuasive happenings, but few social movements have adequate leadership, membership, energy, and funds to satisfy these appetites over long periods while fending off counter efforts by opponents. Old events that drag on receive less and less attention and produce serious drains on a movement's resources. Social movements often resort to rhetorical events such as ceremonies, annual meetings, and anniversary celebrations to remain visible to members and nonmembers. They may alter old symbols or select new ones. The movement may create one or more official newspapers in order to communicate directly with members because the commercial press seems to ignore the movement or treat it "unfairly."

We have devoted little attention to persuasive efforts designed to explain setbacks and delays or to maintain viability and visibility. How, for instance, do movements sustain the zeal created during the early stage of its life cycle? How do they deal with over-confidence and inflated expectations? How do movements maintain commitment to the cause and recruit new members after the excitement of the enthusiastic mobilization stage subsides? How do they use the movement's martyrs and heroes, victories and tragedies, saints and devils to sustain the movement? How are persuasive efforts during ceremonies, conventions, and celebrations similar to and different from persuasive efforts in the streets or before mixed or hostile audiences? The majority of our studies have focused on external persuasive interactions such as the second, but we need to pay more attention to internal interactions such as the first.

Conclusion

A functional approach appears to be a good vehicle by which we may approach Leland Griffin's vision of discovering "rhetorical patterns" or a "consistent set of forms" in the persuasion of social movements. The journey will be neither simple nor quick, and, undoubtedly, the functional scheme presented in this chapter will undergo refinement as our knowledge and experience grow. As functional studies accumulate, we should be able to piece together the persuasion puzzle of social movements and to formulate answers to the many questions posed in this chapter.

Chapters 13, 14, and 15 apply this functional scheme to songs, slogans, and obscenity used in social movements. The functional approach produces insights into how movements use these persuasive channels to further their goals and to counter resistance movements and established orders.

Endnotes

Significant portions of this chapter are reprinted with permission from Charles J. Stewart, "A Functional Approach to the Rhetoric of Social Movements," *Central States Speech Journal*, 31 (Winter, 1980), 298-305.

[1] Leland M. Griffin, "The Rhetoric of Historical Movements," *Quarterly Journal of Speech*, 38 (April, 1952), 188.

[2] See for example, "James R. Andrews, "Confrontation at Columbia: A Case Study of Coercive Rhetoric," *Quarterly Journal of Speech*, 55 (February, 1969), 9-16; Donald H. Smith, "Martin Luther King, Jr.: In the Beginning at Montgomery," *Southern Speech Journal*, 34 (Fall, 1968), 8-17; Wayne E. Brockriede and Robert L. Scott, "Stokely Carmichael: Two Speeches on Black Power," *Central States Speech Journal*, 19 (Spring, 1968), 3-13.

[3] This definition was developed from a discussion of the meaning of the term "function" in Robert K. Merton, *Social Theory and Social Structure*, 2nd ed. (Glencoe, IL: Free Press, 1957), 19-25.

[4] Richard B. Gregg, "The Ego-Function of the Rhetoric of Protest," *Philosophy and Rhetoric*, 4 (Spring, 1971), 71-91.

[5] Dale G. Leathers, "The Rhetorical Strategy of the New Right Movement," unpublished paper presented at the annual convention of the Speech Communication Association, 1972.

[6] Michael C. McGee, "In Search of the 'People': A Rhetorical Alternative," *Quarterly Journal of Speech*, 61 (October, 1975), 248.

[7] Herbert W. Simons, "Requirements, Problems, and Strategies: A Theory of Persuasion for Social Movements," *Quarterly Journal of Speech*, 56 (February, 1970), 1-11; Herbert W. Simons, Elizabeth W. Mechling, and Howard N. Scheier, "The Functions of Human Communication in Mobilizing for Action from the Bottom Up: The Rhetoric of Social Movements," *Handbook of Rhetorical and Communication Theory*, Carroll C. Arnold and John W. Bowers, eds., (Boston: Allyn and Bacon, 1984), 807-808.

[8] Bruce E. Gronbeck, "The Rhetoric of Social-Institutional Change: Black Action at Michigan," *Explorations in Rhetorical Criticism*, Gerald Mohrmann, Charles Stewart, Donovan Ochs, eds. (University Park, PA: Pennsylvania State University Press, 1973), 96-113.

[9] See also Charles J. Stewart, "A Functional Perspective on the Study of Social Movements, *Central States Speech Journal*, 34 (Spring, 1983), 77-80.

[10] Michael Lipsky, "Protest as a Political Resource," *The American Political Science Review*, 52 (1968), 1144-1148; and James Q. Wilson, "The Strategy of Protest: Problems of Negro Civic Action," *Journal of Conflict Resolution*, 3 (1961), 291-303.

[11] See Ernest G. Bormann, "Fantasy and Rhetorical Vision: The Rhetorical Criticism of Social Reality," *Quarterly Journal of Speech*, 58 (December, 1972), 396-407; and Richard B. Gregg, "A Phenomenologically Oriented Approach to Rhetorical Criticism," *Central States Speech Journal*, 17 (May, 1966), 83-90.

[12] *Historical Fact No. 1. Did Six Million Really Die? The Truth At Last* (Chapel Ascote, Ladbroke, Southam, Warks: Historical Review Press, n.d.).

[13] From tapes of radio addresses by Billy James Hargis on March 11 and 12, 1963 and others that are undated.

[14] Karlyn Kohrs Campbell, "The Rhetoric of Radical Black Nationalism: A Case Study in Self-Conscious Criticism," *Central States Speech Journal*, 22 (Fall, 1971), 157.

[15] Gary C. Woodward, "Mystifications in the Rhetoric of Cultural Dominance and Colonial Control," *Central States Speech Journal*, 26 (Winter, 1975), 301.

[16] See for example *Aborted Baby Discarded in Hospital Bucket* (n.p., n.d.); *Life or Death* (Cincinnati: Hayes Publishing Company, n.d.); *The U.S. Supreme Court Has Ruled It's Legal to Kill a Baby* . . . (Cincinnati: Hayes Publishing Company, n.d.).

[17] Eugene V. Debs, "The Issue, delivered in Girard, Kansas, May 23, 1908, in *Debs: His Life, Writings and Speeches* (Chicago: Charles H. Kerr, 1908), 489.

[18] Robert Welch, *The Blue Book of the John Birch Society* (Boston: Western Islands Publishers, 1961), 1.

[19] See E.J. Hobsbaum, *Primitive Rebels*, 2nd ed. (New York: Praeger, 1963); Melvin J. Lasky, *Utopia and Revolution* (Chicago: University of Chicago Press, 1976).

[20] See Martha Solomon, "The Rhetoric of STOP ERA: Fatalistic Reaffirmation," *Southern Speech Communication Journal*, 44 (Fall, 1978), 42-59; and Philip C. Wander, "The John Birch and Martin Luther King Symbols in the Radical Right," *Western Speech*, 35 (Winter, 1971), 4-14.

[21] Karlyn Kohrs Campbell, "The Rhetoric of Women's Liberation: An Oxymoron," *Quarterly Journal of Speech*, 59 (February, 1973), 74-86.

[22] Parke G. Burgess, "The Rhetoric of Black Power: A Moral Demand?" *Quarterly Journal of Speech*, 54 (April, 1968), 122-133; and Robert L. Heath, "Dialectical Confrontation: A Strategy of Black Radicalism," *Central States Speech Journal*, 24 (Fall, 1973), 168-177.

[23] Robert L. Scott and Donald K. Smith, "The Rhetoric of Confrontation," *Quarterly Journal of Speech*, 55 (February, 1969), 7-8.

[24] G. Thomas Goodnight and John Poulakos, "Conspiracy Rhetoric: From Pragmatism to Fantasy in Public Discourse," *Western Journal of Speech Communication*, 45 (Fall, 1981), 299-316.

[25] Gregg (1971), 79.

[26] Jerry Farber, *The Student as Nigger* (North Hollywood: Contact Books, 1969).

[27] Campbell (1971), 156.

[28] Brockriede and Scott, 6.

[29] McGee, 235-249; Campbell, 74-86; Brockriede and Scott, 3-13.

[30] Aaron Gresson, III, "Phenomenology and the Rhetoric of Identification—A Neglected Dimension of Coalition Communication Inquiry," *Communication Quarterly*, 26 (Fall, 1978), 14-23.

[31] Campbell (1973), 74-86; and James W. Chesebro, John F. Cragan, and Patricia McCullough, "The Small Group Technique of the Radical Revolutionary: A Synthetic Study of Consciousness Raising," *Speech Monographs*, 40 (June, 1973), 136-146.

[32] John Wilson, *Introduction to Social Movements* (New York: Basic Books, 1973), 91.

[33] John Wilson, 89-134.

[34] Barbara A. Larson, "Samuel E. Davies and the Rhetoric of the New Light," *Speech Monographs*, 38 (August, 1971), 207-216; and Richard J. Ilkka, "Rhetorical Dramatization in the Development of American Communism," *Quarterly Journal of Speech*, 63 (December, 1977), 413-417.

[35] Wilson, 91-97.

36 Hans Toch, *The Social Psychology of Social Movements* (Indianapolis: Bobbs-Merrill, 1965), 30.

37 Samuel Gompers, "Address to the Machinists Convention," *American Federationist*, 8 (1901), 251.

38 Leland M. Griffin, "The Rhetorical Structure of the 'New Left' Movement: Part I," *Quarterly Journal of Speech*, 50 (April, 1964), 114-127; and Malcolm O. Sillars, "The Rhetoric of Petition in Boots," *Speech Monographs*, 39 (June, 1972), 92-104.

39 Charles J. Stewart, "Labor Agitation in America: 1865-1915,: *America in Controversy: History of American Public Address*, DeWitte Holland, ed., (Dubuque, IA: W.C. Brown, 1973), 159-167.

40 Saul D. Alinsky, *Rules for Radicals: A Pragmatic Primer for Realistic Radicals* (New York: Vintage Books, 1972), 165-183.

41 Wilson, 306.

42 John W. Bowers and Donovan J. Ochs, *The Rhetoric of Agitation and Control* (Reading, MA: Addison-Wesley, 1971), 34.

43 Eric Hoffer, *The True Believer* (New York: Harper and Row, 1951), 18.

44 Mayer N. Zald and Roberta Ash, "Social Movement Organizations: Growth, Decay, and Change," *Social Forces*, 44 (1966), 327-341.

Chapter 9

A Burkean Approach to Social Movement Persuasion

The study of social movements is an interdisciplinary endeavor. It requires familiarity with theories and concepts from the disciplines of sociology, psychology, history, and communication. A social movement, as we have noted in previous chapters, is a complex, dynamic, evolving, and synergistic entity with communication as its life blood. Human communication, in all of its forms, gives life to ideas and, consequently, to behavior. How we communicate determines how we relate to each other as social beings. This notion is true whether we are discussing our one-to-one relationships or our relationships within the larger society.

It is difficult, therefore, to find a comprehensive theory of human communication that accounts for the various forms and levels of human interaction. The writings of Kenneth Burke, however, provide a synthesis of the views of symbolic action. He offers a philosophy of human communication, a theory of social behavior, and a method for analyzing symbolic acts so that we can recognize the important relationship between symbolic acts and the environment in which they occur. As a theorist, Kenneth Burke demonstrates how motives and behavior arise and exist in communication. As a methodologist, he provides tools for analyzing the effects of symbols on human motivation. In this chapter we will discuss Kenneth Burke's philosophy of human communication, his theory of dramatism, his methodological considerations, and the implications of his notions for the study of persuasion and social movements.

Kenneth Burke's Philosophy of Human Communication

Burke's philosophy of human communication provides the basis for a general conception of human beings and human relations. Burke defines the human being as the "symbol-making," "symbol-using," and "symbol-misusing" animal.[1] It is our symbol-using capacity that distinguishes us from other animals. Language, as the medium of communication, is the defining characteristic and essence of human life. We use symbols to define, accept, or reject situations.

Burke makes an important distinction between the realms of "motion" and "action." The realm of "motion" is the physical animal world that is deterministic and in which nature continues its endless process of life (i.e., "the splashing of waves against the beach"). In contrast, the realm of "action" consists of acts that occur because of the symbolic nature of "man." Burke writes that "'Action' is a term for the kind of behavior possible to a typically symbol-using animal (such as man) in contrast with the extra symbolic or nonsymbolic operations of nature."[2] It is within this realm of "action" that humans may overcome the deterministic nature of the world and may mold, shape, or create "reality" for themselves.

This distinction is important, and its value lies in understanding better how people constantly mold and shape "reality" to fit themselves within the realm of "motion." For further explanation, Burke writes:

> This distinction is generalized in dramatism as one between "sheer motion" and "action." It involves an empirical shift of circumference in the sense that although man's ability to speak depends upon the existence of speechless nature, the existence of speechless nature does not depend upon man's ability to speak.[3]

In short, "the difference between a thing and a person is that the one merely *moves whereas the other acts*."[3] As a result, there are three propositions that sum up the distinction between the realms of action and motion:[5]

1. There can be no action without motion;
2. There can be no motion without action; and
3. Action is not reducible to terms of motion.

The implications of the distinction between the realms of "action" and "motion" are twofold. First, our "reality" is a product of our "symbol-making," "symbol-using," and "symbol-misusing" behavior. "However important to us is the tiny sliver of reality each of us has experienced firsthand," Burke argues, "the whole overall 'picture' is but a construct of our symbol systems."[6] Second, our social behavior is grounded in symbolism. Symbolic forms influence conduct because motives arise in human communication. As Burke states, "If man is the symbol-using animal, some motives must derive from his animality, some from his symbolicity, and some from mixtures of the two."[7]

Leaders of social movements are continually competing with other political leaders in defining and redefining our world. The "reality" of American life for civil rights activists was one of discrimination, oppression, and social inequality. The Vietnam War was, for many Americans, an international act of aggression threatening world peace and democracy. Protestors, however, viewed the Vietnam conflict as a limited civil war—a divided country's struggle for "self-determination." Over time and after much debate and confrontation, the "realities" or definitions of the quality of life for blacks and the Vietnam War were altered for many Americans. Through language, resulting from human symbol-making capacity, human action occurs and society—or at least our perceptions—changes.

"Motive" for Burke is a key term that is not used as causal explanation of human behavior, but rather as "short hand terms for situations."[8] This term refers to action by way of communicative behavior. Almost any behavior, because of the ambiguity of language, can be rationalized or justified by appealing to a motive that is simply a linguistic label for a situation. Thus, Kenneth Burke is primarily interested in the attribution of motives to action through communicative behavior. This is important because if we can determine the motive of a speaker, writer, or singer, then we should be able to determine with an acceptable degree of accuracy the persuader's view of reality.

Burke is concerned about order in society, hence the relevance of his philosophy of human communication and action to the study of social movements. For Burke, society is a process of symbolic interaction. Social life is a product of establishing and re-establishing mutual relations with others. Because the human condition is one of imperfect communication, we solve our problems in society through "recalcitrant and mystifying" symbols.[9] Ironically, symbols cause many problems among people. "But, however remote and strange the mystery of another may become," Burke writes, "there must be some way of transcending this separateness if social order is to be achieved."[10]

Finally, it is important to appreciate Burke's view of the persuasive nature of human symbolic behavior. His orientation emphasizes subtle, psychological, and subconscious attempts at persuasion. In fact, persuasion is inherent in the nature of symbolism and language. For Burke, the use of language is a "symbolic means of inducing cooperation in beings that by nature respond to symbols."[11] Thus, "there is no chance of our keeping apart the meanings of persuasion . . . and communication (the nature of the rhetoric as 'addressed')."[12]

Kenneth Burke's Theory of Dramatism

Dramatism, created and developed by Kenneth Burke, is grounded in the symbolic nature of humans. Burke argues that as symbol-using animals, we must stress symbolism as a motive in any discussion of social behavior. By 1968, he had promoted dramatism to an equal status with "symbolic interaction" and "social exchange" as being one of three areas of "interaction" discussed in the *International Encyclopedia of the Social Sciences*.[13] In his article, Burke summarizes dramatism as:

> A method of analysis and a corresponding critique of terminology designed to show that the most direct route to the study of human relations and human motives is via a methodical inquiry into cycles or clusters of terms and their functions.[14]

He calls his method *dramatism* "since it invites one to consider the matter of motives in a perspective that, being developed from the analysis of drama, treats language and thought primarily as modes of action."[15]

Thus, action is at the heart of dramatism, for dramatism is a means for analyzing human action.[16] An "act" is a "terministic center" from which many related influences and considerations derive.[17] Daily "actions" constitute dramas with created and attached significance. Drama, for Burke, serves as an analytic model of the social world. He explains:

> Though a drama is a mode of "symbolic action" so designed that an audience might be induced to "act symbolically" in sympathy with it, insofar as the drama serves this function it may be studied as a "perfect mechanism" composed of parts moving in perfect adjustment to one another like clock-work.[18]

As already noted, the human being is a symbolic creature. Thus, distinctively human behavior and interaction are carried on through the medium of symbols and their attached meanings. We alone can create, manipulate, and use symbols to control our behavior and the behavior of others.

Nearly all human action is symbolic. Human action usually represents something more than what is immediately perceived. Symbols form the basis of our overt behavior, so human action is the by-product or the stimulus of symbols. Before we can formulate a response to any situation, we must define and interpret the situation to ensure an appropriate response to the specific situation. Without exaggerating, therefore, symbols are the foundation of social life and human civilization. We derive meanings for symbols from interactions in specific social contexts. Reality, therefore, is a social product arising from interaction or communication and is limited, specific, and circumscribed.

According to Kenneth Burke, "if action is to be our key term, then drama is the culminative form of action. But if drama, then conflict. And if conflict, then victimage. Dramatism is always on the edge of this vexing problem, that comes to a culmination in tragedy."[19] This process is readily apparent when we consider social movements. Social movements are created and sustained through action: people articulating problems, defining issues, offering solutions, identifying enemies, stating courses of action, and both recruiting and activating followers. Such actions lead to confrontation and often to conflict and, in society, conflict must be explained, justified, or rationalized. Usually there are identifiable victims and corresponding human tragedy. This evolution is true both for individual and society-wide events.

Classical rhetoric stressed the explicit design of persuasion. Humans, as rational animals, responded to arguments supported by reasons, information, and evidence. Today, we view rhetoric as more complex and subtle because we believe that our beliefs, attitudes, and values are often impacted without conscious direction by a particular agent. Elements of the drama seem to impact all of our senses.

The mass media and news industries have heightened the nature of political drama and, in many ways, have become the nervous system of our society. The media are the major sources of information about politics and the state of the polity. Americans receive political information from the media through political advertising, news stories, and feature stories; the media are now perceived as more truthful and accurate than our families and friends.

Broadcast media attract, focus, and direct attention to specific social problems (while ignoring others) quickly and efficiently while serving as channels for public persuasion and mobilization. In mobilizing groups or "kinds of public," the media help to sustain these groups and their causes and confer status and legitimacy to the groups, issues, and ideas.

The result of this transformation of the role of the media in American society, according to Dan Nimmo and James Combs, is that few people learn about politics or social issues from direct experience.[20] Nimmo and Combs argue that political realities are "mediated" through group and mass communication. A result is the "creation, transmission, and adoption of political fantasies as realistic views of what takes place."[21] Fantasy is defined as:

> A credible picture of the world that is created when one interprets mediated experiences as the way things are and takes for granted the authenticity of the mediated reality without checking against alternative, perhaps contradictory, realities so long as the fantasy offers dramatic proof for one's expectations.[22]

Thus, from Nimmo's and Combs' perspective, television news is storytelling and employs elements of the dramatic narrative, utilizing verbal and nonverbal symbols, sound, and visual imagery.

News must be entertaining and highly visual because of the demands of television. News crews trim stories to support film and visual elements, so film footage is no longer used to *illustrate* stories but to *tell* the story.[23] Footage often stands alone with little or no perspective or analysis. Peter Jennings, anchor of ABC's "World News Tonight," states that "television is afraid of being dull . . . in television, you're obligated to write to the pictures."[24] Lane Vernardos, executive producer of "The CBS News with Dan Rather," builds news stories around exciting video rather than the strongest hard news stories.[25] The news industry looks for and shares "news that wiggles," and the more in-depth the coverage, the less "wiggle" attained. Thus, the elements of action and movement are stressed over cognitive elements. Emotional responses are the ones the public remembers. Such responses help define future reactions to people and events. The important point is that for both participants and spectators, the elements of drama, social movements, and events consume the public.

Dramatism is clearly illustrated in the 1970 anti-war demonstrations at Kent State University that resulted in the killing of four students and the wounding of nine others by Ohio National Guardsmen.[26] The decade of the 1960s experienced much discussion, debate, and protest over the issues of civil rights and the Vietnam War. By 1970, student opposition to the war was strong, but the intensity of protest appeared to be declining. There was a drop in draft calls and, on April 20, 1970, President Nixon announced withdrawal of an additional 150,000 troops from Vietnam over the next twelve-month period. Ten days later, Nixon appeared to back away from his promises when he announced that American troops had invaded Cambodia to eliminate enemy strongholds and that American troops would penetrate farther in Indochina. Students felt betrayed by Nixon's announcement and viewed the Cambodia action as an escalation of what seemed to be an "endless" war.

Symbolic actions began to occur on the campus of Kent State University. On Friday night, students met at the center of campus, built a large bonfire, chanted anti-war slogans, and delivered speeches. The students soon marched downtown, broke windows, and had minor skirmishes with police. The drama had begun. The symbolic activities of speeches, slogans, obscene gestures, and stone throwing articulated the issues, grievances, hopes, desires, and frustrations of the protestors. Conflict followed. On Saturday, Mayor LeRoy Satrom of Kent closed the bars, issued an emergency proclamation, placed a curfew on the campus, and requested help from the Ohio National Guard. Rioting developed that evening. Students started fires, threw rocks and bottles at Guardsmen, shouted obscenities and threats at the Guardsmen, and attempted to burn down the R.O.T.C. building. By Monday morning, the National Guardsmen (some of them with minor injuries) had little patience or sympathy for the demonstrators, and the students were angry over the harassment, curfew, and National Guard tear gas. At 12:18 p.m., May 4, 1970, while attempting to disperse demonstrators at an illegal rally, several Guardsmen turned their rifles on a crowd of students and killed four of them. Only two of those killed were demonstrators: one was returning from class and one was going to lunch. After conflict comes victimage. The tragedy at Kent State University shocked the nation. It seemed to be the time for reflection, understanding, and justification. Scapegoats and victims of the event were identified, discussed, and by some, condemned. Official and unofficial sources questioned the National Guardsmen: Were they sufficiently provoked? Were they in serious danger? Were they murderers? Were they properly trained? Was the force justified or excessive? Was the shooting planned ahead of time? Other questions were aimed at the demonstrators: Were they lawless? Were they communists? Were they "hippies"? Were they attempting to attack the National Guardsmen? Did they get what was coming to them? And other questions were directed to Ohio Governor James Rhodes: Was the National Guard needed at Kent State? Were loaded weapons necessary? Were his instructions to "keep the university open at all costs" and "to restore civility" necessary?

The initial statement from the White House included the observation that, "when dissent turns to violence it invites tragedy." Thus, Kenneth Burke's final component of drama—tragedy—is recognized. The event at Kent State University was a series of symbolic actions in the form of a human drama. The era of people in masses taking their grievances to the streets, to demand equal rights and an end to the war in Vietnam, ended with the tragedy at Kent State. The demonstrations and tragedies of the 1960s and 1970s had finally created a consensus in America that our involvement in Vietnam had been a tragic mistake and that laws were needed to end racial discrimination in American society. As Kenneth Burke proclaims, "politics above all is drama."[27]

As a method of analysis, then, dramatism provides a framework for investigating human communication behavior. It is primarily descriptive in nature, but dramatism can provide guidelines for enhancing and understanding communication between people. Hence, dramatism is a "communication theory of human behavior." The value of the method, according to Burke, is that it makes us "sensitive to the 'ideas' lurking in 'things' which might even as social motives seem reducible to their sheerly material nature, unless we can perfect techniques for disclosing their 'enigmatic' or 'emblematic' dimension."[28]

Key Concepts in Burkean Theory

As is true of all methodologies, key concepts function as fundamental tools of analysis. We need to understand several important concepts in Burke's theories of persuasion in order to understand clearly the perspective of dramatism and its application to the persuasive efforts of social movements.

Identification

There is a great deal of division in our society, but communication can help us to articulate our differences and to relate to one another. In communicating we "transcend" to higher plains of meaning that enable us to overcome differences. Thus, in communicating with one another, we seek similarity or common references—Burke calls this process "identification."[29] All people are different, but we have common factors in which we are "consubstantially" or substantially the same. The process of identification reduces ambiguity and, hopefully, encourages cooperation.

For Burke, identification is more than merely relating to others; it is an instrument of transformation. At some level, reality, an event, or a group makes sense (is rational) even though one person's rationalization is another's factuality. Our responses and conclusions, however, are the results of the process of transformation, the end results of the awareness or knowledge of division. In the *Rhetoric of Motives*, Burke argues that "the statement of the thing's nature before and after the change is an *identifying* of it."[30]

Division is the counterpart of identification. Because of division, which is constant and certain, we seek transformation resulting in identification—a level of understanding if not harmony. Transformation occurs at various levels from the most obvious to the most subtle. Death is the ultimate "we." War is the "disease" of cooperation. From Kenneth Burke's perspective, "in pure identification there would be no strife."[31] Thus, when you "put identification and division ambiguously together, so that you cannot know for certain just where one ends and the other begins, you have the characteristic invitation to rhetoric."[32]

There are several levels of identification. Perhaps the most obvious is a persuader's attempt to establish "common ground" with an audience. This happens, for instance, when a United Farm Worker organizer wears work clothes while speaking to farm laborers, proclaims a farm worker (and perhaps Mexican and Roman Catholic) background, and advocates programs that will benefit farm workers. But for Burke, identification is a more encompassing notion than the simple expressions of common ground. Through interaction and identification, we can become involved in many groups, causes, or movements; formulate or change allegiances; and vicariously share in the role of leader or spokesperson.

There are at least seven ways that we can enhance or create a sense of identification with audiences.[33] First, when we become involved in groups or participate in group actions, we may become more tolerant, if not sympathetic, to the views of persuaders or groups. For example, as we will see in Chapter 14, group chants of slogans may create feelings of unity, solidarity, and tacit approval of the issue or action espoused in the chant.

Second, we may share aspects of appearance with the group. Dorothy Mansfield studied the 1960s ministry of the Rev. Arthur Blessitt to the so-called "hippies." In appearance "his hair was trimmed well below his ears; his vestments were a brightly printed, full-sleeved shirt, leather vest, bell-bottom hip-hugger trousers, and boots."[34]

A third form of identification is adapting language to audiences. Two speeches of Stokely Carmichael, leader of SNCC (Student Nonviolent Coordinating Committee), on "Black Power" illustrate this method of identification.[35] He gave one of the speeches to a predominantly black audience in Detroit on July 30, 1966 and the other to a predominantly white audience in Whitewater, Wisconsin on February 6, 1967. The addresses were surprisingly similar in content and examples, but they differed greatly in style and persuasive appeals. For the black audience, Carmichael personified the ideology he was advancing—in delivery, style, and attitude, while for the white audience, he dwelt mainly on an explanation of ideology. For the black audience, he interpreted the notion of "black power" in terms of pride, self-identity, and political mobilization, while he interpreted this slogan for the white audience in terms of mainstream American ideals, using such phrases as "social and political integration" and "pluralistic society." He advocated violent resistance in the Detroit speech, but in the Whitewater address he used milder references to violence and used them in a context of self-defense. Carmichael's delivery to the black audience was "cool and very hip," while his delivery to the white audience was that of an intellectual or "politically enlightened leader." The Detroit address contained more slang than the Whitewater address. Clearly, Carmichael "identified" with each of his audiences.

A fourth form of identification is content adaptation. Content adaptation refers to attempts by persuaders to use examples easily understood by listeners or readers in order to emphasize similarity between persuader and audience. Frederick Douglass, a free slave speaking before a white audience commemorating the Fourth of July in 1852, illustrated the similarity between "slaves" and "masters" in terms of abilities, jobs, and domestic roles:

> Is it not astonishing that, while we are plowing, planting, and reaping, using all kinds of mechanical tools, erecting houses, constructing bridges, building ships, working in metals of brass, iron, copper, silver, and gold; that, while we are reading, writing, and ciphering, acting as clerks, merchants, and secretaries, having among us lawyers, doctors, ministers, poets, authors, editors, orators, and teachers; that while we are engaged in all manner of enterprises common to other men, digging gold in California, capturing the whale in the Pacific, feeding sheep and cattle on the hillside, living, moving, acting, thinking, planning, living in families as husbands, wives, and children, and above all, confessing and worshipping the Christian's God, and looking hopefully for life and immortality beyond the grave, we are called upon to prove that we are men![36]

A fifth means of identification is the attempt to reflect a group's values. The day after the Kent State University shootings, President Nixon expressed full agreement with the goals of the demonstrators: "They are trying to say they want peace. They are trying to say they want to stop the killing. They are trying to say that we ought to get out of Vietnam. I agree with everything that they are trying to accomplish."[37]

A sixth method of identification is the use of visual symbols. It is not unusual for a leader or "outsider" to wear a symbol such as a cross, a button, an article of clothing, or an armband common to an audience, or to make symbolic gesture that communicates a similarity of feelings or experiences. For instance, New York Mayor John Lindsay ordered the flag to half-staff at City Hall to honor those killed at Kent State University.[38] This symbolic gesture communicated sympathy and agreement with anti-war sentiment.

And seventh, a persuader may create identification by referring to individuals or organizations that an audience approves, honors, or respects. Then Vice President Hubert Humphrey, a well-known advocate of black rights, used this tactic several times in an address before the annual convention of the National Association for the Advancement of Colored People on July 6, 1966. He declared:

> I am proud to be back among my friends of the NAACP who have led this march for 57 years...the road to freedom is stained with tears and the blood of many Americans—including men such as Medgar Evers—men already counted among authentic American heroes. . . . And through the years the NAACP has played a role second to none in terms of dedication and determination of sacrifice and courage.[39]

At the heart of the notion of identification, then, is the belief that symbols unite people. Language, as symbols, reveals the persuader's attitude about an issue or group, and the persuader can induce cooperation, or at least insure a fair hearing under most circumstances, by demonstrating similarities with the audience. But there is competition. To unite with one group, cause, or movement is to separate ourselves from some other group, cause, or social movement. If there were no divisions, there would be no need for rhetoric. Perfect identification would require no further communication. Burke relates that, "Since identification implies division, we found rhetoric involving us in matters of socialization and faction."[40]

By analyzing a persuader's language, the rhetorical critic may be able to reveal the substance of the persuader's attempts at identification and thereby to structure the persuader's strategies. The result should be a better understanding of the failures and successes of social movement leaders in their efforts to communicate with a wide variety of audiences: movement members, movement sympathizers, legitimizers, the mass media, and the agents and agencies of established institutions.

The Pentad

Kenneth Burke developed the "dramatistic pentad" in order to understand the dynamic interrelatedness of action. The pentad consists of five elements—act, scene, agent, agency, and purpose—and provides a way to view or to reconstruct action. Burke explains the five elements of dramatism as follows:

> For there to be an act, there must be an agent. Similarly, there must be a scene in which the agent acts. To act in a scene, the agent must employ some means, or agency. And there cannot be an act, in the full sense of the term, unless there is a purpose.[41]

The pentad forces us to become aware of the many elements and influences in each persuasive situation and how key individuals, groups, and/or institutions attempt to "construct reality." It serves as an "elegant" organizing function by providing dynamic interlocking elements that limit courses of action. As Michael Overington notes, this orientation is valuable when assessing political definitions of situations:

> As a method, dramatism addresses the empirical questions of how persons explain their actions to themselves and others, what the cultural and social structural influences of these explanations might be, and what effect connotational limits among the explanatory (motivational) terms might have on these explanations, and hence, on action itself.[42]

Thus, the pentad provides "a kind of simplicity that can be developed into considerable complexity."[43] A systematic application enables an observer to reconstruct various perspectives of "reality."

Three levels of application of the pentad can aid us in sorting out motivational elements. First, any specific event, episode, or sociodrama may be analyzed by investigating its elements. For example, suppose there was a mass demonstration on a college campus against the expansion of nuclear weapons in Europe. In pentadic terms, the act was the mass student demonstration; the scene was the college campus where the demonstration occurred; the agents were the students participating in the demonstration; the agency of the act might have been speeches and marches by the students; and the purposes of the act were to create awareness of the problem and to protest further deployment of nuclear weapons in Europe by the United States. This brief scenario seems simple and obvious. Each element, however, could be investigated further. Suppose the students shouted obscenities (agency) that resulted in a violent confrontation with police (act). What elements of the scene encouraged the conflict? Were all of the agents students or were some professional agitators? The point is that, as an organizing device, the pentad can provide categorical headings under which further analytical and evaluative observations can be rendered.[44]

A second level of application may be a specific social movement. We could use the pentad to isolate movement stages, strategies, tactics, goals, ideology, and organization. For example, in terms of the pro-life movement, the agent might be a national organization, a local affiliate of a national organization, or a splinter group. Analysis of the scene might reveal a reaction to the growth of a secular society with its threat to the family and religion, the women's liberation movement, or the predominate concern over individual rights regardless of age, sex, or race. Acts may include lawsuits, demonstrations, media events, or disruptions of abortion clinics. Agency considerations include posters, newspapers, television reports, buttons, pamphlets, and bumperstickers. Such analyses not only emphasize the interrelatedness of the various elements but can reveal which were most important at a given time.

And a third level for applying the pentad to society might prove beneficial in isolating societal factors that encourage the formation, organization, decline or rejection of a specific social movement. The goal is to account for as many motivational influences upon symbolic behavior as possible. The pentad provides the framework for analyzing the element or elements that persuaders dwell upon in a specific message or situation: act, scene, agent, agency, or purpose. Such analyses may reveal the perceptions (of self, others, situation, the world), motives, and character or personality of persuaders or their audiences.

For Kenneth Burke, therefore, all discussions of human motivation arise out of investigations of the five elements of the pentad. We may discover upon analysis that one element is the key and all others seem to grow out of this single term. The featuring of a single term in a drama may lead to different conclusions about human motivation. For illustrative purposes, let us return to the drama at Kent State University. The act was the shooting of the four students. The scene was the culmination of three days of demonstrations and rioting. The agents were the Ohio National Guardsmen. The agency was the rifles. The purpose of the act remains debatable, but it would seem to have been either planned retaliation or spontaneous self-defense. In analyzing this drama, we might stress the act of shooting the students as the organizing element. Those who believe that the National Guard should not have been called to the campus might argue that the *act-agent* ratio is the key to understanding the drama. The Guardsmen, in defending their actions, might focus on a *scene-act* ratio, arguing that the three days of demonstrations and provocations best explains the other elements. The victims of the drama might argue from a *purpose-act* ratio in explaining the event. For them, the purposes or motives of the shooting were prejudice, intolerance, and retaliation. For some governmental investigators, the cause of the tragedy is revealed in an *agent-agency* consideration. The Guardsmen should not have been allowed to carry weapons; alternatively, empty rifles or blanks rather than live ammunition could have been employed.

This example shows the utility and versatility of the pentad. The various ratios reveal attitudes and motivations of participants in dramas. This enables the critic of the persuasive efforts of social movements to develop a more complete understanding of the perspectives and arguments in a drama. The pentad allows for division and unity and, as individual elements, provides singular focus and organization. Taken together, the elements work in unison to provide understanding of dramatic symbolic behavior.

Burkean Analysis of Social Movements

Nature of Society

Historically there have been two dominant approaches to understanding society. From a dramatistic perspective, each approach is too deterministic. The sociological approach emphasizes structure: behavior results from factors such as status, position, cultural prescriptions, norms, values, social sanctions, role demands, and general system requirements. These factors are viewed as causes of behavior while ignoring the social interactions that influence each of them. Similarly, the psychological approach emphasizes motives, attitudes, hidden complexes, and general psychological processes as ways to account for behavior, but it ignores social interaction. Rather than focusing on causative factors, the psychological approach focuses on the behavior such factors produce.

From a dramatistic perspective, social interaction is of vital importance. Herbert Blumer, a founder of this perspective, views symbolic interaction as "a process that forms human conduct instead of being merely a means or a setting for the expression or release of human conduct."[45] Thus, dramatism—like the social systems approach presented in Chapter 7—emphasizes the dramatic, changing nature of society. Society arises, matures, and continues to exist through communication. Individuals are constantly interacting, developing, and shaping society. People exist in action and consequently must be viewed in terms of action. To analyze human society, then, the student of persuasion and social movements must begin with an analysis of the human beings who are engaging in action. Society may be defined as individuals in interaction, individuals acting in relation to each other, individuals engaging in cooperative acting in relation to each other, individuals engaging in cooperative action, and individuals communicating with self and others. From this definition we may argue that people "make society" and society "makes people." As Blumer argues:

> The activity of human beings consists of meeting a flow of situations in which they have to act and their action is built on the basis of what they note, how they access and interpret what they note, and what kind of projected lines of action they map out."[46]

Social Control

Social control is usually viewed as a result of institutional influences such as laws, the police, or Congress. But social order is not entirely dependent upon "agencies of control." No regime can long survive on a threat of force alone. Communication is the most important means of social order, for within the communication lies the power to create and to control the images that legitimize authority. Communication joins all people. Hugh Duncan, a student of Kenneth Burke, observes that:

> Images, visions, and all imaginings of the future are symbolic forms, for when the future becomes the present, and thus becomes "real" new futures are created to guide our search for solutions to problems in the present which emerge as we try to create order in our relationships.[47]

Social order, according to Duncan, is always expressed in some kind of hierarchy. Hierarchy differentiates people into ranks based on many variables—age, sex, race, skill, wealth, education, etc. "All hierarchies," Duncan argues, "function through a 'perfection' of their principles in final moments of social mystification which are reached by mountings from lower to higher principles of social order."[48] Thus, the task for authorities is to invest local symbols with universal symbols that "transcend" local, isolated concerns.

The community "lives" because of frequent and intense reenactment by its members of key roles believed to be necessary to social order. "We learn to act, not simply by preparing to act, or by thinking 'about' action, but by playing various kinds of dramas."[49] For Hugh Duncan, there are seven basic forms of social drama: games, play, parties, festivals, ceremonies, drama, and rites. In terms of government, ceremonies, rites, and ritual are the most formalized types of social dramas. Success is dependent upon the elements of glory and efficiency:

> Glory is a dignification achieved through style (a way of life) which inferiors use to identify themselves with superiors. Superiors, in turn, use styles of performance (their "presence") to move the hearts and minds of inferiors to loyalty and reverence.[50]

Social order, therefore, is legitimized through symbols grounded in nature, man, society, language, or God. When followers, through socialization, have been taught "significant symbols" which uphold social order, they require their leaders to "play" their roles within the principles established.

Conversely, disorder originates in society through disorder in communication. Duncan argues that "when people cannot communicate they cannot relate. Disrelationships are not *reflected* in communication; they *originate* in communication."[51] According to Burke,the division of labor and the handing down of property gave rise to classes.[52] Order among the classes involves the distribution of authority. This distribution, in turn, establishes a hierarchical form. "Thus," Burke observes, "the purely *operational* motives binding a society become inspirited by a corresponding condition of mystery."[53] And, Leland Griffin—interpreting Burke—concludes:

> Wherever there is mystery there is corresponding communication that results in understanding—the understanding that makes piety possible. But the maintenance of piety involves the need for obedience—which is to say, the painful need for self-control (self-restraint, self-moderation) and out of this obligation comes the possibility of disobedience . . . [54]

Social Movements

As we noted in Chapters 2 and 7, social movements do not instantaneously occur and develop or "just happen." When the seeds of discontent are planted, much nurturing and microscopic growth occurs long before the first leaf breaks the soil for all to see. A social movement is a process of transformation from societal order (the prevailing hierarchy, beliefs, attitudes, values, goals, and cessation of identification with the prevailing hierarchy), action (symbolic behavior of articulating grievances, altering perceptions of society, providing courses of action), drama (symbolic acts, events, episodes), conflict (separation, confrontation, violence, tragedy), victimage (identification of the causes of societal evil, conflict, and violence that must be destroyed), transcendence (the purging and removal of social ills while establishing new levels of social identification, cooperation, and unity), redemption (forgiveness of social sins), and order (hierarchy and societal values accepted, sanctioned, and legitimized). When one phase ends and another begins is often difficult, and sometimes impossible, to isolate.

Leaders and superiors must create and use symbols that unite and transcend individual and collective differences. "The legitimation of authority," argues Duncan, "is based on persuasion."[55] Leaders, in their struggles for power and attempts to stay in power, must provide integrative symbols for the masses to transcend the ambiguities and conflicts of heroes and villains, of loyalty and disloyalty, of concern and indifference, of confidence and fear, of obedience and disobedience, of hierarchy and anarchy, of peace and violence. The notions of faith and reason are on the side of order. Faith is expressed by accepting the authority of others as legitimate. Reason is expressed by the acceptance of authority based upon the quality of performance and positive impact upon the quality of life. The temptations of emotions and prevalence of imagination are on the side of disorder. Emotions are articulated through dramatic actions, issues, and statements. Imagination creates a new order, governmental system, or social utopia. In simple terms, therefore, when division in society is so great that symbols no longer possess common meanings, people will turn to leaders who will create new symbols. When symbols can no longer transcend differences among people, conflict can only be resolved through violence.

Michael Osborn argues that contemporary rhetoric is dominated "by strategic pictures, verbal or nonverbal visualizations that linger in the collective memory of audiences as representatives of their subject when rhetoric has been successful."[56] He calls a strategic picture a "depiction" that has become a significant and recurring form of public address. Masses of people are joined and sustained by simple mythic pictures that embody common goals and values.

Osborn identifies five functions of depiction that directly relate to the drama of social movements.[57] The first function of depiction is presentation of the world. Rhetoric is not reflective but constructive. Our world, as noted before, is symbolic, mediated, and purposeful. The second function is intensification of feeling. Depiction adds color, shading, and emphasis to people, places, and events. War, for instance, can be presented as heroic or tragic with each extreme generating emotional responses. The third function is a resource for identification. Commonality in all forms contributes to a sense of community and oneness. The fourth function, implementation, refers to "time of action." Implementation articulates the future, provides plans of action, and sustains group activity. And the fifth function is reaffirmation of reality. In a ceremony, for example, a group's heroes and martyrs are praised, and rituals are developed to maintain the symbols and memories of the group.

Thus, within depiction, one can note the "strings of consciousness" or the view of the world as seen by others. Depiction is a process composed of many "snapshots" of the world. From this perspective, the creation of a social movement lies in the failure of communication among groups, and the results are rejection of the symbols of those in power, cessation of identification with the prevailing hierarchy, and the spreading of disloyalty. The civil rights movement of the 1960s was successful in rejecting the symbols of American society. The movement redefined the heritage of "negro" into "Afro-American;" reinforced a positive self-concept of "Black is beautiful"; and declared a new political activism in "Black

Power," Once separated from the existing order, although with a sense of guilt, the disaffected are moved to articulate grievances and to dream of salvation—a state of redemption. Blacks defined American society as one of discrimination, oppression, and inequality. The Reverend Martin Luther King, Jr. articulated their dream beautifully from the steps of the Lincoln Memorial in Washington, D.C.:

> I have a dream . . . that this nation will rise up and live out the true meaning of its creed . . . that all men are created equal; . . . that one day on the red hills of Georgia the sons of former slaves and the sons of former slaveowners will be able to sit down together at the table of brotherhood; . . . that one day even the state of Mississippi . . . will be transformed into an oasis of freedom and justice; . . . that my four little children will one day live in a nation where they will not be judged by the color of their skin but by the content of their character; . . . one day right there in Alabama little black boys and black girls will be able to join hands with little white boys and white girls as sisters and brothers; . . . and the glory of the Lord shall be revealed, and all flesh shall see it together.

Now, with a sense of duty and purpose, the followers of the social movement act, shout "**No**" to the existing order and proclaim a new beginning. In the words of Martin Luther King:

> This is no time to engage in the luxury of cooling off or to take the tranquilizing drug of gradualism. Now is the time to make real the promises of Democracy. Now is the time to rise from the dark and desolate valley of segregation to the sunlit path of racial justice. Now is the time to lift our nation from the quicksands of racial injustice to the solid rock of brotherhood. Now is the time to make justice a reality for all of God's children . . . . Go back to Mississippi, go back to Alabama, go back to South Carolina, go back to Georgia, go back to Louisiana, go back to the slums and ghettos of our northern cities, knowing that somehow this situation can and will be changed.

Burke states that four basic motives arise in human communication: hierarchy, guilt, victimage, and redemption.[58] For him, these motives are revealed in observing human relationships, and they encompass all human motivation. These motives describe the process of birth, maturation, and death of social movements. "Hierarchy" stems from human desire for order, and rejection of an established hierarchy produces a sense of "guilt." From Burke's perspective, "Language produces hierarchies, hierarchies produce categorical guilt as well as provide man with a means of purging and redeeming himself through the dialectic of transcendence made possible by symbolic action and the verbal hierarchy."[59] Guilt is relieved through "victimage" or the sacrifice of a scapegoat that epitomizes the evils of society: Jews, capitalists, communists, landlords, agitators. Victimage, then, is a mode of purification. The extreme forms of victimage are homicide (of others) and suicide (of selves). In homicidal victimage, there is the polluted and the pure. The former is the scapegoat; the latter is the sacrificial. The act of making others suffer for *our* sins is at the heart of victimage. Thus, one person's or group's guilt demands some other person's or group's death or injury.[60] In primitive societies, purification came from sacrificing animals to a god. In the sophisticated and complex societies of today, however, purification comes from endowing a person, government, idea, or practice with social evils that dictate removal. Removal can range from redefinition to murder. Burke identifies three ways a person is made "worthy" of sacrifice.[61] First, a person may be made worthy of sacrifice legalistically, as an offender against legal or moral principles of justice. Second, a person may be worthy because of a subtle kind of poetic justice. And third, a person may be worthy of sacrifice because of "fate," perhaps the least rational of the three. Scapegoats become the "sacrificial animal" upon whose back is ritualistically placed all of a social movement's real or perceived evils.

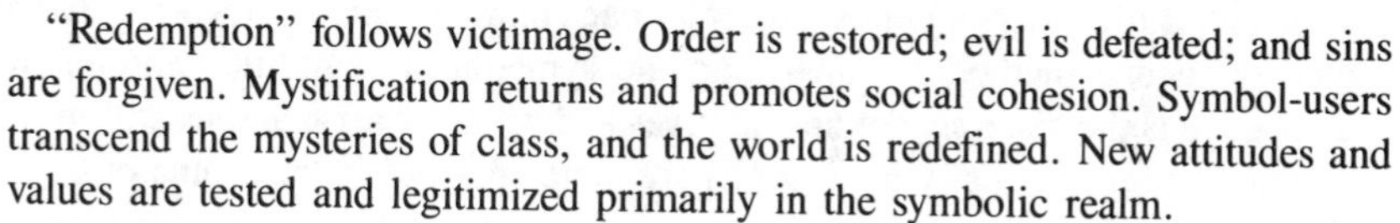

"Redemption" follows victimage. Order is restored; evil is defeated; and sins are forgiven. Mystification returns and promotes social cohesion. Symbol-users transcend the mysteries of class, and the world is redefined. New attitudes and values are tested and legitimized primarily in the symbolic realm.

Sociodramas

Because aspects of the transformation and development of entire social movements are difficult to isolate and to manage, individual episodes or sociodramas are easier to investigate. Wherever there is action there is drama, and, as Hugh Duncan writes, "failure to understand the power of dramatic form in communication means failure in seizing and controlling power over men."[62] Sociodramas are not merely symbolic screens or metaphors; they are social reality because they are forms of social interaction and integration.

We need to identify some act or action in order to analyze a social drama. If we focus on dramas of authority, we might ask: Under what conditions is the act being presented? What kind of act is it? What roles are the actors assuming? What forms of authority are being communicated? What means of communication are used? What symbols of authority are evoked? How are social functions staged? How are social functions communicated? How are the messages received? What are responses to authority messages?

The scope of a social drama is prescribed by the investigator. The drama may involve one person or many, a symbolic (rhetorical) event or a physical event; one moment or a specified period in time. Sociodramas are the acts and scenes that comprise our lives. Individual photographs capture moments and evoke reflection, memories, analysis, and emotions of joy or sadness. Taken together and shown sequentially, the snapshots produce movement, action, and behavior. Although a drama can be analyzed frame by frame, it is essentially a composite of individual acts.

Summary

In Burkean terms, then, a social movement is a study of drama composed of many acts. They are acts of hierarchy, transformation, transcendence, guilt, victimage, redemption, and salvation. With acts as the pivotal concept, Burke suggests that we investigate the scenes that encompass and surround the act, for scenes provide the context for an act. Next, he suggests that we consider the agents involved in the act—the actors who mold, shape, create, and sustain movements. Likewise, consideration of the agency or the channels of communication in an act reveal the impact of persuasive activities. And consideration of the purpose of an act aids in discovering the ultimate motives or meaning of an act.

Conclusions

Kenneth Burke offers a philosophy of human communication, a theory of social behavior, and a method for analyzing the symbolic act. At the heart of his perspective is the discovery of how motives and behavior arise and exist through communication. Our daily interactions are mere episodes in the drama of social life. Order is created, manipulated, sustained, and altered through symbols.

A social movement is a process of transformation from order, division, drama, conflict, victimage, transcendence, redemption, and reestablished order. As symbol-using animals, we transcend our animal nature by giving rise to property, rights, duty, loyalty, and obligation. These items and concepts must be guarded, defended, and negotiated. Division breeds conflict, and conflict results in associated guilt and the corresponding cancellation of the guilt—the process of victimage and redemption. Thus, we encounter the "mystification" of social interaction. Our task, however, is more than simply understanding the "social mystery" of collective behavior. Rather, our task in a democratic society is to participate actively in sociodramas that enhance the quality of our lives. "For better or worse," Burke writes, "the mystery of the hierarchy is forever with us, let us, as students of rhetoric, scrutinize its range of entrancements both with dismay and in delight."[63]

Kenneth Burke's perspective of human action and his method of analysis are useful to students of social movements because they allow us to investigate all phases and aspects of social movement phenomena. We may analyze any level of symbolic behavior and any action: a single message; an individual persuader over time; a large event with many participants; a group, organization, or collectivity; social cultures or societies; and historical timeframes.

When investigating individual persuaders and messages, each Burkean concept may help us to discover stylistic characteristics; beliefs, attitudes, and motivations; or persuasive strategies. In terms of symbolic event, episode, or sociodrama, Burkean concepts can help us to identify the correlations and strategies of participants; to reveal basic or recurring rhetorical patterns and strategies; or to investigate the stages or phases in the dramatistic process. The methodology, in short, is applicable to many "symbol-making, symbol-using, and symbol-misusing" behaviors.

Endnotes

[1] Kenneth Burke. *Language as Symbolic Action*, (Berkeley: University of California Press, 1966), 6.

[2] Kenneth Burke, "Interaction-Dramatism," *International Encyclopedia of Social Sciences* (New York, 1967), 447.

[3] Burke, *IESS*, 447.

[4] Burke, *Language as Symbolic Action*, 53.

[5] Burke, *IESS*, 447.

[6] Burke, *Language as Symbolic Action*, 5.

[7] Burke, *Language as Symbolic Action*, 63.

[8] Kenneth Burke, *Permanence and Change (New York: Bobbs-Merrill, 1965), 29-30.*

[9] Burke, *Permanence and Change*, xvii.

[10] Burke, *Permanence and Change*, xxxiii.

[11] Kenneth Burke, *A Rhetoric of Motives (Berkeley: University of California Press, 1969), 43.*

[12] Burke, *A Rhetoric of Motives*, 46.

[13] Burke, *IESS*, 445-452.

[14] Burke, *IESS*, 445.

[15] Kenneth Burke, *A Grammar of Motives (Berkeley: University of California Press, 1969), xxii.*

[16] Michael Overington, "Kenneth Burke and the Method of Dramatism," *Theory and Society*, 4 (Spring, 1977), 129-156.

[17] Kenneth Burke, "Dramatism," *Communication Concepts and Perspectives*, Lee Thayer, ed., (Washington, DC: Spartan Books, 1967), 332.

[18] Burke, *IESS*, 449.

[19] Burke, *Language as Symbolic Action*, 55.

[20] Dan Nimmo and James Combs, *Mediated Political Realities (New York: Longman, 1983).*

[21] Nimmo and Combs, xv.

[22] Nimmo and Combs, 8.

[23] David Altheide and Robert Snow, *Media Logic* (Beverly Hills, CA: Sage, 1979), 109-110.

[24] As quoted in Martin Schram, *The Great American Video Game* (New York: William Morrow, 1987), 58.

[25] Schram, 51.

[26] For an excellent account of the Kent State shootings, see Milton Viorst, *Fire in the Streets* (New York: Simon and Schuster, 1979), 508-543.

[27] Kenneth Burke, *The Philosophy of Literary Form*, 3rd ed. (Berkeley: University of California Press, 1973), 310.

[28] Burke, *Language as Symbolic Action*, 429.

[29] Burke, *A Rhetoric of Motives*, 21-45.

[30] Burke, *A Rhetoric of Motives*, 20.

[31] Burke, *A Rhetoric of Motives, 25.*

[32] Burke, *A Rhetoric of Motives, 25.*

[33] These seven ways of identification are discussed by Wayne Thompson, *The Process of Persuasion* (New York: Harper and Row, 1975), 430-431.

[34] Dorothy Mansfield. "A Blessitt Event: Reverend Arthur Blessitt Invites Youth to 'Tune In, Turn On, Drop Out,'" *Southern Speech Communication Journal* 37 (Winter, 1971), 165.

[35] For speeches and excellent analysis, see "Stokely Carmichael: Two Speeches on Black Power," by Wayne Brockriede and Robert Scott, *The Rhetoric of Black Power* (New York: Harper and Row, 1969), 84-131.

[36] Frederick Douglass. "An Ex-Slave Discusses Slavery, July 4, 1852," *A Treasury of the World's Greatest Speeches*, Houston Peterson, ed. (New York: Simon and Schuster, 1965), 481.

[37] As reported by Milton Viorst, *Fire in the Streets*, 540.

[38] Viorst, 540.

[39] Hubert Humphrey. "Address at the NAACP Convention, July 6, 1966," in Scott and Brockriede, 66.

[40] Burke. *A Rhetoric of Motives*, 45.

[41] Burke, "Dramatism," 332.

[42] Overington. pp. 129-156.

[43] Burke. *A Grammar of Motives*, xvi.

[44] Richard Crable and John Makay. "Kenneth Burke's Concept of Motives in Rhetorical Theory," *Today's Speech*, 20 (Winter, 1972), 13.

[45] Herbert Blumer. *Symbolic Interactionism* (Englewood Cliffs, NJ: Prentice-Hall, 1969), 8.

[46] Blumer. 16.

[47] Hugh Duncan. *Symbols in Society* (New York: Oxford University Press, 1968), 48.

[48] Duncan, 73.

[49] Duncan, 61.

[50] Duncan, 205.

[51] Duncan, 130.

[52] Burke, *Permanence and Change*, 276.

[53] Burke, *Permanence and Change*, 276.

[54] Leland Griffin. "A Dramatistic Theory of the Rhetoric of Movements," *Critical Responses to Kenneth Burke*, William Rueckert, ed., (Minneapolis: University of Minnesota Press, 1969), 457.

[55] Duncan. 200.

[56] Michael Osborn. "Rhetorical Depiction," in Herbert Simons and Aram Aghazarian (eds.), *Form, Genre, and the Study of Political Discourse* (Columbia, SC: University of South Carolina Press, 1986), 79.

[57] Osborn. 81.

[58] Burke. *Permanence and Change*, 274.

[59] William Rueckert, *Kenneth Burke and the Drama of Human Relations* (Berkeley, CA: University of California Press, 1982), 145.

[60] Rueckert. 146.

[61] Burke. *Philosophy and Literary Form*, 40.

[62] Duncan. 25.

[63] Burke. *A Rhetoric of Motives*, 333.

Part Three

Studies of Social Movement Persuasion

Chapter 10

The Authoritarian Character of the John Birch Society

There is widespread agreement among students of social movement persuasion that recruitment and consolidation are essential functions. Without recruitment there are no members, and without consolidation the members do not constitute a collectivity.[1] This chapter explicates the means by which one organization, the John Birch Society, selectively recruited the adherents best suited to its organizational efforts, while simultaneously excluding potential mutineers.

Chapter 7 presented a social systems approach to persuasion and suggested that personality (or character type) and message are interdependent. This chapter explains how Birch Society rhetoric provides primarily psychological (rather than political, social, or philosophical) gratifications to those of "authoritarian character" while alienating those of "democratic character."

The John Birch Society

The John Birch Society was founded in 1958 as a secret, activist, anti-communist organization by Robert H.W. Welch. A retired candy executive and former official of the National Association of Manufacturers, Welch wanted a cadre of dedicated and disciplined patriots who would help him take America back from the communists. Importantly, he did not desire a large organization (large organizations being difficult to discipline).[2]

Conventional wisdom holds that the John Birch Society disintegrated in the mid-1960s as a consequence of two phenomena. The first of these was the Goldwater debacle of 1964—a campaign in which the Birch Society was quite active and visible. The second was the belief dilemma posed for Birchers by the anti-war protests of the 1960s: Birchers opposed both the war (as an effort by American communists to squander our national resources) and protestors of virtually all political stripes (as Communist-inspired troublemakers).[3] The Birch Society's visibility diminished, and public and scholars alike inferred that the Society had become insignificant.

But the John Birch Society did not disband in the mid-1960s; it entered a new phase and continued to grow. This is evident in the circulation of two publications—*The John Birch Society Bulletin* (the members-only monthly), and *American Opinion* (Welch's general circulation monthly). The average readership of *American Opinion* during the 1963-1965 "peak" was 29,190 as compared to 29,361 for the period 1979-1981. Yet the number of mailed subscriptions (an index of readers' continuing commitment) actually rose by 50%—from 15,218 during the 1963-1965 "peak" to 22,893 in 1979-1981. Furthermore, *American Opinion* did not reach its average annual circulation for the 1958-1981 period until after the "peak" period (1966 for general circulation and 1971 for mailed subscriptions). Finally, the mailed circulation of the *Bulletin* (available only to members and some libraries) averaged 61,073 for the period of 1976-1981 and reached 107,776 in 1981—more than any known estimate of the Society's "peak" membership.[4]

These circulation data strongly suggest that the John Birch Society did not disintegrate in 1966—it simply became less public. Unfortunately, most scholars mistook visibility for vitality (a common mistake in the case of secret organizations) and ceased studying the Society. Dale Leathers, the most insightful critic of Birch rhetoric, argues that the Birch ideology, like other reactionary rhetoric, exhibits the characteristics of a closed-mind:

> reactionary rhetoric is dominated by the three most significant properties of the closed mind. Reactionaries absolutely reject all beliefs opposed to their own, that is, disbeliefs; their own belief system is totally isolated from their disbeliefs; the reactionary is unable to distinguish between the strikingly diverse set of beliefs which are opposed to his own.[5]

But in describing the characteristics of the closed-mind, Leathers neglects the relative importance of Rokeach's three regions of belief-disbelief systems. These three regions are the "central region" ("the nature of the physical world. . . , the nature of the 'self' and of the 'generalized other' "), the "intermediate region" (beliefs and disbeliefs about the nature of authority and those who exercise it), and the "peripheral region" (containing beliefs and disbeliefs derived from authorities).[6] For Leathers, therefore, the key to reactionary persuasion is that, "He does not concentrate on what he believes. . . but on what he disbelieves" *whether it relates to the physical world, the self, authority, or inconsequential matters*.[7]

There are at least two reasons for seeking alternative explanations to the closed-mind thesis. The first reason is the lack of ideological satisfaction found among Birchers during their purported "peak" activity in 1964-1965. The closed-mind thesis suggests that members need a tight, consistent set of beliefs as protection against a threatening environment.[8] Indeed, in his survey of members (conducted with the assistance of Birch headquarters), Fred W. Grupp found that 61% reported *joining* the Birch Society for "ideological reasons," but only 19% reported finding ideological satisfaction.[9] *Yet despite their unsatisfied need, these people remained members of the John Birch Society.*

The second reason for modifying the closed-mind explanation derives from the anti-war belief dilemma. Closed belief systems serve a protective function by providing clear and consistent explanations. When a closed belief system fails to explain an environment, it is "dysfunctional" and is replaced by a more efficient closed belief system. Since the believer needs an efficient set of beliefs, the closed-minded person can rarely tolerate ambiguities or contradictions. Thus, the persistence of the anti-war belief dilemma should have caused major defections from the ranks of the Society as the closed belief system functioned inefficiently.[10] Instead, readership of *American Opinion* increased from 25,761 in the Goldwater year of 1964 to 35,400 in 1965 and 43,262 in 1966—an increase of 68% during the period of expected decline.

Although two sets of available data contradict the closed-mind explanation of Birchism's appeal, Leathers' case is otherwise quite convincing. His analysis derives from Milton Rokeach's efforts to discover the nature of "topic-free authoritarianism." But Rokeach's work was the culmination of previous interest in authoritarianism—a personality type dominated by a concern with superior-inferior relationships. This earlier research (conducted most notably by Abraham Maslow, Erich Fromm, and Theodor W. Adorno and his colleagues) emphasized *rightist* authoritarianism for the better understanding of Nazi sympathizers.[11] While their work was later criticized by Rokeach and others for its political bias (conservatives were always more authoritarian than liberals), that bias is only pertinent when attempting to understand leftist or moderate authoritarians. Their pioneering work should be quite helpful to students of rightist movements such as the John Birch Society. Let us turn, therefore, to a brief overview of that research.

Characteristics of Authoritarianism

Psychological study of the "authoritarian character structure" was based primarily upon clinical observation until Adorno *et al* presented their California F-Scale (for the measurement of Fascist tendencies) in 1950. These works were directed at understanding rightist authoritarianism and are pertinent to an understanding of the John Birch Society. The dominant feature is what Rokeach called the "intermediate region": beliefs about authority and those who exercise it. For the authoritarian character, everything revolves around authority. The three major premises of the authoritarian worldview are: the world as a jungle, a need for hierarchical organization, and the glorification of dominance and submission.[12]

The fundamental premise of the authoritarian world view is that life is essentially threatening. Maslow explained that:

> Like other psychologically insecure people, the authoritarian person lives in a world which may be conceived to be pictured by him as a sort of jungle in which every man's hand is necessarily against every other man's, in which the whole world is conceived of as dangerous, threatening, or at least challenging, and in which humans are conceived of as primarily selfish or evil or stupid.... This jungle is peopled with animals who either eat or are eaten, who are either feared or despised. One's safety lies in one's own strength and this strength consists primarily in the power to dominate. If one is not strong enough the only alternative is to find a strong protector.

Since danger is all around, the protector can and will demand total obedience. And since the protected must sustain the relationship with the protector, submission is willing and, when the danger is keenly felt, ecstatic. *Within this jungle the protector-protected relationship predominates.*

The authoritarian character's antithesis—the "Democratic Character"—tends to see the world as a basically friendly, supportive place—more greenhouse than jungle. Since there is little danger, there is little need for protection and, therefore, little need for submission, discipline, or orders.

To the extent that the world really *is* a jungle, the authoritarian's worldview is advisable. It is foolish to wander off from a safari to negotiate with lions and tigers. Authoritarians therefore express only contempt for those who fail to recognize the world as a very threatening place.

In the jungle, all creatures compete relentlessly and unmercifully for the means of survival. Every creature must, therefore, be quickly categorized as "superior" (and thus "to be feared, resented, bootlicked, and admired") or as "inferior" (and therefore "to be scorned, humiliated, and dominated"). Time is precious in the jungle since anyone slow to recognize enemies cannot long survive. Thus, everyone must be quickly and easily ranked in a hierarchy from strong to weak.

While the authoritarian sees all differences between people as vertical, the democratic character tends to view differences between people as horizontal. Since unity is essential for survival, the authoritarian can tolerate neither diverse goals nor diverse means. All people, achievements, and events are measured on one scale. Various authoritarians may stress different scales, but none can stress tolerance or diversity because multiple scales compound the danger to all by confounding the process of ranking everyone on a superior-inferior scale.

The person judged superior on that one scale is judged universally superior, and the inferior universally inferior. But the democratic character judges superiority-inferiority in specific functional terms. The authoritarian assigns holistic superiority while the democrat appraises specific capabilities, functions, and performances.

Since these judgments of superiority must be made quickly, and since superiority is inherently generalizable, the authoritarian judges by externals. These externals include titles, physical stature and grooming, wealth, family name, or behavior.

This is useful precisely because a superior person is consistently so. Conversely, the democratic personality prefers to judge others—when judge one must—on the basis of performance. As Maslow explained:

> He (sic) customarily gives his permanent respect only to people who are worthy of respect for functional reasons. He doesn't give his respect automatically simply because he is supposed to, or because everybody else respects this person.

But the authoritarian does precisely that.

In short, external characteristics are noted by the authoritarian, measured against the single vertical scale, and generalized to ascertain the person's leader-follower relationship. The democratic character examines functional characteristics, adjudicates them (only as necessary) according to diverse values and creates a leader-follower relationship (when necessary) for the attainment of some specific goal.

Given the foregoing context for the leader-follower relationship, the authoritarian naturally believes that any leader's kindness is a weakness. Maslow explained that:

> If he (sic) is in dominance status, he will tend to be cruel; if he is in subordinate status, he will tend to be masochistic. But because of the tendencies in himself, he will understand, and deep down within himself will agree with the cruelty of the superior person, even if he himself is the object of the cruelty. He will understand the bootlicker and the slave even if he himself is not the bootlicker or the slave. The same principles explain both the leader and the follower in an authoritarian group, both the slave-owner and the slave.

Significantly, then, the follower glories in subservience to the leader. This relationship and the generalization of superiority-inferiority preclude negotiation of control since neither party finds such negotiations either valid or productive. Both realize that the worthless inferior is fortunate to have the protector, and both realize that the protector should feel little beyond contempt for the follower.

Since the authoritarian sees people as fundamentally selfish, evil, stupid, and unable to survive alone, inferiors are to be used as the superior sees fit. Other people are "tools" or "pawns on a chessboard" and may even be seen as sub-human. The democratic character views humans as partners rather than rivals and is reluctant to use or to manipulate them.

This sado-masochistic tendency leads to an authoritarian value system in which brutality, cruelty, selfishness, and hardness are exalted and in which sympathy, kindness, and generosity are reviled *by leaders and followers alike*. Importantly, the democratic character has no comparable tendency: there is room for both selfishness and generosity, for hardness and compassion since different people value differently.

Maslow lists several other characteristics of authoritarianism which deserve passing attention. These include an "abyss between men and women," (men being purportedly better able to survive through strength), the soldier ideal, the importance of humiliation as a mechanism for establishing superiority, antagonism toward the education of inferiors, avoidance of responsibility for one's own fate, and the pursuit of security through order, discipline, and other compulsive-obsessive outlets.

Pervading all of these characteristics is the impossibility of satisfaction. The best one can hope for in the jungle is temporary relief from constant danger. But the jungle is, after all, the jungle. And one must be most vigilant when the jungle seems safest. The democrat can be happier for longer since his or her basic needs have been satisfied and danger—not safety—is the exception in life.

Before moving on to an examination of the authoritarian dimension of John Birch Society persuasion, we must observe with Maslow that the authoritarian character is a construction of internally consistent beliefs or tendencies, all of which revolve around the premise that the world is a very threatening, dangerous place. The authoritarian worldview is a functional framework for interpreting one's environment. Implicit in the authoritarian character is the need for communication. Maslow's description of survival is interpersonal: the inferior is doomed unless he or she can create and sustain a relationship with a sufficiently strong protector. The persuasive process through which this help is enlisted is central to the authoritarian's psychological survival.

The Authoritarian Dimension of Birch Society Persuasion

The central arguments of the John Birch Society provide for all of the psychological needs of the authoritarian character while alienating those of the democratic character. These central arguments are found in *The Blue Book of the John Birch Society*, a transcription of Welch's address at the Society's founding in 1958 that remains the Society's formal ideological statement.[13] By analyzing this core ideology for evidence of authoritarianism and democratic character, *we hope to demonstrate that the Society is built around its leader first and its/his closed belief system secondarily.* This enables the leader to reconcile subsequent belief dilemmas for his followers.

The Birchist World as Jungle

The theme of the *Blue Book* is the danger of *subversive* communism. If people are not aroused to that danger, says Welch, "in a few short years we shall all be hanging from the same lamp posts while Communist terror reigns all around us (p. x)." He tells the reader that:

> the truth I bring you is simple, incontrovertible and deadly. It is that, unless we can reverse forces which now seem inexorable in their movement, you have only a few more years before the country in which you live will become separate provinces in a world-wide Communist dominion ruled by police-state methods from the Kremlin (p. 1).

But unlike most other Americans during the Cold War of the 1950s, Welch regarded the danger as neither Soviet aggression nor nuclear war. Instead, Welch identified the danger as subversion. Lenin's strategy, he said:

> is taking us over by a process so gradual and insidious that Soviet rule is slipped over so far on the American people, before they ever realize it is happening, that they can no longer resist the Communist conspiracy as free citizens (p. 19). This subversion comes from a gigantic conspiracy to enslave mankind; an increasingly successful conspiracy controlled by determined, cunning, and utterly ruthless gangsters, willing to go to any means to achieve its end (p. 21).

These conspirators are "like an octopus so large that its tentacles now reach into all of the legislative halls, all of the union labor meetings, a majority of the religious gatherings, and most of the schools *of the whole world* (p. 60)." Indeed, Welch warns that: "The human race has never before faced any such monster of power which has determined to enslave it. There is certainly no reason for underrating its size, its efficiency, its determination, its power, or its menace (p. 61)." The John Birch Society's world is not a friendly place.

The worldview of the John Birch Society stresses constant, imminent, hidden, ruthless danger. It is difficult to read much of its material without experiencing some sense of duress. But each of us adapts to such duress differently. While the prototypical democrat rejects the argument's central premise (often rejecting valid arguments along with the invalid ones), the authoritarian is inclined to recognize the fundamental theme and read on. Having accepted the premise than an illusive, dangerous conspiracy is afoot, the authoritarian must find a protector.

The Birch Tendency Toward Autocracy

The authoritarian character of the Society's argument becomes more evident when we examine Welch's alternative to communist enslavement. The democratic character would likely prefer a cooperative effort based upon functional abilities, while the authoritarian would look for leadership and protection.

Welch dismisses democracy as "merely a deceptive phrase, a weapon of demagoguery, and a perennial fraud (p. 147)," He observes that a republican form of government has "many attractions and advantages, under certain favorable circumstances. . .but it lends itself too readily to infiltration, distortion and disruption (p. 146)." That leaves autocracy: "The John Birch Society is to be a monolithic body [which] will operate under completely authoritative control at all levels (pp. 146-147)." This autocratic structure is necessary since "no collection of debating societies is ever going to stop the Communist conspiracy from taking us over. . .and we mean business every step of the way (p. 147)."

Welch's autocratic structure does not tolerate negotiations over control. The Society, he says, "cannot stop for parliamentary procedures or a lot of arguments among ourselves" because "we are now being more and more divided and deceived, by accepting within our walls more and more Trojan horses (p. 147)." Therefore, "we are not going to have factions developing on the two-sides-to-every-question theme (p. 149)." Thus, Welch offers his readers the prototypical authoritarian solution for danger: a strict autocratic relationship.

But the Society's hierarchy is not simply Welch above the membership. He explains that the Society:

> will function almost entirely through small local chapters, usually of from ten to twenty dedicated patriots. . . . Each will have a Chapter Leader *appointed by headquarters* . . . or appointed by officers in the field who have themselves been duly *appointed by headquarters* (p. 51, emphasis added).

Welch's description of the John Birch Society's organizational structure emphasizes the danger of the world, a preference for clearly ordered hierarchy in which all authority flows down from the Belmont, Massachusetts headquarters to the local chapters, and intolerance for dissension and democratic procedures. *Even if a democratic character should find Welch's alarmist worldview tempting, such a person would be psychologically repelled from* the Society because of its rigid, monolithic, autocratic structure. But an authoritarian tempted by the alarm would seek precisely this sort of autocracy for protection. Welch's organizational plan, therefore, meshes neatly with his alarm to entice the authoritarians and to repel democrats.

A second manifestation of the authoritarian tendency to hierarchy is the Society's generalization of superiority from external characteristics. The reader of the *Blue Book* is introduced to all 26 members of the Council positionally: a "Boston surgeon," a "worthy son of a famous 'free enterpriser' in the Northwest lumber industry," a "well-known and highly successful Texas businessman" and several corporate, religious, and military figures (p. 172). Not only does Welch fail to indicate the specific, functional relevance of their impressive credentials to an understanding of communism or conspiracies (for the benefit of democratic characters), but he explicitly states that the primary purpose of the Council is "to show the stature and standing of the leadership of the Society (p. 172)." Stature and standing are important to the authoritarian, but generally unimportant to the democrat. Again, the Council should attract authoritarians while avoiding the kind of appeal that could attract democrats.

In addition to stature, the John Birch Society tends to generalize superiority based upon one's willingness to acknowledge the danger and the solution (in this case Birchism). *Others are judged by their agreement or disagreement with Robert Welch*. Historian Oswald Spengler's work "fits the known facts of history" while Arnold Toynbee is a "meretricious hack . . . who is one of the worst charlatans that ever lived (p. 34)." Presidents Roosevelt, Truman, and Eisenhower all allegedly furthered the communists' goals because Welch disagreed with them.[14] Barry Goldwater and Ronald Reagan are applauded because they understand, while William F. Buckley and Russell Kirk are chastised because they do not.[15] This distinction serves to isolate members from the kind of two-sides-to-every-question controversy that Welch disdains. Metaphorically, anyone who fails to follow the safari leader endangers the whole safari. Yet the democratic character who fears communists might find some value in the thoughts of Buckley or Kirk. Welch appears to be stressing safety through autocracy rather than safety through conservatism. Let us turn our attention, then, to the nature of the autocratic relationship that he prescribes.

Birchist Sado-Masochism

The *Blue Book* is replete with references to communists' sadistic treatment of their followers. We are told of the communists' "police state features" that impose "brutal rule" and "slavery" upon "Party members who are wholly subservient (pp. 20, 17, 28, 60)." This is important because communism "has been imposed and must always be imposed, from the top down, by trickery and terror; and then it must be maintained by terror (p. 61)." This terror is directed not only at the slaves but at recalcitrant Party members themselves who "are shot in some dark alley or pushed off a subway platform in front of a moving train (p. 162)." Given this alarming picture of sadistic rule by the communists, the democratic character might reasonably expect Welch to offer an alternative of kindness, rather than brutality, of cooperation rather than slavery, of participation rather than subservience, and of bottom-up rather than top-down organization.

But Welch's alternative to sadistic communist domination is the Birch Society's organizational structure that *mirrors* the communist monolith. The Society is ordered from the top-down with members obeying official directives and subject to removal for non-compliance (p. 162). Indeed, Welch observes that:

> the biggest of all organizational mistakes is to set up a local group for some continuing purpose, exhort them to do a good job, and then leave them alone to do it. It is the leadership that is most demanding, most exacting of its followers not the one which asks the least and is afraid to ask more that achieves really dedicated support (p. 72).

Contrast conservative-authoritarian Welch's organizational philosophy with that of conservative-democrat Ronald Reagan: "Surround yourself with the best people you can find, delegate authority, and don't interfere as long as the policy you've decided upon is being carried out."[16] The difference between Welch and Reagan stems not from differences in their conservatism but from their differing conceptions of authority. In true sado-masochistic fashion, Welch stresses (1) the leader's responsibility to push his selfish, lazy, and stupid followers to their limits, (2) the followers' ecstatic submission to that direction, and (3) his ability to understand and to empathize with the followers pushed to their limits even though "he himself is not the bootlicker." It is important here that Welch argues not only that such leadership is effective (efficiency need not always be popular), but that it encourages "really dedicated support" rather than defection or mutiny. These tendencies are unlike anything in the democratic character, as evidenced by President Reagan's position.

Thus, the *Blue Book* suggests supplanting communist dominance with Welch's dominance until the quantity of government can be drastically reduced and a largely anarchistic polity created in which strength and protection determine survival.[17] This program functions psychologically for the authoritarian and is dysfunctional for the democratic character who prefers partnership. But the important point is that Welch's program parallels the psychological continuum of authoritarianism, rather than the political continuum running from freedom to control.

A second manifestation of the Birch Society's sado-masochism is the pattern of gratifications afforded members for following Welch. Whereas the democrat would look for functional, practical benefits, the authoritarian seeks submission to a protector. In this regard, Welch announces that:

> The men (sic) who join the John Birch Society during the next few months or few years are going to be doing so primarily *because they believe in me and in what I am doing*. . . . And we are going to use that [personal loyalty], like every other resource, to the fullest advantage that we can (p. 149).

Even the criterion for continued membership is loyal submission: "those members who cease to feel the necessary degree of loyalty can either resign or will be put out before they can build up any splintering following of their own inside the Society (p. 149)."

But on what basis is the potential Bircher expected to develop this deep personal loyalty to Welch? He explains his credentials as follows:

> with all my shortcomings, there wasn't anybody else on the horizon willing to give their whole lives to the job, with the determination and dedication I would put into it. . . . Whatever I have in me, of faith, dedication, energy, I intend to offer that leadership to all who are willing to help me (pp. 114-115).

Put simply, while others might have better functional credentials for fighting communists, we should attach ourselves to Robert Welch (and only to him) because he alone is obsessed with this safari. The quantity of work and the willingness to spend himself thoroughly are regarded as more important than either the kind or quality of work, or the efficiency or prudence of the effort.

Welch's demand for personal loyalty on the basis of his obsession is all the more startling when we recognize that his practical, functional credentials are quite impressive. But the reader of the *Blue Book* does not learn that Welch studied at the University of North Carolina, the U.S. Naval Academy, and Harvard Law School; nor that he wrote a primer on salesmanship and served in various official capacities for the National Association of Manufacturers.[18] These seemingly pertinent facts are not divulged until a short postscript to the second printing of the *Blue Book* (pp. 166-167). *The point here is that Welch, a master salesman,* could *have sold his leadership to democratic characters by stressing his functional expertise. Instead, he emphasized (whether intentionally or not) his energy, his commitment, his constant reading of communist materials, and his willingness to exercise authority, dominance, and control—a package highly attractive to authoritarian characters.*

Maslow explained that authoritarians revel in superior-inferior relationships. Inferiors know that they deserve to be controlled, while superiors find temporary satisfaction in the exercise of control. This theme pervades *The Blue Book of the John Birch Society* as Welch condemns communist control and offers only his own control as the alternative. He sells the necessity for "dynamic, personal leadership" and personal loyalty based primarily upon his compulsive-obsessive efforts and his readiness to punish those of dubious loyalty *rather than* on the basis of his notable, and apparently relevant, credentials. *Potential members are asked to join the John Birch Society not because it will succeed, not because its tactics are well-conceived, not because they can participate or shape its directions, but because they want to be personally loyal to Robert Welch.*

In summary, *The Blue Book of the John Birch Society* depicts a dangerous, threatening world in which ruthless conspirators abound. It suggests a monolithic, autocratic organization built around members' personal loyalty to one man on the basis of his dedication and energy. This organization to combat totalitarianism will, however, tolerate neither discussion nor parliamentary procedure, and anyone quibbling with the leader will be expelled. Thus, the John Birch Society may be said to exemplify all three major characteristics of the authoritarian character structure: a view of the world as a threatening place, a tendency toward hierarchy, and a sado-masochistic tendency.

The Authoritarian vs. Closed-Mind Theses Compared

Earlier in this chapter we suggested that the closed-mind thesis of Birchism's appeal did not fit the available data. Recall that the two problems with the closed-mind explanation were that (1) Grupp's survey of members indicated both ideological disappointment and continued membership, and (2) circulation of *American Opinion* increased dramatically (rather than decreased) during the anti-war belief dilemma.

Our authoritarian hypothesis suggests that people joined the Society because of their desire for the "dynamic, personal leadership" of Robert Welch—because they believed in *him* and in what *he* was doing. Unfortunately and surprisingly (given Welch's portrayal of member gratifications), Grupp failed to ask members whether their membership was attributable to Welch's personal leadership, and the nature of Grupp's questions prevents our drawing informed inferences about our hypothesis.

However, the authoritarian explanation offers two clearly measurable hypotheses regarding the belief dilemma. Since danger increases the need for protection, the belief dilemma should increase member's dependence on Welch for authoritative interpretations. This hypothesis is supported by the 68% increase in *American Opinion* circulation during the 1964-1966 belief dilemma. The second hypothesis is related to the first: when the danger subsides, the need for protection and leadership decreases. The circulation data reveal a decrease in *American Opinion* readership from 43,262 in 1966 to 37,835 in 1967 and 34,098 in 1968 following the resolution of the Vietnam War belief dilemma in 1966. After acquiring 18,000 new readers during the two-year belief dilemma, *American Opinion* lost 9,000 of them during the next two years. The circulation data lend considerably more support to the authoritarian explanation for Birchism than to the closed-mind explanation.

Conclusions

This analysis of the John Birch Society's central arguments suggests three conclusions. The first is that the Society's *Blue Book* depicts a threatening world and stresses the need for ecstatic submission to a dynamic, personal leader within an autocratic hierarchy—a depiction congruent with the archetypal authoritarian character structure and antithetical to the democratic character structure. Through this happy coincidence, Robert Welch in one rhetorical stroke (1) recruits the ardent, dedicated followers he needs and wants, (2) alienates potentially troublesome democrats, and (3) consolidates his recruits into a band of loyalists who will (4) become more, not less, reliant on him during times of ideological dissonance.

Second, the psychological gratifications provided for authoritarian characters by Welch permit his ironic and often contradictory arguments (the protection of freedom through dictatorial leadership, the protection of capitalism through non-competitive organization, and strength through submission). These arguments seem to require the authoritarian character's world view for proper completion: the protector determines and provides what the protected need for society. In this case, Welch's alarmist discourse reinforces the authoritarians' conviction that the world is dangerous, thereby increasing their need for a protector. Welch then offers his own form of demanding "dynamic, personal leadership" to fill that need. By creating a strong protector-protected relationship with these protector-hungry authoritarians, Welch reserves for himself the ability to resolve belief dilemmas for his followers—a loophole unavailable unless the belief system is derived from the protector-protected relationship. Indeed, belief dilemmas may lead to ideological defections, *unless* a leader like Robert Welch reconciles them.

If rhetoric serves the function of adjusting ideas to people and people to ideas (as Donald Bryant has suggested), then this chapter suggests that Welch's *Blue Book* message is clearly adapted to an archetypal personality type. It is likely to appeal to authoritarian types and to offend or alienate democratic character types.

It excludes from membership those persons most likely to disrupt it while gratifying the compulsive-obsessive workers who want to work diligently for a revered leader. The argument works for members so that members will work for their leader. These psychological gratifications offer a plausible explanation for the endurance of the Society during a period of declining visibility and political efficacy. We need to ascertain whether the Birch experience is typical of other organizations in this regard.

And third, this chapter has demonstrated that persuasive functions do not necessarily bear a linear relationship to social movement messages. It is possible for a leader to recruit, confront, and consolidate—all in one message. And whether Welch the salesman planned it that way or it simply reflects his own character, it seems clear that the John Birch Society's alarmist discourse is more than mere "paranoia"—it works for them, and it works well.

The net result is an organization with an authoritarian character. Not all members of the John Birch Society will fit precisely the description of the authoritarian character structure (it is only archetypal). But its message speaks to the authoritarian tendencies in each of us, creating for its members an organization which is probably still more authoritarian than most of its individual members because they are bound together by their shared mistrust of the world and their need for protection against it. Future research should investigate the interdependence of personality and the persuasive efforts of other social movements.

Endnotes

[1] In addition to Chapter 8, see Charles J. Stewart, "A Functional Approach to the Rhetoric of Social Movements," *Central States Speech Journal*, 31 (Winter, 1980), 298-305; Herbert W. Simons, "Requirements, Problems, and Strategies: A Theory of Persuasion for Social Movements," *Quarterly Journal of Speech*, 56 (February, 1970), 1-11; and Bruce E. Gronbeck, "The Rhetoric of Social-Institutional Change: Black Action at Michigan," *Explorations in Rhetorical Criticism*, G.P. Mohrmann, C.J. Stewart, and D.J. Ochs, eds. (University Park: Pennsylvania State University Press, 1973), 96-123.

[2] For background on the John Birch Society, see J. Allen Broyles, *The John Birch Society: Anatomy of a Protest* (Boston: Beacon Press, 1966); Gerald Schomp, *Birchism Was My Business* (New York: Macmillan, 1970); and two reports by the Anti-Defamation League of B'nai B'rith: Benjamin R. Epstein and Arnold Forster, *Report on the John Birch Society, 1966* (New York: Random House, 1966), and *The Radical Right: Report on the John Birch Society and Its Allies* (New York: Random House, 1967). Welch's account of Birch's life is presented in *The Life of John Birch* (Chicago: Henry Regnery, 1954). A more dispassionate and informative treatment is James Hefley and Marti Hefley, *The Secret File on John Birch* (Wheaton, IL: Tyndale House, 1980). By either account, Birch was a fundamentalist Baptist missionary in China who became involved in American intelligence operations during World War II. Despite his compatriots' efforts to restrain him, Birch seems to have displayed too much bravado in an encounter with a Chinese officer. Welch regards Birch as the first casualty in the final struggle against communism.

3 Stephen Earl Bennett, "Modes of Resolution of a 'Belief Dilemma' in the Ideology of the John Birch Society," *Journal of Politics*, 33 (1971), 735-772.

4 Circulation data are published in accordance with federal statute in the December issues of these publications. Circulation is the best index of Society membership since their rolls remain secret and their primary activities are educative. The dearth of published materials about the Society since 1971 reassures us that the data are not inflated by subscriptions from researchers.

5 Dale Leathers, "Belief-Disbelief Systems: The Communicative Vacuum of the Radical Right," in Mohrmann, Stewart, and Ochs, 131.

6 See Milton Rokeach, *The Open- and Closed-Mind* (New York: Basic Books, 1960), 39-51.

7 Leathers, 111.

8 Rokeach, 67.

9 Fred W. Grupp, "Personal Satisfaction Derived from membership in the John Birch Society," *Western Political Quarterly*, 24 (1971), 79-83; and "The Political Perspectives of Birch Society Members," *The American Right Wing*, Robert A. Schoenberger, ed. (Atlanta: Holt, Rinehart, and Winston, 1969), 83-118. Grupp's survey indicates that 62% joined for "ideological" reasons (only 21% found such satisfaction), 18% "to associate with like-minded people" (19% found it), 11% to become informed (16% found it), and 8% for political commitment (36% found this).

10 Bennett, 735-749.

11 See Abraham Maslow, "The Authoritarian Character Structure," *Journal of Social Psychology, 18 (1943), 401-411; Erich Fromm, Escape from Freedom*, (New York: Avon Library, 1965); and T.W. Adorno, Else Frenkel-Brunswik, Daniel J. Levinson, and R. Nevitt Sanford, *The Authoritarian Personality* (New York: Harper, 1950).

12 These characteristics are derived from Maslow's article, 403-411, unless otherwise noted.

13 Unless otherwise noted, all references to Welch or the John Birch Society's persuasion refer to Robert H.W. Welch, Jr., *The Blue Book of the John Birch Society*, (Belmont, MA: Western Islands, 1961).

14 Robert Welch, *The Politician*, (Belmont, MA: Belmont Publishing, 1963), see esp. 279.

15 Welch strongly supported the Goldwater candidacy as early as the 1958 organizational session (see 109). But Welch believed that the conspiracy had the political process rigged so as to prevent Goldwater's election. For his part, Goldwater was not a Welch supporter. After reading *The Politician*, Goldwater "urged him not to print it. I said I couldn't accept his theory that Ike was either a dunce and a dupe or a conscious sympathizer. Most of the John Birchers are patriotic, concerned, law-abiding, hardworking and productive. There are a few whom I call Robert Welchers, and these are the fanatics who regard everyone who doesn't totally agree with them as communist sympathizers." Barry Goldwater, *With No Apologies*, (New York: William Morrow, 1979), 119.

16 Ann Reilly Dowd, "What Managers Can Learn from Manager Reagan," *Fortune*, (September 15, 1986), 33-41. The same management philosophy was expressed during the first debate between Reagan and Mondale published in *The Weekly Compilation of Presidential Documents*, 20 (October 7, 1984), 1446.

17 Welch's utopia is a highly individualistic society epitomized by his slogan, "Less Government and More Responsibility" (117). The problem with government, he says, is neither its form nor its quality, but its quantity: "the increasing quantity of government

in all nations has constituted the greatest tragedy of the twentieth century" (123). If the authoritarian conceives of life as taking place in a jungle, then government represents civilization—which distorts the natural order of survival.

[18] Several sources (including *Who's Who*) have reported that Robert Welch served in important capacities with the National Association of Manufacturers during the 1950s. The N.A.M. disputes this contention, insisting that Mr. Welch was only one of some two hundred honorary officials and that he never held a position of responsibility in their organization. Personal correspondence with Dr. Jane Work, Department of Legislative Planning, National Association of Manufacturers, April 15, 1983.

Chapter 11

A Rhetoric of Transcendence

Pro-Life Responds to Pro-Choice

As a social movement challenges established norms, values, hierarchical relationships, symbols, and rhetorical strategies and as it proceeds from the genesis and social unrest stages to the enthusiastic mobilization stage, its newfound strength, "creates doubts about the legitimacy and morality of the establishment."[1] Established institutions cannot ignore this threat. Together with other resistance forces, they respond to the movement's provocations by challenging its fragile claim of legitimacy, means and ends, norms and values, and credibility.

Confrontations between institutional forces and social movements serve three essential functions. They establish the movement as a serious threat; they contrast the two collectives; and they reveal the ugly side of the establishment. Robert Cathcart claims that confrontation is "the necessary ingredient" for a social movement to come into being and to proceed with its cause, while Kenneth Burke notes that "drama requires a conflict."[2] As necessary as confrontation appears to be for social movements, however, its results are often a mixed bag of blessings and curses. Resistance rhetoric threatens the movement's existence by attacking its foundations: ideology, structure, and legitimacy. Unless it can develop an effective rebuttal strategy, the social movement may be pushed back to an earlier stage, may stall, or may perish.

A Rhetoric of Transcendence

Some social movements appear to rely heavily upon a "rhetoric of transcendence" to counter the persuasive efforts of institutions and resistance movements. In a rhetoric of transcendence, persuaders argue that a person, group, goal, thing, right, action, or proposal *surpasses*, is *superior* to, or was *prior* to others of its kind. When operating at the highest level of transcendence, persuaders claim that a goal or group, for instance, is superior to or greater than *all* of its kind. When operating at the lowest level of transcendence, persuaders claim that a goal or group is superior to or greater than *one* or *a few* of its kind.[3] Kenneth Burke writes that transcendence is "the building of a *terministic bridge* whereby one realm is *transcended* by being viewed *in terms of* a realm 'beyond it'."[4]

There appear to be four common points of comparison in establishing transcendence, Burke's terministic or language bridge: quantity (more-less), quality (good-bad), value (important-unimportant), and hierarchy (high-low).[5] A persuader bases an argument on "quantity," writes Kenneth Burke, when contending that one group is *larger than* a competing group or that one organization is *more inclusive* than one or more organizations with which it is identified.[6] For instance, a person advocating censorship may claim to speak for the American people that transcends political parties, special interest groups, or liberals. Leaders of an "industrial union" that is open to all workers may claim that their organization transcends a "trade union" that represents only one trade such as carpenters, plumbers, or control tower operators. Thus, many groups struggle to become the *largest* or *most inclusive* of all grass roots, people's, workers, professional, reform, or political organizations.

A persuader uses the point of "quality" when arguing that one goal, proposal, or strategy is *good* while a competing goal, proposal, or strategy is *bad* or *evil*. Truth is contrasted with falsehood, justice with injustice, freedom with slavery, equality with inequality, nonviolence with violence, rationality with irrationality, reason with emotion. Aristotle noted many centuries ago, however, that "it often happens that people agree that two things are both useful but do not agree about which is the more so, the next step will be to treat of relative goodness and relative utility."[7] Thus, a persuader may contend that one proposal promises a *greater Good* than a competing proposal or that one strategy is *less evil* than another strategy. Debaters, litigants, and legislators often argue about "comparative advantages" or "comparative disadvantages" of proposals and actions. For instance, persons warning of the potential catastrophic results of acid rain may recognize that solutions will cause economic hardships for some companies and workers, or persons advocating censorship of textbooks or gun control measures may admit that their proposals will place some limits on our constitutional rights. The potential benefits, however, far outweigh the potential harms.

A persuader uses the point of "value" when arguing that a group's *ends* are so important that *any means* (invective, dishonesty, obscenity, espionage, disruptions, violence, terrorism) is justified or that the need to meet a crisis takes *precedence over factional differences*. For example, government agencies use "national security" to justify spying on American citizens and the issuance of "disinformation." Political parties use "for the good of the people" to justify dirty campaign tricks. And "revolutionary" social movements use "freedom" and "independence" to justify bombings, assassinations, and terrorism.

A persuader bases an argument on "hierarchy," according to Kenneth Burke, when attempting to establish that one thing, act, right, or ideal exceeds another because it is of a *higher order* along a gradation or continuum: human above animal, spiritual over temporal, supernatural over natural, universal over the individual or local.[8] Scientists, for example, argue that it is ethical to experiment on *animals* because these experiments will eventually help to save the lives of *humans*, a higher order of life. Persons of particular religious organizations may refuse to recite the "Pledge of Allegiance" or to go to war for a country because these human, political acts violate religious principles that are of a higher order. The notion of "hierarchy" is a versatile argumentative tactic for collectives such as social movements. For instance, if a member or leader does something to discredit the movement, a persuader might argue that the "power of truth" for which the movement is fighting "transcends the limitations of the personal agent who propounds it."[9] To counteract feelings of guilt or accusations of blame for the consequences of a movement's actions, a persuader might argue that the act was not an "inferior kind of crime" (breaking-and-entering, trespassing, petty theft, vandalism) but a "transcendent kind of crime" actually "required by traditional values" or to further a just cause.[10]

The strategy of transcendence, then would seem to provide social movements with a variety of lines of argument for defending organizations, enhancing positions, and avoiding the necessity of denying the undeniable. This strategy may strengthen a movement's support among "the people" and important legitimizers because it refutes the opposition by identifying the movement (including its prescribed course of action, mobilization efforts, and claims to legitimacy) symbolically with what is large, good, important, and of the highest order in society. Kenneth Burke writes:

> Hence, to some degree, solution of conflict must always be done purely in the symbolic realm (by "transcendence") if it is to be done at all. Persons of moral and imaginative depth require great enterprise and resourcefulness in such purely "symbolic" solutions of conflict (by the formation of appropriate "attitudes").[11]

In the remainder of this chapter, we will illustrate the rhetoric of transcendence by analyzing the persuasive efforts of the pro-life movement to respond to rhetorical attacks by the pro-choice resistance movement. These attacks have posed major dilemmas for pro-life persuaders.

The Abortion Issue

"Right-to-life" committees formed in several states during the late 1960s to resist efforts to liberalize laws governing abortion. But on January 22, 1973, the United States Supreme Court dealt this fledgling resistance movement an "unqualified legal defeat."[12] The Court, in *Roe v. Wade*, decided (1) that a woman's constitutional right of privacy precludes a state from prohibiting her from obtaining an abortion on demand during the first trimester of pregnancy, (2) that a state could regulate abortions during the second trimester only for the purpose of protecting the woman's life, and (3) that a state could regulate abortions during the third trimester to preserve the life of the child.[13] Thus, the Court viewed *fetal life* as *human* only after the first six months of pregnancy.

Right-to-life groups recovered quickly from the shock of this unexpected defeat and began to create a "pro-life" revivalistic movement, guided primarily by the National Right to Life Committee, Inc., to make abortion unlawful once again and to reaffirm society's respect for human life. The solution and the means of obtaining it were a constitutional amendment defining human life as beginning at the moment of conception and prohibiting the termination of a *child's* life except in situations in which the *mother's* life is in *certain* danger. This amendment would overturn the Supreme Court decision and preclude further court and legislative actions (state and national) to liberalize abortion. The National Right to Life Committee, state affiliates, Baptists for Life, and allied groups began at once to mobilize massive political pressure from the "grass roots level" to move an amendment through the Congress and eventually through two-thirds of the state legislatures.

Pro-Choice Confronts Pro-Life

"Pro-Choice" organizations such as the National Abortion Rights Action League and the Religious Coalition for Abortion Rights (along with allies such as Planned Parenthood and the National Organization for Women) have defended the Supreme Court decision and countered the persuasive efforts of the pro-life movement. "Safe, legal abortion," pro-choice advocates argue, is both "something personal" and a "constitutional right."[14] The belief that abortion is murder because the fertilized egg is a person, they contend, "is a theological belief, not a biological fact," and this theological belief "is not shared by the majority of Jewish and Christian denominations."[15] In fact, they point out, it is "a religious belief held by the Roman Catholic Church."[16] Pro-choice sources warn that since abortion is a religious issue and since *most* religious groups favor legal abortion, an amendment restricting access to abortion would be a serious "infringement on the First Amendment principles of separation of church and state."[17] The pro-life movement is depicted as a coalition of a "few small Protestant denominations and Orthodox Judaism," "radical right wing forces," "the electric churchmen," "anti-women's rights organizations" and, above all, the Roman Catholic Church and its hierarchy that act as the force and orchesrator behind the movement.[18] A "Handful of people," a pro-choice newspaper advertisement warns, wants "to impose their religious views on everyone."[19]

The controversy over abortion has become ugly at times as elements of pro-life have resorted to violent and non-violent actions. Pro-choice has branded all pro-life supporters as "anti-choice fanatics" who "in a frenzy amounting to hysteria" have resorted to arson, shootings, bombings, vandalism, assaults, disruptions, and kidnappings. Such actions, one source concludes "prove just how little is really meant by the 'right to life' catch-phrase."[20]

Pro-choice resistance poses serious rhetorical dilemmas for pro-life persuaders. For example, an attack on the constitutional rights of women to choose an abortion would enhance the image of pro-life as reactionary and anti-women's rights, but failure to respond might result in a no-win stand-off between equal constitutional rights. The pro-life movement must resolve the separation of church and state issue, but it cannot deny the "moral" nature of the abortion issue because individuals and organizations tend to support the movement on "moral" grounds. The pro-life movement must answer incessant charges that it is a small, Catholic-run movement allied with a few right-wing groups devoted to single-issue politics, but it cannot deny the abundant and growing evidence of Roman Catholic and right-wing involvement (particularly the Rev. Jerry Falwell and his "Moral Majority" and the efforts in Congress of Senator Jesse Helms of North Carolina) without being transparently deceitful and running the risk of splintering the movement. Neither can the movement accept nor ignore these charges because it needs a broad base of support to exert pressure on Congress and state legislatures. Finally, the pro-life movement must refute charges of fanaticism, but simple denial is impossible and efforts to suppress elements might lead to further factionalizing of the movement at a critical time in its crusade.

Pro-Life Responds to Pro-Choice

The heart of pro-life rhetoric is the attempt to establish that the fetus, regardless of age, is a *human being*. Leaflets such as "Love and Let Live" and "We Care, We Love, We Are Pro-Life" include pictures of fetuses and chronological charts that demonstrate how quickly an identifiable and functioning human being (always referred to as a child or a baby) comes into existence after conception. Accounts by nurses and physicians relating instances when they had to starve, smother, or bash in the head of an aborted fetus because it refused to die often accompany gory, full-color pictures of tiny bodies in buckets and trash cans and decimated bodies resulting from various types of abortion.[21] Perhaps the most spectacular and controversial effort to show life and death in the womb is the film and video entitled "The Silent Scream" that purports to show the struggle for life of a fetus being "murdered" by an abortion procedure. Joseph Scheidler, founder and director of the Pro-Life Action League, often narrates the struggle of the fetus in "The Silent Scream" against a vacuum aspirator: "She retreats frantically from the device. But it pulls her legs off. Then it disembowels her. She struggles violently with her arms. Her head falls back; her mouth opens in anguish."[22]

Pro-life leaflets and pamphlets quote medical, legal, philosophic, and scientific authorities to prove that life begins at conception.[23] A "President's Report" to the membership of the Indiana Right to Life organization following successful state and congressional elections in 1978 underscores the importance of rhetorical efforts to establish the fetus as a human being: "Once people are aware that the heart of an unborn child beats at just 18 days after conception and that 'termination of pregnancy' really refers to 'abortion,' not birth, then people want to know what they can do to restore protection to the unborn child."[24] Scheidler of the Pro-Life Action League contends that if he could show "The Silent Scream" on network television, the debate over abortion would end in one week.[25]

Pro-life's gruesome accounts, narratives, pictures, and videos are not merely efforts to play upon audience emotions or to bypass "rational" debate. For, if pro-life can persuade audiences that the fetus is a *human being* and not a *thing*, then it has established the premise upon which it bases much of its persuasion—that abortion violates the most basic and fundamental of human rights: the Right to Life. This premise places the right to life at the pinnacle of the human rights hierarchy and allows pro-life to argue from the highest level of transcendence. Persuaders refer to the right to life as an inalienable right that cannot be abridged and cite the 5th and 14th Amendments as support. Full-page newspaper advertisements entitled "A Declaration of Respect for Life" headlines the second paragraph of the Declaration of Independence: "We hold these truths to be self-evident, that all men are created equal; that they are endowed by their Creator with certain unalienable rights; that among these are life, liberty, and the pursuit of happiness."[26] Leaflets and newspapers cite Thomas Jefferson's statement that "The care of human life and happiness—and not their destruction—is the first and only legitimate object of good government," and Albert Schweitzer's declaration, "If a man loses his reverence for any part of life—he will lose his reverence for all of life."[27] The right to life is placed at the pinnacle of several hierarchies: "the most basic value of our society," "our first civil right," the "absolute value" or "root" of western culture, the Indo-European tradition, of all civilized society, and a God-given right that transcends all civil law.[28]

A Contrasting of Rights

Although pro-life persuaders may fail to see (or choose to ignore) the contradictions in their hierarchical potpourri, they draw attention to federal and state laws designed to guarantee lesser rights or the rights of lower beings—a combination *value* and *hierarchy* argument. For example, one writer notes that state laws guarantee "the right of inheritance, to damages received while yet unborn, to get a blood transfusion over the mother's objection, to have a guardian appointed, and other rights of citizenship" but not the "most basic right of all—the right to life."[29]

While pro-life persuaders rarely argue against women's rights, they often question the limitations and hierarchical order of these rights. For instance, a publication entitled "The Abortion Connection," exclaims that in contrast to the right to life, "There is **no** 'constitutional' right of abortion. There is only a Supreme Court-created right from the split-decision in *Roe v. Wade* on January 22, 1973."[30] In a leaflet bearing a picture of an unborn but fully developed fetus and entitled *Is This Life Worth a Postage Stamp?* the author asks, "But do her [the woman's] rights include dealing out a death sentence to another human being who is completely defenseless?"[31] This point appears to be a reverse value argument: the end (preserving a woman's right of privacy) does not justify the means (depriving the unborn child of the right to life). Pro-life persuaders frequently compare the woman's need or right to solve a "personal" or "social" problem with the unborn child's right to live: both are good but the right to life is a far greater good. The author of a leaflet entitled *The U.S. Supreme Court Has Ruled It's Legal to Kill a Baby*, asks: "Have we ever, in a civilized society given to one person (the mother) the complete right to kill another (the baby) in order to solve the first person's personal problem?" When pro-life persuaders address the possibility that a pro-life amendment might force women to turn to dangerous illegal abortions, they argue (based on the notion of transcendent quality) that death due to "tragic" illegal abortions is a lesser evil than "the extermination of well over 1,000,000 unborn babies yearly in the U.S. alone."[32] Two recent pro-life posters encapsulate the struggle over rights: "Equal Rights for Unborn Women" and "Half the People Entering Abortion Clinics Never Come Out Alive."[33]

The ultimate paradox, according to pro-life persuaders, is American concern for animal life and not human life. In Newspaper advertisements entitled "Eagles, Beagles, Babies and 'There Oughta Be a Law,'" there are large pictures of a bald eagle, two beagle puppies, and an unborn fetus. A caption reads: "Ours is a peculiar society. We have laws protecting wildlife and dogs, but not defenseless human beings.[34] The advertisements report that stealing one eagle egg may result in a $5,000 fine, one year in jail, or both and that both houses of congress overwhelmingly approved a federal law prohibiting the use of dogs in tests of chemical, biological, or radioactive warfare materials. While these laws protect the life and rights of eagles and beagles, the advertisements note, "Last year... more than 1,000,000 unborn babies were 'terminated' through 'abortion on demand.' Terminated means killed. Killed without penalty. Unless someone got a parking ticket in front of an abortion mill." The line of argument is clear: Although the United States has laws to protect the rights of privacy, to solve personal problems, and to protect animal life, there are no laws to guarantee the *human* right to life—the right at the pinnacle of the rights hierarchy.

In Defense of the Movement

Pro-life persuaders also rely upon a rhetoric of transcendence to explain and defend their movement. A common charge (particularly during political campaigns) is that the pro-life movement is devoted to a single issue when the nation and its leaders are facing a multitude of problems, including hunger, war, ecological disaster, and nuclear holocaust. The movement cannot deny its "one-issue" stance because it has campaigned against many senators and congressmen on the basis of their abortion position alone, so it turns to a rhetoric of transcendence and handy points of comparison. For example, an "Indiana Right to Life Political Action Committee" report counters this accusation by arguing that abortion transcends other *unquestioned* single issues:

> Many pro-life people have been labeled "single issue voters." This is meant to charge them with being narrow-minded and other things.
>
> **But: think again.**
>
> Would you vote for: members of Congress who in the past have been indicted for misuse of public funds (remember no one was killed)?—or did that disqualify them from holding public office?
>
> Would you vote for: a candidate who would do nothing to stop, or who would endorse legal child abuse or torture?—or would that disqualify him or her from holding office?
>
> Then would you vote for: any person running for public office who either agrees with, who has publicly stated that he or she will do nothing to stop, or will resist any effort to stop the killing of over one million innocent pre-born babies a year?—or does such active (or passive) approval of this killing disqualify such a person from holding office?[35]

Thus, this single issue—abortion—transcends other single issues that society would readily accept as justification for voting against a candidate because it is of greater value or worth. Nancy Koster, editor of the *Minnesota Citizens Concerned for Life Newsletter* used several analogies to answer the "one-issue" charge: "If your house were on fire, would you rush out for shingles to fix its leaky roof? Or if your son was hit by a car, would you stop on the way to the hospital so your daughter could visit the dentist?"[36] "Of course not," she replied, "You would set priorities—stop the blaze, save the dying child. Everyone would understand and share your priorities." "In America today," she concluded, our house is on fire and our children are dying. If we don't set the right priorities, the killing will continue and the blaze will spread."

Pro-life persuaders often compare abortion to the single issue that people readily accept as perhaps the greatest concern—war. A leaflet entitled *The Fact of Death*, written by Gilbert Durand, declares that "The #1 killer is not *war*. The #1 killer is abortion!"[37] "In 1972 alone," Durand claims, "more babies were killed by 'legal' abortion in California than were American servicemen killed in the Vietnam, Korean, Spanish, Mexican, 1812, and Revolutionary wars put together." "If you are concerned about war," he concludes, "be *more* concerned about abortion." Newspaper advertisements on July 4, 1978 entitled "American War Casualties," include one cross for each 25,000 people killed in the Revolutionary War, Civil War, World War I, World War II, Korean War, Vietnam War, and "War on the unborn." The crosses for the unborn overwhelm the World War II crosses in second place 200 to 22.[38] Abortion, then, transcends war in the hierarchy of killers because of the quantity of deaths.

As the pro-life movement has expanded its ideology to include infanticide, euthanasia, and protection of the "less than perfect," its persuaders have increasingly countered the "single-issue" charge by noting that the movement is not *merely* anti-abortion. The pro-life movement, they contend, is "striving to retain the dignity of human life in all stages" from inception to the grave and to "guarantee equal protection and due process of law for all human beings."[39] Thus, the movement's concerns are greater than or more inclusive than (using the argumentative point of quantity) a single issue, even a life or death issue such as abortion.

Pro-life rhetoric does not confront directly the highly important controversy over separation of church and state. Instead, it addresses such questions as, "Is abortion a religious issue?" One leaflet, captioned "Aborted Baby Discarded in a Hospital Bucket," contains the answer in bold print: **"Abortion is a human issue—not just a religious one."**[40] A typical answer appears in a leaflet entitled "Life or Death":

> Theology certainly concerns itself with respect for human life. It must turn to science, however, to tell it when life begins. The question of abortion is a basic human question that concerns the entire civilized society in which we live. It is not just a Catholic, or Protestant, or Jewish issue. It is a question of who lives or dies.[41]

Thus, persuaders infer that since the concern for life transcends (is more inclusive than) "theology" and "religious denominations" and is not, therefore, merely a religious issue, the movement's actions and demands do not infringe upon the principle of separation of church and state. Pro-life rhetoric enhances this inference by relying upon non-religious medical, scientific, and philosophic sources for support. Only two leaflets out of dozens studied were religiously oriented to any extent. Quotations from scripture and clergy rarely appear in pro-life literature. In twenty-eight issues of Indiana's Right to Life monthly newspaper, *The Communicator*, clergy appear in only two pictures and are authors of only three brief articles. "God" or "the Lord" is alluded to in less than a half-dozen issues. In 1977 the National Right to Life Committee listed no clergy among its officers, its Executive Committee, or its fifty-three member Board of Directors. The reader of pro-life literature must look very closely to detect any link between religion and the abortion issue or religion and the movement. This use of "transcendence" seems dangerously close to placing the natural (human life) above the supernatural (theology and religion). Apparently pro-life persuaders and followers perceive theology and religion to be inherently human or organizational concerns and, hence, lower on the hierarchical scale than "life."

The pro-life movement uses this same method of transcendent argument—based on quantity or inclusiveness—in responses to accusations that it is a Roman Catholic movement in disguise. In a letter dated January 16, 1978, Bishop Raymond J. Gallagher urged members of the Roman Catholic Diocese of Lafayette in Indiana to observe Respect Life Sunday, and he declared:

> In observing this date I ask the interest of all Catholic people to this issue, not because it is a pet project of the Roman Catholic Church in the United States but because it deals with a right and value so fundamental that it goes beyond any sectarian theological objective.[42]

An editorial in *The Communicator* entitled "The Right to Life—A Catholic Issue and a *catholic* Issue" exclaims: "The right to life *is* a Catholic issue. . . . but it is even more a *catholic* issue, for what would be more universal than the sanctity of human life?"[43] This editorial and other sources cite teachings and support of other religious and non-religious groups (Baptists for Life, Democrats for Life, Clergy for Life, and Nurses Concerned for Life) to show the pro-life movement is *larger* and more *inclusive* than the resistance rhetoric of the pro-choice movement would lead people to believe—an argument based on quantity.

Similarly, pro-life literature argues by implication that the movement transcends—is larger than—the Roman Catholic Church. Fliers mailed to homes and distributed at fairs, churches, and shopping centers describe pro-life organizations as "non-denominational" and "a non-profit, non-sectarian group of concerned citizens." Pro-life writers refer to the movement as a "great people's movement," "the largest grassroots citizen's movement in recent history," and a "majority movement."[44] Members of the movement are "some of the finest minds in the country," "people from all across the country and in every walk of life," and "moms, dads, business people, retired people and children."[45] Full-page newspaper advertisements containing hundreds of names of local "concerned citizens... who are opposed to abortion" suggest widespread support among all types of people although the majority of names are solicited after Sunday masses at Roman Catholic churches. Donations, membership fees, and requests for materials are never sent to religious organizations, let alone a Catholic church. The value of non-clerical national, state, and local organizations is obvious. In twenty-eight issues of *The Communicator*, there was not one picture of a Catholic priest, only one article by a Catholic priest, and occasional small news items about events at Catholic churches or schools. People (particularly politicians) and events at non-Catholic churches and non-religious events such as marches, demonstrations, meetings with legislators, and right to life conventions dominate the newspaper. Only one leaflet out of dozens studied can be described as Catholic. Increasing emphasis in the pro-life movement on concern for the crippled, the aged, and the infirm—and not just abortion—may help to disassociate the movement from the Catholic Church. While abortion has a long association with the Church, infanticide and euthanasia do not. Thus, the reader of pro-life literature is given the clear message that the movement is *far larger* and *more inclusive* than Roman Catholicism. This notion of transcendence was epitomized in the headline announcing the 1987 convention of the National Right to Life Committee: "WE THE PEOPLE. . . Working to Restore Protection for Life in the Constitution."[46]

The claim that the pro-life movement transcends the Roman Catholic Church has always been true to the extent that Catholic and non-Catholic lay people have outnumbered and outperformed the Roman Catholic hierarchy in the movement, but it becomes truer each year as non-Catholic denominations, television evangelists, political groups, and conservative politicians have joined the cause. When the United States Senate defeated an anti-abortion constitutional amendment in June, 1983, the director of the Life Amendment Political Action Committee (one of many new groups that are challenging established movement leadership) accused the National Right to Life Committee and the National Conference of Catholic Bishops of handing "the pro-life movement the greatest single legislative setback in its 10-year history" and of driving "a mammoth wedge into the movement itself."[47] Public involvement of these recent recruits in the movement and vocal in-fighting prove that the pro-life movement transcends the Roman Catholic Church, but it also supports pro-choice claims that the movement is strongly allied with (perhaps being taken over by?) right wing political groups, anti-women's rights organizations, and the electric churchmen (television evangelists). Thus, this transcendent argument would seem to be of dubious value to the pro-life movement, particularly the National Right to Life Committee.

Perhaps the greatest rhetorical dilemma facing the "pro-life" movement centers on its growing militancy that led during the 1980s not only to sit-ins, demonstrations, and harassment of abortion clinic personnel and clients but to vandalism, arson, bombings, and kidnapping. Pro-life persuaders cannot deny the sometimes violent acts of their fellow true believers (29 bombings and arsons were committed in the name of the movement in 1984 alone), nor can they unconditionally condemn such acts and their perpetrators without the risk of further factionalizing the movement.[48] Some pro-life spokespersons and organizations take this risk, however. For example, a consortium of right-to-life groups in New York offered a $5,000 reward for information leading to those responsible for bombing an abortion clinic, and the Reverend Jerry Falwell (leader of the Moral Majority) called violent elements "common criminals" and warned that violence does "great damage to the anti-abortion cause."[49] Some leaders of major pro-life organizations deny that their members have committed violent acts and urge members to refrain from violence. Dr. J.C. Willke, President of the National Right to Life Committee, issued this appeal to supporters of the movement: "Let us witness peacefully in work, in picketing, by sit-ins, in letters, by prayers, and at the ballot box. It is they who live by violence and the modern sword, the suction curvette. Violence is not our way."[50]

Although a number of movement leaders and followers condemn violence perpetrated in support of the pro-life cause, others use at least six different arguments based on transcendence to justify the new militance of the movement or to explain why they cannot condemn it. First, persuaders vindicate militant pro-lifers because militants allegedly defend *higher principles* and do not act through self-interest. A writer in the *National Right to Life News* claims "the appeal of the pro-life movement is to those principles of justice and nondiscrimination which transcend self-seeking."[51] Second, pro-life apologists argue that violence for *noble purposes* transcends violence for ignoble purposes and, thus, is acceptable. Cal Thomas of the Moral Majority compares pro-life violence with the civil rights riots of the 1960s and concludes that both were "equally wrong, but served a higher and nobler purpose in that they moved lethargic government leaders to action."[52] Third, persuaders argue that militance is justified in defense of a *higher law*. For example, Monsignor Thomas C. Corrigan defended the "Cleveland Eleven" by contending that when "the laws of God (which say abortion is wrong) are in opposition to the laws of man (which say abortion is legal), people are justified in siding with the Gospels and challenging man-made laws."[53] Fourth, persuaders claim that the *end justifies or transcends the means*. During his trial for trespassing in an abortion clinic sit-in, Daniel Avila of Fort Wayne, Indiana, declared that "when life or property is in danger. . .a person does have a right to go in. He has a right to attempt in a reasonable manner to stop the destruction of life or property."[54] The Cleveland Eleven, arrested for disrupting an abortion clinic, concluded, "It's a small price to pay in view of the millions of lives annually being snuffed out."[55] Fifth, persuaders argue that *lesser violence* is justified if it stops a *greater violence*. Jan Carroll of the National Right to Life Committee refuses to apologize for violence because "violence that goes on inside the clinic is much more damaging to the moral fiber of the nation."[56] And sixth, pro-life persuaders contend that *extraordinary circumstances* justify violent means that are ordinarily considered unacceptable in society. Elsie Lewis, active in the American Life League, explains that:

> For the most part, where there is an unjust law, you obey it, and you try to change it. But when they are killing two million babies a year—it is so heinous an injustice. While working to change the law, many lives are being lost. Since 1973 a holocaust has been going on . . . . If you believe that an abortuary is murdering thousands of babies and thirty are scheduled for tomorrow, how can you condemn someone for destroying it?[57]

Thus, pro-life persuaders defend militant tactics by using six lines of argument that develop three of the four points of comparison that establish transcendence: hierarchy (higher principles, higher law), quality (noble purposes, lesser crime or evil), and value (end over means, extraordinary circumstances). These points of comparison allow persuaders both to condemn and to praise militant actions and thereby to answer challenges of the pro-choice opposition and to avoid factionalizing the movement over choice of tactics. Violence, like war, is generally to be condemned, but there are circumstances when violence is the lesser of two evils and is the only viable course of action. After all, many pro-life persuaders contend, they are soldiers in a war on the unborn.

Conclusions

The pro-life movement relies heavily upon a rhetoric of transcendence to resolve dilemmas created by the resistance rhetoric of the pro-choice movement. Pro-life persuaders base their refutations on the premise that the right to life is at the pinnacle of the human rights hierarchy—the most fundamental, God-given right that transcends all other rights, values, and laws. With this premise as a basis, they do not deny the woman's rights of privacy, control over her body, or to resolve personal or social problems, but using the points of quality, value, and hierarchy, pro-life persuaders argue that the right to life is a greater good, is of more worth, and is uppermost in the hierarchy of rights. Employing the points of quality and quantity, they see *potential* deaths due to illegal abortions as a lesser evil than the greater number of deaths that *are occurring* through legal abortions, and they argue that the end—guaranteeing women's rights—does not justify the means—killing unborn children. Pro-life advocates, basing arguments on value and hierarchy, decry the laws of a society that protect lesser rights and the rights of lower forms of life—eagles and beagles—while denying superior rights to superior beings—humans.

Pro-life responds to attacks on the movement by arguing that its "single issue" is more inclusive than abortion (quantity), is more important than other readily accepted single issues such as political corruption and child abuse (value), and involves more deaths than war which appears at the top of the list of national and personal concerns (quantity and hierarchy). Persuaders refute charges that their movement violates the principle of separation of church and state and is a small band of right wing fanatics led by the hierarchy of the Roman Catholic Church by arguing and implying that the movement's concerns and membership are larger than and more inclusive than religion or theology and the Roman Catholic Church or the political-religious right wing in this country (quantity). The issue of life and death, they argue, is more important and supersedes the principle of separation of church and state (value and hierarchy). Pro-life persuaders defend the growing militancy of their movement by noting that trespassing and disruptions are lesser evils than abortion (quality), that the end—to save millions of lives—takes precedence over means (value), and that God's laws protecting human life surpass man-made laws governing trespassing and nonviolent resistance (hierarchy).

Pro-life's efforts to gain "terministic control" in the struggle over abortion are critical in the movement's arguments from transcendence. For example, calling the fetus (a low form of life) a baby or child (the highest form of life) allows the movement to develop its major premise that abortion destroys tiny beings who are human from the moment of conception. Calling abortion (an amoral, routine medical procedure) killing or murder (an immoral, brutal, premeditated act) allows the movement to argue from the highest levels of principle, ethics, law, and morality. And calling the struggle an effort to end the "war on the unborn" and the "American holocaust" allows the movement to justify its single-issue politics and militant actions because "war" permits the righteous to use any means to achieve noble ends: saving millions of lives and preserving the moral fiber of the nation.

The pro-life movement's rhetoric of transcendence is a fragile interdependent network of premises based on a major premise that is denied by the opposition and questioned by many, including movement sympathizers. This premise is that a *human being* exists from the *moment of conception*. If the recipient of a pro-life message questions or denies this premise, the network of transcendent arguments crumbles. A *non-human* fetus, a thing, does *not* have an inalienable right to life and is *not* above and perhaps is below some animals or things. Therefore, the *woman's* rights (a human's rights) are transcendent, and the issue appears to be *religious*, not political or legal. Thus, political activities on behalf of a "human life" amendment would give credence to the claim that the movement is threatening the principle of separation of church and state. Appeals to God's laws are irrelevant.

Pro-life arguments often *imply* or *assume* transcendence rather than state it overtly. This would seem to be a wise strategy. For some audiences, the mere mention of the separation of church and state issue or the Roman Catholic connection (particularly in areas of the country with anti-Catholic feelings) would endanger the acceptance of the argument. An implicative strategy is risky, however, because some audiences may not detect the implication or, worse yet, may perceive the implication as a clever deception. A rhetoric of transcendence, particularly an implied transcendence, may be less effective with audiences that know little about the issue or have been exposed to pro-choice counter rhetoric.

A rhetoric of transcendence would seem to be a highly functional rhetorical strategy for the pro-life movement and for other social movements as well. For example, social movements take "moralistic" stances portraying their causes and members as being *above* or *superior* to established norms, values, and institutions. Social movements also suffer from limited resources and thus often find it difficult to *prove* that an institution, norm, or value is utterly without value. A rhetoric of transcendence allows a movement to address *degrees* of size, importance, goodness, or risk. For instance, a social movement need not establish that it, its cause, or its methods are without flaw but only that it is larger than counter rhetoric claims, that it is more honorable than established institutions, that its plan is safer than current policies, or that its tactics are less evil than ones employed by police or regulatory agencies. Social movements must also strive to maintain unity among supporters of the cause and to attract support from the public, legitimizers, and established institutions. A rhetoric of transcendence allows a movement, or a faction of a movement, to stress its superiority without having to destroy other factions or antagonize institutions that might be potential allies. Thus, the movement may reduce the risk of factionalizing the movement or of scaring away potential supporters.

This chapter has illustrated how the pro-life movement has employed a rhetoric of transcendence—arguing from the points of quantity, quality, value and hierarchy—to resolve major rhetorical dilemmas posed by pro-choice resistance rhetoric and has noted potential values of this persuasive strategy for social movements. More studies are needed to see if and how other social movements have used this strategy. Such studies will add to our knowledge of persuasion and social movements as well as the rhetoric of transcendence.

Endnotes

1 Robert S. Cathcart, "Defining Social Movements by Their Rhetorical Form," *Central States Speech Journal*, 31 (Winter, 1980), 271.

2 Robert S. Cathcart, "New Approaches to the Study of Social Movements," *Western Speech Communication Journal*, 36 (Spring, 1972), 88; Kenneth Burke, "Catharsis—Second View," *Centennial Review*, 5 (1961), 130; Leland M. Griffin, "A Dramatistic Theory of the Rhetoric of Movements," *Critical Responses to Kenneth Burke*, William Rueckert, ed., (Minneapolis: University of Minnesota Press, 1969), 456.

3 These levels are apparent in Kenneth Burke's usage of the term transcendence and many synonyms in *Roget's International Thesaurus* (New York: Crowell, 1958), entries 33.5 and 33.8.

4 Kenneth Burke, *Language as Symbolic Action* (Berkeley: University of California Press, 1966), 187.

5 Marcus Tullius Cicero, *Topics*, trans. H.M. Hubbell (Cambridge: Harvard University Press, 1959), 433; Kenneth Burke, *A Rhetoric of Motives* (Berkeley: University of California Press, 1969), 231.

6 Burke, *Rhetoric of Motives*, pp. 11-12; Kenneth Burke, *Dramatism and Development* (Barre, MA: Clark University Press, 1972), 23-24.

7 Aristotle, *The Rhetoric*, trans. W. Rhys Roberts (New York: Modern Library, 1954), Book I, 1362a37-b2 and 1363b5-13. See also Karl R. Wallace, *Francis Bacon on Communication and Rhetoric* (Chapel Hill: University of North Carolina Press, 1943), 60-65.

8 Kenneth Burke, *A Grammar of Motives* (Berkeley: University of California Press, 1969), 424, 425, and 428; Burke, *Rhetoric of Motives*, 14, 16, 76, and 138; Kenneth Burke, *The Rhetoric of Religion* (Berkeley: University of California Press, 1970), 58, 83, and 156.

9 Burke, *Rhetoric of Motives*, 76.

10 Burke, *Rhetoric of Religion*, 230; Barry Brummett, "Burkeian Scapegoating, Mortification, and Transcendence in Political Campaign Rhetoric," *Central States Speech Journal*, 32 (Winter, 1981), 256 and 259.

11 Kenneth Burke, *The Philosophy of Literary Form* (Berkeley: University of California Press, 1973), 312.

12 Richard D. Orlaski, "Abortion: Legal Questions and Legislative Alternatives," *America*, 10 Aug. 1974, 50.

13 United States Supreme Court Reports, vol. 35 (Rochester, NY: Lawyers Co-Operative Publishing Company, 1974), 147-149.

14 "Abortion Is Our Right," (ad.) *Newsweek*, 29 Oct. 1979, n. pag.; "In 1982, If You Have a Miscarriage, You Could Be Prosecuted for Murder," (ad.) Lafayette, Indiana *Journal and Courier*, 26 May 1981, B-4.

15 *Religious Coalition for Abortion Rights: What is RCAR?* (Washington, DC: Religious Coalition for Abortion Rights, 1979), n. pag.

16 *Legal Abortion: Arguments Pro & Con* (New York: Westchester Coalition for Legal Abortion, 1978), n. pag.

17 *The Abortion Rights Crisis* (Washington, DC: Religious Coalition for Abortion Rights, 1979), n. pag.

18 *Abortion Q. and A.* (Washington, DC: National Abortion Rights Action League, n.d.), n. pag.; "Abortion Is Our Right," n. pag.; *Do You Want to Return to the Butchery of Back Alley Abortion* (New York: National Association for Repeal of Abortion Laws, n.d.), n. pag.; *The Abortion Rights Crisis*, n. pag.

19 "In 1982, If You Have a Miscarriage," n. pag.

20 Mailings in 1982 by the National Abortion Rights Action League entitled "FANATICISM" and "Violence Against the Right to Choose."

21 See for example, *Aborted Baby Discarded in Hospital Bucket*, n.p., n.d., n. pag.; *This Life Is In Your Hands* (Houston, TX: Houston Right to Life, n.d.), n. pag.; "California Doctor on Trial," *The Communicator*, April 1978, 3-4.

22 *Newsweek*, 14 Jan. 1985, 25.

23 See for example, John Lippis, *The Challenge to be "Pro Life"* (Santa Barbara, CA: Santa Barbara Pro Life Education, Inc., 1978), John C. Willke, *Handbook on Abortion* (Cincinnati: Hayes, 1975).

24 *The Communicator*, December 1978, 2.

25 *Newsweek*, 14 Jan. 1985, 25.

26 Lafayette, Indiana *Journal and Courier*, 4 July 1976, H-8; 22 Jan. 1977, A-9; and 23 Jan. 1978, B-5.

27 Lippis, p. 19; *The Communicator*, March 1977, 2; *Choose Life* (Toledo, OH: Ohio Right to Life Society, n.d.), 6.

28 *Give to the Unborn Their First Civil Right—Life* (Houston: Houston Right to Life, n.d.), n.pag.; *Life or Death*, n.p., n.d., n.pag.; Ken Unger, *What You Don't Know Can Hurt You*! (Ashtabula, OH: Protestants Protesting Abortion, n.d.), n.pag.; Maureen Boisclair and Mary Senander, *Abortion: A Catholic Issue* (n.p., 1977), n.pag.; *Abortion?* (Boston: Daughters of St. Paul, 1971), 2-3, 5.

29 Unger, n.pag.

30 *The Abortion Connection*, n.p., n.d., n.pag.

31 *Is This Life Worth a Postage Stamp?* n.p., n.d., n.pag.

32 Unger, n.pag.

33 *Americans Against Abortion*, Summer 1986, 17.

[34] Lafayette, Indiana *Journal and Courier*, 22 Jan. 1979, A-8; 22 Jan. 1980, B-4; 11 May 1980, B-7.
[35] *Indiana Right to Life Political Action Committee* (Indianapolis: Indiana Right to Life Political Action Committee, 1978), 1.
[36] Nancy Koster, "If Your House Were on Fire . . ." *National Right to News*, 23 October 1986, 1 and 8.
[37] Gilbert Durand, *The Facts of Death* (Glendale, CA: Committee of Ten Million, 1973), n.pag.
[38] Lafayette, Indiana *Journal and Courier*, 4 July 1978, A-2.
[39] John F. Seidensticker, *The Euthanasia Debate* (n.p., 18 Oct. 1973), n. pag.; *Why Vote Pro-Life*, n.p., n.d., n.pag.
[40] *Aborted Baby Discarded in Hospital Bucket*, 2.
[41] *Life or Death* (Cincinnati: Hayes Publishing, 1975), 4.
[42] Mimeographed copy.
[43] *The Communicator*, Oct. 1976, 2.
[44] See for example, *The Communicator*, June 1978, 2; and May 1977, 2.
[45] See for example, *The Communicator*, Sept. 1978, 2; Nov./Dec. 1977, 2; and Oct./Nov. 1980, 3.
[46] *National Right to Life News*, 5 March 1987, 5.
[47] Lafayette, Indiana *Journal and Courier*, 29 June 1983, 1, col. 1.
[48] "Abortion Terrorism: The Toll Rises," *MS*, March 1985, 19.
[49] "More Ads, No More Bombs," *America*, 8 February 1986, 82; "Violence Against Abortion Clinics Escalates Despite the Opposition of Prolife Leaders," *Christianity Today*, 1 Feb. 1985, 45.
[50] J.C. Willke, "Violence—The Answer?" *The Communicator*, May, 1978, 2.
[51] *Indiana Right to Life*, n.p., n.d., 3, reprinted from *National Right to Life News*, Feb. 1980, n.pag.
[52] "Violence Against Abortion Clinics," 45-46.
[53] Cleveland, OH *Catholic Universe Bulletin*, 17 Sept. 1976, 2, col. 4.
[54] *The Communicator*, Jan. 1978, 3.
[55] *Catholic Universe Bulletin*, 17 Sept. 1976, 2, col. 2.
[56] "Violence Against Abortion Clinics," 46.
[57] Judith Adler Hennessee, "Inside a Right-to-Life Mind," *Mademoiselle*, April 1986, 261.

Chapter 12

The Panama Canal Treaties and Argument from Narrative Vision

This chapter examines how some people help other people to see the world "properly." We shall focus on (1) how people coalesce around preferred frameworks for interpreting reality, (2) how a social movement can challenge the establishment's framework, (3) how subsequent events can determine the outcome, and (4) how the framework and events are interdependent. Let us begin with the theory before studying the Panama Canal controversy.

Narrative and Rhetorical Vision

Historian David Carr writes that, "Human existence and action . . . consist not in overcoming time, not in escaping it or arresting its flow, but in shaping and forming it."[1] Time matters as it is experienced by people, and people experience time through narratives. Carr maintains that each person (1) lives in a present that embodies his or her remembered past, and (2) acts in expectation of a future that is a projection of past and present. In short, we cast ourselves in an unfolding story and act it out. Since we *choose* the appropriate story and our role in it, we can change stories at any time.

Philosopher Howard Kamler explains that stories perform five important psychological functions that help us to "know" and to protect what we "know" from counterargument. Stories let us believe what we want (or need) to believe by defining what constitutes relevant evidence and what does not. Stories also cover gaps in our understanding by explaining the otherwise unexplainable. Stories give structure to our lives by contextualizing otherwise ambiguous episodes. Stories protect our beliefs because each comes with the explicit defense mechanism, "other things being equal," that spares any story and its evidence when it can be proven irrelevant. And finally, Kamler writes, stories enable us to communicate because we make our private stories public and personally adopt public stories (such as cultural myths and ideologies).[2]

Thus, each individual searches for self-understanding by imposing narrative structure on life. The social systems model presented in Chapter 7 discussed the general importance of characterized environments; the functional approach to movement persuasion explained in Chapter 8 outlined social movements' specific need to transform perceptions of both history and society. All of these are accomplished through narrative. Each narrative structures the past, projects a future, and prescribes a preferred course of conduct *from a particular vantage point*. Each narrative has an author, a narrator, a protagonist, and an audience, and we strive to narrate our own lives.

The narrator's vantage point—in time, intellect, wisdom, values, and character—positions the narrative for the audience. The reader-narrator identification is central. Readers who identify with the narrator can step into the story, enact it,and retain the experience. Stories that facilitate these processes, in turn, foster identification. Readers repelled by the narrator may use the narrative for its opposite lesson, and an ill-defined or unconvincing narrator can be ignored. Thus, the narrator's image and audience appeal are important to the narrative. Personal identification overpowers logical rigor.[3]

Charles Dickens's *The Christmas Carol* exemplifies the basic point. Dickens devised a narrative in which despicable protagonist Ebeneezer Scrooge is haunted by Christmas spirits who reacquaint him with his Past, Present, and Future. The spirits help Scrooge to see a happier Past, an unseen Present, and an unwanted Future. He avoids the unwanted Future by reweaving threads from his forgotten Past with the opportunities of the previously unseen Present. But the reader is not led to identify with the despicable Scrooge lest the reader rationalize Scrooge's behavior and defend it. The reader instead views Scrooge's transformation from the perspective of his kind, loving, forgiving, and charitable nephew—the perspective readers are induced to take on as a universal guide to life.

David Carr further theorizes that we organize our social relationships and communities through the telling and retelling of stories. Stories or myths link us to our contemporaries and to our predecessors and successors.[4] The story-telling process engages people in a communicative relationship defined by the narrator-audience relationship.

The narrator and listener create a "We" through their identification. "My story" becomes "our story" as teller and listener become one through the co-creation of the story. Publics or communities coalesce around clusters of stories as each "We" has its own folklore and narrators. Narrators embellish the story by emphasizing different characters, motives, events, chronology, or plotlines. Carr distinguishes between stories that endure ("retentions") and those that can be remembered if necessary ("recollections").[5] Differences develop when one person's retention is another's mere recollection. For example, conservatives retold the Alger Hiss-Whitaker Chambers story for some twenty years after most others had forgotten it; labor movement songs retold the ballads of Joe Hill and Sacco and

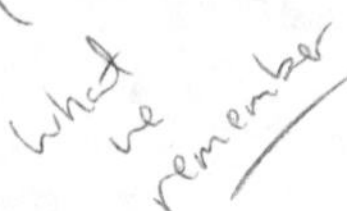

Vanzetti after they had been forgotten; and Christians retell biblical stories that non-Christians have shelved. Social movements often weave a variety of recollections into a new narrative and raise it to the level of retention.

If history is the creation of explanatory stories, and if social relationships form around these explanatory stories, then some of these narrative groups must inevitably conflict. Consider the historic conflicts among Christian denominations, all based upon their varying interpretations of the story of Jesus of Nazareth. Similarly, most American social movements evoke conflicting narratives of the *real* meaning of America and the essence of "The American Dream."

Walter Fisher argues that each narrative enacts a set of values and that these enacted values govern the narrative's audience appeal. Each narrative is judged, according to Fisher, by its *narrative coherence* (does the story work?) and by its *narrative fidelity* (does the story square with audience beliefs and values?). Thus, Fisher argues that audiences look for *good reasons*, which they regard as stories that are:

(1) true to and consistent with what we think we know and what we value,

(2) appropriate to whatever decision is pending,

(3) promising in effects for ourselves and others, and

(4) consistent with what we believe is an ideal basis for conduct.[6]

This view of persuasion hinges less upon changing beliefs, attitudes, or values than upon integrating the desired belief or behavior into a narrative regarded as coherent, relevant, compatible, promising, and proper by the appropriate audience.

The narrative position is largely compatible with a popular rhetorical perspective known as "fantasy theme analysis." Ernest Bormann's studies of small-group communication confirmed Robert F. Bales' observation that individuals working together frequently "dramatize" or act out a "fantasy" (a recollection or an estimation of the future).[7]

The verbalizing, expressing, or dramatizing of a fantasy orients listeners to the present by drawing upon past and future. Some fantasies fall flat. But when listeners recognize the fantasy as one of their own, they respond emotionally as well as cognitively. They hitch-hike on the original comment and extend the fantasy by polishing the image, adding examples, and extending it. Then a third person recognizes the shared fantasy and joins the fun. Soon the individuals have drawn on their individual pasts and futures to create a shared present. Thus, they develop a common orientation to their present, and *they are bound to one another both by the shared vision and by the process of creating it*. This process is called "chaining" (as in "they created an elaborate fantasy chain" or "the fantasy chained out to the entire group").

Ernest Bormann's primary contribution is his suggestion that fantasy-chaining transcends the small-group experience. If small groups create shared identities through group fantasizing, he reasons, so might large groups: audiences, organizations, social movements, and societies. Bormann identifies rhetorical visions as "the composite dramas which catch up large groups of people in a symbolic reality."[8] They arise through communication and provide the themes, heroes, villains, values, and motivations which are invoked in later communication.

Rhetorical visions are particularly pertinent where clear explanations are elusive. Bormann observes that:

> When the authentic record of events is clear and widely understood, the competing visions must take it into account . . . [But] Whenever occasions are so chaotic and indiscriminate that the community has no clear observational impression of the facts, people are given free rein to fantasize within the assumptions of their rhetorical vision.[9]

Narrative and rhetorical vision are not identical frameworks. The narrative model is more perceptually grounded, more cognitive, and offers more analytical guidance. Fantasy theme analysis draws rather more heavily upon imaginings than recollections, (although most would agree that our fantasies and imaginings grow out of our experiences).

The connection between narrative and rhetorical vision should be evident. Fantasies and rhetorical visions are narrative in form. Some fantasies/narratives stimulate recognition and empathy, thereby: (1) enhancing audience-narrator identification, (2) inducing the audience to participate in the narrative itself, (3) inviting the audience to join in the creative process, (4) fostering identification with like-minded auditors, and (5) motivating the auditor to retain and advance the story as narrator. We shall use the term "narrative vision" to encompass both Carr's sense of configured time and Bormann's collective imagining with respect to the New Right movement of the 1970s.

The Politics of Renegotiation, 1964-1978

President Lyndon Johnson responded to 1964 Panamanian protests by initiating a reexamination of the treaties governing ownership and use of the canal, a process continued by President Richard Nixon. Congressman Daniel Flood (R. PA) wrote several times during 1974 warning Nixon of threats to our navigational freedom: "In the current struggle for the domination of strategic waterways . . ., a line must be drawn somewhere and I can think of no better place to do so than at Panama where Soviet agents are already ensconced in its government."[10] Nixon, more concerned with stonewalling the impeachment proceedings than with Panamanians, responded that: "at stake is not just our control of the canal—vital as that may be—but relations with the Republic of Panama, the nations of the Caribbean and

Latin America, and by extension with much of the Third World, all of which feel a concern and involvement in the resolution of this matter."[11] Flood and Nixon were expressing the core themes of the controversy ("Drawing a line in the dust" versus "nurturing relations with smaller nations") four years and two presidents before the treaty would come to a vote.

When Gerald Ford succeeded Nixon, the treaty wheels kept turning. Henry Kissinger remained as Secretary of State, and his people (notably Ambassador Ellsworth Bunker) continued to negotiate. But the Ford administration was insecure. Nixon holdovers had little respect for the newcomers, and Ford's loyalists mistrusted both the holdovers and those jockeying for the 1976 nomination. President Ford had never been endorsed by voters beyond Grand Rapids, Michigan, and the Presidency had been disgraced through the Watergate scandal. In this atmosphere, White House staffers avoided controversy by sidestepping questions, keeping few informal memoranda, and avoiding explanations.

One exchange of letters illustrates both the process and its impact on the canal controversy. William Douglas Pawley of Miami, a former ambassador to Peru and Brazil, wrote President Ford to oppose the treaty process. The letter went to the White House, to the National Security Council, to the State Department for a draft reply, back to the National Security Council which returned it to the White House Director of Correspondence, Roland Elliott. Elliott's reply to Ambassador Pawley, dated October 6, 1975, said in part:

> (our) interest in the Panama Canal, therefore, is that it continue to be efficiently operated on a nondiscriminatory basis and that it be secure.... The achievement of a cooperative relationship with Panama would constitute neither a surrender nor an apology to it, but rather would strengthen the mutual interests of both countries in maintaining a well run canal.[12]

But Elliott's letter omitted major portions of the State Department draft that would have illuminated the administration's thinking. For example, the ambassador was *not* told that:

> In this new treaty relationship we are seeking the specific treaty rights which *allow the United States to operate and defend the canal effectively for an extended period of time and the option to expand canal capacity* either by enlarging the current canal or constructing a new sea level canal. *We believe that a new treaty* embodying... such rights *will fulfill our most basic interest* in the Panama Canal *and at the same time satisfy Panamanian aspirations* for full sovereignty over their territory and for increased participation in the Canal's operation and defense [emphasis added].[13]

In these and other letters to influential citizens, the Ford administration withheld its rationale and thereby avoided the chance to advance the narrative vision in which treaty negotiation made sense.

Consequently, few Americans learned much of the treaty process and rumors ran rampant. Without knowing the administration's policy rationale, critics like the Veterans of Foreign Wars charged that "The Battle is now clearly joined between those who would cede our Canal to the Panamanians and those who would not" without pondering the *reasons* for "ceding our Canal."[14] Senator Jesse Helms (R. N.C.) characterized Secretary of State Kissinger as a diplomatic Santa Claus:

> After having given away our nuclear superiority, our wheat, our technology, our production capacity, and our money, Secretary Kissinger has now graduated to giving away our territory itself. The Panama Canal Zone is ours, bought and paid for as indisputably as the Louisiana Purchase, or California or Alaska.[15]

And Phillip Harman of the American Education League railed that: "It is hardly the hallmark of diplomatic genius to consider surrendering our canal lifeline—vital for our national defense and economic health—to the specious claims of an unstable, totalitarian government closely tied to history's most dangerous tyranny."[16] These and similar statements flourished among conservatives because they enunciated the conservative concerns about Soviet influence, military security, insecure Third World countries, public demonstrations, and disrespect for the law. They also flourished because they had no competing narrative from the establishment which preferred to handle renegotiation as an administrative rather than as a political issue.

When President Ford announced his intention to run for election, the already divided Republicans coalesced around Ford and Ronald Reagan. Nowhere are their contrasting styles more evident than in their handling of Harman and his American Education League. Robert McFarlane of Ford's National Security Council scrawled "Don't answer it" on Harman's letter, while Reagan signed Harman on as an advisor on the Panama Canal and Central America.[17] Reagan garnered considerable support, but Ford handily won his party's nomination to face Jimmy Carter. Reagan's moment occurred in North Carolina where he used the canal issue to win the primary in Jesse Helms's state. Ford answered canal questions from reporters but continued to avoid a major speech on the canal treaties, perhaps realizing that he could alienate conservatives in his party.

Reagan's problem was that most Americans were unconcerned about Panama, the canal, or anything else in the world at large. Although Americans agreed with Reagan in principle that American should retain sovereignty over the canal (by a 76% to 16% margin), Gallup's "most important issue" poll in May, 1976 indicated that Americans were worried about high prices (38%), unemployment (24%), government dishonesty (13%), and crime (8%); foreign policy as an umbrella category concerned only 5% of the public.[18] Reagan beat Ford on the canal issue, but only 5% of the public seemed to care.

There were those who urged President Ford to take charge of the canal issue. Aide Terry O'Connell suggested a National Security Council paper on the canal "so we can catch Reagan in the midst of his lie." Godfrey Harriss of Harriss-Ragan Management, consultants to Panama, wrote to suggest that the canal could be "used *positively* by the President to advance his position" against Reagan. He also pointed out, for the first time in the White House Central Files on Panama, what was to become a crucial semantic wedge: the original treaty did not grant America sovereignty over the Canal Zone but granted all rights *as if* America had sovereignty. Ford's staffers recognized the delicacy of taking advice from a consultant to Panama and expressed their appreciation for the spirit in which Harriss had made the offer. Staffers similarly appreciated the "active and constructive support" of a publisher who urged Ford "to explode Ronald Reagan's campaign myths about the Panama Canal in a nationwide television address."[19] But these concerns, it seemed, could be handled with administrative rhetoric (as discussed in Chapter 6). When ready, the treaties would be debated by the Senate—not by the House, not by referendum, and not by the courts. These were delicate matters for skilled negotiators, Ford and Kissinger believed, not fodder for public campaigning.

The canal did not become an issue during the 1976 campaign because Ford and Carter agreed, and the public was apathetic. With Ford and Nixon out of the picture, however, it fell to President Carter and the Democrats to advocate ratification. Once the treaties were ready for debate, the public's interest increased. Now Republicans saw ratification as a Democratic plan, and conservative opponents were ready to lead the fight against the treaties and, in the process, to wrest control of the Republican Party from the Nixon-Ford-Kissinger-Rockefeller wing.

Richard Viguerie claimed that "No political issue in the last 25 years so clearly divided the American establishment from the American people as the Panama Canal treaties." The proposed treaties were truly supported by the establishment: two Democratic and two Republican presidents, the Democratic leaders in both houses or Congress, all members of the Joint Chiefs of Staff, "Big Labor, Big Business, Big Media, the big international banks, and just about every liberal political and cultural star you could name." Opposed to the treaties were "the American people—about 70% of them . . . probably 85% of registered Republicans" and a coterie of conservative spokespersons who would become known as the "New Right": Senators Paul Laxalt, Jake Garn, and Bill Scott, Congressmen Philip Crane, Larry McDonald, and Mickey Edwards, and organizers Paul Weyrich, Howard Phillips, William Rhatican, Terry Dolan, and Viguerie himself.[20] The treaties passed the Senate by a two-vote (68-32) margin (a significant victory for President Carter), but many Americans remained deeply opposed to the treaties.[21]

The "New Right" movement used the proposed Panama Canal treaties to energize the conservative imagination. By advancing a narrative that warranted treaty rejection (rather than conceding the worldview and arguing technicalities), the New Right engaged less active conservatives in group fantasizing. The process aroused public sentiment, developed a massive public relations machine, defined

its identity, created a list of political "villains," and transformed treaty ratification into a rhetorical success. As Viguerie explains:

> Our campaign to save the Canal gained conservative converts around the country—added more than 400,000 new names to our lists—encouraged many of the movements leading figures... to run for public office—and produced significant liberal defeats. The New Right came out of the Panama Canal fight with no casualties, not even a scar. Because of Panama we are better organized. We developed a great deal of confidence in ourselves, and our opponents became weaker. That November [1978] the New Right really came of age.[22]

In short, the New Right campaign accomplished four of the five functions of social movement persuasion despite losing the treaty vote. It enabled them to (1) transform perceptions of history, (2) transform perceptions of society, (3) prescribe courses of action, and (4) mobilize for action. Let us use narrative vision to explain how they did it.

We shall contrast pro- and anti-treaty narratives from the 1974-1978 period to see how the New Right movement used the canal issue to weave diverse public recollections and fantasies into a narrative vision that aroused and united conservatives and, ultimately, reoriented American foreign policy. We shall pay particular attention to the narrative advanced by the movement's primary spokesman, Illinois Republican Congressman Philip Crane, and by the addresses and remarks of the establishment's major advocate, President Jimmy Carter.

President Carter spoke for the foreign policy establishment (the leadership of both parties, the diplomatic corps, the State Department, the CIA, and the Pentagon), and Crane's book was the New Right movement's definitive critique of that bipartisan foreign policy. Congressman Crane (like anti-war Senators Eugene McCarthy, George McGovern, and Alan Cranston) served as an elected member of the established order while energetically advocating the position of an uninstitutionalized collectivity. Crane's office surely enhanced his credibility.[23] But as a member of the House of Representatives rather than the Senate, Crane was outside the institutionalized structure for debating treaty ratification. On treaty ratification, congressmen carry no more legitimate authority than ordinary citizens.

Moreover, Carter and Crane advanced comparable narratives. Each (1) recounted our past, (2) depicted our present situation, (3) envisioned desirable and undesirable futures, (4) dramatized and reconciled significant American values and symbols, and (5) espoused a preferred course of action consistent with the narrative and its values.

The Past: America's Claim to the Canal

President Carter's narrative contrasted characteristic American fairness and morality with the unfair 1903 Hay-Bunau-Varilla Treaty. He found it shameful that

"No person from Panama ever saw that treaty before it was signed. No Panamanian, of course, was involved in the signing of that treaty."[24] But the new treaties would reaffirm America's fairness since it "is what is right for us and what is fair to others."[25]

Carter further argued that even the unfair treaty failed to grant America sovereignty over the canal. He told a questioner that: "the treaty . . . gave Panama sovereignty over the Panama Canal Zone itself. It gave us control over the Panama Canal Zone *as though* we had sovereignty. So, we've always had a legal sharing of responsibility over the Panama Canal Zone."[26] Since Panama retained sovereignty even under an unfair treaty, we should affirm it with a fair treaty.

But Congressman Crane and many others worried about the sovereignty issue. He argued that America's claim to the canal was legally derived from a succession of treaties culminating in the Hay-Bunau-Varilla Treaty of 1903. But neither Crane nor Mr. Hay himself tried to argue that our claim to the canal derived from a fair treaty. Both readily conceded that the treaty was advantageous to America, disadvantageous to Panama, and likely to have been rejected by Panama upon reconsideration.

Instead, Crane argued that a clever and legal treaty had granted America sovereignty over the canal zone. His narrative covered the negotiation of the Hay-Bunau-Varilla Treaty by which newly independent Panama granted America the right to build, operate, maintain, and defend the canal, and relinquished its claim of sovereignty over the newly designated Canal Zone.[27] America's claim to the canal stemmed from shrewdness and opportunism:

> When any nation goes to the bargaining table it does so with the determination to act in its own best interests and to derive as many benefits as possible from the ensuing negotiations. Our 1903 agreement with Panama was no exception. There is no doubt that the Hay-Bunau-Varilla Treaty was very favorable to the United States, a shrewd bargain.[28]

Crane's account of the original treaty's imbalance was fully consistent with that of its negotiator, Mr. Hay.[29]

Congressman Crane further maintained that the legal treaty ceded *all* sovereignty over the Canal Zone to the United States. He refuted Carter's claim that America was granted control "as though" we had sovereignty with a 1904 memorandum from the Panamanian secretary of government to the effect that Panama ended its jurisdiction over the Canal Zone upon ratification in 1904.[30] But the thrust of Carter's argument had been that the treaty provided for Panamanian sovereignty and American jurisdiction as if we had sovereignty. Crane cited Henry Kissinger's pro-treaty references to "restoring Panamanian sovereignty" and several examples of American acts usually associated with sovereignty and inferred that "the very yielding to Panama of certain small pieces of control proves that the United States has full control—*de facto* sovereignty—in the first place."[31] But Carter's concern was that very discrepancy between our *de facto* sovereignty and Panama's *de jure* sovereignty.

Curiously, President Carter's most authoritative and cogent handling of the sovereignty issue came three months before Crane's book and four months before his "Fireside Chat." Carter explained to a Denver audience that:

> We [Americans] have never owned the Panama Canal Zone. We've never had title to it. We've never had sovereignty over it . . . the Supreme Court has confirmed since then [sic] that this is Panamanian territory. People born in the Panama Canal Zone are not American citizens. We've always paid them an annual fee, since the first year of the Panama Canal Treaty that presently exists, for the use of their property . . . . People say we bought it; it's ours; we ought not to give it away. We've never bought it. It's not been ours. We are not giving it away.[32]

Although Carter and Crane built *prima facie* arguments on sovereignty, each failed to engage the other's argument directly. Crane's account sidestepped the treaty's grant of control *as if* America held sovereignty. Even as reprinted in his book Article III of the 1903 treaty states that: "The Republic of Panama grants to the United States all the rights, power and authority within the zone . . . *which the United States would possess and exercise if it were the sovereign of the territory* within which said lands and waters are located (emphasis added).[33] Thus, Crane's reliance on signs of sovereignty exploited the fact that the treaty preserved Panamanian sovereignty while granting the appearance of sovereignty. Crane skirted the fundamental issue and misconstrued the treaty text in his own book's appendix.

For his part, Carter too often summarized and asserted while Crane used detailed extrinsic support like testimony and court decisions. Carter's claim that "the Supreme Court has confirmed since then that this is Panamanian territory," for example, is refuted with Crane's specific references to *Wilson v. Shaw* (1907), *The United States v. Husband* (1972), and a "veteran American diplomat and international law authority."[34]

Carter and Crane presented strikingly divergent histories which constrained their audiences' reactions. If the treaty were grossly unjust and exploitive, even an explicit Panamanian grant of sovereignty to America might be discounted. But if the treaty were honorably negotiated, then even implicit Panamanian concessions should be binding. Moreover, if America held sovereign control over the Canal Zone, then *any* sharing of that power could be construed as "surrender," "retreat," or a "giveaway"; but if Panama itself held sovereignty, then there was nothing to surrender.

Crane's narrative dramatized an American success based on legality, shrewdness, pride, and self-interest. Carter's narrative dramatized an American embarrassment and intimated that our collective past was less noble than we had believed. Fisher's first test for "good reasons" is the degree to which the narrative is "true to and consistent with what we think we know and what we value."[35] Crane's history met the first narrative test better than did Carter's, even though it appears to misuse its own evidence.

The Present: The Western Hemisphere Today

President Carter depicted Panama among our "historic allies and friends" headed by a "stable government which has encouraged the development of free enterprise" and will hold democratic elections.[36] But Crane described a "banana republic" dominated by "forty influential families" where "poverty is abysmal and in which General Omar Torrijos runs a "corrupt, vicious police state . . . built with the help of his Marxist allies" and kept from bankruptcy only by "the New York banking community."[37]

Moreover, Carter and Crane advanced contrasting views of Pan-American relations. Carter described legitimate disaffection in the hemisphere and depicted the canal as "the last vestige of alleged American colonialism."[38] Thirteen years of negotiations had "built up hopes of new friendship, new trade opportunities, and a new sense of commonality and equality of stature between their governments and our government that never existed before."[39] The cornerstone of these hopes and expectations was a "new sense . . . of improved friendship and common purpose . . . not based on grants or loans or financial aid from us to them but based on the fact that this treaty corrects a longstanding defect in our relationships with countries to the south."[40] Carter eagerly anticipated this "new partnership" and spoke of defending the canal with Panamanian forces "joined with us as brothers."[41] The Carter narrative dramatized Panamanian resentment of America against the background of America's uncharacteristic deceit.

But where President Carter saw our exploitation and injustice as contributors to Panamanian resentment, Crane saw only American generosity:

> The United States did for Panama what the Spanish, Simon Bolivar, the French Company, and the Colombians had all failed to do: built and operated a magnificent interoceanic canal that pumped commercial vitality and opportunity into the stagnant economic bloodstream of Panama. We also rid the country of the scourges of malaria and yellow fever, brought good jobs and opportunity to thousands of needy Panamanians, and promptly paid increasingly large subsidies to the Panamanian government—all after helping Panama to win independence in the first place.[42]

Thus, where Carter advanced a story of legitimate resentment, Crane told of childish ingratitude: "To the extent that Panama exists and is a viable state today, it is because a strong America, which could have taken what it wanted without giving anything in return, has been a generous friend of Panama from the moment of ratification of the 1903 treaty. But . . . gratitude soon grows old."[43] Crane's view of Pan-American relations was distinctly paternalistic: the American parents bestowed countless favors upon baby Panama only to be resented. Crane implied that Panama needed to be taught a lesson.[44]

Carter and Crane agreed that the canal would be crucial to Panama's future. Crane's account highlighted the danger that Panama might close the canal as economic and political blackmail. General Torrijos was ready to seize the canal.[45] Crane cited a speech wherein Torrijos predicted his own violent death fighting for the canal, and warned that:

> it is precisely the kind of incendiary appeal that has sent thousands of Latin American rioters into the streets in the past, and might very well do so again in the future—especially in the face of a passive, docile America that has demonstrated a pattern of yielding to threats instead of dealing from a position of strength.[46]

Crane warned that it would be a "criminal blunder" to turn the canal zone over to a "corrupt dictator" who is "a flagrant violator of human rights" and is "surrounded by criminals and Marxists," "an intimate friend of Fidel Castro, a rabid anti-American, and a seeker after advice, technicians, and aid from the Soviet Union" because we would risk both blackmail and closure of the canal."[47] "The real threat of violence to the canal," writes Crane "would crest *after* the departure of American security forces, not while they were in place to protect the zone."[48]

Carter examined Panama's economic interests and argued that "Panama wants the canal open and neutral—perhaps even more than we do" because "Much of her economy flows directly or indirectly through the canal." For this reason "Panama would be no more likely to neglect or close the canal than we would be to close [our] Interstate Highway System." The threat to the canal comes "not from any government of Panama, but from misguided persons who may try to fan the flames of dissatisfaction with the terms of the old treaty."[49]

If Americans were concerned by the bleak picture sketched by Crane, then President Carter might well have reiterated his October 22nd comments about defending the canal. The President compared a canal defense to our military involvements in Korea and Vietnam:

> With the passing of these two treaties, . . . if we should later have to go into Panama, it will be with the endorsement of the Panamanian Government, the Panamanian people. It will be with the endorsement of 30 or 40 or 50 other nations who will sign the neutrality treaty going into effect after the year 2000, . . . So it gives us a legitimacy and an endorsement of the rest of the world to keep the canal open, well managed, and to meet the security needs, the trade needs of our own country.[50]

The crux of Carter's position is that any attempt to defend or recapture the canal *under the existing treaty* would be a violation of Panamanian sovereignty. But the proposed treaties explicitly commit Panama to an open, neutral canal under international law.

The Carter and Crane narratives dramatized divergent values. President Carter's story was one of a friendly, honest, rational, democratic, capitalist nation ready, willing, and worthy to be our military and economic partner. But Congressman Crane told of a hostile, corrupt, childish, socialist nation ready and willing but unworthy of partnership with America. Accuracy aside, Crane's story built upon his audience's belief in American superiority and generosity but asked them to be suspicious and protective in this particular case. Carter's account undermined his audience's belief in our tradition of fairness and military strength, and asked his audience to demonstrate its trusting and generous nature in this particular case.

The Future: The Kind of Power We Wish to Be

President Carter and Congressman Crane agreed that the canal decision would demonstrate "the kind of great power we wish to be."[51] Carter claimed that Theodore Roosevelt "would join us in our *pride* for being a *great and generous* people, with the *national strength* and *wisdom* to do what is *right for us* and what is *fair to others* (emphasis added)."[52] The President told reporters that ratification would be "a show of strength... national will... fairness and... confidence in ourselves." He explained that we need not "run over a little country. It's much better for us to show our strength and our ability by not being a bully and by saying to Panama, let's work in harmony."[53] Carter said that ratification would demonstrate that "we are able to deal fairly and honorably with a proud but smaller sovereign nation... [because] we believe in good will and fairness, as well as strength."[54] He spoke of the "new partnership" as a "source of national pride and self-respect."[55]

Panama was to be transformed from "a passive and sometimes deeply resentful bystander into an active and interested partner" who will "[join] with us as brothers against a common enemy" should the canal need military defense.[56] The treaties would not create a "power vacuum" but would "increase our nation's influence in this hemisphere, help to reduce any mistrust and disagreement, [and] remove a major source of anti-American feeling." In the Carter vision, the United States was a powerful, fair, generous neighbor ready and willing to demonstrate those admirable traits by sharing the canal with the Panamanians.

But Congressman Crane painted a different future based upon the nature of the world and the proper places of property and generosity. Crane bluntly differentiated his world from Carter's: "The world is not a Sunday school classroom in Plains, Georgia. It is a violent, conflict-ridden place where peace and freedom only survive when they are protected... Peace comes only to the prepared and security only to the strong."[57] Although generosity among friends is noble, generosity in a jungle is foolish and cowardly.

Crane therefore argues that ratification would be "one more crucial American step in a descent into ignominy—to the end of America's credibility as a world power and a deterrent to aggression."[58] Crane's future envisions neither friendship nor generosity but a reputation for cowardice and weakness:

> Edmund Burke warned that, "the concessions of the weak are the concessions of fear." There can be no question but that, in the eyes of a Soviet Union engaged in a massive naval and military build-up, and in the eyes of third-world countries envious of America's affluence, surrender in Panama would appear as not a noble act of magnanimity, but as the cowardly retreat of a tired, toothless paper tiger.[59]

The futures envisioned by Carter and Crane directly conflict. Crane saw danger, Carter security. Crane wanted superiority, Carter partnership. Crane implied force and punishment, Carter generosity and kindness. Crane thought America weak, Carter thought us strong. Crane saw shame in "surrender," Carter in continued imperialism. Each believed that the other indirectly helped America's enemies.

Discussion

The Panama Canal controversy illustrates how the New Right movement took exception to a bipartisan consensus, developed a coherent narrative vision that aroused and united potential supporters by dramatizing their fears, and eventually elected its best narrator and early spokesman to the presidency. Carter and Crane advocated choices that made sense within their respective narratives, and the choice of narrative dictated the direction of American policy.

New Right organizers saw the canal issue as a symbolic vehicle for energizing their movement. Because the debate was between narrative visions, defenders of the establishment narrative risked losing, and in fact did lose, their entire policy framework. The New Right undermined public confidence in the assumptions underlying our foreign policy and provided an alternative narrative framework through which subsequent events in Iran, Afghanistan, Nicaragua, Grenada, El Salvador, and the Persian Gulf would be interpreted by the "great communicator," Ronald Reagan.

Dramatic rhetorical narratives that excite the imagination are more persuasive than those that are more technical in nature. Both Crane and Carter claimed to have "the facts," and both established their authority and expertise (although Crane never explained why a congressman would devote so much of his constituents' representation to an issue on which he could not cast a vote).[60] But Crane was better able than Carter to involve his audience in the process of collective fantasizing because his narrative provided themes that his audience interpreted as "good reasons."

Let us appraise the narratives with respect to Fisher's four criteria of narrative rationality.[61] First, Crane's narrative dramatized American heroism, strength, generosity, legality, and cleverness while Carter's narrative required us to revise our sense of history and national character to admit that our "Bully President" had himself been a bully who had tricked our unsuspecting neighbors. Crane's narrative was therefore more true to and consistent with what we "knew," "believed," and "valued" than Carter's. Ironically and importantly, the social movement used existing perceptions of history while the President sought to transform them, an unusual reversal brought about by the Ford administration's avoidance of issue definition.

Second, both narratives were appropriate to the ratification decision because they framed the issues and compelled a conclusion. Neither left its audience to ask, "So how does this affect treaty ratification?" But Crane's account was self-supporting. His conflict with the President and defense establishment clouded the decision and made momentary caution (his position) seem more prudent than trust. Carter, like Ford, tried to respond to aroused concern with administrative rhetoric (see Chapter 6), but even this required him to allay the fears aroused by the social movement. This left Americans to ask two questions: "After fourteen years of negotiating, what's the hurry?" and "If you are right, Mr. President, why is this convincing congressman so worried?"

Third, Crane's narrative was the more "promising" in effects for ourselves and others. It promised that the choice of cowardice and weakness would lead to the possibility of a friendship devoid of respect, while stern resolve would lead to power and respect. Carter's narrative promised that the choice of generosity and honor would lead to friendship, respect, and security while intransigence would lead to greater antagonism and vulnerability. Crane's account invites audience fantasizing because its stakes are so dramatic.

And fourth, Crane's narrative was the more internally consistent because of its simplicity. Carter's narrative presented several apparent inconsistencies. Why should we grant anything to people who are increasingly resentful? How are these resentful people developing this new sense of mutual purpose and trust with America? If Panama is friendly and stable, why need we worry about defending the canal? If we need to worry about defending the canal, why voluntarily relinquish any of our claim to it? Carter answered these questions reasonably well, but his answers were complex and strung-out over several months. Crane's narrative provided few apparent inconsistencies. He did commit a critical logical error by arguing that the presence of all the signs of American sovereignty over the canal proved American sovereignty, since the treaty—as he himself reprinted it—(1) preserved Panamanian sovereignty and (2) granted America all rights and privileges *as if* we had sovereignty over it. But this inconsistency was buried deep in his argument and it was obscured by his references to memoranda and court decisions on related points.

In short, President Carter advanced a technically sound argument for treaty ratification that did not meet the tests of good narrative. Crane's arguments against ratification, flawed as they were, met the narrative tests and involved audience members in the social movement. The treaty was ratified on administrative and technical grounds, but the movement established its narrative framework as a viable alternative and used it a year later to frame events in Iran and Afghanistan and overthrew the Ford-Carter-Kissinger "friendly giant" scenario.

Conclusions

A choice between narrative frameworks ultimately boils down to the question of believability, and believability hinges on the individual's personal inventory of words, meanings, experiences, associations, social influences, values, needs, and sense of causation. We believe what we need to believe to keep ourselves afloat in the world. A narrative that embodies and dramatizes our experiences and fantasies "makes sense" to us, as Fisher suggests, because it has coherence and fidelity. It excites us, and we wonder why no one noticed it before. As Bormann explains, we share it excitedly with our associates, creating through the act of collective fantasizing a sense of community that is embodied in the shared vision.

President Carter asked support for treaty ratification on technical grounds, relying upon the testimony of establishment figures to create a bandwagon of support. But the New Right transformed the controversy into a movement vs. establishment conflict. Crane's office legitimized his advocacy, and his reliance upon old memoranda, court cases, testimony, and reprinted treaties created what Barnet Baskerville once called "the illusion of proof."[62] When Crane's narrative accounted for subsequent developments in Iran and Nicaragua, moderate Republicans like Richard Nixon and Gerald Ford were perceptually exiled to the Carter position.

In 1964, Senator J. William Fulbright lamented the "divergence between the realities of foreign policy and our ideas about it" and warned against "policies based on old myths rather than current realities." Such policies were both dangerous and unnecessary, he warned, "dangerous because it can reduce foreign policy to a fraudulent game of imagery and appearances, unnecessary because it can be overcome by the determination of men in high office to dispel prevailing misconceptions through candid dissemination of unpleasant but inescapable facts."[63] With two decades of political and rhetorical hindsight, we can better understand that political realities are experienced only through language and that policy debates must either be conducted *within* a narrative vision or *between* two (or more) competing visions.

In a debate between narratives, the struggle over images, heroes, villains, values, and motives is central, not irrelevant. These symbolic struggles determine how Americans—whether policy-makers or ordinary citizens—will order the world around them and therefore how they will define their policy alternatives. Narrative visions are the frameworks within which specific people, motives, and incidents are interpreted. As people recognize, share, and apply their vision, they recruit members and consolidate them into a working group.

This analysis of the New Right's Panama Canal campaign illustrates four important points about social movements and narrative vision. First, activists coalesce around a narrative framework for interpreting political realities. Second, even a logical establishment narrative advanced by the president can be credibly challenged by an emerging social movement with a clear and convincing narrative. Third, the movement's narrative transcends its particular focus, and short-term losses frequently become long-term wins. And fourth, because narratives help us to interpret events, and because events help us to validate our choice of narrative, political history is a series of narrative visions.

Endnotes

[1] David Carr, *Time Narrative, and History* (Bloomington: Indiana University Press, 1986), 89.

[2] Howard Kemler, *Communication: Sharing Our Stories of Experience* (Seattle: Psychological Press, 1983), 27-58.

[3] Walter R. Fisher, *Human Communication as Narration: Toward a Philosophy of Reason, Value, and Action* (Columbia: University of South Carolina Press, 1987), 66-67.

[4] Carr, 112-113.

[5] Carr. 23.

[6] Fisher, 194.

[7] Ernest G. Bormann, "Fantasy and Rhetorical Vision: The Rhetorical Criticism of Social Reality," *Quarterly Journal of Speech*, 58 (December, 1972), 396-407; and "Fantasy and Rhetorical Vision: Ten Years Later," *Quarterly Journal of Speech*, 68 (August, 1982), 288-305. See also Dan Nimmo and James E. Combs, *Mediated Political Realities* (New York: Longman, 1983); and Murray Edelman, *Constructing the Political Spectacle* (Chicago: University of Chicago Press, 1988).

[8] Bormann (1971), 398.

[9] Bormann (1972), 405.

[10] Daniel J. Flood, Letter to President Richard M. Nixon, June 3, 1974, White House Central Files: Foreign Policy, Panama Canal (Ann Arbor, MI: Gerald R. Ford Presidential Library). Hereafter referred to as Ford Central Files.

[11] Richard M. Nixon, Response to Congressman Flood, May 29, 1974, Ford Central Files.

[12] William Douglas Pawley, Letter to President Ford, July 2, 1975, Ford Central Files.

[13] Roland Elliott, Response to William Douglas Pawley, October 6, 1975, Ford Central Files.

[14] Col. F.P. Jones (Ret.), "The United States Canal on the Isthmus of Panama: The Showdown Approaches" (Washington, DC: Official Memorandum to officers and publications of the Veterans of Foreign Wars, September 25, 1975), Ford Central Files.

[15] Quoted in Jones, "The United States Canal. . . ."

[16] Phillip Harman, "Our Panama Canal: A Vital Asset" (Buena Park, CA: mimeographed flier, December 16, 1975), Ford Central Files.

[17] Robert McFarlane, memorandum attached to the Harman flier, Ford Central Files.

[18] Although available from other sources, these data are from the files of Foster Channock who tracked issues for the administration and suggested strategy. They represent not

just what pollsters saw in America but what the Ford White House saw in America. See White House Staff Files, White House Operations, Foster Channock Files, 1975-1976, Gallup Polls of May 16, 1976 (hereafter referred to as Channock Files).

19 See the Memorandum from Terry O'Donnell to Jerry Jones on May 5, 1976; the Letter from Godfrey Harriss to John Marsh on May 5, 1976; Marsh's reply to Harriss; and the telegram from Stan Rose to Robert Dole. All of these are in the Ford Central Files.

20 Richard A. Viguerie, *The New Right: We're Ready to Lead* (Falls Church, VA: The Viguerie Company, 1981), 65-67.

21 Although both Carter and Crane refer to 70-80% public opposition to the treaties, an August, 1977 Gallup Poll reports only 47% opposition. See American Institute of Public Opinion, *The Gallup Poll: Public Opinion, 1972-1977*, Vol. 2 (Wilmington, DE: Scholarly Resources, 1978), 1181-1183. In his memoirs, *Keeping Faith* (New York: Bantam Books, 1982), Carter calls his efforts to win support for the Canal treaties his most difficult political battle (184).

22 Viguerie, 70-71.

23 About 100,000 copies of Crane's book were distributed in January, 1978 by Richard Viguerie's associates. Phillip M. Crane, *Surrender in Panama: The Case Against the Treaty* (New York: Dale Books, 1978), 1-2; and Jimmy Carter, "Panama Canal Treaties," *Public Papers of the President of the United States: Jimmy Carter, 1978* (Washington, DC: United States Government Printing Office, 1979), 259.

24 Jimmy Carter, "Radio-Television News Directors Association," *Public Papers of the Presidents: Jimmy Carter, 1977* (Washington, DC: United States Government Printing Office, 1978), 1597 (referred to hereafter as 9-15-77).

25 Carter, "fireside Chat," 262 and 263.

26 Jimmy Carter, "'Ask President Carter' on CBS Radio," *Public Papers of the Presidents: Jimmy Carter, 1977* (Washington, DC: United States Government Printing Office, 1978), 325 (referred to hereafter as 3-5-77).

27 The treaty chain included the 1901 Hay-Paunceforte Treaty with Britain permitting American involvement in any Central American canal, the 1903 Hay-Herran Treaty (unanimously rejected by the Colombian Senate) which would have granted America complete control over the canal area to build and operate a canal, and the 1903 Panamanian secession from Colombia in which America played "a secondary role." See Crane, 23-33.

28 Crane, 41.

29 Crane quotes a Hay warning that American failure to ratify the Hay-Bunau-Varilla Treaty could mean the failure of any American canal effort: "As it stands now as soon as the Senate votes we shall have a treaty in the main very satisfactory, vastly advantageous to the United States . . . not so advantageous to Panama. If we amend the treaty and send it back some time next month, the . . . period of enthusiastic unanimity, which . . . comes only once in the lifetime of a revolution, will have passed away, and they will have entered on the new fields of politics and dispute . . . . If it is again submitted to their consideration they will attempt to amend it in many places, no man can say with what result." Quoted in Crane, 38.

30 Crane, 36.

31 Crane, 37.

32 Jimmy Carter, "Denver, Colorado," *Public Papers of the Presidents: Jimmy Carter, 1977*

(Washington, DC: United States Government Printing Office, 1978), 1886 (referred to hereafter as 10-22-77).

[33] Quoted by Crane, 136.

[34] Crane, 36-37.

[35] Fisher, 194.

[36] Carter, "Fireside Chat," 262.

[37] Crane, 56-57, 71, and 66.

[38] Carter, "Fireside Chat," 258 and 261.

[39] Jimmy Carter, "Interview with the President," *Public Papers of the Presidents: Jimmy Carter, 1977* (Washington, DC: United States Government Printing Office, 1978), 1513 (referred to hereafter as 8-27-77).

[40] Carter, 9-15-77, 1597.

[41] Carter, "Fireside Chat," 260 and 262.

[42] Crane, 41.

[43] Crane, 41.

[44] Carter disdained Crane's sort of South American policy as "kind of like a big brother giving handouts to small nations to the south to buy their friendship," Carter, 10-22-77, 1886.

[45] Crane, 93.

[46] Crane, 93.

[47] Crane, 82.

[48] Crane, 102.

[49] Carter, "Fireside Chat," 262.

[50] Carter, 10-22-77, 1888.

[51] Carter, "Fireside Chat," 262.

[52] Carter, "Fireside Chat," 263, emphasis added.

[53] Carter, 10-22-77, 1890.

[54] Carter, "Fireside Chat," 259 and 262.

[55] Carter, "Fireside Chat," 262.

[56] Carter, "Fireside Chat," 260.

[57] Crane, 113-114.

[58] Crane, 113.

[59] Crane, 112.

[60] Jimmy Carter, "The President's News Conference, August 23, 1977," *Public Papers of the Presidents: Jimmy Carter, 1977* (Washington, DC: United States Government Printing Office, 1978), 1488 (referred to hereafter as 8-23-77); and Carter 8-27-77, 1514.

[61] Fisher, 194.

[62] Barnet Baskerville, "The Illusion of Proof," *Western Speech*, 25 (Fall, 1961), 236-242.

[63] J. William Fulbright, *Old Myths and New Realities* (New York: Random House, 1964), 4.

Chapter 13

The Persuasive Functions of Songs

The persuasive potential of music has attracted attention for centuries, particularly when social agitators have composed and performed protest songs. Plato warned in *The Republic*, written in the fourth century B.C., that "any musical innovation is full of danger to the whole state, and ought to be prohibited."[1] Jeremy Collier, famous for his controversial pamphlets and moral essays that demanded social reforms in seventeenth century England, remarked that music is "as dangerous as gunpowder."[2] Slaves on southern plantations before the Civil War used songs disguised as religious hymns ("Steal Away," "Run to Jesus," "Follow the Drinking Gourd," and "Many Thousand Gone") to urge slaves to run away from plantations and to use the underground railroad to Canada.

It was not until the 1960s and 1970s that researchers began to study the persuasive nature and effects of protest music. Songs of this period demanded civil rights for blacks, criticized American society, condemned the war in Vietnam, and raised the consciousness of women. For the first time in American history, protest music became popular and commercially lucrative. Records by the Kingston Trio; the Chad Mitchell Trio; Peter, Paul, and Mary; Simon and Garfunkle; Bob Dylan and others sold in the millions. Establishment elements became frightened when "The Eve of Destruction" sung by Barry McGuire reached the number one position on popular music charts and when leftist singers of the 1930s such as Peter Seeger, Woody Gutherie, and The Weavers were rediscovered and "white-washed" into union or labor singers. Decca Records countered with "The Dawn of Correction" and "Better Days Are Yet to Come" by the Spokesmen. The American Broadcasting Company warned its affiliates of their responsibility and accountability to the American public. And David Noebel warned in his book, *The Marxist Minstrels: A Handbook on Communist Subversion of Music*, that "The communist infiltration into the subversion of American music has been nothing short of phenomenal and in some areas, e.g., folk music, their control is fast approaching the saturation point under the able leadership of Pete Seeger."[3] The impact and danger of popular protest songs were greatly exaggerated. Sociologist R. Serge Denisoff discovered in a study of the "The Eve of Destruction" that only 36% of young listeners interpreted the song in the composer's terms and that of these only 44% approved of the message while 39% disapproved.[4]

Some research focuses on persuasive aspects of music. For instance, James Irvine and Walter Kirkpatrick theorize that rhythm reduces inhibitions and defense mechanisms of listeners and makes them more susceptible to rhetorical elements.[5] Cheryl Thomas notes that music sets a mood for the audience and that repetition in songs can create a kind of light hypnosis.[6] Stephen Kosokoff and Carl Carmichael find that both speeches and songs are more effective when they accompany one another.[7] And John Bloodworth writes that the musical artist has a greater freedom of expression than the speaker or essayist.[8]

Other research has focused on music as persuasive message and has produced a litany of generalizations. David Carter claims that protest music presents a negative present and a bright future, focuses on the enemy, encourages action, exposes the movement's ideology, and solidifies the movement.[9] Bloodworth notes that protest music dwells on self-perception and self-identity, unites people behind a cause, and creates anxiety about the future. Thomas says that songs extol famous martyrs, recruit people to the movement, provide sentimental trips into the past with its emotional associations, and glorify the movement. And Ralph Knupp finds that music deals more with adversaries than the social movement, does not propose specific solutions, is present-oriented, appeals more to activity than to ideology, appeals little to outsiders, and promotes group unity.[10]

These studies and others reveal the persuasive nature and potential of music for social movements. However, some conclusions conflict, and most sweeping generalizations have come from unsystematic studies of small samples of songs taken from one or two twentieth century social movements.

This chapter focuses on the persuasive functions songs have performed for American social movements from the Revolutionary era to the 1980s, and attempts to answer four questions: (1) have the functions of protest songs changed over the past two centuries, (2) have specific persuasive functions dominated protest songs over the past two centuries, (3) have persuasive functions varied from stage to stage of long-lived social movements, and (4) have persuasive functions varied between moderate and radical elements of the same movement? Answers to these questions come from an analysis of the manifest content of 714 songs written for or adopted by 21 American social movements (see Figure 1).[11] Each song was coded according to how it appeared to perform the general and specific functions presented in Chapter 8. If a song, for example, called for "freedom" or "equality," this was coded as including general demands under prescribing courses of action.[12] If a song called for the right to vote or for an eight-hour workday, this was coded as including a specific demand. Because songs are brief messages, no count was made of each occurrence of the same persuasive function in each song. The procedure was to note if and how each function was performed in a given song. Frequency counts were limited to social movements for which a minimum of ten songs were available for analysis.

Figure 1: Distribution of Songs Included in This Study

Social Movement	**Sample of Songs**
American Independence Movement	5
Anti-American Aristocracy Movement	2
Anti-Slavery/Abolition Movement	33
Labor Movement	
Pre-Civil War: 1800-1860	23
Post-Civil War: 1865-1900	71
Eight-Hour Movement	24
Twentieth Century: 1900-1940	48
I.W.W. (radical unionism)	54
Black Rights Movement: 1865-1954	42
Civil Rights Movement: 1954-1980	59
Temperance Movement	10
Woman's Rights/Suffrage Movement	19
Women's Liberation Movement	48
Anti-War Movement: Civil War	7
Anti-War Movement: 1865-1940	5
Anti-Vietnam War Movement	39
Populist Movement	17
Farm Movement: 1925-1980	12
Counter-Culture Movement: 1930-1940	3
Counter-Culture Movement: 1960-1975 (moderate)	43
Counter-Culture Movement: 1960-1975 (radical)	12
Resistance Movement: 1954-1975	20
Migrant Worker Movement	4
Gray Power Movement	1
Gay Liberation Movement	23
Anti-Nuclear Power Movement	28
Socialism	62

Let us turn first to a discussion of how social movement music attempts to transform perceptions of history: past, present, and future.

Transforming Perceptions of History

The Past

Only 13% of the songs referred to the past, and most of those references were brief. Only one song dealt solely with the past—a nursery rhyme ballad of the civil rights movement entitled "Grey Goose." There were no apparent differences between songs of moderate and radical elements or life cycles of movements. Twentieth century songs tended to be more concerned with the past than nineteenth century songs, perhaps because more history was available for reference. More than two-thirds of the songs that dealt with the past portrayed it as negative. For instance, the civil rights song entitled "Freedom Is A Constant Struggle" exclaimed that "we've struggled so long," "cried so long," "sorrowed so long," and "died so long." The socialist song "The Long-Haired Kings" described the brutal life under the "warrior kings of old." There were few exceptions to such negative portrayals, even in songs of movements with pasts worth recalling. For example, only occasionally did a labor song look to the pre-industrial era, an anti-war song refer to recent peaceful times, or a counter-culture song relate how America had been before its corruption. Exceptions to this finding were resistance songs. For instance, the song "We're Not for Integration" declared that "Our southland got along just fine" before the civil rights agitators arrived.

The Present

Sixty-one percent of the selected protest songs portrayed the present, ranging from 91% of moderate Counter-Culture songs to 8% of radical counter-culture songs. The life cycle of social movements may determine the amount and frequency of attention to the present. For instance, songs of movements such as the black rights and farm movements seem rarely to have gone beyond a stage of social unrest. Their portrayals of the present were 81% and 83%. In contrast, the civil rights and populist movements had lengthy periods of enthusiastic mobilization, and their treatments of the present were 39% and 29%. Perhaps social movements devote more attention to history when they are attempting to create awareness of an urgent problem and less attention to history when they become dynamic forces and clash with institutions.

An overwhelming 96% of songs that dealt with the present contained only negative portrayals, and many of these portrayals dominated the songs. Forty-two of the 76 songs that served a single major persuasive function dealt solely with a negative vision of the present. For example, the anti-slavery song "Sometimes I Feel Like a Motherless Child," describes the plight of the slave. The resistance song entitled "The Great Society" describes the terrible state of the country under Lyndon Johnson. And the satirical anti-Vietnam War song "Kill for Peace" exclaims that when Americans do not like the way people walk, talk, or threaten their status, they "kill, kill, kill, burn, burn, burn."

The Future

Only 18% of the songs dealt with the future, with the great day coming. There are no obvious patterns. For instance, songs of the labor movement, nineteenth and twentieth century movements, and movements demanding revolutionary changes were at both ends of the scale.

Unlike treatments of the past and the present that were usually negative, 73% of the portrayals of the future were positive. For example, the eight-hour movement song "Divide the Day" envisioned a day when there would be work for all, plenty of food, and joy in the homes of the workers. In "When the Revolution Comes," socialists sang of a future when robbers, editors, policemen, landlords, and capitalists would no longer frighten workers and would have to "live by honest labor!" Not all portrayals were positive, however. Resistance, anti-nuclear power, and counter-culture movements presented negative visions of the future. The majority of both negative and positive portrayals were brief. For example, the anti-slavery song "My Father, How Long" alluded to a time when "The Lord will call us home... where pleasure never dies" and "We'll walk the golden streets of the New Jerusalem." Not a single song was devoted solely or predominantly to transforming perceptions of the future.

Social movement songs are clearly present-oriented. Few songs included in this study address the past or future, and ones that do tend to present brief negative visions of the past or brief positive visions of the future. Social movement music seems to emanate during the stages of social unrest and enthusiastic mobilization when movements are preoccupied with immediate intolerable conditions and conflicts. Thus, social movement songs expound on a negative present rather than on a past that is past or a future that is distant.

Transforming Perceptions of Society

The Opposition

Sixty percent of the selected songs identified the social movement's devil—its major antagonist. Songs of movements that engaged in frequent conflicts with institutions and other social movements and were generally regarded as radical and revolutionary contained the most devil appeals, while songs of social movements that were moderate, less confrontative, or both contained the fewest devil appeals. See Figure 2 for frequency of devil appeals in the selected songs.

The majority of songs that cited devils (80%) identified nebulous, unnamed evil forces, groups, or things such as capitalists, men, bankers, bosses, landlords, integrators, war machines, generals, nuclear power plants, and demon rum. Few songs identified a specific devil such as Henry Ford, Lyndon Johnson, Martin Luther King, Jr., the Pullman Palace Car Company, and the Nuclear Regulatory Commission (NRC). Lack of specificity is not surprising because few protest songs, unlike speeches, are created for specific situations or events. Most songs are sung in a variety of situations over a period of years or decades and do not become dated when an antagonist dies or resigns or an event fades from memory. Indeed many songs, for example "We Shall Overcome," are passed on from movement to movement. This song began as a southern labor song in the 1920s and 1930s, was revised slightly for the civil rights movement, became an important song for black nationalist movements in Africa, and was eventually the anthem for the Catholic rights movement in Northern Ireland. The citation of specific devils (persons or groups) would be dangerous for members of social movements such as anti-slavery and labor. Also, social movements tend to be concerned about large problems such as suffrage, civil rights, and working conditions rather than individuals or specific organizations. Songs introduced during periods of confrontation are most likely to refer to specific devils. For example, anti-nuclear power groups sang "The Meldrim Thompson Song" during their efforts to stop construction of a nuclear power plant in Seabrook, New Hampshire. The Labor song "Ballad of the Chicago-Memorial Day Massacre of 1937," composed after a bloody confrontation at Republic Steel, attacked its owner Tom Gilder. And civil rights songs, particularly during the marches, sit-ins, and demonstrations in Alabama and Mississippi, referred to George Wallace, Ross Barnett, and Jim Clark.

Figure 2: Frequency of Devil Appeals

Most Devil Appeals		Fewest Devil Appeals	
Radical Counter Culture	83%	Moderate Counter-Culture	42%
Populist	82%	Anti-Slavery/Abolition	42%
I.W.W. (radical)	81%	Civil Rights	41%
Labor 1900-1940	79%	Anti-Nuclear Power	36%
Resistance	75%	Temperance	30%
Socialist	71%	Women's Liberation	25%

Only 3% of the songs contained conspiracy appeals—claims that groups were making secret and concerted efforts to harm the movement. The populist movement and the 1900-1940 period of the labor movement used conspiracy appeals most frequently. Populists sang about "the cursed snare—the Money Ring," spying and plotting by landlords, banks, and merchants, and the banding together of monopolies. Labor songs referred to members being "framed up by the law," mine owners "framing men to jail," and "The bosses' justice" ordering "cops and thugs to give them lead."

The most surprising finding is the number and nature of social movements whose songs contained *no* conspiracy appeals: I.W.W., resistance, anti-Vietnam War, counter-culture (moderate and radical), socialist, temperance, women's rights, women's liberation, gay liberation, anti-slavery, and the pre-Civil War labor movement. Many of these movements clashed frequently with a variety of institutions and resistance movements, encountered organized opposition, and (researchers have claimed) had a paranoid flavor in their persuasive efforts. Perhaps conspiracy appeals are too complex for songs; it is simpler to list a devil or two. Or perhaps theorists have overestimated the role of conspiracy appeals in social movement rhetoric.

The selected songs employed surprisingly mild language toward the opposition. Only 27% used invective. Most invective was limited to names for the movement's devils: tyrants, usurpers, thugs, agitators, oppressors, masters, and lords. A small number sang about "race hate fascists," "ghouls of gain," "mule-hearted screwers," "fornicating preachers," and "mean... wicked... heartless... cruel deceivers." Few songs approached the level of verbal venom exhibited in the labor movement's "You Low Life Son of a Bitch" with its profanity and references to the boss as thief, snitch, skunk, pimp, swine, snake, cheat, and "baby-starving... organizer of death." Movements that perceived themselves as locked into a "no holds-barred" mortal conflict with vicious institutions or other social movements resorted to invective far more often than reform-oriented movements noted for moderate persuasive tactics. Figure 3 shows this contrast.

Figure 3: Use of Invective

Most Often		**Least Often**	
I.W.W.	57%	Moderate-Counter Culture	9%
Eight-Hour	54%	Civil Rights	5%
Resistance	50%	Women's Liberation	4%
Radical Counter-Culture	50%	Gay Liberation	4%
Labor 1865-1900	48%	Anti-Vietnam War	3%

Although many practitioners and students of social protest agree with Saul Alinsky that "Ridicule is man's most potent weapon,"[13] *Only one of ten selected songs used ridicule.* Radical-revolutionary movements used ridicule most often. The songs of moderate reform movements such as the following used *no* ridicule: black rights, civil rights, farm movement, temperance, and anti-nuclear power. Ridicule, when it was used in social movement music, tended to be heavy-handed efforts to degrade the opposition. Thus, civil rights advocates were called niggers, apes, and jigaboos; police were called pigs; factory owners were cowardly fobs; and workers and blacks who supported institutions or did not join the movement were scabs, Uncle Toms, stools, cruel knaves, or slackers. Resistance songs such as "Banjo Lip," "Who Likes a Nigger," and "That's the Way a Nigger Goes" contained vicious caricatures of blacks. Labor songs such as "The Scabs Crawl In," "Casey Jones the Union Scab," and "Scissor Bill" attacked non-union workers, especially ones that helped owners to break strikes.

A small percentage of songs, approximately 3%, employed satire or parody. The majority of these songs appeared in two twentieth century movements:

anti-Vietnam War and moderate counter-culture. Anti-war protestors, for instance, sang "The Draft Dodger Rag," "With God on Our Side," "Feel Like I'm Fixin' to Die Rag," and "Kill for Peace." Counter-culture protestors sang "The Merry Minuet," "The Lament of a Minor Dean," "Mine Eyes Have Seen the Horror of the Coming of the Reds," and "Hex on Sex." Interestingly, most of the music of these two movements, unlike social movement music of earlier periods, was composed, and/or sung by professional, commercial artists. The labor movement 1865-1900 did have its parody of "America"; the I.W.W. satirized "Christians at War"; and the abolitionists had a special version of "My Country." The majority of social movement songs, however, were either devoid of humor or employed a meat cleaver approach to ridicule that appealed to the gutteral instincts of *movement members* rather than a scalpel approach of satire and parody that would have appealed to a variety of audiences.

The Self

Contrary to claims of several writers, a relatively small 38% of the selected songs dealt overtly with self-concept or attempted to enhance the self-concept of social movement members and potential members. As expected, social movements that have felt a critical need to establish or to defend self-identity or self-worth delved most often into the self. However, only about a third of women's liberation songs, a movement famous for its consciousness-raising groups and attempts to create a feeling of self-worth among women, addressed the self overtly. Songs dealing with self-concept tended to cry out: We are somebody; We are important; We make contributions; or We are strong! These declarations dominate songs such as "I Am Woman," "Don't Put Her Down," and "The Liberated Woman's Husband's Talking Blues" of the women's liberation movement; "The Farmer Is the Man," "A Hayseed Like Me," and "The Hand that Holds the Bread" of the populist movement; and "Okie from Muskogee," "Segregation Wagon," and "Nigger Hatin' Me" of the resistance movement. Some songs described the achievements or contributions of the social movement's primary audience. For example, the socialist "Hymn of the Proletariat" asked:

> Who hammers brass and stone?
> Who raiseth from the mine?
> Who weaveth cloth and silk?
> Who tilleth wheat and vine?
> Who worketh for the rich to feed,
> Yet lives himself in sorest need?
> It is the men who toil, the Proletariat.

More than half of the songs that appealed overtly to self-concept attempted to activate audiences rather than to enhance feelings of self-identity or self-worth. These attempts appeared in 50 labor songs. One tactic was to challenge singers and listeners to "show the world you're a man" (resistance); "Be brave, be human, not a slave" (socialist); "Come forth and prove your manliness . . . come forth, ye women, be true mothers" (labor 1865-1900); and "Dare to be a union man: Dare to stand alone" (labor 1865-1900). A second tactic, related to the first one, was to pose challenging rhetorical questions. The civil rights version of "Which Side Are You On" asked, "Will you be an Uncle Tom or will you be a man?" A labor song of the 1865-1900 period asked, "Shall we yield our manhood, and to oppression bow?" And the eight-hour song "Freedom" asked, "Has nature's thrift given thee naught but honey's gift? See! the drones are on the wing, have you lost your will to sting?" A third tactic was to relate personal conversion experiences. The populist song "A Hayseed Like Me" began the first verse with "I was once a tool of oppression" and began the last verse with "But now I've roused up a little." The gay liberation song "Second Chance" contained the following verse:

> You know once I was something like you
> I was scared to try anything new
> Well then love it conquered
> Let's see what it can do for you.

The 1930s labor song "Boom Went the Boom" told how "I thought the boss was my best friend" but "I wish I had been wise, next time I'll organize." A fourth tactic was to arouse guilt feelings. For example, the anti-Vietnam War song "Better Days" admitted that "I remember I was smiling as they sent you off—to where? I don't remember." The civil rights song "The Ballad of Bill Moore" related the bravery of an assassinated civil rights protestor and noted, "he dared to walk there [Alabama] by himself, none of us here were walking with him." "Radiation Blues," an anti-nuclear power song, had a child of the future asking:

> Tell me Papa why you didn't say no
> To nuclear power years ago
> Tell me Papa why you didn't say no
> You let it slip away

Labor movement songs of the nineteenth century alluded to the bravery of the American revolutionaries and the cowardliness of their children. "The Working Men" song declared, "To break, we should be ashamed, the bond our fathers framed." And the song "Swell Our Ranks" lamented:

> Oh, ye old and peerless heroes!
> Who did battle for us all,
> In the days of freedom's life-throes,
> Look not earthward on our fall!
> Look not on your servile offspring,
> Who to brothers bend the knee,
> Afraid to utter thoughts within them,
> Or do battle with the free.

A fifth tactic was to portray the terrible status of the oppressed. "Woman Is Nigger of the World" related how we force women to behave, dress, and think—how we have turned women into "the slave of the slaves." The black rights song "Ain't It Hard to Be a Nigger" described how blacks were treated in society and at work. One verse read:

Nigger and white man
Playin' seven-up;
Nigger win de money.
Skeered to pick it up.

The importance of creating we-they distinctions in social movement persuasion is undisputed. Social movement music does a good job of creating and attacking the "they"—the devils, but relatively few social movement songs contain overt content designed to enhance the "we." An interesting question is whether the medium of music alone devotes less attention to the self than to "devils" or whether this characteristic is representative of social movement literature in general—speeches, leaflets, pamphlets, and journals. Perhaps social movements see more need to attack devils than to create self-identity or to enhance feelings of self-worth.

Prescribing Courses of Action

The What

Demands and solutions appeared in 54% of the songs, but most of these appearances were ambiguous references to freedom, liberty, justice, equality or equal rights, reform, fair share, rights or human rights, and dignity. Of those classified as "specific" demands or solutions, the majority were vague allusions to ending the war, gaining civil rights, killing Jim Crow (southern segregation laws), achieving integration, attaining fair compensation (rewards for toil, higher wages, just pay), working shorter hours, obtaining leisure time, and having peaceful homes with quiet firesides. Some songs were more specific, demanding equal pay for equal work, a limit to the workday (ranging from four to twelve hours), the right to vote, collective bargaining, greenbacks and bonds, and an end to nuclear tests and nuclear power plants. Highly specific demands tended to appear in songs from single-issue oriented movements (an eight-hour workday from the eight hour movement and universal suffrage from the suffrage phase of the women's rights movement) or in songs from social movement campaigns ("No Seabrook" in the anti-nuclear power effort to end construction of the Seabrook power plant and "60 Cents a Ton" during a coal miner's strike in the 1900-1940 period of the labor movement).

Only 5% of the selected songs included "solutions," and most of these were simple and nondetailed. For example, the I.W.W. proposed "One Grand Union"; an anti-Vietnam War song proposed to "Stop the War, right now"; an anti-nuclear power song recommended that America "look toward the sun and the wind" for power; socialists proposed a "worker's commonwealth"; and two versions of the same song ("Talking Union" and "Talking Lesbian") urged listeners and singers to "build you a union." Even fewer songs provided some detail for solutions. For instance, "Arise Ye Garvey Nation," a song popular during Marcus Garvey's "back to Africa movement" of the 1920s, mentioned getting ships and materials strong enough to withstand the storms of the seven seas, training Black Cross nurses, and creating a "motor corps" to "take up the wounded dead" from the battlefields to come. Detailed demands and solutions were few probably because both would seem inappropriate for the musical medium.

Songs of social movements that dealt with fairly concrete issues tended to include demands and/or solutions, most frequently, while songs of social movements that were preoccupied with general conditions included demands least often. See Figure 4.

Figure 4: Frequency of Demands and Solutions

Most Often		**Least Often**	
Eight-Hour	96%	Moderate Counter-Culture	21%
Socialist	82%	Radical Counter-Culture	17%
Labor 1865-1900	77%	Farm	17%
Civil Rights	75%	Black Rights	14%

The Who

Only 27% of the songs addressed who must bring about or stifle change, including mentions of the movement, an organization, a leader, or an elite (the true believers of the movement). Contrary to assertions by some contemporary writers, only 3% of the selected songs alluded to "the movement." A slightly higher percentage, but still small proportion of the selected songs, alluded to the organization (e.g., the union) or to a specific organization such as the Knights of Labor, I.W.W., the Weathermen, or Coxey's Army. Highly organized social movements and ones that espoused organization as a means to an end referred to organization most often. Songs from minimally organized movements and ones that did not stress organization as a means were very low on the scale. For example, black rights, anti-slavery, temperance, moderate counter-culture, women's liberation, and anti-nuclear power did not refer to organization in their songs included in this study.

A mere 4% of the selected songs mentioned "leaders" or named specific leaders such as Martin Luther King, Jr., Coxey, Marcus Garvey, and U.S. Stevens (founder of the first national labor union in America). The highest frequencies were populists and labor 1900-1940 who named leader-heroes in their songs such as Coxey and his army of unemployed workers, Eugene Debs and the Pullman Strike, and Joe Hill and his miners. The typical social movement song contained no references to leaders, including all of the selected songs from such movements as pre-Civil War labor, I.W.W., anti-slavery, resistance, farm, temperance, counter-culture, women's liberation, anti-nuclear power, and gay liberation.

Only 11% of the selected songs referred to the "elite" of true believers who would carry out the social movement's cause. Civil rights songs mentioned freedom riders and freedom fighters; radical counter-culture songs praised the Weathermen; and the I.W.W. lauded the "wobblies," as they called I.W.W. members. Few songs praised the elite more profusely than the "Noble Knights of Labor" in the post-Civil War labor movement. One verse read:

> Oh, the great Knights, the noble Knights of Labor,
> The true Knights, the honest Knights of Labor,
> Like the good old Knights of old, they cannot be bought or sold,
> The great Knights, the noble Knights of Labor.

Highly organized movements and ones confronting established institutions referred to the elite most often. It is obvious that social movement songs have not devoted much attention to the elite. As noted during the discussion of transforming perceptions of society, social movement songs tend not to be self-centered. Songs are more concerned with perceptions of the opposition than the self and more concerned with what must be changed or stifled than with the movement, organization, leadership, or elite who must further the cause. "Self" appears to be a secondary concern in social movement music.

The How

Nineteen percent of the songs prescribed how—strategies, tactics, and communication channels—movements should accomplish their goals. Recommendations, included picket lines, marches, demonstrations, strikes, boycotts, votes, sit-ins, stand-ins, agitation, singing, non-violent protest, disruptions, freedom rides, talk, thoughts, organization, and running away. Some suggestions were "original." The song "Over 65" by the gray power movement explained, "And when a nose needs tweaking, I'm right at it and critiquing everywhere." The resistance song "Black Power Never" urged audiences to "wear your *never* buttons, and wave your rebel flags." And the labor song "Stick 'Em Up" recommended placement of black and red stickerettes "on every slave-pen in the land, on every fence and tree" so "No matter where you look you'll see a little red stickerette."

The songs of only three social movements advocated violence. One resistance song recommended running civil rights leaders out of town on a rail, and another proposed shipping "twenty million jigaboos" back to Africa on leaking boats. One women's liberation song, "Don't Say Sister (Until You Mean It)," urged violence in self-defense: "When they stab you in the back, Give me a knife and watch me use it." Only one movement, radical counter-culture, advocated violence over persuasion in several songs. For example, this movement advocated assassination in "Stop Your Imperialist Plunder," gasoline bombs in "We Are the Trashmen," armed struggle and riots in "White Riot," and attacks on police in "Fa La La La La."

The most common strategy was the ballot box. Even socialists who advocated "revolution" and the I.W.W. with its radical image proposed the ballot as the primary means of bringing about change. All phases of labor advocated change through peaceful, constitutional means. A Knights of Labor song entitled "The Grand Labor Cause" declared that "the ballot's our only salvation." Another song declared, "Not by cannon nor by saber..., Thought is stronger far than weapons." Although society often perceives social movements as collections of radical bomb-throwers, most social movement songs have advocated moderate and legitimate means of change.

Highly organized social movements in the stage of enthusiastic mobilization and preoccupied with means referred most frequently to strategies, tactics, and channels. This conclusion is obvious when we contrast the civil rights (22%) with the black rights movement that contained no references to strategies, tactics, or channels.

Sociologist R. Serge Denisoff claims that as social movements have become less ideological during this century, their songs have grown less ideological.[14] But if *what, who,* and *how* are the primary elements of ideology,[15] it would seem that twentieth century protest songs are neither more nor less ideological than their nineteenth century counterparts. Most songs present highly simplified versions of movement ideology. If we look only at *what*—demands and solutions—twentieth century songs rank close to nineteenth century songs in frequency of treatment. See Figure 5.

Figure 5: References to Demands and Solutions

Socialist	82%
Labor 1800-1900	78%
Civil Rights	75%
Anti-Nuclear Power	68%
Gay Liberation	65%

Degree of organization, movement life cycle, and particular cause appear to be more influential than historical period on whether and to what extent a movement's music delves into ideological concerns.

Mobilizing the Movement

Calls to Action

Sixty percent of the selected songs called upon audiences to act. Most calls echoed prescribed courses of action such as to sing, march, demonstrate, picket, vote, organize, strike, talk, disrupt, agitate, and run away. A few challenged listeners to "stand up and be counted," to "go tell it to the mountain," to "give your hands to the struggle," or to "dump the bosses off your back." The most common plea was to unite while only one in twenty songs called upon listeners to organize. While some researchers have noted that songs are primarily instruments for recruiting, only 10% of the songs urged listeners to join movements. If songs recruit members, they do so indirectly.

Songs of many related social movements varied considerably in the frequency of calls to action. See Figure 6.

Figure 6: Frequency of Calls to Action

Moderate Counter-Culture	30%	*and*	Radical Counter-Culture	58%
Black Rights	33%	*and*	Civil Rights	64%
Women's Rights	26%	*and*	Women's Liberation	73%
Farm	42%	*and*	Populist	70%

There are no obvious generalizations because, in the examples given in Figure 6, there is no consistent pattern of radicalness, organization, stage, cause, or historical period.

Because songs are usually sung either by highly credible sources or by audiences themselves, they would seem to present excellent opportunities for persuasion through statements of personal intent. The first format urges listeners to follow the example of leaders, and the second format is a form of self-persuasion. For example, a black rights song declared, "Well now I shall not be moved"; a civil rights song exclaimed, "I gotta fight for my freedom"; a labor song said, "I'm too old to be a scab"; an anti-nuclear power song declared, "I'm gonna stand here and protest"; a gray power song warned, "so I'll take on anybody, foul or fair"; and a migrant workers song intoned, "The picket sign, the picket sign, I carry it all day long." Although we might expect profuse use of such statements in social movement songs, they actually appeared in only 11% of the selected songs. Surprisingly, statements of personal intent never appeared in radical counter-culture, temperance, labor 1865-1900, and eight-hour songs. Only 4% of the I.W.W. and labor 1900-1940 songs included personal intents. Twentieth century songs contained more personal intents more frequently than did nineteenth century songs, but there is no obvious reason for this change.

Appeals Beyond the Movement

Following a comparison of small samples of labor songs with anti-Vietnam War songs, Ralph Knupp concludes that *"The rhetorical patterns in protest songs suggest that they are largely in-group activities."*[16] The present study supports this conclusion. Only 3% of the 714 selected songs appealed overtly to outsiders or to potential legitimizers for sympathy or assistance. Occasionally a song would appeal to the feelings and consciences of outsiders. For example, the labor song "Thirty Cents a Day" tells of a young maiden dying from long hours, brutal work, and starvation. The last verse begins, "Too late, Christian ladies! You cannot save her now; she breathes out her life—see the death damp on her brow." The anti-slavery song "A Pilgrim of God" describes the condition of slaves and their pleas for help. It ends:

> But while your kindest sympathies
> To foreign lands do roam,
> I would ask you to remember
> Your own oppressed at home.

"Links on a Chain" by Phil Ochs appealed to labor unions to help blacks in their struggle for equal rights and jobs. With slight changes, a great many movement songs could have appealed to a larger variety of audiences for understanding and support.

Only 10% of the selected songs made overt threats to established institutions or their agents. The anti-slavery song "Nat Turner," written shortly after Nat Turner's bloody slave uprising, warned slave owners:

> You might be as rich as cream,
> And ride you a coach and four-horse team;
> But you can't keep the world from moving around,
> And Nat Turner from gaining ground.

The I.W.W. tune "Harvest War Song" warned, "We are coming home, John Farmer, We are coming home to stay." The civil rights song "Oh Wallace" warned the Alabama governor: "Oh Wallace, you never can jail us all, Oh Wallace, segregation's bound to fail." Thus, social movement music talked a great deal more *about* the opposition than *to* the opposition. Songs tend to be for in-house consumption.

Victory is Near

Only 11% of the songs predicted that victory was at hand. For instance, the black rights song "One Day Old and No Damn Good" portrayed a hard present and then reassured audiences, "This nightmare, babe, can't last the night; We'll end it soon, both black and white." Other songs said that "Freedom's comin' and it won't be long"; Oppressions expiring, and soon will be past;" "The joyful hour is coming, 'tis the dawn before the day"; and "It's coming fast—our turn, at last—the social revolution." The majority of social movement songs tend to be dreary and pessimistic. This is particularly true of twentieth century songs. All of the movements with the fewest musical references to immediate victory were in the twentieth century.

Sustaining the Movement

Justifying Setbacks and Delays

Not one of the 714 selected songs attempted to explain setbacks and delays movements had had or were experiencing. Music would seem to be an inappropriate medium for this specific persuasive function. Songs are not designed to explain complex matters.

Commitment to the Movement

Twenty-one percent of the songs dealt with commitment to social movements. Some songs assured listeners that "perseverence conquers all," that "the union makes us strong," and that "Our hearts and hands in union strong, not fear or threats can swerve." Other songs urged listeners to "stick together," to "hang in there a little bit longer," to "hold the fort," to "fight on undaunted," and to "be firm and valient-hearted." Others involved audiences in singing pledges of commitment. A Revolutionary War era song proclaimed, "We are the troop that will never stoop to wretched slavery." A Ku Klux Klan resistance song promised, "we always can be counted on, when there's a job to do." And a civil rights song pledged, "We're gonna keep on fighting for freedom, in the end we will be free." Only 3% of the selected songs included personal pledges or intentions to remain committed to the cause. A woman's rights song pledged not to be silenced: "No, I will speak my mind if I die for it." A labor song of the 1930s declared, "I'm a miner's son, and I'll stick with the union, 'til every battle's won." A civil rights version of this labor song exclaimed, "I'm a freedom son, I'll stick right with this struggle until the battle's won." Interestingly, the black rights song "I Shall Not Be Moved" was changed to "We Shall Not Be Moved" during the civil rights movement. Perhaps this was an effort to stress the need for collective action and unity. Social movement songs tended to urge people to remain committed or to include collective pledges rather than resort to potentially more persuasive personal pledges. These preferences reduced opportunities for the influence of highly credible sources of self-persuasion.

Ultimate Victory

Twenty-four percent of the selected songs assured movement supporters that victory would come ultimately for their efforts. Perhaps the most famous of all social movement songs, "We Shall Overcome" (an altered version of the 1930s labor song "We Will Overcome"), proclaimed that "We shall overcome someday" and "we'll walk hand in hand someday." The temperance song "Victory" predicted that "In the sweet by and by, we'll conquer the demon of rum." The resistance song "Better Days Are Yet to Come," designed to lessen the influence of counter-culture's "Eve of Destruction," pleaded "Listen to me everyone, better days are yet to come." And the Knights of Labor song "The Good Time Coming" began with this verse:

There's a good time coming, boys,
A good time coming;
We may not live to see the day,
But earth shall glisten in the ray,
Of the good time coming.

Optimism was higher in nineteenth century songs than in twentieth century songs, and more frequent in songs of highly organized and less confrontational movements. The overall level of optimism, however, was much lower than expected.

The Movement's Heritage

A number of writers have claimed that social movement songs rely heavily upon references to past heroes, martyrs, victories, and tragedies to sustain commitment of supporters and the movement's forward progress. The findings of this study do not substantiate these claims. *Only 13% of the selected songs mentioned heroes or martyrs*. The majority of these songs referred to assassinated leaders or followers such as Medgar Evers, Bill Moore, Malcolm X, and Martin Luther King, Jr. of the civil rights movement; to persons unfairly arrested and convicted or executed such as Joe Hill and Sacco and Vanzetti of the labor movement and the Scottsboro boys and the Ferguson brothers of the black rights movement; or to victims such as peasants in Vietnam, coal miners, "labor's sons and daughters," child factory workers, and mythical workers such as John Henry. A small number of songs referred to heroes such as the Founding Fathers, Abraham Lincoln, Mother Jones (an early labor leader), Momma Rosa Parks (a black seamstress who refused to give up her seat to a white male passenger and thus sparked the Montgomery bus boycott led by the young Rev. Martin Luther King, Jr.), James Meredith (the first black student at the University of Mississippi), and Harriet Tubman (a black anti-slavery leader). References to heroes and martyrs appeared more often in twentieth century protest songs than in nineteenth century songs.

Less than 2% of the selected songs referred to tragedies or victories. A handful of labor songs (all seven that dealt with tragedies) related the details of disasters such as "The Ludlow Massacre," "1913 Massacre at Calumet, Michigan," "The Marion, North Carolina, Massacre," and "The Ballad of the Chicago-Memorial Day Massacre of 1937." The six songs that recalled victories dealt with successful strikes, passage of important legislation such as an eight-hour law in Illinois, or the bringing down of Chicago during the 1968 Democratic National Convention.

Results of this study suggest that few songs are designed to sustain social movements. Most songs were composed during the social unrest and enthusiastic mobilization stages, before most tragedies and victories took place, and before most heroes and martyrs were enshrined. When movements sing during the maintenance stage, they apparently select from among the movement's traditional songs such as "We Shall Overcome," "Solidarity Forever," and "We Shall Not Be Moved" rather than compose new ones.

Conclusions

All of the general and specific persuasive functions except justifying setbacks and delays appeared in at least one of the 714 social movement songs analyzed during this study. This specific function would seem to be most inappropriate for the musical medium. The majority of songs described the present, identified one or more devils, listed demands or solutions, and urged listeners or participants to act.

The selected social movement songs from 21 movements tended to be negative rather than positive, pessimistic rather than optimistic, general rather than specific, and mild rather than abrasive in language. While most songs were addressed to the in-group rather than to potential legitimizers or the opposition, they were not "movement centered." A minority attempted to enhance self-concept (identity or self-worth) and even fewer praised the movement, movement organizations, leaders, or the elite. Songs were concerned with present circumstances rather than the past or the future. They dwelt upon large problems rather than individuals and tended to identify abstract demands (freedom, equality, liberty, justice) rather than specific problems or solutions. Songs issued few threats and prescribed few violent actions. They pleaded for "fair" treatment and urged followers to use lawful means—primarily the ballot box—to bring about change. Few songs seemed designed to sustain social movements through overt appeals. A minority urged audiences to remain committed to the cause and assured them of ultimate victory. A tiny minority mentioned movement heroes, martyrs, tragedies, or victories.

The persuasive content of songs varied drastically from song to song within the same movement, between movements, and over time. Many differences were inexplainable, but there were some apparent patterns. For instance, twentieth century songs referred to the past and to movement heritage more often than did nineteenth century songs, perhaps there was more of each to talk about. Twentieth century songs also included tasteful satire more often (perhaps because of involvement of commercial composers in the 1960s and 1970s), more statements of personal intent, and a greater degree of pessimism. The songs of highly organized social movements exuded more optimism, were (not surprisingly) more movement centered, and addressed more often the strategies, tactics, and communication channels movements should employ to achieve their goals. Songs of single-issue movements or composed during social movement campaigns were more specific, especially when treating demands and solutions. Songs of radical social movements and ones in desperate struggles with established institutions dealt more with the opposition and employed more ridicule and invective. Attempts to transform perceptions of history (past, present, and future) appeared more often in and tended to dominate songs composed during the social unrest stage of social movements.

This study substantiated many of the claims from earlier studies but called others into question. For example, contrary to some claims, there were very few conspiracy appeals in the 714 selected songs. Few songs dealt overtly with self-concept, the "movement," or the movement's heritage—especially the movement's triumphs and heroes. Few songs included overt efforts to unify the movement or to get people to join. There was little attention given to ideology in either the nineteenth or the twentieth century songs. And although songs tended to be highly simplistic, they were seldom devoted to a single function as some writers have claimed. Eighty-nine percent of the selected songs performed two or more major persuasive functions. A larger percentage of songs performed all five major functions than performed a single major function.

Although many social movement songs seemed admirably suited to perform persuasive functions, a surprising number failed to perform important functions. For example, more attention to the past and the future could have aided in legitimizing movements both to members and non-members, could have helped to establish the urgency of problems, and could have portrayed more effectively the glorious future that was desired or the gloomy future movements wished to avoid. More attention to self (concept, identity, worth) could have reduced feelings of inferiority and illegitimacy and counteracted attacks by established institutions and resistance movements. Social movement songs used satire and ridicule too infrequently. Both of these tactics can make protest fun, build self-concept by making the opposition look ugly and foolish, and are difficult to counteract. More statements of personal intent by audiences and highly credible sources could have enhanced commitment of members and prompted them to act as desired. Since social movements tend to be long-term persuasive efforts, songs should have assured audiences more frequently that victory was near or at least inevitable and should have urged audiences to remain committed to the cause. And finally, social movement songs should have appealed to audiences beyond social movement members and sympathizers, especially to potential legitimizers. Nearly all of the selected songs appealed only to the in-group.

Endnotes

[1] Plato, *The Republic*, trans. B. Jowett (New York: Modern Library, n.d.), Book IV, 424, 135.

[2] R. Serge Denisoff, *Sing a Song of Social Significance* (Bowling Green, OH: Bowling Green University Popular Press, 1972), 19. Cited from Jerome Rodnitzky, "The New Revivalism: American Protest Songs, 1945-1968," paper delivered at American Studies Association convention, 1969.

[3] David Noebel, *The Marxist Minstrels: A Handbook on Communist Subversion of Music* (Tulsa: American Christian College Press, 1974), 1.

[4] Denisoff, 137-145.

[5] James R. Irvine and Walter G. Kirkpatrick, "The Musical Form in Rhetorical Exchange: Theoretical Considerations." *Quarterly Journal of Speech*, 58 (October, 1971), 272-284.

[6] Cheryl Irwin Thomas, "'Look What They've Done to My Song, Ma': The Persuasiveness of Song," *Southern Speech Communication Journal*, 39 (Spring, 1974), 260-268.

[7] Stephen Kosokoff and Carl W. Carmichael, "The Rhetoric of Protest: Song, Speech, and Attitude Change," *Southern Speech Communication Journal*, 35 (Summer, 1970), 295-302.

[8] John David Bloodworth, "Communication in the Youth Counter Culture: Music as Expression," *Central States Speech Journal*, 26 (Winter, 1975), 304-309.

[9] David A. Carter, "The Industrial Workers of the World and the Rhetoric of Song," *Quarterly Journal of Speech*, 66 (December, 1980), 365-374.

[10] Ralph E. Knupp, "A Time for Every Purpose Under Heaven: Rhetorical Dimensions of Protest Music," *Southern Speech Communication Journal*, 46 (Summer, 1981), 377-389.

[11] Texts for the songs came from records, tape recordings, and printed sources such as Philip S. Foner (ed), *American Labor Songs of the Nineteenth Century* (Urbana: University of Illinois Press, 1975); Tom Glazer (ed), *Songs of Peace, Freedom, and Protest (New York: David McKay, 1970); John Greenway (ed), American Folksongs of Protest* (Philadelphia: University of Pennsylvania Press, 1953); David M. Rosen (ed), *Protest Songs in America* (Westlake Village, CA: Aware Press, 1972); and *Songs of the Workers: To Fan the Flames of Discontent* (Chicago: Industrial Workers of the World, 1974).

[12] Each song was coded twice and students in a persuasion course at Purdue University coded a sample of songs both to refine the coding scheme and to reduce the problem of identifying persuasive functions that were not apparent in the *content of the songs*.

[13] Saul D. Alinsky, *Rules for Radicals: A Practical Primer for Realistic Radicals* (New York: Vintage, 1972), 128.

[14] Denisoff, 78-79.

[15] John Wilson, *Introduction to Social Movements* (New York: Basic Books, 1973), 89-150.

[16] Knupp, 388.

Chapter 14

The Persuasive Functions of Slogans

The drastic increase in social activism within the United States since 1960 has been accompanied by such memorable and sometimes infamous, slogans as: "Hey, Hey, LBJ, How Many Kids Have You Killed Today"; "Hell No, We Won't Go"; "Fuck the Draft"; "Freedom Now"; "Free Huey"; "Dare to Struggle, Dare to Win"; "Black Power"; "Don't Trust Anyone Over 30"; "America, Love It or Leave It"; "America, Change It or Lose It"; "Gray Power"; and "Black Is Beautiful." Protestors have chanted, shouted, and sung slogans; printed them in leaflets, pamphlets, and social movement newsletters and newspapers; worn them on buttons, tee-shirts, jackets, and the seats of their pants; and have written, painted, or pasted them on billboards, posters, banners, automobile bumpers, buses, subways, sidewalks, and walls. But in spite of the use and visibility of slogans, they have received little attention in studies of strategies, tactics, and communication channels employed by social movements.[1]

"The Report of the Committee on the Advancement and Refinement of Rhetorical Criticism," published in *The Prospect of Rhetoric* in 1971, encouraged study of "any human act, process, product, or artifact which, in the critic's view, may formulate, sustain, or modify attention, perceptions, attitudes, or behavior."[2] We believe that slogans clearly fall within the realm of rhetoric or persuasion envisioned in the Committee's charge. In this chapter, then, we will identify the nature, types, and persuasive functions of slogans as an important languaging strategy in the persuasive efforts of social movements.

The Nature of Slogans

"Sloganeering" did not originate in the 1960s. The term has a rich history. It originated from the Gaelic word *slaugh-gharim*, which signified a "host-shout," "war cry," or "gathering word or phrase of one of the old Highland clans; hence the shout or battle cry of soldiers in the field."[3]

English-speaking people began using the term by 1704. The term at that time meant "the distinctive note, phrase or cry of any person or body of persons." Slogans were common throughout the European continent during the middle ages, and they were utilized primarily as "passwords to insure proper recognition of individuals at night or in the confusion of battle." The American revolutionary rhetoric would not have been the same without "the Boston Massacre," "the Boston Tea Party," "the shot heard around the world," and shouts of "no taxation without representation."

John Bowers and Donovan Ochs define slogans as "imperative statements...single words or short phrases with the imperative mood strongly implied."[4] But slogans are more than "imperative statements"—commands, decrees, edicts, or fiats; they also invoke impressions and elicit emotional responses. George Shankel defines a slogan as "some pointed term, phrase, or expression, fittingly worded, which suggests action, loyalty, or which causes people to decide upon and to fight for the realization of some principle or decisive issue."[5] This definition recognizes that slogans perform a variety of persuasive functions. Murray Edelman has discussed the "dynamic" function of language in stimulating mental or behavioral action. For him, this dynamism is the key to understanding the persuasive use of symbols such as slogans within the realm of politics:

> The employment of language to sanctify action is exactly what makes politics different from other methods of allocating values. Through language a group cannot only achieve an immediate result but also win the acquiescence of those whose lasting support is needed. More than that, it is the talk and the response to it that measures political potency, not the amount of force that is exerted.[6]

Thus, slogans operate in society as "social symbols" and, as such, their intended or perceived meanings may be difficult to grasp and their impact or stimulation may differ between and among individuals and groups. Edelman notes that "Because language is so efficient a tool for reifying the abstract, it is central to the practice endemic in contemporary culture of dealing in abstractions."[7] Hugh Duncan emphasizes that "it is the ambiguity of symbols which makes them so useful in human society. Ambiguity is a kind of bridge that allows us to run back and forth from one kind of meaning to another, until we take firm resolve to cross the bridge into new, and fixed meanings."[8] From this "new and fixed meaning," we think, we feel, and ultimately we may act.

Robert Brooks demonstrated the phenomenon of symbolic bridgecrossing in his investigation of how three groups—black college students, white college students, and white policemen, interpreted the meaning of the slogan "Black Power."[9] He discovered three dominant dimensions in the meaning of "Black Power." The first dimension was "aggression." Whites, more frequently than blacks, perceived aggression, violence, confrontation, and racial domination inherent in the concept of "Black Power." The second dimension was "goals." Blacks, more frequently than whites, tended to associate various political goals such as equal rights and equal opportunity with the slogan. And the third dimension, "mystique," referred to endowing the slogan with nonmaterial attributes such as self-identity, pride, and awareness. The words "black power," therefore, had different meanings for different groups ranging from positive notions such as political goals and pride to negative notions such as aggression, confrontation, and violence. Slogans, then, may serve as the symbolic justifications for feelings and actions and provide a bridge or direct link to social action. Hugh Duncan concludes:

> Symbols, then, create and sustain beliefs in ways of acting because they function as names which signify proper, dubious, or improper ways of expressing relationships. As we are taught in the Bible, we act in the name of the Father, the Son, and Holy Ghost.[10]

Because slogans may operate as "significant symbols" or as key words that have a standard meaning in a group, they serve both expressive and persuasive functions. Harold Laswell recognized that the influencing of collective attitudes is possible by the manipulation of significant symbols such as slogans.[11] He believed that a verbal symbol might evoke a desired reaction or organize collective attitudes around a symbol. Murray Edelman writes that "to the political scientist patterning or consistency in the contexts in which specific groups of individuals use symbols is crucial, for only through such patterning do common political meanings and claims arise."[12] Thus, the slogans a group uses to evoke specific responses may provide us with an index of the group's norms, values, and conceptual rationale for its claims.

Slogans as Tools of Persuasion

Slogans are so pervasive in today's society that it is easy to underestimate their persuasive power. They have grown in significance because of the medium of television and the advertising industry. Television, in addition to being the major advertising medium, has altered the nature of human interaction. Political images are less personal and shorter. They function as summaries and conclusions rather than bases for public interaction and debate. The style of presentation in television is more emotional, but the content is less complex or ideological. In short, slogans work well on television.

The advertising industry has made a science of sloganeering. Today, communication itself is a problem because we live in an "overcommunicated" society. Advertisers have discovered that it is easier to link product attributes to existing beliefs, ideas, goals, and desires of the consumer rather than to change them. Thus, to say that a cookie tastes "homemade" or is as good as "Mom used to make" does not tell us if the cookie is good or bad, hard or soft, but simply evokes the fond memories of Mother's baking. Advertisers, then, are more successful if they present a product in a way that capitalizes on established beliefs or expectations of the consumer. Slogans do this well by crystallizing in a few words the key idea or theme one wants to associate with an issue, group, product, or event. "Sloganeering" has become institutionalized as a virtual art form, and an advertising agency may spend months testing and creating the right slogan for a product or a person.

Slogans have a number of attributes that enhance their persuasive potential for social movements. They are unique and readily identifiable with a specific social movement or social movement organization. "Gray Power," for instance, readily identifies the movement for elderly Americans, and "Huelga" (strike in Spanish) identifies the movement to aid Mexican-American field workers in the west and the southwest. Slogans are easy to say and to remember, but they are difficult to imitate. In the abortion controvery, for example, the "right to choose" does not sound as potent and urgent as the "right to life." Slogans are often fun because they contain active verbs and adjectives, are witty, and rhyme. Examples of slogans with these characteristics are: "Make Love, Not War" (anti-Vietnam War movement); "Keep Your Morality Off My Body" (pro-choice and gay rights movements); "Not the Church, Not the State, Women Must Decide Their Fate" (women's liberation movement); and "We Are Here and We Are Not Going to Disappear" (Gray Panthers). Slogans are often repetitious or are designed to be repeated or chanted. The Black Action Movement at the University of Michigan chanted "Open It Up or Close It Down" during demonstrations demanding an open admissions policy and an active minority recruitment program at the University. Demonstrators and participants in mass rallies shouted "Free Huey" again and again in their efforts to obtain the release of arrested Black Panther Party leader and Minister of Defense Huey P. Newton from jail. Slogans may serve as a way to release pent-up emotions and frustrations and, like name-calling and obscenity—as we will see in Chapter 15, may act as a verbal surrogate for physical aggression. And finally, slogans may create a "blindering" effect by preventing audiences from considering alternative ways of thinking, feeling, and/or acting.[13] Slogans tend to be definitive, Platonic statements of the social movement's "truths" and rely on audience predispositions to achieve xpected responses.

Three things should be evident about slogans. First, they are more than a 1ode of expression or information; they are *persuasive* in nature. Second, y recognizing the "symbols" to which audiences have been conditioned to espond, social movement persuaders may formulate slogans that will have rofound, persuasive, organizing effects. And third, the analysis of slogans f various social movements and social movement organizations (such as he John Birch Society, the Black Panthers, and the American Indian Aovement) may reveal their implicit norms, values, and claims.

Types of Slogans

There appear to be three types of slogans in the persuasion of social novements. *Spontaneous slogans* tend to be "original" and to rely upon ndividual protestor initiative for their creation and use during demonstra-ons and movement meetings. Spontaneous slogans are often short, rhyth-nical chants such as "Shut It Down" (anti-war protestors in Chicago uring the 1968 Democratic National Convention); "Freedom, Freedom, reedom" (civil rights movement); "ROTC Has to Go" and "Pigs Off 'ampus" (anti-war demonstrations at Kent State University); and "Viva ,a Causa" (Chicano movement). Other spontaneous slogans are longer, ometimes more issue-oriented, and appear on signs carried by protestors. ;xamples are "Don't Cook Dinner, Starve a Rat Today" and "House-vives Are Unpaid Slaves" (women's liberation movement); "We Have Our Bible, We Don't Need Your Dirty Books" (movement to censor school text-ooks and books in public libraries); "The Racist Pigs Must Free Huey or he Sky's the Limit" (Black Panther Party demonstration for Huey Newton); and "We Build Up, We Don't Tear Down" (pro-Vietnam War novement).

Sanctioned slogans are "official" slogans of social movements or ones adopted by the movement or a specific social movement organization. They are placed on movement produced buttons, leaflets, posters, and news-etters, and are often chanted at movement meetings. Examples are pro-life's "Give to the Unborn Child Their First Civil Right—Life," "Never to ,augh or Love," and "We Are Protestants, Protesting Abortion." The counter-culture movement employed such slogans as "Don't Trust Anyone Over 30" and "All Power to the People." The official slogan of the Knights of Labor was "An Injury to One Is an Injury to All." Highly organized ,ocial movements that publish their own newspapers, magazines, and pamphlets tend to use an official slogan or motto on the front pages or the covers of publications, and these slogans may accompany or be part of the official logo. For example, the masthead of *The Call,* published by the

Marxist-Leninist October League, contains the slogan, "People of the World Unite to Defeat Imperialism." The native American newspaper *Wassaji* uses the slogan "Let My People Know." *The Rebel Worker,* published by the radical left Workers Party and Rebel Worker Organization, has the slogan "Freedom, Justice, Social Equality" on a banner held in the beak of a Bald Eagle. And publications of CARE (Citizens Against a Radioactive Environment) has a circular logo with a half-sunburst in the top part and the words "No Nukes" in the bottom part.

Advertising slogans are found most frequently on buttons, bumperstickers, and tee-shirts. They tend to be short statements that emphasize a single demand or remind us of the social movement or a particular social movement organization. "Issue" examples are "recall Ralph Nader" (radical right resistance groups); "Employ, Don't Destroy" (anti-nuclear power and weapons groups); and "Solar Employs, Nuclear Destroys" and "Don't Waste America" (anti-nuclear power). "Organizational" slogans are "Black Panthers," "Gray Panthers," "Right to Life," and "The Wobblies Are Coming" (Industrial Workers of the World).

Let us turn now to a discussion of the persuasive functions that these three types of slogans perform for social movements.

Persuasive Functions of Slogans

In the remainder of this chapter, we attempt to determine the persuasive functions that social movement slogans perform. Our analysis is based on a sample of 585 spontaneous, sanctioned, and advertising slogans used by 18 contemporary American social movements.[14] We selected contemporary social movements so that we would be aware of how, when, where, and by whom the slogans were used—all important factors in determining the persuasive functions of such brief and ambiguous messages as slogans. The movements and samples of slogans are shown in Figure 1.

Our procedure was similar to that employed in studying music (Chapter 13). The content of each slogan was coded according to how it appeared to perform the general and specific persuasive functions presented in Chapter 8. Frequency counts were limited to movements for which a minimum of ten slogans were available for analysis.

Let us turn first to a discussion of how social movement slogans attempted to transform perceptions of history: past, present, and future.

Transforming Perceptions of History

The Past. Not one of the 585 slogans included in this study attempted to transform perceptions of the past. Social movements tend not to dwell on the past in their persuasive efforts, and the simplicity of slogans would seem to make them an inappropriate source for treating any event, issue, or concept

Figure 1: Distribution of Slogans in This Study

Social Movement	Sample of Slogans
Anti-Nuclear Power Movement	32
Anti-Nuclear Weapons Movement	6
Anti-Vietnam War Movement	79
Black Rights Movement	66
Ecology Movement	21
Gay Rights Movement	14
Gray Power Movement	15
Kidvid Movement	4
Native American Movement	19
Movement to Reform Marijuana Laws	3
Pro-Choice Movement	19
Pro-Life Movement	38
Pro-Nuclear Power Movement	8
Radical Left Movement	45
Radical Right (Resistance) Movement	114
Save the Whales Movement	3
United Farm Workers/Chicano Movements	28
Women's Liberation Movement	71

that requires explanation. Audiences must be able to attach instant meanings to the slogans that they see, hear, or say.

The Present. Only 16% of the selected slogans portrayed the present, and these slogans tended to appear in a few social movements that felt an urgent need to transform perceptions of "reality." Eighty-nine percent of the slogans that dealt with the present were efforts to make audiences aware of intolerable situations. Typical examples were:

No playing today kids—smog by General Motors (ecology)
Abortion: The American Holocaust (pro-life)
Housewives are unpaid slaves (women's liberation)
War is not healthy for children and other living things (anti-Vietnam War)
How can we make ends meet? (Gray Panthers)
You can't be free in St. Louis with slavery in Birmingham (black rights)

Protestors often included graphic pictures with their slogans to enhance their persuasive impact. For instance, the ecology movement's slogan "Ecology is for the birds" was accompanied by a picture of an oil-soaked duck. The anti-Vietnam War slogan "The real tragedy of war is its survivors'' was accompanied by a picture of crippled Vietnamese children. And the United Farm Worker slogan ''Every grape you buy keeps this child hungry'' was accompanied by a picture of a starving child in filthy surroundings. Some social movements have attempted to ''redefine reality'' through such slogans as:

Fetus is Latin for child (pro-life)
Peace is more than the absence of war (anti-nuclear weapons)
Porn is violence disguised (women's liberation)
Abortion is something personal—not political (pro-choice)

The pro-choice slogan ''If men could get pregnant, abortion would be a sacrament'' seems to have been an attempt to redefine abortion and the motives of the male-oriented opposition to it.

The Future. Only 4% of the 585 slogans studied attempted to transform perceptions of the future, and these slogans (unlike social movement songs) attempted to create negative expectancies in the minds of readers and listeners, expectancies that would come about unless a change was initiated or stifled. The anti-nuclear weapons movement declared that ''nuclear war is nuclear suicide'' and the ecology movement pleaded, ''Save our grandchildren now, not when it's too late.'' Some movements seemed to play verbal ping-pong with their adversaries. For example, pro-life warned that ''Abortion today justifies euthanasia tomorrow'' while pro-choice asked ''Do you want to return to the butchery of back-alley abortion?'' And anti-nuclear power advised, ''Better active today than radioactive tomorrow'' while pro-nuclear power warned, ''No nukes, no heat, no lights.''

Most social movement slogans were brief and seemed to emanate during the stage of enthusiastic mobilization when movements were preoccupied with demands and confrontations with established institutions. Thus, social movement slogans dwell little on history and, when doing so, tend to be negative and to expound upon an intolerable present.

Transforming Perceptions of Society

The Opposition. Only 15% of the selected slogans identified the social movement's devil—its major antagonist. Slogans of movements that engaged in frequent conflicts with institutions and other social movements and were generally regarded as ''radical'' and ''revolutionary'' contained the most devil appeals. See Figure 2.

These figures reveal that devil appeals appear far less often in slogans than in songs (see Chapter 13). And, in contrast to songs, only a simple majority of slogans identified nebulous, unnamed evil forces, groups, or things such as men, anyone over 30, communism, the rich, capitalists, oil profiteers, and blacks. On the other hand, nearly half of

Figure 2: Devil Appeals in Slogans

Most Devil Appeals		Fewest Devil Appeals	
Radical Right	29%	Gray Panthers	7%
Anti-Vietnam War	23%	Native American	5%
Gay Rights	21%	Pro-life	3%
Radical left	20%	Pro-choice	0%
United Farm Workers	18%	Anti-nuclear power	0%

the selected slogans identified specific devils such as Ronald Reagan, Lyndon Johnson, Richard Nixon, Anita Bryant, Jane Fonda, the SDS (Students for a Democratic Society), Gallo Wines, General Electric, and the National Council of Churches. Unlike songs, slogans (especially spontaneous ones) are often created for specific situations or events and may become dated or obsolete within hours, days, or weeks. It is not surprising, then, that they would be more specific than songs. None of the slogans contained conspiracy appeals or used the word conspiracy.

The selected slogans employed surprisingly mild language toward the opposition. Only about 4% (compared to 27% for songs) used invective or name-calling. The following were some of the more colorful slogans:

Don't cook dinner—starve a rat today (women's liberation)
Boycott Campbell's Cream of Exploitation Soup (United Farm Workers)
Let's stop supporting the bandit state of Israel (radical right)
Pill-em or kill-em groups make $'s from abortion (pro-life)
Green Pigs (anti-Vietnam War protest at Kent State University)
Anita Bryant—Empress of the bigots (gay rights)

Only about 2% of the 585 slogans (compared to 10% for songs) employed ridicule. Typical examples were:

The SDS is a social disease (radical right)
The peace dove is a chicken (radical right and pro-Vietnam war)
Judas William Foolbright (radical right and pro-Vietnam War protest against anti-war Senator William Fulbright)
Why can't white men act like human beings? (native American)
Bless those who declare war, they're usually too old to fight and die (anti-Vietnam War)
If you liked Hitler, you'll love Wallace (black rights protest against Alabama Governor George Wallace who was running for President)

The brevity of slogans may explain the near-absence of ridicule and satire in social movement slogans, but brevity would not explain the mild language of slogans. Perhaps during the enthusiastic mobilization stage of movements, protestors are preoccupied with making demands and pressuring the opposition rather than identifying devils and calling names, a rhetoric more appropriate for earlier stages of protest and less confrontative times.

Social movement slogans tend to have more specific targets than do protest songs, but they tend to be less abrasive in language than songs. These are interesting contrasts when we consider that songs are generally sung in safe surroundings somewhat removed from both the public and the opposition, while slogans are usually displayed, chanted, or shouted in public places or in the face of the opposition and on the opposition's territory.

The Self. A surprisingly small 12% of the 585 selected slogans dealt with self-concept. As expected, the slogans of social movements that have felt a critical need to establish or to defend the "self" included the most frequent appeals to self-concept. See Figure 3.

Figure 3: Slogans Dealing with Self-Concept

Most Frequent		Least Frequent	
Gay rights	43%	Pro-choice	5%
Gray Panthers	33%	Pro-life	3%
Native Americans	31%	Anti-Vietnam War	2%
Women's liberation	22%	Anti-nuclear power	0%
Radical right	17%	Ecology	0%

The selected social movement slogans contained only about one-third as many appeals to self-concept as did the social movement songs studied in Chapter 13. Slogans appear to be used less often than songs to transform perceptions of society.

The most common appeal was to self-worth, proclaiming that "I am somebody," "I am important," "I am of value," or "I should be in positions of authority." Typical of these slogans were direct appeals such as the following:

> Women are not chicks (women's liberation)
> A woman's place is in the house—and in the Senate (women's liberation)
> We build the city up, not burn it down (radical right)
> Discover America with real Americans (Native American)
> Seniors count too (Gray Panthers)
> Say it loud, I'm Black and I'm Proud (black rights)
> God loves Gays (gay rights)
> I am special, I am me (women's liberation)

Less direct, but clever, attempts to enhance self-concept were the women's liberation slogan "Trust in God, *She* will provide" and the gay rights slogan "I am your worst fear, I am your best fantasy."

Another common appeal was to feelings of power and strength. The simple but persuasive slogan "Black power" generated a host of imitations: "Brown power," "Red power," "White power," "Gray power," "Woman power," "Senior power," "Poor power," "Gay power," and "All power to the people." Other slogans expressed the strength of movement members or their capacity to bring about change. For instance, a women's liberation slogan declared, "The hand that rocks the cradle should rock the boat;" a Chicano slogan stated, "We are not a minority;" a NORML (National Organization for Reform of Marijuana Laws slogan) assured audiences that "You can change the world;" and a Gray Panther slogan declared, "Panthers on the prowl." Such slogans as these appear to be designed to alter the image of movement members as well as to give them feelings of strength and the will to act. There were only 28 appeals to power and strength among the 585 selected slogans. This small figure, however, does not reveal the frequency with which protestors used specific slogans. Undoubtedly the slogan "black power," for example, was more significant in both frequency and impact than dozens of other black rights slogans combined.

Twenty percent of appeals to self-concept dealt with self-identity. These slogans seemed to reflect a need among protestors to express who they were. Examples were:

I'm proud to be an American (radical right)
Meet a woman who's had an abortion (pro-choice)
I am a [sic] Indian and I am pretty dam [sic] proud of it (native American)
Vietnam vets for peace (anti-Vietnam War)
I am a lesbian and I am beautiful (gay rights)

These slogans exuded pride, a declaration of beliefs or support for a cause, and the willingness to reveal one's self for a cause. Other slogans identified persons with specific groups or organizations:

Feminism lives (women's liberation)
I am a secret member of the John Birch Society (radical right)
I am an American Nazi (radical right)
We care, we love, we are Pro-Life (pro-life)
We are pro-choice and we vote (pro-choice)
Young Americans for Freedom (radical right)

As we will see later in this chapter, slogans such as the above serve important organizational and unifying functions as well as the need to enhance self-concept.

Only 12% of the selected slogans (compared to 22% of songs) attempted to "activate" audiences by challenging them to act through appeals to self-concept. The following examples were typical of such slogans:

Don't be half a man, join the Klan (radical right)
Whose side are you on...their's [soldiers] or Nixon's (anti-Vietnam War)
Be counted this time, march to end the war (anti-Vietnam War)
Why shop where you can't eat? (black rights)
Dare to struggle, dare to win (radical left)

Although the importance of creating we-they distinctions through social movement persuasion is undisputed, few social movement slogans seem to be designed either to attack the "they" or to enhance the "we." Slogans, like the songs studied in Chapter 13, do a better job of attacking others than enhancing the self.

Prescribing Courses of Action

The What. Demands and solutions appeared in 43% of the slogans, and they tended to dominate the slogans of several contemporary social movements. Notice in Figure 4 that the percentages are fairly high (with the exception of the United Farm Workers whose slogans tended to urge action) for all of the contemporary social movements included in this study.

Figure 4: Demands and Solutions in Slogans

Most Often		Least Often	
Anti-nuclear power	74%	Women's liberation	38%
Black rights	64%	Radical left	33%
Pro-choice	53%	Gay rights	28%
Native American	53%	Ecology	24%
Radical right	47%	United Farm Workers	0%

Many slogans made vague references to equality, happiness, free speech, freedom, justice, rights, and peace, but 37% of all demands and solutions were quite specific. For example, a radical right slogan demanded "Freedom for Rudolf Hess" (the former German Nazi leader); a black rights slogan urged institutions to "Ban the Krugerrand" (a South African gold piece being sold in America); a native American slogan demanded that authorities "Free the Wounded Knee 300"; and anti-nuclear power advocates chanted "Close Indian Point" (a nuclear power plant) while pro-nuclear power advocates tried to prevent the closing of a nuclear power plant with the slogan "Save No. One." Nearly all slogans that addressed demands and solutions were what Bowers and Ochs have referred to as "imperative statements"—commands, edicts, or fiats.

One of the most important persuasive functions of slogans is their simplification of complex issues, problems, solutions, and relationships. Thus, some of the selected slogans polarized complex issues:

America—love it or leave it (radical right and pro-Vietnam War)
Make love not war (anti-Vietnam war)
Abortion kills babies—choose life (pro-life)
Employ: don't destroy (anti-nuclear power)
Separation or death (radical right and the KKK)

Other slogans proposed simple solutions without recognizing the complicated steps involved or the ramifications of implementation:

No more nukes (anti-nuclear power)
Save the whales (save the whales)
Dump Israel (radical right and American nazis)
Humanize America (radical left)
Get out of Vietnam (anti-Vietnam War)

Many slogans revealed the impatience of movement members and leaders during the enthusiastic mobilization stage. In John Wilson's words, protestors had grown "tired of being sick and tired."[15]

Enough! Out now (anti-Vietnam War)
End the arms race now (anti-nuclear weapons)
Equal rights now (women's liberation)
Jobs or income now (radical left)
Abortion rights now (pro-choice)
We demand an FEPC law now (black rights)

Other social movement slogans espoused vague dreams, hopes, or visions, such as the following:

Peace on earth, good will to people (women's liberation)
Every child a wanted child, every mother a willing mother (women's liberation and pro-choice)
For a bicentennial without colonies (native American)
What if they gave a war and nobody came? (anti-Vietnam War)
Live and let live (pro-life)

Slogans allow social movement members and leaders to simplify and to "package" their pictures of the world—their ideologies—that produce "impressions" of action, direction, analysis, and thoroughness.[16] If, as Joseph Lelyveld claims, television has reduced the "attention span of the ordinary viewer" to "fractions of minutes" and "has made political communication a matter of fleeting impressions," then social movement slogans would seem to be important persuasive vehicles for contemporary social movements.[17]

The Who. Only 4% of the 585 selected slogans addressed who must bring about or stifle change, including mentions of movement organizations (e.g., "Gray Panthers: age and youth in action"; "Young Americans for Freedom"; and "The KKK likes Cubans, if they are in Cuba") and the naming of social movement leaders (e.g., "Viva Chavez," "We stand with Fr. Dan Berrigan," and "We protest the arrest of Rev. Dr. King in Birmingham"). An important persuasive characteristic of such slogans is their potential for creating a strong personal identification with and commitment to a cause, particularly when protestors wear these slogans on buttons or tee shirts, place them on their automobiles, or carry them on placards. The following examples reveal this persuasive potential:

I am an American Nazi (radical right)
Nurses for Life (pro-life)
We are Protestants protesting abortion (pro-life)
Pro-family, pro-choice (pro-choice)
Panthers on the prowl (Gray Panters)
Americans *FOR* nuclear power (pro-nuclear power)

Thus, slogans provide both an opportunity for self-expression of beliefs and membership and a means of exhibiting or communicating these to a variety of audiences. Too few contemporary slogans take advantage of this opportunity.

The How. Only three slogans addressed how (strategies, tactics, and communication channels) movements should accomplish their goals. The United Farm Workers slogan "No violencia es neustra fuerza" urged nonviolence; the radical right (pro-Vietnam War) slogan "Why be violent—debate" chided the anti-Vietnam War movement for resorting to violence when it opposed violence in Vietnam; and the anti-Vietnam War slogan "No negotiations" inveighed against negotiation as a means of resolving either the protest or the military conflict. Slogans are obviously not used for prescribing or discussing tactics.

Mobilizing for Action

Calls to Action. Twenty-seven percent of the selected slogans called upon audiences to act. Some were ambiguous pleas to repent, fight, picket, support, wake up, vote, help, "do it," "do your part," and encouragements such as "Right on sister." Unlike musical calls to action, many slogans prescribed specific actions:

Boycott Chiquita bananas (United Farm Workers)
Sign here to keep Taiwan free (radical right)
Be the voice of the unborn—vote no on B (pro-life)
Vote yes: change the abortion law—November 7 (pro-choice)
Occupy Seabrook (anti-nuclear power)
Support "Operation Shutdown" (black rights)

Calls to action were second only to courses of action in frequency of appearance in slogans. Very small percentages of slogans called upon audiences to join the cause, to unite, or to organize. Although slogans are personal expressions of self, belief, commitment, and action, they rarely proclaimed actions in the first person. A rare exception was radical right's "I think it's time for us to stand up and be counted."

Appeals Beyond the Movement. Unlike protest songs that are largely in-group persuasive activities, slogans appeal implicitly and explicitly to a variety of audiences: the uncommitted "oppressed," the "people," "legitimizers," and the mass media. When the United Farm workers demonstrated in front of supermarkets and liquor stores, for example, they carried and chanted such slogans as "Don't buy Red Coach Iceberg lettuce," "Help the grape workers win their strike," and "Don't swallow Gallow's wine." Their appeals were primarily to the public, customers, and the media, not to movement members. The same was true when save the whales protestors used the slogan "Wake up! to the alarming facts"; and when the ecology movement urged people to "Breathe deeply, then revolt." Many slogans urged audiences to get involved. A black rights slogan protesting the control of local schools asked black people on the streets of New York, "Do you want your child to be a big dummy?" An anti-nuclear weapons slogan pleaded, "Americans unite and disarm." And a pro-choice slogan entreated readers, "Don't stand by silently and let outrage become law—fight back."

Slogans are a primary means of getting attention and making people conscious of a problem. Claus Mueller has noted that:

> Articulated dissent presupposes that political symbols (terms, concepts, and ideological interpretations) be attached to subjectively experienced conditions that do not correspond to expectations or needs. Political consciousness is perforce bound to a symbolic interpretation of socio-political experience....as long as no political interpretations were attached to deplorable conditions, these conditions remained inert, posing no threat to the status quo.[18]

The save the whales slogan "Our look can kill," for example, attempted to make people aware that whales were being slaughtered to provide cosmetics. The NORML slogan "This little plant can turn your life upside down" warned audiences that violation of unfair marijuana laws could cost them their money and their freedom. In 1966 Stokely Carmichael, chairman of the Student Nonviolent Coordinating Committee, began to contemplate a slogan and an act that would capture the attention of the mass media, instill new life into the black rights movement, and redefine the image of blacks, their demands, and their allies. On June 5, 1966 James Meredith undertook a one-man voting rights pilgrimage from Memphis, Tennessee to Jackson, Mississippi, but he was ambushed and shot on June 6. Numerous black rights leaders, including Carmichael, immediately took over the march. The SNCC group led by Carmichael chanted the new slogan whenever marchers met hostile treatment along the way. On the evening of June 17, about half-way through the march, Stokely Carmichael introduced the new slogan to the nation in a speech at Greenwood, Mississippi. He stated in part: "The only way we gonna stop them white men from whuppin' us is to take over. We been saying 'freedom' for six years and we ain't got nothing. What we gonna start sayin' now is Black Power!" "Black power" quickly became one of the best known, most controversial, and more influential slogans in American history. It monopolized the attention of the mass media for weeks, became a rallying cry and ego-enhancer for blacks, catapulted Stokely Carmichael into the top echelon of black leaders, divided the black rights movement into "civil rights" and "black power" factions, purged the movement of unwanted white liberals, and threatened a variety of institutions.

Slogans can unite, or at least create a perception of unity among people "with widely varying motives and beliefs," by focusing upon a common characteristic, value, belief, or goal.[19] This is particularly true, Murray Edelman writes, when political and social issues are unclear—as is the case with most social movements.[20] An obvious example of a unifying slogan is the native American movement's adoption of the classic slogan, "All for one, one for all." The women's liberation movement reaches beyond its membership with the slogan, "Rape is a crime against *all* women." In a similar fashion, the pro-life movement attempts to appeal to all women with the slogan, "Unborn women have rights too." And the anti-nuclear power slogan "In case of nuclear accident kiss your children goodbye" appeals to parents and to the universal love of children and the motive to protect them at all costs. Slogans such as these allow people to rally around a common belief or value when they might disagree over many specific aspects of a social movement.

Pressuring the Opposition. The majority of the 585 selected slogans, unlike social movement songs, applied direct or indirect pressure against other movements, institutions, or agents of institutions. Nearly every demand, for example, was phrased as an imperative statement and shouted or displayed in public or on location: state legislatures or Congress, corporations, churches, court houses or chambers, colleges, stores, beauty contests, and so on. Such slogans as "Ratify ERA now" (women's liberation), "No bus for us" (radical right), "Convert Rocky Flats" (anti-nuclear power), and "Free Huey" (black rights) applied at least indirect pressure on the opposition. The same is true for expressions of power such as "Black power," "White power," "We are everywhere" (gay rights), "We are back: National Socialist White People's Party" (radical right), and

"Feminism lives" (women's liberation). When social movements call upon people to act or to unite, they pose threats to oppositions, and these oppositions cannot remain indifferent when movements employ such slogans as "talk about what we can do, do what we talk about" (women's liberation), "Books are weapons, use them" (radical right), "Support Indian resistance" (native American), and "Buy war guns" (black rights).

Some social movements applied direct pressure upon oppositions through calls to action against them or overt threats. Not surprisingly, social movements involved in confrontations resorted most often to overt threats. The most common threats were calls for action against various oppositions:

> Tell him what to do with the broom! (women's liberation)
> Look for the label, boycott scab grapes (United Farm Workers)
> Don't trade here! Owners of this business surrendered to race mixers (radical right)
> Shut it down (radical left)
> Kill the pigs (anti-Vietnam War)
> Stop Diablo—join the blockade (anti-nuclear power)

As Bowers and Ochs have pointed out, oppositions, particularly established institutions, cannot afford to take threats lightly.[21] If they are caught unprepared, they may experience loss of sales, votes, property or, most importantly, the support of "the people." Over-preparation or over-reaction, however, may make institutions look foolish or ugly or lead to tragedy. The morning after students at Kent State University tried to burn down the ROTC building and before the fatal shooting of four students, a large banner hanging from a tree asked, "Why is the ROTC building still standing?" Undoubtedly such slogans added to the atmosphere that prompted National Guardsmen to fire upon the students. Some social movement slogans applied direct pressure through questions and threats:

> Would you be more careful if it was you who got pregnant? (women's liberation)
> Hey, hey, LBJ, how many kids have you killed today? (anti-Vietnam War)
> We will remember (United Farm Workers)
> Niggers beware! Hands off whites or die (radical right)
> Keep your laws and your morality off *my* body (pro-choice)
> Free Huey now or the sky's the limit (black rights)

Thus, social movement slogans, unlike songs, were not merely or primarily for in-house consumption. They appealed to a variety of audiences, applied both direct and indirect pressure upon oppositions, and talked more *to* than *about* their opponents.

Victory is near. Not one of the 585 selected slogans predicted that victory was at hand. Most slogans tended to be neither optimistic nor pessimistic about ultimate victory.

Sustaining the Movement

Since most slogans addressed the "here and now" during the mobilization stage, they did not refer to setbacks or delays (brevity would prevent explanations of either) and did not urge followers to remain committed. A few slogans assured audiences that victory would come ultimately for their efforts. Examples were "Failure is impossible" (women's liberation), "We shall overcome" (United Farm Workers and black rights), and "When women decide this war should end, this war will end" (anti-Vietnam War).

A small percentage of slogans referred to hero-victims, victories, or tragedies to sustain commitment and the movement's forward progress. Examples included:

Remember the Augusta Six (black rights)
Tyrone had a right to live (radical left)
We got the Rosenbergs (radical right)
Remember Kent [State] and Jackson [State] (Anti-Vietnam War)
Remember 3 Mile Island (anti-nuclear power)

It appears that most slogans are created during the enthusiastic mobilization stage before most tragedies and victories take place and before heroes and martyrs are enshrined. Few new slogans appear during the maintenance stage when demonstrations and confrontations dwindle or disappear.

Conclusions

Slogans, with us for centuries, act as social symbols and symbolic justifications. Social movements employ them to create impressions, to alter perceptions, to elicit emotional responses, to make demands, and to pressure oppositions. The ambiguity of slogans enable them to serve as verbal bridges from one meaning to another and allow individuals and groups to interpret them according to their own perceptions and needs. They simplify complex problems, solutions, and situations while demanding instant corrective actions. Many slogans are unique to and readily identifiable with specific social movements or social movement organizations.

All of the general and most of the specific persuasive functions appeared in at least a few of the 585 social movement slogans analyzed for this study. Slogans, particularly spontaneous ones, were created during the enthusiastic mobilization stage of movements. Thus, they tended to reflect concern for the moment rather than for the past or the future. They made uncompromising and often highly specific demands and urged immediate action rather than attacking the opposition or enhancing the self. They appealed to a variety of audiences (movement sympathizers, "the people," legitimizers, and the mass media) rather than to the in-group as social movement songs do. And they applied both indirect and direct pressures upon oppositions. Although many of the 585 slogans were imperative statements, a small percentage of them used name-calling or abrasive language. A large percentage of the selected slogans were situation or event specific and became obsolete once a strike or a campaign ended, an opposition leader left office, or a movement leader was released from prison. A number of slogans, particularly sanctioned and advertising slogans, such as "black power," "Gray Panthers," and "I am an American Nazi" appealed to feelings of power and strength and created a personal identification with and commitment to a cause. Slogans tend to be a highly personal form of protest because individuals wear them, carry them, shout them, and place them on possessions such as automobiles.

In Chapter 15, we will focus on the use of obscenity in social protest, including the functions of slogans that include obscene language.

Endnotes

1 Robert E. Denton, "The Rhetorical Functions of Slogans: Classifications and Characteristics," *Communication Quarterly*, 28 (Spring, 1980), 10-18.

2 Lloyd F. Bitzer and Edwin Black, eds., *The Prospect of Rhetoric*, (Englewood Cliffs, NJ: Prentice-Hall, 1971), 220.

3 George E. Shankel, *American Mottoes and Slogans* (New York: Wilson, 1941), 5.

4 John W. Bowers and Donovan J. Ochs, *The Rhetoric of Agitation and Control* (Reading, MA: Addison-Wesley, 1971), 22.

5 Shankel, 7.

6 Murray Edelman, *The Symbolic Uses of Politics* (Urbana, IL: University of Illinois Press, 1967), 114.

7 Edelman, 117.

8 Hugh Duncan, *Symbols in Society* (New York: Oxford University Press, 1968), 8.

9 Robert D. Brooks, "Black Power: The Dimensions of a Slogan," *Western Speech*, 34 (Spring, 1970), 108-114.

10 Duncan, 22.

11 Harold D. Laswell, "The Theory of Propaganda," *American Political Science Review*, 21 (1927), 627.

12 Edelman, 115.

13 John Makay and William Brown, *The Rhetorical Dialogue: Contemporary Concepts and Cases* (Dubuque, IA: W. C. Brown, 1972), 374.

[14] The 585 slogans were obtained from social movement buttons, posters, bumperstickers, newspapers, journals, leaflets, pamphlets, books, photographs of slogans being displayed during demonstrations, and accounts of social movements and their actions.
[15] John Wilson, *Introduction to Social Movements* (New York: Basic Books, 1973), 89-90.
[16] Nelson Polsby and Aaron Wildavsky, *Presidential Elections* (New York: Scribners, 1971), 178.
[17] Joseph Lelyveld, "The Selling of a Candidate," *New York Times Magazine*, 18 March 1976, 16.
[18] Claus Mueller, *The Politics of Communication* (New York: Oxford University Press, 1973), 113.
[19] George F. Rude, *The Crowd in History* (New York: Wiley, 1964), 246.
[20] Murray Edelman, *Politics as Symbolic Action* (Chicago: Markham, 1971), 119.
[21] Bowers and Ochs, 40.

Chapter 15

Obscenity and Social Protest

Obscenity, by definition, violates accepted custom and language, so we would expect that the use of obscenity in public would invite negative sanctions from "the people" and institutions. This was only partially true during the student, counter-culture, and anti-Vietnam War movements of the 1960s and 1970s that frequently employed verbal and nonverbal obscenities. While some groups, institutions, and individuals decried obscenity, the movements seemed to signal an increase in the general use of obscenity in American society—particularly profanity. And, as "radical" social protest waned, so too did the outcry and shock over the *public* use of obscene language. Profanity became commonplace in film and on television, and by 1973 Paul Cameron found that in large samples of everyday speech, every fourteenth word contained some form of profanity.[1]

The Act of Swearing

The act of swearing has always been a part of human social interaction. Sigmund Freud suggests that "the first human being who hurled a curse instead of a weapon against his adversary was the founder of civilization."[2] Many philologists argue that before humans developed a systematic means of communication, there were constant evocations of highly charged or emotional sounds. These sounds were in response to daily events of physical exertion, shock, pain, or anger. Such expressions were primarily physiological and secondarily psychological. The sounds were determined by the shape of the human chest and form of nasal cavities, throat, and larynx. The argument is that today's short expletives are mere remnants of those earlier sounds.[3]

Anthropologists have found the use of swearing and obscenity common practice among nonliterate tribes and peoples.[4] Most cultures, for example, have at least two words for parts of the body—one proper and one derogatory. There is no claim, however, that the act of swearing is instinctive or innate. In fact, some groups such as native Americans, Japanese, Mayans, and Polynesians do not swear, and this suggests that swearing is a culturally learned behavior.[5]

The limited research on swearing suggests that swearing is a response to individual stress, frustration, or anger and follows the pattern of swearing-relief-purification-pacification. Some studies suggest that swearing increases in social settings, reduces stress, decreases under extreme stress, and is both contagious and mutually reinforcing in certain situations.[6]

Obscenity has played an important role within the realm of politics. The noted political scientist, Harold Laswell, wrote that "politics is the process by which the irrational bases of society are brought out into the open."[7] Obscenity is a form of conflict. And "conflicts," according to Robert Doolittle, "can only be manifested by or through some form of communicative behavior. . . . We can certainly have communication without conflict, but we cannot have conflict without some form of communication."[8]

In a democracy, conflict and violence are usually expressed at the symbolic level. Protestors of the 1960s expressed their separateness and independence by violating the conventions of hair, clothing, appearance, actions, and language. Student "violence" was primarily verbal or gestural. Jonathan and Alfred Bingham report that of 232 campus protests, 76% involved no physical violence or destruction.[9]

Obscenity is the ultimate form of symbolic violence aimed at people. Thus, obscenity is likely to appear when conflicts occur between individuals, within groups, between groups, in the community, and in the larger society. Wendell Phillips, noted for his agitation against slavery before the Civil War, observed:

> The scholar may sit in his study and take care that his language is not exaggerated, but the rude mass of men is not to be caught by balanced periods—they are caught by men whose words are half battles. From Luther down, the charge against every reformer has been that his language is too rough. Be it so. Rough instruments are used for rough work.[10]

Definitions and Forms of Swearing

Many researchers use the terms of profanity and obscenity interchangeably. However, Ashley Montagu, in his book entitled *The Anatomy of Swearing*, identifies seven forms of swearing.[11]

1. Swearing—the act of verbally expressing the feeling of aggressiveness that follows upon frustration in words possessing strong emotional associations.
2. Cursing—a form of swearing distinguished by the fact that it invokes or calls down some evil upon its object.
3. Profanity—a form of swearing in which the names or attributes of the figures or objects of religious veneration are uttered.

4. Blasphemy—the act of vilifying or ridiculing the figures or objects of religious veneration.
5. Obscenity—a form of swearing that makes use of indecent words or phrases.
6. Vulgarity—a form of swearing that makes use of crude words.
7. Euphemistic swearing—a form of swearing in which mild, vague, or corrupted expressions are substituted for the original strong ones.

For our purposes, obscenities may be verbal or nonverbal and usually appear as adjectives. They utilize indecent words, phrases, and actions that may be classified into three categories: religious, excretory, and sexual. Sexual obscenities, the most abundant, fall into three groups: copulative, genital, and sexual irregularities. Robert Bostrom, John Basehart, and Charles Rossiter, in studying the impact of various obscenities, found that sexual obscenities were most offensive, followed by excretory, and then religious obscenities.[12]

Categories and classification of obscenities are not crucial to our discussion. It is important, however, to recognize that the rhetorical impact and significance of different obscenities are influenced by the type of obscenity and other influences to be discussed later. In this chapter, we will investigate the uses of obscenity by social protestors to understand better the types and effects of symbolic behavior in social movements.

Obscenity as Rhetoric

Some readers may wonder if obscenity is rhetoric and, if so, why the use of obscenity is worthy of discussion in light of the many issues, actors, events, and types of social movements in American history. We believe that obscenity is a potentially powerful persuasive weapon for social protestors. "Dissent," argue Fabrizio, Karas, and Menmuir, "has its own rhetoric, one that can be studied in its full range of tones—resentful or resigned, angry or agonized, irate or ironic, furious or downright funny."[13] As recently as 1976, Ashley Montagu observed that "swearing constitutes a species of human behavior so little understood, even by its most devoted practitioners, that an examination of its meaning and significance is long overdue."[14]

John Bowers and Donovan Ochs define rhetoric as "the rationale of instrumental, symbolic behavior."[15] This definition recognizes a broad range of human behavior that possesses the potential for rhetorical significance. Such potential is grounded in the symbolic nature of human beings, for, as Kenneth Burke writes, symbols are the realities of human existence. Since people are symbol-using animals, symbolic acts demonstrate the essence of humankind and hence deserve study and appreciation regardless of their fashionable popularity. Burke argues that "the use of symbols, by one symbol-using entity to induce action in another (persuasion properly addressed) is in essence not magical but realistic."[16] This chapter, then explores the notion of obscenity as confrontational rhetoric, its rhetorical characteristics and functions, and its potential persuasive effects.

Obscenity as Confrontational Rhetoric

The counter-culture movement in the 1950s began to set the tone, stage and strategies for protest in the 1960s.[17] The "beatniks," although small in number and located primarily in major cities and near college campuses, offered a different set of values, lifestyle, and modes of expression from the general society. Individualism became the doctrine of personal liberation ("spiritual emancipation from constraints of society") that called into question the conventions of behavior, sex, politics, and degree of free speech. "Progress," the beatniks claimed, resulted in corporate prosperity at the expense of individuals, the threat of the atomic bomb, and a plastic, synthetic world of food, dress, and environment. By the end of the 1950s, all of the major art forms (novels, poems, painting, theatre, movies, and music) were addressing the need for change, new values, and the condition of social life.[18]

Verbal and nonverbal obscenity became an important public issue in the political and social protests of the 1960s and 1970s. Protestors against the war in Vietnam relied heavily upon obscenities to express their rage, frustrations, and perceptions of American society. They argued that obscene rhetoric was appropriate for describing and attacking an obscene society. Early protestors of the civil rights and anti-war movements had utilized more traditional languaging strategies and forms of protest, but when these efforts failed to change policies of the establishment, they turned to less traditional methods, including obscenity. Denied the instruments of power and easy access to the mass media, protestors created a new language of protest and means of attracting attention and publicity.

Many rhetorical scholars studied the rhetoric of dissent, confrontation, alienation, and revolution during the 1960s and 1970s. Robert Cathcart argued persuasively that a social movement can be identified by its confrontational form.[19] For Cathcart, a social movement is a ritual conflict whose most distinguishing form is confrontation. Robert Scott and Donald Smith argued that confrontation is inherently symbolic: "The act carries a message. It dissolves the lines between marches, sit-ins, demonstrations, acts of physical violence, and aggressive discourse. In this way it informs us of the essential nature of discourse itself as human action."[20] Robert Browne lamented in 1970 that "the older rhetoric might well be described as a rhetoric of continuity; continuity between groups, classes, generations. The newer rhetoric is a rhetoric of discontinuity."[21] Edward Corbett concurred by stating that "a good deal of contemporary rhetoric is nonconciliatory.

By this I mean that whereas speakers and writers once took special pains to ingratiate themselves with their audience, today many speakers and writers seem actually to go out of their way to antagonize or alienate their audience."[22] The point is, every desire and emotion is a valid reason to initiate symbolic exchange. Emotional responses may be bad reasons for action, but they are valid when grounded in one's reality. "The real art," Wayne Booth asserts, "lies always in the proper weighing—and what is proper is a matter finally of shared norms, discovered and applied in the experience of individuals whose very individuality is forged from other selves." Thus, "every protest implies an affirmative ground for protest; every affirmation implies many negations."[23]

The use of obscenity fits within the notion of confrontation and politics. Political issues are usually controversial and emotional, so political rhetoric is nearly always charged with emotion. Emotional responses to issues, of course, can be positive and uplifting or negative and frustrating. Saul Alinsky explains why:

> The passions of mankind have boiled over into all areas of political life, including its vocabulary. The words most common in politics have become strained with hurts, hopes, and frustrations. All of them are loaded with popular opprobrium, and their use results in a conditioned, negative, emotional response.[24]

An obscene word or gesture can provide a summation of the group situation that lends emotion to the group's political interests and serves to abstract, reify, and magnify the issues at hand.

The audiences of protestors nearly always range from the sympathetic to the indifferent to the hostile. This mixed audience contributes to the frustration and emotional intensity that is reflected in the agitator's rhetoric. The more distant or separated people feel from a political institution, church, or social group and the less probability they have of airing their complaints, the more they will turn to alternative, unconventional means of persuasion. The use of obscenity, therefore, reflects a "political" reality of frustration with and separateness from institutions.

Rhetorical Characteristics of Obscenity

Obscenities as symbols do not have singular meanings or singular functions. In order to identify characteristics of obscenity, then, we need to address the nature of symbols: verbal and nonverbal.

Symbols provide shared meanings, perceptions, and security among groups. For Richard Weaver, language is a "social and cultural creation functioning somehow within the psychic constitution of those who use it. ...The question of stability in language cannot be considered apart from the psychic stability of the culture group."[25] Language usage or styles can signal conformity or rebellion in a society,[26] and although subtle in some cases and overt in others, symbols help to create, sustain, or define role behavior. In an Army barracks, the use of obscenity about job and sex is not only accepted but may signal that the user is a "tough soldier." In contrast, the same obscenities by a college professor, corporate executive, congressman, or minister would elicit scorn and condemnation.

The use of obscenity may have little rhetorical significance when separated from situation and context. No symbol is intrinsically or literally "dirty." Obscenity, like beauty, is in the eye or mind of the beholder. Words become dirty or taboo because of social conventions, not logical bases of argument. In addition, specific words, phrases, or gestures may be viewed as less obscene over time, but the notion of societal acceptance is crucial to the rhetorical nature of obscenity.

The contextual elements of *who* and *where* are vital to the use of obscenity. Sex, position, age, and degree of status influence our perceptions of taboo symbols. The use of obscenities by women, children, teenagers, and individuals of high perceived status is more shocking than its use by middle-aged men or dock workers. Police officers have reacted most angrily to obscenities by young people, particularly females. The public reacted with disgust to obscenities used by politicians such as Nelson Rockefeller, Richard Nixon, and Spiro Agnew. Where obscenity is used may influence its rhetorical impact; indeed obscenity appears to be largely "situational." Every rhetorical act, of course, occurs in a setting. But political scenes often provide an emotional context for the acts that occur. Murray Edelman argues that "the politically relevant setting is not merely physical but also social in character" and "is fundamental to symbol formation."[27] Language, as a result of political settings, may be reduced to a "sequence of Pavlovian" cues rather than an instrument of reasoned discourse. Public use of obscenity is usually perceived to be more serious, threatening, and challenging than private use of obscenity.

The notion of verbal taboo, according to Dan Rothwell, is a throwback to a primitive confusion of words with things.[28] The purpose of designating some language as taboo is to protect society from the perceived danger of language that would destroy the moral and social fabric of a culture. Using taboo language, therefore, challenges societal values, attitudes, and religious beliefs and thus jeopardizes social order. Identifying taboo language and behavior maintains the status quo and protects society from the corrupt, the unknown, the unclean, and the undesirable. Mary McEdwards defines agitative language as belonging to a "particular type of rhetoric whose end is movement away from the *status quo.* Some may argue that all rhetoric has this same end. However, the rhetoric we call *agitation* evokes extreme movement away from the *status quo*—usually a complete reversal of existing conditions or situations."[29]

In its broadest sense, obscenity may be characterized as *metaphor* and *imagery*. According to Richard Weaver, all language is metaphorical in its origin.[30] If metaphor implies symbolism because metaphor disengages the word from the thing signified and if language is metaphorical, then verbal obscenity is metaphorical. In public usage, verbal obscenity usually links a person, group, or object to some religious, sexual, or excretory reality. To call someone a "son of a bitch" is to imply more than birth heritage. Rather, it is an attack upon an individual by linking the person to a construct that society views as negative. The strength of the obscenity, then, lies in the linking or comparative process. Michael Hazen observes that:

> By making comparisons with those things which are at the heart of a culture's values, a verbal obscenity draws on the strength and vitalness of a society. The values that are being drawn on are those which are important to society. Sex, bodily functions, and religion are at the heart of how we perceive ourselves and our relationship to the world. Thus, the verbal obscenity, as a metaphor, draws its strength from the culture's definition of what is proper in several inherent realms of human values.[31]

Verbal obscenities violate societal norms and expectations. The more obscene the language, the greater is the violation against social norms and the greater the potential impact upon an audience.

Imagery is closely related to the notion of metaphor. Kenneth Burke writes that, "any representation of passions, emotions, actions, and even mood and personality is likely to be treated as falling under the heading of 'images,' which in turn explicitly or implicitly involve 'imagination'."[32] Imagery and ambiguity are important rhetorical concepts. One image created rhetorically may imply several ideas. Ambiguity of language allows for various transformations of meanings attached to each word. Thus, to call someone a "bastard" may be a friendly, a hostile, or a factual reference. Because of imagery and ambiguity, it is impossible to remove "corrupting" elements from language. Negative connotations, therefore, can always be associated with any sign or symbol so designated by society. The most instructive endeavor is to attempt to isolate the purposes such connotations serve when used in a public setting.

Within the realm of social protest, obscenity is emotional and intense. Its use often reflects the extent of the persuader's pessimism, futility, and anger. Obscenities are expressions of inner feelings.

The Persuasive Functions of Obscenity

Let us turn now to the persuasive functions that obscenity has performed for social movements. Remember that the ambiguous nature of obscene symbols and symbolic acts, their brevity, and the variety of situations in which they are used may enable each to fulfill several functions, often at the same time.

Transforming Perceptions of History

During the Vietnam War, anti-war protestors turned to obscenities in an effort to alter the way the American people viewed the military conflict and American society. Jerry Rubin argued that a new language of protest was a critical need because the institutions controlled the old language and thus the perceptions of the war and its opposition:

> When they control the words, they control everything, and they got the words controlled. They got "war" meaning "peace;" they got "fuck" being a "bad word" they got "napalm" being a good word—they got "decency" that to me is indecent. The whole thing is like backwards, and we gotta turn it around.[33]

To turn it around, Theodore Windt writes, anti-war protestors resorted to verbal obscenities and public sexual acts to communicate their belief that "while sex is natural and creative" and exhibits love, "war is unnatural and destructive" and exhibits hatred.[34] Windt concludes: "To commit public sexual acts is to attempt to shock people into recognizing that the very same customs that suppress sex sustain wars."

Jerry Farber wrote a popular and highly controversial essay entitled "The Student as Nigger" while he was a member of the English faculty at San Diego State College. He used obscenity and sexual metaphors to influence the way his readers viewed the American educational system, particularly the universities.[35] He wrote that "In California state colleges the faculties are screwed regularly and vigorously by the Governor and the Legislature." For students "There is a kind of castration that goes on in schools. It begins, before school years, with parents' first encroachment on their children's free unashamed sexuality and continues right up to the day when they hand you your doctoral diploma with a bleeding, shriveled pair of testicles stapled to the parchment." "At my school," he remarked, "we even grade people on how they read poetry. That's like grading people on how they fuck." In short, the entire university system according to Farber consisted of "academic bullshit."

Farber and the anti-Vietnam War protestors used obscenity to shock people out of their apathy and to convince them that an intolerable situation existed that warranted urgent action. Obscenities tend to be present rather than past or future oriented.

Transforming Perceptions of Society

A primary use of obscenity is to polarize the social movement from its opposition. J. Dan Rothwell argues that:

> The principle effect of verbal obscenity is polarization, which emanates from the social disapproval of this type of language.... The results of this polarization are sometimes profound and diverse. Few people are capable of remaining apathetic to the use of verbal obscenity by anyone, much less agitators. Consequently, the agitator wins at least a superficial, if not a consequential victory by forcing the majority into separate and opposing camps preparing for battle.... It is important that the agitator know his allies and his foes.[36]

Agitators have employed obscenities in a variety of ways to establish this necessary we-they distinction between movement and establishment.

The Opposition. Social movements that resort to obscenities, the most extreme form of invective, tend to heap them upon their perceived devils. Jerry Farber called his fellow faculty members "chickenshit" and said that "teachers **are** short on balls."[37] Students at Kent State University called National Guardsmen "fascist bastards;" students at Jackson State College called the police "motherfuckers;" and the demonstrators in Chicago during the 1968 Democratic National Convention called the police "fucking pigs," "brainless assholes," and "shitheads" and shouted "the CIA sucks."[38] Eldridge Cleaver, a leader of the Black Panthers, exclaimed in a speech on the UCLA campus in 1968 that all of his hatred and hostility was for a "fucked up system, that has fucked up our lives, and fucked up the world we live in, that we have to deal with for ourselves and for posterity."[39] Obscenities such as these are not purposeless, gutter profanities. They allow social movements to define and to stereotype the opposition as vile, hypocritical, impotent, and stupid—in essence as obscene. They exhibit a profound contempt for and revolt from established institutions, norms, and values that are responsible for a truly obscene situation. Obscenities, then, are used to discredit and humiliate oppositions.

Some social movements want to do more than define and label their devils. They attempt to goad institutions into exhibiting their "true" natures for all to see. Scott and Smith write that the confronter communicates to opponents: "We know you for what you are. And you know that we know."[40] And "the confronter who prompts violence in the language or behavior of another has found his collaborator. 'Show us how ugly you really are,' he says, and the enemy with dogs and cattle prods, or police billies and mace, complies." Protestors in Chicago in 1968 bombarded the police with nonstop cries of "motherfuckers," "pigfuckers," "cocksuckers," "bastards," "fuck the pigs," "fuck the nazis," "goddamn sons of bitches," "Who's your wife with now," and "Your wife sucks cock." They threw toilet paper, urine, and feces at the police and, particularly young female agitators, made all manner of obscene gestures. For example, a policeman later reported that "a 'female hippie' came up to him, pulled up her skirt and said, 'You haven't had a piece in a long time'."[41] These taunts and actions eventually resulted in what "The Walker Report to the National Commission on the Causes and Prevention of Violence" termed "unrestrained and indiscriminate police violence"—a "police riot." Officers gassed, clubbed, kicked, and used automobiles and motorcycles to runover innocent onlookers, pedestrians, residents, delegates to the Democratic National Convention, photographers, and reporters as well as protestors. They resorted to the ugly rhetoric of the demonstrators. Police charged into crowds with cries of "Get their fucking cameras"; "Let's get these fucking bastards"; "Fuck your press credentials"; "Get the bastards"; "We fucked one of the motherfuckers"; "Get out of the park you motherfuckers"; and "You better get your fucking dirty cunt out of here."[42] The demonstrators in Chicago had indeed found their collaborators. Members of the establishment had discredited and humiliated themselves because they had lost control—a major sin for institutions—and because they had "proven," to the satisfaction of the demonstrators at least, that they were nazis, fascists, and pigs.

The Self. The obscenities that discredit and humiliate the opposition may enhance the self-concept of protestors. Richard B. Gregg writes that "By painting the enemy in dark hued imagery of vice, corruption, evil, and weakness, one may more easily convince himself of his own superior virtue and thereby gain a symbolic victory of ego-enhancement."[43] When members of the labor movement sang the following verse of the song entitled "You Low Life Son of a Bitch," they were "establishing, defining, and affirming" their self-hood "by engaging in a rhetorical act."[44]

You low life truffling bastard,
You low life son of a bitch,
You selfish, greedy, low down thief,
You goddamn thieving snitch.
You yaller-back, piss-complected skunk,
You scheming, conniving bastard.
That's what I call a greedy rich thief,
Now what do you think of that?

Verses such as these and more contemporary exclamations such as "Fuck you, LBJ"; "Up against the wall motherfuckers"; "Fuck the draft"; and "Hell no, we won't go" not only establish self-hood but each, according to Gregg, "proclaims, extols, and describes in exaggerated fashion the strengths and virtues of the ego sought after."[45] The sexual mocking of authority figures relieves the protestor of personal feelings of inadequacy and thus serves to lower authority figures below the protestor's own perceived level of social worth. Each obscenity gives the user the *power* to reduce and to challenge the most powerful of foes, and each challenge is fairly safe. Rarely is the boss (unnamed in the labor song), the President, the draft board, or other institutional agents—aside from the police officer or the member of the National Guard—present to answer the charges hurled so bravely. For instance, no authority was present at the UCLA rally to revoke Eldridge Cleaver's parole and to take him back to prison when he shouted to an absent Governor Ronald Reagan: "Well I'm not goin'! Fuck him in his ass! Fuck him! I'm not goin'!"

The use of obscenity may also demonstrate the user's "sexual, social, and political liberation" from a repressive, "parental establishment."[46] Stephen Spender writes that obscenity "is based on speaking the unspeakable. It is a style of protest, the basic protest being against censorship: not just official censorship but social censorship which inhibits you from saying [doing] anything you like to anyone anytime."[47] Thus, obscenity demonstrates social and political independence, exhibits freedom (at least over one's mouth or body), and is a symbolic tactic the established order cannot easily coopt.

Prescribing Courses of Action. Social movements that rely heavily upon obscenities often divorce themselves totally from the societies around them—societies they believe have no norms or values worth redeeming. As for themselves, these movements may have no clear demands or solutions, no courses of action. Obscenity is a convenient means of putting down the system and escaping the need or responsibility of finding a replacement. Protestors at a demonstration following the Democratic National Convention carried signs saying "Bullshit"—no demands or solutions, merely a condemnation of everything.[48] During the fall before the Convention, Abbie Hoffman advocated "Revolution for the hell of it," and remarked: "There's no doubts about it. We're going to wreck this fuckin' society. If we don't, this society is going to wreck itself anyway so, we might as well have some fun doin' it."[49] A January 1968 issue of the *New York Free Press* outlined a strategy for confusing the enemy and preventing the enemy from responding effectively to the movement:

> We've got to get crazy. Craziest motherfuckers they ever seen in this country. Cause that's the way we're gonna beat them. So fucking crazy that they can't understand it at **all.** They know something's up, something's going on down there, something's happening, some change coming on in this country.... We won't tell 'em what it is. What do you want to tell them for? Don't tell 'em shit. **Never**.... That's the problem you have when you focus in on an issue, when you make a demand. They can deal with a demand. We put a finger up their ass and tell them, "I ain't telling you what I want," then they got a problem.[50]

H. Rap Brown outlined a somewhat different strategy for confusing the enemies of those struggling for black power: "If white folks say gray suits are fashionable, you go buy a pink one. If they say america [sic] is great, you say america ain't shit. Chairman Mao says, 'Whatever the enemy supports, we oppose. Whatever the enemy opposes, we support'."[51] The obvious results of these obscenity-laced strategies are no meaningful courses of action and no dialogue with the enemy. Obscenity does, however, express an extreme contempt for society's standards and a burning desire for revolutionary change. "Civility," Dan Rothwell observes, "is an instrument of the status quo; verbal obscenity is a symbol of rebellion against the power structure. Agitators seek profound change, and profanity offers a profound change from the accepted style of dissent."[52]

Mobilizing for Action. Social movements must attract *attention* if they are to grow, to pressure the opposition, and to survive. When orthodox means of persuasion fail to gain attention, some movements have resorted to what Theodore Windt calls the "diatribe"—"moral dramaturgy intended to assault sensibilities, to turn thought up-side-down, to turn social mores inside-out, to commit in language the same barbarisms one condemns in society."[53] Haig Bosmajian writes that "The dissenter wants to be heard, to be listened to and if shouting obscenities is the only way he can get people to listen to him, so be it."[54] A student who took part in the 1967 march on the Pentagon and the 1968 demonstrations at Columbia University commented: "I and the others had reached the point where we could no longer tolerate being disregarded. I and the others had to own our lives."[55] The outrageousness of obscenity—particularly when it is used in public, in "sacred" places, and by young people, women, and professionals such as Jerry Farber who "should know better"—jolts people into awareness that a social movement exists and that a significant number of people are disenchanted enough with society to violate its fundamental rules of conduct.

Verbal obscenities and symbolic acts not only gain attention from immediate observers, but they also—and perhaps more importantly—gain the attention of the mass media. Jerry Rubin, a founder of the Yippies, wrote about efforts to manipulate the media:

> We're living TV commercials for the revolution. We're walking picket signs. Every response to longhairs creates a moral crisis for straights. We force adults to bring all their repressions to the surface, to expose their raw feelings.[56]

Simple "obscene" acts have drawn the attention of the mass media to social movements. On March 3, 1964, a young man unaffiliated with the University of California at Berkeley wandered throughout campus wearing a sign stating "fuck."[57] Students gathered together and denounced his arrest. One speaker called for a thousand "fuck communism" signs to be distributed; a "fuck defense fund" was established; and a student read a passage publicly from *Lady Chatterly's Lover* that contained the word "fuck." This spontaneous incident received national attention through the mass media and created discussions about freedom of speech and obscenity. Jerry Rubin, Abbie Hoffman, and other agitators of the 1960s and 1970s learned quickly that obscenity not only gained the attention of the media, but it gave them a degree of control. Radio and television could not broadcast oral obscenities, and they, along with the print media, could not show pictures of obscene acts. All three, however, could report the sights and sounds of police reactions to obscenities and other provocations. Abbie Hoffman, speaking in Lincoln Park in Chicago on August 27, 1968, instructed demonstrators on media control and coverage:

> If you don't want it on TV, write the word "**Fuck**" on your head, see, and that won't get on TV, right? But that's where the theatre is at, it's TV. I mean our thing's for TV. We don't want to get on Meet the Press. What's that shit? We want Ed Sullivan, Johnny Carson Show, we want the shit where the people are lookin' at it and diggin' it.... The media distorts. But it always works to our advantage.[58]

As we noted earlier, obscenity is an effective means of provoking the necessary *confrontations* with established orders. It is the most intense form of symbolic aggression, and studies of language intensity have revealed a strong correlation between the use of obscenity and "perceived" agression.[59] Obscenity often entices the opposition into performing the first act of physical violence, an act that may gain sympathy for the social movement and justify its verbal and nonverbal retaliations. Studies singled out obscenity as the most important element in the escalation of violence in the Chicago riots of 1968.[60] As a byproduct, these ugly symbolic and sometimes violent confrontations may make more moderate elements of the movement and critics within the system more respectable to the public and to institutional leaders. Windt writes:

> In contrast to the obscenity-shouting Yippies and the popular image of the bomb-hurling Weatherpeople, Senators Fulbright, Kennedy, Church, and McGovern seemed to the American public models of responsible criticism. Just as Stokely Carmichael legitimized the moderate, nonviolent posture of Martin Luther King, Jr., so too, the violent acts of the Weatherpeople and the absurd acts of the Yippies contributed to acceptance of traditional criticism of the war and enhanced the *ethos* of those critics who held positions of power.[61]

Obscenity-laden threats *force institutions to prepare for the worst possible scenario* even if such preparations are costly and may make them look ridiculous. Institutions cannot afford to be caught unprepared, especially when the public welfare is at stake. During the months prior to the Democratic Convention, the Yippies issued all manner of outrageous plans and threats, knowing that Chicago authorities had to take each seriously. Obscene threats included intentions to "fornicate in the parks and on Lake Michigan's beaches," "to fuck nuns," "to wreck this fuckin' society," to have Yippie women pose as "hookers" to attract Convention delegates and dose their drinks with LSD; and "to gather 230 'hyper-potent' hippie males into a special battalion to seduce wives, daughters, and girlfriends of convention delegates."[62]

Obscenities may *enhance the credibility* of movement leaders, members, and organizations because they have the nerve to say what others feel. For instance, Rothwell notes that "the Black Panthers' obscene vilification of police apparently expresses the private feelings of many black Americans. Although they may not approve of the Panther terminology, they may admire those who have the courage and audacity to insult policemen."[63]

Obscenity may contribute to *movement cohesiveness.* Humans have a basic need to identify with others in similar circumstances, and obscenity can create this sense of interpersonal identification. Robert Cathcart contends that "movements are carried forward through language, both verbal and non-verbal, in strategic ways that bring about identification of the individual with the movement."[64] Obscenity may bring about this identification among protestors and between protestors and potential sympathizers and legitimizers. Abbie Hoffman told agitators to "always use the symbols, props, dress and language of the people you are working with."[65] Social action organizer Saul Alinsky explained why he used the obscene:

> Every now and then I have been accused of being crude and vulgar because I have used analogies of sex or the toilet. I do not do this because I want to shock, particularly, but because there are certain experiences common to all, and sex and toilet are two of them. Furthermore, everyone is interested in those two — which can't be said of every common experience.[66]

Group chanting of obscenities makes everyone equal in the movement, involves everyone in the protest, and both shares and reduces the risk involved. Peter Farb maintains that "the common denominator of all slang whether it be the speech of adolescents or the jive talk of musicians, is that it tests who belongs to the group and who is an intruder."[67] This would seem to have been Eldridge Cleaver's purpose when, after a brief greeting to his audience on the UCLA campus, he declared: "Before I go any further, I want to get into this by saying what some people don't like to hear, and what others seem to not mind. Fuck Ronald Reagan! Fuck Ronald

Reagan!" The audience cheered as they identified with Cleaver and his hatred for the Governor of California. Cleaver belonged.

And finally, obscenity may provide a means for movements and their individual members *to release pent-up hostility and fear.* Psychologist Chaytor Mason asserts that obscenity serves as a safety valve that helps society to function without excessive frustration.[68] Verbal aggression is often a surrogate for physical aggression and, consequently, may have a therapeutic value for society and spare it from bloodshed—or at least extreme bloodshed. Verbal aggression permits youth to challenge society verbally to ascertain the boundaries of expression. "Profanity," according to Mason, "is the essence of the human being. Like scratching, it releases tension, and like sex, it's one of those very personal, satisfying acts."[69]

Adverse Effects of Obscenity on Social Protest

We have cited a variety of valuable persuasive functions that obscenity can perform for social movements, but obscenity can also have a variety of adverse effects on social movements.

First, although obscenity is an effective means of capturing attention of the public and the mass media, it tends to draw attention to itself and away from the demands and solutions for which the movement is fighting. The issue becomes not *what* is being said but *how* it is being said and by *whom.* David Dellinger, the defender of the Chicago Seven in the trial that followed the Democratic National Convention, warned the movement:

> We become intoxicated by the slogan "By any means necessary," and forget the interrelationship of means and ends. Like the hot-rod who was caught in a traffic jam and bottomed out by racing across a field, we rush into shortcuts that take us for an exciting ride but don't get us where we want to go. The movement falls into its own brand of tokenism, preferring the showy symbolism of insulting a "pig" or trashing a window to the reality of winning over the people to resist the authority of the state and the corporation.[70]

Saul Alinsky in his book *Rules for Radicals* berated those who forget the cause: "These rules make the difference between being a realistic radical and being a rhetorical one who uses the tired old words and slogans...and has so stereotyped himself that others react by saying, 'Oh, he's one of those,' and then promptly turn off."[71]

Second, attention gained through obscenity tends to be short-lived. As Windt writes, "Once attention has been gained and criticism voiced, the diatribe diminishes in usefulness. People demand serious remedies, seriously treated. Moral dramaturgy must give way to conventional rhetorical forms."[72] When the shock of hearing and seeing obscenities wears off, there is nothing left. The Yippie "movement" is an excellent illustration of this problem.

Third, since obscenity is the most extreme form of verbal aggression, it is difficult, if not impossible, to make the movement more "radical" without resorting to violence. People soon grow tired of the same old words. How long, for example, can a person remain excited about chanting "fuck" or carrying signs that read "bullshit?" As Saul Alinsky warns, "A tactic that drags on too long becomes a drag."[73] If a social movement resorts to obscenity that is too extreme, it will lose the attention of the mass media it desperately desires.

Fourth, the social unacceptability of verbal and nonverbal obscenity relegates its use to minorities in both society and social movements. "Most people castigate those who dare to speak obscenities in the public forum," Rothwell writes, "despite the fact that a substantial portion of the 'Silent Majority' seems to have little aversion to private cursing."[74] The President's Commission on Campus Unrest warned: "Students should be reminded that language that offends will seldom persuade. Their words have sometimes been as offensive to many Americans as the words of some public officials have been to them."[75] Theodore Windt writes that "In 1968 the Survey Research Center of the University of Michigan found that nearly seventy-five percent of the people reacted negatively to protestors."[76] Reasons tended to be dress, actions, language, and life-style. The President's Commission wrote of a "public backlash against campus unrest." Rather than turning against the institutions involved in campus violence, the Commission concluded, "many Americans came to believe that only harsh measures could quell campus disturbances."[77] This repugnance for the public use of obscenity denies to social movements that use this persuasive tactic the support of important legitimizers outside of and moderates within the movements. Neither group desires or can afford to condone or be associated with elements that resort to obscene language and acts. Leaders of the anti-Vietnam War movement became concerned about the divisive effect of obscenity on the movement. Tom Hayden chastized his fellow SDS (Students for A Democratic Society) members at a meeting in 1968:

> There is no reason to call McCarthy kids motherfuckers or assholes. There's no reason to continue to verbally put down white liberals for only contributing money or legal defense and going no further. There's no reason to verbally antagonize anyone unnecessarily—that is a form of pseudo politics, a substitute for action.[78]

Verbal obscenity in social protest seems to become both contagious and noxious over time to growing numbers of people.

And fifth, obscenity often helps to produce violent responses that memers of social movements do not expect. Shortly after noon on May 4, 1970, group of approximately 50 protestors approached a line of Ohio National Guardsmen on the Kent State University campus. Many of the protestors were shouting obscenities, and a photograph clearly shows several students making obscene gestures with their middle fingers, some with both hands. The Guard moved forward to dispell the students from the Commons; confrontations occurred; and at approximately 12:25 the Guardsmen lowered their rifles and fired into the crowd. Seconds later four students were dead and nine were wounded.[79] Several of the victims had been hundreds of ards away from the confrontation and were either watching the activities or going to class. On May 14, 1970, a group of between 75 and 200 students on the Jackson State College campus in Mississippi confronted state and ocal police after two days of rock and bottle-throwing and incessant obcenities. Shortly before midnight police fired into a crowd and into nearby dormitory windows. Two students were killed and twelve were wounded.[80] During the five days of the Democratic National Convention in Chicago, 92 police officers and approximately 1,000 demonstrators and non-demonstrators were treated for injuries and 668 people were arrested.[81] Social movements must weigh the possible benefits of obscenity with the potential costs. The social movements of the 1960s and 1970s apparently did not do so.

Conclusions

Verbal and nonverbal obscenity is not a "socially acceptable" form of ocial interaction or protest, but it has been with us for centuries and is a iable means of persuasion. Obscenity is beneficial to society because it llows the disenchanted to vent their frustrations through verbal rather than iolent aggression. And obscenity is beneficial to social movements because t provokes the confrontations necessary for furthering their goals.

Social movements have resorted to obscenity to transform perceptions of history—to make people perceive situations to be obscene. They have polarized friends from enemies by defining and stereotyping oppositions as obscene, by provoking establishments into losing control and thus exhibiting their ugliness, and by showing profound contempt for the oppressors. Obscenities establish self-hood for protestors, exaggerate their strengths and virtues, and liberate them sexually, socially, and politically from a 'parental" establishment. Some social movements have employed obscenities to show contempt for all social processes and efforts to bring about change and to avoid the necessity and responsibility for prescribing demands and solutions of their own. Obscenity helps movements to mobilize for action by capturing the attention of the establishment, the people, and the mass media. Institutions find it difficult to ignore incessant verbal and nonverbal obscenities and to avoid clashes with their "foul-mouthed" and "obscene" antagonists. Authorities must prepare for the worst scenario when confronting outlandish demands and threats by anti-social elements, even when such preparations may be costly and humiliating. Shared obscenity may enhance the cohesiveness of the social movement and serve as a test to determine who belongs in the ranks of the dedicated true believers.

But the use of obscenity may have a variety of adverse effects on the persuasive efforts of social movements. Obscene words and actions tend to draw attention to themselves and away from the movement's cause. Attention gained through obscenity tends to be short-lived. Since obscenity is often the "last resort" of a social movement, there is often no rhetorical strategy to turn to that is more exciting or shocking. The social unacceptability of obscenity relegates its users to minorities within society and within social movements because neither legitimizers nor moderates want to use or be identified with obscenity. And the obscenity-provoked confrontations with established orders are often costly in arrests, injuries, and deaths.

Regardless of the problems associated with obscenity, however, some protestors of the past have determined that the risks were acceptable when there seemed to be no other means of getting attention, of being heard. Undoubtedly some protestors of the future will come to the same conclusion. We hope this chapter will help you to understand this decision and what protestors hope to accomplish by stepping beyond social norms for language and behavior.

Endnotes

[1] Paul Cameron, "Frequency and Kinds of Words in Various Social Settings, or What the Hell's Going on?" *Pacific Sociological Review*, 12 (1969), 101-104.

[2] As reported in "A Good Word for Bad Words, *Time*, 14 December 1981, 77.

[3] Ashley Montagu, *The Anatomy of Swearing* (New York: Macmillan, 1967), 5.

[4] Montagu, 9.

[5] Montagu, 55-56.

[6] Montagu, 65-89.

[7] Harold Laswell, *Psychology and Politics* (New York: Prentice-Hall, 1960), 184.

[8] Robert J. Doolittle, *Orientations to Communication and Conflict* (Chicago: Science Research Associates, 1976), 2.

[9] Jonathan B. Bingham and Alfred M. Bingham, *Violence and Democracy* (New York: World, 1970), 43.

[10] As reported in Mary G. McEdwards, "Agitative Rhetoric: Its Nature and Effect," *Western Speech*, 32 (Winter, 1968), 38.

[11] Montagu, 104-105.

12 Robert Bostrom, John Basehart, and Charles Rossiter, "The Effects of Three Types of Profane Language in Persuasive Messages," *The Journal of Communication*, 23 (December, 1973), 473.

13 Ray Fabrizio, Edith Karas, and Ruth Menmuir, *The Rhetoric of No* (New York: Holt, Rinehart, and Winston, 1970), vi.

14 Montagu, 2.

15 John W. Bowers and Donovan J. Ochs, *The Rhetoric of Agitation and Control* (Reading, MA: Addison-Wesley, 1971), 2.

16 Kenneth Burke, *A Rhetoric of Motives* (Berkeley: University of California Press, 1974), 46.

17 See Milton Viorst, *Fire in the Streets: America in the 1960's* (New York: Simon and Schuster, 1979).

18 For example, novels such as Norman Mailer's *The Naked and the Dead*, Kerouac's *The Dharma Bums*, Lillian Burrough's *Naked Lunch*, and the republishing of D.H. Lawrence's *Lady Chatterley's Lover* in 1959 were controversial and stimulated public debate over obscenity.

19 Robert Cathcart, "New Approaches to the Study of Movements: Defining Movements Rhetorically," *Western Speech*, 36 (Spring, 1972), 86.

20 Robert L. Scott and Donald K. Smith, "The Rhetoric of Confrontation," *Quarterly Journal of Speech*, 55 (February, 1969), 7.

21 Robert M. Browne, "Response to Edward P.J. Corbett, 'The Rhetoric of the Open Hand and the Rhetoric of the Closed Fist'," *College Composition and Communication*, 21 (May, 1970), 187.

22 Edward P.J. Corbett, "The Rhetoric of the Open Hand and the Rhetoric of the Closed Fist," *College Composition and Communication*, 20 (December, 1969), 294-295.

23 Wayne Booth, *Modern Dogma and the Rhetoric of Assent* (Chicago: University of Chicago Press, 1974), 164 and 193.

24 Saul Alinsky, *Rules for Radicals: A Practical Primer for Realistic Radicals* (New York: Vintage, 1971), 48.

25 Richard Weaver, *Language as Sermonic* (Baton Rouge: Louisiana State University Press, 1970), 120-121.

26 Murray Edelman, *Politics as Symbolic Action* (Chicago: Markham, 1971), 74-75.

27 Murray Edelman, *The Symbolic Uses of Politics* (Urbana, IL: University of Illinois Press, 1977), 103.

28 Dan Rothwell, *Telling It Like It Isn't: Language Misuse and Malpractice* (Englewood Cliffs, NJ: Prentice-Hall, 1982), 92-93 and 96.

29 McEdwards, 271.

30 Richard Weaver, *Visions of Order* (Baton Rouge: Louisiana State University Press, 1964), 142.

31 Michael Hazen, "The Rhetorical Functions of Verbal Obscenity in Social Protest: The Limits of Cultural Values," unpublished paper presented at the annual convention of the Speech Communication Association, San Antonio, Texas, November 1979.

32 Burke, 81.

33 As reported in Theodore Otto Windt, Jr., "The Diatribe: Last Resort for Protest," *Quarterly Journal of Speech*, 58 (February, 1972), 10.

34 Windt, 11-12.

[35] Jerry Farber, "The Student as Nigger," in Fabrizio, Karas, and Menmuir, 414, 416, 417.
[36] J. Dan Rothwell, "Verbal Obscenity: Time for Second Thoughts," *Western Speech*, 35 (Fall, 1971), 240-241.
[37] Fabrizio, Karas, and Menmuir, 414.
[38] *The Report of the President's Commission on Campus Unrest* (Washington, DC: U.S. Government Printing Office, 1970), 266 and 439; Daniel Walker, *Rights in Conflict: The Violent Confrontation of Demonstrators and Police in the Streets of Chicago During the Week of the Democratic National Convention* (New York: Bantam Books, 1968), 135, 146, 154.
[39] Eldridge Cleaver, Speech at UCLA, 4 October 1968, from a tape recording.
[40] Scott and Smith, 7, 8.
[41] Walker, 248.
[42] See for example, Walker, 1, 5, 8, 139, 154, 155, 158, and 181.
[43] Richard B. Gregg, "The Ego-Function of the Rhetoric of Protest," *Philosophy and Rhetoric*, 4 (Spring, 1971), 82.
[44] Gregg, 74.
[45] Gregg, 76.
[46] Haig A. Bosmajian, "Obscenity and Protest," *Dissent: Symbolic Behavior and Rhetorical Strategies* (Boston: Allyn and Bacon, 1972), 298.
[47] Stephen Spender, *The Year of the Young Rebels* (New York: Random House, 1969), 7-8.
[48] Mitchell Goodman, *The Movement Toward a New America: The Beginnings of a Long Revolution* (Philadelphia: Pilgrim Press, 1970), 95.
[49] Walker, 41, 43.
[50] Walker, 46.
[51] As reported in Rothwell, "Verbal Obscenity," 234.
[52] Rothwell, "Verbal Obscenity," 234.
[53] Windt, 7-8.
[54] Bosmajian, 299.
[55] As reported in Bosmajian, 299.
[56] As reported in Windt, 13.
[57] As reported in Viorst, 300-301.
[58] Goodman, 361-362.
[59] Rothwell, *Telling It Like It Isn't*, 118.
[60] See Walker, 1: and Donald Myrus, *Law and Disorder: The Chicago Convention and Its Aftermath* (Chicago: Myrus and Joseph, 1968).
[61] Windt, 14.
[62] Walker, 43 and 86.
[63] Rothwell, "Verbal Obscenity," 236.
[64] Cathcart, 86.
[65] Abbie Hoffman, *Revolution for the Hell of It* (New York: Bantam Books, 1968), 153.
[66] Alinsky, 83-84.
[67] Peter Farb, *Word Play: What Happens When People Talk* (New York: Bantam Books, 1975), 86.
[68] Rothwell, *Telling It Like It Isn't*, 106.
[69] John Leo, "A Good Word for Bad Words," *Time*, 14 December 1981, 77.

[70] As reported in Bosmajian, 296.
[71] Alinsky, xviii.
[72] Windt, 8-9.
[73] Alinsky, 128.
[74] Rothwell, "Verbal Obscenity," 232-233.
[75] *Report of the President's Commission*, 14-15.
[76] Windt, 13.
[77] *Report of the President's Commission*, 40.
[78] As reported in Bosmajian, 296.
[79] *Report of the President's Commission*, 265-410.
[80] *Report of the President's Commission*, 421-444.
[81] Walker, 351-358.

Part Four

Conclusions and Bibliography

Chapter 16

Summary and Conclusions

The first edition of this book was undertaken to synthesize, to extend, and to apply many of the findings, theories, and approaches to persuasion and social movements generated since the 1960s. It seems appropriate to close the second edition by summarizing our view of social movement persuasion.

We defined a social movement as "an organized, uninstitutionalized, and significantly large collectivity that emerges to bring about or to resist a program for change in societal norms and values, operates primarily through persuasive strategies, and encounters opposition in what becomes a moral struggle." Although it is a definition difficult to operationalize, it neatly distinguishes our conception of social movements from political parties, political action committees, riots, trends, revolutions, and Farm-Aid concerts. Some readers responded to our definition by arguing the importance of riots, individual protests, and benefit concerts as symbolic acts. We agree that they matter, and perhaps someday we shall discuss them in another project. They are persuasion, but they are not social movement persuasion. Social movements face a unique set of rhetorical problems stemming from their need to attract, to unify, to mobilize, and to sustain great numbers of people in the absence of institutionalized resources, authority, or sanctions.

Readers familiar with the first edition will notice that we have modified our definition in two subtle but meaningful ways. The first edition said that social movements "are countered by an established order," and the new chapter on resistance explains how established orders do it. Social movements also "encounter opposition" from sources other than the established order. Examples include indifference, inertia, surrogates for established orders, and competing social movements that undergird and sustain the established order; the chapter on resistance demonstrates this as well.

A social movement never emerges from quiet times unless its needs and interests have been frustrated by opposition. That frustration invites movement adherents to reexamine their purposes and motives. Having lost on the grounds of practicality and legality, social movements turn to a general sense of rightness. Most movements soon ground their objectives in a superior morality which necessarily defines the established order as morally corrupt and generates conflict that is moral in tone. Certainly most American political rhetoric is moral in tone, and one can argue that every argument contains a moral dimension. We have added the moral tone to our definition for two reasons. Social movements have few resources at their disposal, and they need moral arguments as the cores of their ideologies. Moreover, opponents typically characterize movements as evil threats to the prevailing morality. Rhetoric that is moral in tone need not come from a social movement,but every social movement will find itself locked in a rhetorical struggle that is moral in tone.

The efforts of social movements to tackle their unique rhetorical problems creates a characteristic life cycle: genesis, social unrest, enthusiastic mobilization, maintenance, and termination. We see in the women's, civil rights, and labor movements examples of this life cycle and the ability of social movements to turn maintenance into remobilization. We have also seen cases where movements spun their wheels because they failed to recognize their next phase, and we have seen cases where movements failed to handle the rhetorical problems presented by the new stage. Indeed, non-institutionalization itself forces this constant adaptation upon social movements.

Two particular problems facing social movements concern leadership and legitimacy. We have argued that popular images of movement leaders are misleading. Social movements are led by editors, clergy, business people, teachers, and lawyers so frustrated by the injustices they perceive in the world that they take extraordinary action; movements are not spearheaded by some thoughtless, irresponsible, possibly psychotic "lunatic fringe." The leaders are both decision makers and symbols of their movements. They may attain leadership because of their charisma, prophecy, or pragmatism; and they keep it by blending multiple attributes, by adapting to events, by handling diverse or conflicting leadership roles, by changing as the movement changes, by adapting to events, and by not falling behind or getting ahead of their followers.

Political, religious, and social institutions have the presumption of legitimacy, and those who attack such institutions need to prove the legitimacy of their causes. Movements can draw upon constitutional rights such as freedom of speech, freedom to assemble, and the consent of the governed to legitimize their position. The point is that the established order need not bother to prove its legitimacy. We have set forth some of the problems and strategies facing social movements as they search for legitimacy.

Students of social movement persuasion have frequently advanced typologies of movements and inferred rhetorical characteristics from them. We have fought that temptation because it assumes a direct causal relationship between two different levels of analysis: the social movement and the argument. We have instead offered a typology of political arguments related to the desirability of change. It may be that "ultra-conservative" movements want to go back to an earlier time and that "ultra-liberal" movements want to move ahead. But these social movements pursue their objectives through a kaleidoscopic array of arguments. Rather than classifying a movement and deducing its rhetorical style, we should comparatively study the array of arguments across the political spectrum and infer types of social movement persuasion accordingly.

In short, we see in social movement persuasion the evolution of political communities. Representative democracy does not guarantee policy satisfaction, and the dissatisfied may find one another and develop sufficient dissatisfaction to confront the established order and the interests it has seen fit to represent. The emerging dialectic between movement and establishment eventually results in a revised political community supported by a new consensus. Sometimes the social movement overthrows the establishment, sometimes they win minor concessions, and sometimes they are disenfranchised. But usually the struggle results in new distinctions, priorities, and relationships.

We presented three approaches to the study of social movement persuasion that are grounded in a symbolic interactionist perspective. The social systems approach emphasizes the social evolution of political communities through interpretation and depiction. It can help to answer questions such as why did these particular people join the movement? Why did the movement flourish in particular settings? How did the political community develop its unique character? The functional approach highlights the necessary movement tasks that can only be performed by rhetoric. It can help to answer such questions as: Why did a movement suddenly fade from view? How do varied social movements recruit new members? How did the same movement confront the established order at various points in history? And the dramatistic approach of Kenneth Burke emphasizes the attribution and the resolution of guilt in the conflict between opposing groups. It can help to answer questions such as how did the movement assign blame for the problem? How did the movement and establishment characterize their conflict? Through what means was societal redemption achieved? Some concerns overlap among the three perspectives, but each has a useful and unique emphasis.

The third section of the book presented analytical studies that explore theoretical points in detail to explain cases of social movement persuasion. The chapter on the John Birch Society demonstrates how the form and substance of a movement's discourse work psychologically for members so they can work for the movement. The Pro-Life vs. Pro-Choice chapter describes the process through which two competing movements struggle for the moral high ground while the established order and inertia sustain the status quo. The New Right chapter shows how a social movement created a compelling explanatory narrative that dramatized widespread fears and undercut public confidence in institutional legitimacy. The studies of songs, slogans, and obscenities support the hypotheses that rhetoric performs functions for movements and that movement rhetoric reveals clusters of communicative characteristics which in turn suggests rhetorical differences among social movements.

We have tried to present and validate a theoretical framework appropriate for the study of social movement persuasion. Concepts such as legitimacy, moral argument, leadership, resistance, evolution, dramatism, and depiction are not unique to social movements. But the decision to cross the threshold of societal norms takes persuader and audience into a different dimension in which unifying symbolic resources such as norms, myths, and values can no longer be used. Old presumptions that support the established order become conceptual trapdoors leading back to the mainstream. The right to speak and the right to assemble become difficult to exercise in opposition to the agents of authority. For these and other reasons already discussed, social movement persuasion is a unique kind of rhetoric that requires a shift in analytical perspective.

An old friend of one of the authors read the first edition and said, "Hitler would have kept this book at his bedside." Students of rhetoric are well-acquainted with the charge that persuasion can be used for undesirable purposes, and it is worth recalling Plato's answer to that charge nearly two thousand years ago. In his treatise *The Gorgias*, Plato conceded that rhetoric could be used for undesirable purposes, but he argued that it would be impossible to expose immorality, illegality, undesirability, or impropriety without it. Rhetoric is a process of adjusting your own experience to your audience's experience, and it will be used for good or ill in accordance with the persuader's sense of morality and ethics. Perhaps some future Hitler may benefit from books like this one. If so, some future Thomas Jefferson, Susan B. Anthony, Samuel Gompers, Mohandas Gandhi, Martin Luther King, or Cesar Chavez should benefit as well. More importantly, we believe that a fuller understanding of social movement persuasion will enable citizens to understand better the important evolutionary role of social movements in American society: and the more clearly to hear, to understand, and to choose from among them.

A Selected Bibliography of Persuasion and Social Movements

Articles

Abbott, Don. "Ian Paisley: Evangelism and Confrontation in Northern Ireland," *Today's Speech*, 21 (Fall, 1973), 49-55.

Anderson, Judith. "Sexual Politics: Chauvinism and Backlash?" *Today's Speech*, 21 (Fall, 1973), 11-16.

Andrews, James R. "The Ethos of Pacifism: The Problem of Image in the Early British Peace Movement," *Quarterly Journal of Speech*, 53 (February, 1967), 28-33.

____. "Piety and Pragmatism: Rhetorical Aspects of the Early British Peace Movement," *Speech Monographs*, 34 (November, 1967), 423-436.

____. "Confrontation at Columbia: A Case Study in Coercive Rhetoric," *Quarterly Journal of Speech*, 55 (February, 1969), 9-16.

____. "The Rhetoric of Coercion and Persuasion: The Reform Bill of 1832," *Quarterly Journal of Speech*, 56 (April, 1970), 187-195.

____. "The Passionate Negation: The Chartist Movement in Rhetorical Perspective," *Quarterly Journal of Speech*, 59 (April, 1973), 196-208.

____. "Reflections of the National Character in American Rhetoric," *Quarterly Journal of Speech*, 57 (October, 1971), 316-324.

____. "Spindles vs. Acres: Rhetorical Perceptions on the British Free Trade Movement," *Western Speech*, 38 (Winter, 1974), 41-52.

____. "History and Theory in the Study of the Rhetoric of Social Movements," *Central States Speech Journal*, 31 (Winter, 1980), 274-281.

____. "An Historical Perspective on the Study of Social Movements," *Central States Speech Journal*, 34 (Spring, 1983), 67-69.

Asinaf, Eliot. "Dick Gregory Is Not So Funny Now," *The New York Times Magazine*, 17 (March, 1968), 37-45.

Banninga, Jerald L. "John Quincy Adams on the Right of a Slave to Petition Congress," *Southern Speech Communication Journal*, 38 (Winter, 1972), 151-163.

Baskerville, Barnet. "The Cross and the Flag: Evangelists of the Far Right," *Western Speech*, 27 (Fall, 1963), 197-206.

Benson, Thomas W. "Rhetoric and Autobiography: The Case of Malcolm X," *Quarterly Journal of Speech*, 60 (February, 1974), 1-13.

Benson, Thomas W. and Bonnie Johnson. "The Rhetoric of Resistance: Confrontation with the Warmakers, Washington, D.C., October 1967," *Today's Speech*, 16 (September,1968), 35-42.

Berg, David M. "Rhetoric, Reality, and the Mass Media," *Quarterly Journal of Speech*, 58 (October, 1972), 255-263.

Betz, Brian R. "Eric Fromm and the Rhetoric of Prophecy," *Central States Speech Journal*, 26 (Winter, 1975), 310-315.

Bezayiff, David. "Legal Oratory of John Adams: An Early Instrument of Protest," *Western Journal of Speech Communication*, 40 (Winter, 1976), 63-71.

Bloodworth, John D. "Communication in the Youth Counter Culture: Music as Expression," *Central States Speech Journal*, 26 (Winter, 1975), 304-309.

Bormann, Ernest G. "Fantasy and Rhetorical Vision: The Rhetorical Criticism of Social Reality," *Quarterly Journal of Speech*, 58 (December, 1972), 396-407.

——. "The Southern Senator's Filibuster on Civil Rights: Speechmaking as Parliamentary Strategem," *Southern Speech Journal*, 27 (Spring, 1962), 183-194.

——. "Fetching Good Out of Evil: A Rhetorical Use of Calamity," *Quarterly Journal of Speech*, 63 (April, 1977), 130-139.

Bosmajian, Haig A. "The Nazi Speaker's Rhetoric," *Quarterly Journal of Speech*, 46 (December, 1960), 365-371.

——. "Nazi Meetings: The *Sprechabend*, the *Versaamlung*, the *Kundgebung*, the *Feierstunde*," *Southern Speech Journal*, 31 (Summer, 1966), 324-337.

——. "The Sources and Nature of Adolf Hitler's Technique of Persuasion," *Central States Speech Journal*, 25 (Winter, 1974), 240-248.

——. "The Persuasiveness of Nazi Marching and *Der Kampf um Die Strasse*," *Today's Speech*, 16 (November, 1968), 17-22.

——. "Obscenity and Protest," *Today's Speech*, 18 (Winter, 1970), 9-14.

——. "'Speech' and the First Amendment," *Today's Speech*, 18 (Fall, 1970), 3-11.

——. "Freedom of Speech and the Heckler," *Western Speech*, 36 (Fall, 1972), 218-232.

——. "Freedom of Speech and the Language of Oppression," *Western Journal of Speech Communication*, 42 (Fall, 1978), 209-221.

——. "Defining the 'American Indian': A Case Study in the Language of Suppression," *Speech Teacher*, 22 (March, 1973), 89-99.

——. "The Abrogation of the Suffragists' First Amendment Rights," *Western Speech*, 38 (Fall, 1974), 218-232.

Bowen, Harry W. "Does Non-Violence Persuade?" *Today's Speech*, 11 (April, 1963), 10-11, 31.

——. "The Future of Non-Violence," *Today's Speech*, 11 (September, 1963), 3-4.

——. "A Realistic View of Non-Violent Assumptions," *Today's Speech*, 15 (September, 1967), 9-10.

Booth, Wayne. "'Now Don't Try to Reason With Me': Rhetoric Today, Left, Right, and Center," *The University of Chicago Magazine*, 60 (November, 1967), 12.

Brock, Bernard L. "A Special Report on Social Movement Theory and Research: Editor's Commentary," *Central States Speech Journal*, 34 (spring, 1983), 80-82.

Brockriede, Wayne E. and Robert L. Scott. "Stokely Carmichael: Two Speeches on Black Power," *Central States Speech Journal*, 19 (Spring, 1968), 3-13.

Brommel, Bernard J. "The Pacifist Speechmaking of Eugene V. Debs," *Quarterly Journal of Speech*, 52 (April, 1966), 146-154.

____. "Eugene V. Debs: The Agitator as Speaker," *Central States Speech Journal*, 20 (Fall, 1969), 202-214.

Brooks, Robert D. "Black Power: The Dimensions of a Slogan," *Western Speech*, 34 (Spring, 1970), 108-114.

Brummet, Barry. "The Skeptical Critic," *Western Journal of Speech Communication*, 46 (Fall, 1982), 379-382.

____. "Premillennial Apocalyptic as a Rhetorical Genre," *Central States Speech Journal*, 35 (Summer, 1984), 84-93.

Burgchardt, Carl R. "Two Faces of American Communism: Pamphlet Rhetoric of the Third Period and the Popular Front," *Quarterly Journal of Speech*, 66 (December, 1980), 375-391.

Burgess, Parke G. "The Rhetoric of Black Power: A Moral Demand," *Quarterly Journal of Speech*, 54 (April, 1968), 122-133.

____. "The Rhetoric of Moral Conflict: Two Critical Dimensions," *Quarterly Journal of Speech*, 56 (April, 1970), 120-130.

____. "Crisis Rhetoric: Coercion vs. Force," *Quarterly Journal of Speech*, 59 (February, 1973), 61-73.

Burgoon, Michael. "A Factor-Analytic Examination of Messages Advocating Social Change," *Speech Monographs*, 39 (November, 1972), 290-295.

Bytwerk, Randall L. "Rhetorical Aspects of the Nazi Meeting: 1926-1933," *Quarterly Journal of Speech*, 61 (October, 1975), 307-318.

Campbell, Finley C. "Voices of Thunder, Voices of Rage: A Symbolic Analysis of a Selection from Malcolm X's Speech 'Message to the Grass Roots,'" *Speech Teacher*, 19 (March, 1970), 101-110.

Campbell, Karlyn Kohrs. "Feminity and Feminism: To Be or Not To Be a Woman," *Communication Quarterly*, 31 (Spring, 1983), 101-108.

____. "The Rhetoric of Radical Black Nationalism: A Case Study in Self-Conscious Criticism," *Central States Speech Journal*, 22 (Fall, 1971), 151-160.

____. "The Rhetoric of Women's Liberation: An Oxymoron," *Quarterly Journal of Speech*, 59 (February, 1973), 74-86.

____. "Style and Content in the Rhetoric of Early Afro-American Feminists," *Quarterly Journal of Speech*, 72 (November, 1986), 434-445.

Carlson, A. Cheree. "Gandhi and the Comic Frame: 'Ad Bellum Purificandum,'" *Quarterly Journal of Speech*, 72 (November, 1986), 446-455.

Carpenter, Ronald H. and Robert V. Stelzer. "Nixon, *Patton*, and a Silent Majority Sentiment about the Vietnam War: The Cinematographic Bases of a Rhetorical Stance," *Central States Speech Journal*, 25 (Summer, 1974), 105-110.

Carson, Herbert L. "An Eccentric Kinship: Henry David Thoreau's 'A Plea for Captain John Brown,'" *Southern Speech Journal*, 27 (Winter, 1961), 151-166.

Carter, David A. "The Industrial Workers of the World and the Rhetoric of Song," *Quarterly Journal of Speech*, 66 (December, 1980), 365-374.

Cathcart, Robert S. "New Approaches to the Study of Movements: Defining Movements Rhetorically," *Western Speech*, 36 (Spring, 1972), 82-88.

——. "Movements: Confrontation as Rhetorical Form," *Southern Speech Communication Journal*, 43 (Spring, 1978), 233-247.

——. "Defining Social Movements by Their Rhetorical Form," *Central States Speech Journal*, 31 (Winter, 1980), 267-273.

——. "A Confrontation Perspective on the Study of Social Movements," *Central States Speech Journal*, 34 (Spring, 1983), 69-74.

Chapel, Cage William. "Christian Science and the Nineteenth Century Woman's Movement," *Central States Speech Journal*, 26 (Summer, 1975), 142-149.

Charland, Maurice. "Constitutive Rhetoric: The Case of the *People Quebecois*," *Quarterly Journal of Speech*, 73 (May, 1987), 133-150.

Chesebro, James W. "Rhetorical Strategies of the Radical Revolutionary," *Today's Speech*, 20 (Winter, 1972), 37-48.

——. "Cultures in Conflict—A Generic and Axiological View," *Today's Speech*, 21 (Spring, 1973), 11-20.

Chesebro, James W., John F. Cragan, and Patricia McCullough. "The Small Group Technique of the Radical Revolutionary: A Synthetic Study of Consciousness Raising," *Speech Monographs*, 40 (June, 1973), 136-146.

Clark, Thomas D. "Rhetorical Image-Making: A Case Study of the Thomas Paine-William Smith Propaganda Debates," *Southern Speech Communication Journal*, 40 (Spring, 1975), 248-261.

——. "Rhetoric, Reality, and Rationalization: A Study of the Masking Function of Rhetoric in the London Theosophical Movement," *Communication Quarterly*, 26 (Fall, 1978), 24-30.

Condit, Celeste Michelle. "The Functions of Epideictic: The Boston Massacre Orations as Exemplar," *Communication Quarterly*, 33 (Fall, 1985), 284-299.

——. "Crafting Virtue: The Rhetorical Construction of Public Morality," *Quarterly Journal of Speech*, 73 (February, 1987), 79-97.

——. "Democracy and Civil Rights: The Universalizing Influence of Public Argumentation," *Communication Monographs*, 54 (March, 1987), 1-18.

Conrad, Charles. "The Transformation of the 'Old Feminist' Movement," *Quarterly Journal of Speech*, 67 (August, 1981), 284-297.

——. "The Rhetoric of the Moral Majority: An Analysis of Romantic Form," *Quarterly Journal of Speech*, 69 (May, 1983), 159-170.

Corbett, Edward P.J. "The Rhetoric of the Open Hand and the Rhetoric of the Closed Fist," *College Composition and Communication*, 20 (December, 1969), 288-296.

Coughlin, Elizabeth M. and Charles E. Coughlin. "Convention in Petticoats: The Seneca Falls Declaration of Women's Rights," *Today's Speech*, 21 (Fall, 1973), 17-23.

Cox, J. Robert. "The Rhetoric of Child Labor Reform: An Efficacy-Utility Analysis," *Quarterly Journal of Speech*, 60 (October, 1974), 359-370.

——. "Perspectives on Rhetorical Criticism of Movements: Antiwar Dissent, 1964-1970," *Western Speech*, 38 (Fall, 1974), 254-268.

Cragan, John F. "Rhetorical Strategy: A Dramatistic Interpretation and Application," *Central States Speech Journal*, 26 (Spring, 1975), 4-11.

Crandell, S. Judson. "The Beginnings of a Methodology for Social Control Studies in Public Address," *Quarterly Journal of Speech*, 33 (February, 1947), 36-39.

Crocker, James W. "A Rhetoric of Encounter Following the May 4th, 1970, Disturbances at Kent State University," *Communication Quarterly*, 25 (Fall, 1977), 47-56.

Cusella, Louis P. "Real-Fiction Versus Historical Reality: Rhetorical Purification in 'Kent State'—The Docudrama," *Communication Quarterly*, 30 (Summer, 1982), 159-164.

Dees, Diane. "Bernadette Devlin's Maiden Speech: A Rhetoric of Sacrifice," *Southern Speech Communication Journal*, 38 (Summer, 1973), 326-339.

Denton, Robert E. "The Rhetorical Functions of Slogans: Classifications and Characteristics," *Communication Quarterly*, 28 (Spring, 1980), 10-18.

Delia, Jesse G. "Rhetoric in the Nazi Mind: Hitler's Theory of Persuasion," *Southern Speech Communication Journal*, 37 (Winter, 1971), 136-149.

Dick, Robert C. "Negro Oratory in the Anti-Slavery Societies: 1830-1860," *Western Speech*, 28 (Winter, 1964), 5-14.

Doolittle, Robert J. "Riots as Symbolic: A Criticism and Approach," *Central States Speech Journal*, 27 (Winter, 1976), 310-317.

Duffy, Bernard K. "The Anti-Humanist Rhetoric of the New Religious Right," *Southern Speech Communication Journal*, 49 (Summer, 1984), 339-360.

Duncan, Rodger D. "Rhetoric of the Kidvid Movement: Ideology, Strategies, and Tactics," *Central States Speech Journal*, 27 (Summer, 1976), 129-135.

Edwards, Michael L. "A Resource Unit on Black Rhetoric," *Speech Teacher*, 22 (September, 1973), 183-188.

Eich, Ritch K. and Donald Goldmann. "Communication, Confrontation, and Coercion: Agitation at Michigan," *Central States Speech Journal*, 27 (Summer, 1976), 120-128.

Erickson, Keith V. "Black Messiah: The Father Divine Peace Mission Movement," *Quarterly Journal of Speech*, 63 (December, 1977), 428-438.

Erlich, Howard S. "Populist Rhetoric Reassessed: A Paradox," *Quarterly Journal of Speech*, 63 (April, 1977), 140-151.

Ferris, Maxine Schnitzer. "The Speaking of Roy Wilkins," *Central States Speech Journal*, 16 (May, 1965), 91-98.

Fletcher, Winona L. "Knight Errant or Screaming Eagle? E.L. Godkin's Criticism of Wendell Phillips," *Southern Speech Journal*, 29 (Spring, 1964), 214-223.

Flynt, Wayne. "The Ethics of Democratic Persuasion and the Birmingham Crisis," *Southern Speech Journal*, 35 (Fall, 1969), 40-53.

Flynt, Wayne and William Warren Rogers. "Reform Oratory in Alabama, 1890-1896," *Southern Speech Journal*, 29 (Winter, 1963), 94-106.

Foss, Sonya K. "Teaching Contemporary Feminist Rhetoric: An Illustrative Syllabus," *Communication Education*, 27 (November, 1978), 328-335.

Frank, David A. "Shalem Achschav—Rituals of the Israeli Peace Movement," *Communication Monographs*, 48 (September, 1981), 165-182.

Fulkerson, Gerald. "Exile as Emergence: Frederick Douglass in Great Britain, 1845-1847," *Quarterly Journal of Speech*, 60 (February, 1974), 69-82.

Fulkerson, Richard P. "The Public Letter as a Rhetorical Form: Structure, Logic, and Style in King's 'Letter from Birmingham Jail,'" *Quarterly Journal of Speech*, 65 (April, 1979), 121-136.

Gallagher, Mary Brigid. "John L. Lewis: The Oratory of Pity and Indignation," *Today's Speech*, 9 (September, 1961), 15-16, 29.

Gillespie, Patti P. "Feminist Theatre: A Rhetorical Phenomenon," *Quarterly Journal of Speech*, 64 (October, 1978), 284-294.

Glancy, Donald R. "Socialist with a Valet: Jack London's 'First, Last, and Only' Lecture Tour," *Quarterly Journal of Speech*, 49 (February, 1963), 31-39.

Goldzwig, Steven. "A Rhetoric of Public Theology: The Religious Rhetor and Public Policy," *Southern Speech Communication Journal*, 52 (Winter, 1987), 128-150.

Goodman, Richard J. and William I. Gorden. "The Rhetoric of Desecration," *Quarterly Journal of Speech*, 57 (February, 1971), 23-31.

Goodnight, G. Thomas and John Poluakos. "Conspiracy Rhetoric: From Pragmatism to Fantasy in Public Discourse," *Western Journal of Speech Communication*, 45 (Fall, 1981), 299-316.

Gravlee, G. Jack and James R. Irvine. "Watts' Dissenting Rhetoric of Prayer," *Quarterly Journal of Speech*, 59 (December, 1973), 463-473.

Gregg, Richard B. "A Phenomenologically Oriented Approach to Rhetorical Criticism," *Central States Speech Journal*, 17 (May, 1966), 83-90.

——. "The Ego-Function of the Rhetoric of Protest," *Philosophy and Rhetoric*, 4 (Spring, 1971), 71-91.

Gregg, Richard B. and A. Jackson McCormack. "'Whitey' Goes to the Ghetto: A Personal Chronicle of a Communication Experience with Black Youths," *Today's Speech*, 16 (September, 1968), 25-30.

Gregg, Richard B., A. Jackson McCormack and Douglas J. Pederson. "The Rhetoric of Black Power: A Street-Level Interpretation," *Quarterly Journal of Speech*, 55 (April, 1969), 151-160.

Griffin, Leland M. "The Rhetoric of Historical Movements," *Quarterly Journal of Speech*, 38 (April, 1951), 184-188.

——. "The Rhetorical Structure of the 'New Left' Movement: Part I," *Quarterly Journal of Speech*, 50 (April, 1964), 113-135.

——. "On Studying Social Movements," *Central States Speech Journal*, 31 (Winter, 1980), 225-232.

Gunter, Mary F. and James S. Taylor. "Loyalist Propaganda in the Sermons of Charles Inglis, 1717-1780," *Western Speech*, 37 (Winter, 1973), 47-55.

Gustainis, J. Justin and Dan F. Hahn, "While the Whole World Watched: Rhetorical Failures of Anti-War Protest," *Communication Quarterly*, 36 (Summer, 1988), 203-216.

Hagen, Michael R. "Roe vs. Wade: The Rhetoric of Fetal Life," *Central States Speech Journal*, 27 (Fall, 1976), 192-199.

Hahn, Dan F. "Social Movement Theory: A Dead End," *Communication Quarterly*, 28 (Winter, 1980), 60-64.

Hahn, Dan F. and Ruth M. Gonchar, "Studying Social Movements: A Rhetorical Methodology," *Speech Teacher*, 20 (January, 1971), 44-52.

Haiman, Franklyn S. "The Rhetoric of the Streets: Some Legal and Ethical Considerations," *Quarterly Journal of Speech*, 53 (April, 1967), 99-114.

——. "Nonverbal Communication and the First Amendment: The Rhetoric of the Streets Revisited," *Quarterly Journal of Speech*, 68 (November, 1982), 371-383.

Hammerback, John C. "The Rhetoric of Righteous Reform: George Washington Julian's 1852 Campaign against Slavery," *Central States Speech Journal*, 22 (Summer, 1971), 85-93.

____. "George W. Julian's Antislavery Campaign," *Western Speech*, 37 (Summer, 1973), 157-165.

Hancock, Brenda Robinson. "Affirmation by Negation in the Women's Liberation Movement," *Quarterly Journal of Speech*, 58 (October, 1972), 264-271.

Hart, Roderick P. "The Rhetoric of the True Believer," *Speech Monographs*, 38 (November, 1971), 249-261.

____. "An Unquiet Desperation: Rhetorical Aspects of 'Popular' Atheism in the United States," *Quarterly Journal of Speech*, 62 (October, 1976), 256-266.

Heath, Robert L. "Alexander Crummell and the Strategy of Challenge by Adaptation," *Central States Speech Journal*, 26 (Fall, 1975), 178-187.

____. "Black Rhetoric: An Example of the Poverty of Values," *Southern Speech Communication Journal*, 39 (Winter, 1973), 145-160.

____. "Dialectical Confrontation: A Strategy of Black Radicalism," *Central States Speech Journal*, 24 (Fall, 1973), 168-177.

Heisey, D. Ray and J. David Trebing. "A Comparison of the Rhetorical Visions and Strategies of the Shah's White Revolution and the Ayatollah's Islamic Revolution," *Communication Monographs*, 50 (June, 1983), 158-174.

____. "Authority and Legitimacy: A Rhetorical Case Study of the Iranian Revolution," *Communication Monographs*, 53 (December, 1986), 295-310.

Hensley, Carl Wayne. "Rhetorical Vision and the Persuasion of a Historical Movement: The Disciples of Christ in Nineteenth Century American Culture," *Quarterly Journal of Speech*, 61 (October, 1975), 250-264.

Hillbruner, Anthony. "Inequality, the Great Chain of Being, and Ante Bellum Southern Oratory," *Southern Speech Journal*, 25 (Spring, 1960), 172-189.

Hogan, J. Michael. "Wallace and the Wallacites: A Reexamination," *Southern Speech Communication Journal*, 50 (Fall, 1984), 24-48.

Holtan, Orley I. "A.C. Townly, Political Firebrand of North Dakota," *Western Speech*, 35 (Winter, 1971), 30-41.

Hope, Diana Schaich. "Redefinition of Self: A Comparison of the Rhetoric of the Women's Liberation and the Black Liberation Movements," *Today's Speech*, 23 (Winter, 1975), 17-25.

Howe, Roger J. "The Rhetoric of the Death of God Theology," *Southern Speech Communication Journal*, 37 (Winter, 1971), 150-162.

Hunsaker, David M. "The Rhetoric of Brown v. Board of Education: Paradigm for Contemporary Social Protest," *Southern Speech Communication Journal*, 43 (Winter, 1978), 91-109.

Hynes, Sandra S. "Dramatic Propaganda: Mercy Otis Warren's 'The Defeat,' 1773," *Today's Speech*, 23 (Fall, 1975), 21-27.

Ilkka, Richard J. "Rhetorical Dramatization in the Development of American Communism," *Quarterly Journal of Speech*, 63 (December, 1977), 413-427.

Jablonski, Carol J. "Rhetoric, Paradox, and the Movement for Women's Ordination in the Roman Catholic Church," *Quarterly Journal of Speech*, 74 (May, 1988), 164-183.

Jabusch, David M. "The Rhetoric of Civil Rights," *Western Speech*, 30 (Summer, 1966) 176-183.

Japp, Phyllis M. "Esther or Isaiiah?: The Abolitionist-Feminist Rhetoric of Angelin Grimke," *Quarterly Journal of Speech*, 71 (August, 1985), 335-348.

Jefferson, Pat. "The Magnificent Barbarian in Nashville," *Southern Speech Journal*, 3 (Winter, 1967), 77-87.

———. "'Stokely's 'Cool': Style," *Today's Speech*, 16 (September, 1968), 19-24.

Jensen, J. Vernon. "British Voices on the Eve of the American Revolution: Trapped b the Family Metaphor," *Quarterly Journal of Speech*, 63 (February, 1977), 43-50.

Jensen, Richard J. and John C. Hammerback. "'No Revolutions without Poets': The Rhetori of Rodolfo 'Corky' Gonzales," *Western Journal of Speech Communication*, 46 (Winte 1982), 72-91.

———. "Feminists of Faith: Sonia Johnson and the Mormons for ERA," *Central States Speec Journal*, 36 (Fall, 1985), 123-137.

———. "From Muslim to Morman: Eldridge Cleaver's Rhetorical Crusade," *Communicatio Quarterly*, 34 (Winter, 1986), 24-40.

Jorgensen-Earp, Cheryl R. "'Toys of Desperation'—Suicide as Protest Rhetoric," *Th Southern Speech Communication Journal*, 53 (Fall, 1987), 80-96.

Jurma, William E. "Moderate Movement Leadership and the Vietnam Moratoriun Committee," *Quarterly Journal of Speech*, 68 (August, 1982), 262-272.

Katz, Daniel. "Factors Affecting Social Change: A Social-Psychological Perspective," *Journal of Social Issues*, 30 (1974), 159-180.

———. "Group Process and Social Integration: A System Analysis of Two Movements o Social Protest," *Journal of Social Issues*, 39 (Winter, 1983), 109-128.

Kendall, Kathleen E. and Jeanne Y. Fisher. "Frances Wright on Women's Rights: Eloquenc versus Ethos," *Quarterly Journal of Speech*, 60 (February, 1974), 58-68.

Kennicott, Patrick C. and Wayne E. Page. "H. Rap Brown: The Cambridge Incident," *Quarterly Journal of Speech*, 57 (October, 1971), 325-334.

Kennicott, Patrick C. "Black Persuaders in the Antislavery Movement," *Speech Monographs* 37 (March, 1970), 15-24.

Killian L. "Organization, Rationality, and Spontaneity in the Civil Rights Movement," *American Sociological Review*, 49 (December, 1984), 770-783.

King, Andrew A. "The Rhetorical Legacy of the Black Church," *Central States Speec Journal*, 22 (Fall, 1971), 179-185.

———. "The Rhetoric of Power Maintenance: Elites at the Precipice," *Quarterly Journa of Speech*, 62 (April, 1976), 127-134.

King, Andrew A. and Floyd D. Anderson. "Nixon, Agnew, and the 'Silent Majority': A Case Study in the Rhetoric of Polarization," *Western Speech*, 35 (Fall, 1971), 243-255

Klumpp, James F. "Challenge of Radical Rhetoric: Radicalism at Columbia," *Wester Speech*, 37 (Summer, 1973), 146-156.

Knupp, Ralph E. "A Time for Every Purpose Under Heaven: Rhetorical Dimensions o Protest Music," *Southern Speech Communication Journal*, 46 (Summer, 1981), 377-389

Kosokoff, Stephen and Carl W. Carmichael. "The Rhetoric of Protest: Song, Speech, an Attitude Change," *Southern Speech Journal*, 35 (Summer, 1970), 295-302.

Kroll, Becky Swanson. "From Small Group to Public View: Mainstreaming the Women's Movement," *Communication Quarterly*, 31 (Spring, 1983), 139-147.

Lake, Randall A. "Enacting Red Power: The Consummatory Function in Native American Protest Rhetoric," *Quarterly Journal of Speech*, 69 (May, 1983), 127-142.

____. "Order and Disorder in Anti-Abortion Rhetoric: A Logological View," *Quarterly Journal of Speech*, 70 (November, 1984), 425-443.

Larson, Barbara A. "Samuel Davies and the Rhetoric of the New Light," *Speech Monographs*, 38 (August, 1971), 207-216.

Larson, Charles U. "The Trust Establishing Function of the Rhetoric of Black Power," *Central States Speech Journal*, 21 (Spring, 1970), 52-56.

Laufer, Robert S. and Vern L. Bengston. "Generations, Aging, and Social Stratification: On the Development of Generational Units," *Journal of Social Issues*, 30 (1974), 181-205.

Lawson, R. "The Rent Strike in New York City, 1904-1980: The Evolution of a Social Movement Strategy," *Journal of Urban History*, 10 (May, 1984), 235-258.

Lawton, Cynthia Whalen. "Thoreau and the Rhetoric of Dissent," *Today's Speech*, 16 (April, 1968), 23-25.

Leathers, Dale G. "Fundamentalism of the Radical Right," *Southern Speech Journal*, 33 (Summer, 1968), 245-258.

Linkugel, Wil A. "The Rhetoric of American Feminism: A Social Movement Course," *Speech Teacher*, 23 (March, 1974), 121-130.

____. "The Speech Style of Anna Howard Shaw," *Central States Speech Journal*, 13 (Spring, 1962), 171-178.

____. "The Woman Suffrage Argument of Anna Howard Shaw," *Quarterly Journal of speech*, 49 (April, 1963), 165-174.

Lippman, Monroe. "Uncle Tom and His Poor Relations: American Slavery Plays," *Southern Speech Journal*, 28 (Spring, 1963), 183-197.

Lipsky, Michael. "Protest as a Political Resource," *American Political Science Review*, 52 (1968), 1144-1158.

Lomas, Charles W. "Agitator in a Cassock," *Western Speech*, 27 (Winter, 1963), 16-24.

____. "Kearney and George: The Demagogue and the Prophet," *Speech Monographs*, 28 (March, 1961), 50-59.

____. "The Agitator in American Society," *Western Speech*, 24 (Spring, 1960), 76-83.

Lucas, Stephen E. "Coming to Terms with Movement Studies," *Central States Speech Journal*, 31 (Winter, 1981), 255-266.

Makay, John J. "George C. Wallace: Southern Spokesman with a Northern Audience," *Central States Speech Journal*, 19 (Fall, 1968), 202-208.

Mann, Kenneth Eugene. "Nineteenth Century Black Militant: Henry Highland Garnet's Address to the Slaves," *Southern Speech Journal*, 36 (Fall, 1970), 11-21.

Mansfield, Dorothy M. "Abigail S. Duniway: Suffragette with Not-so-common Sense," *Western Speech*, 35 (Winter, 1971), 24-29.

Martin, Howard H. "The Rhetoric of Academic Protest," *Central States Speech Journal*, 17 (November, 1966), 244-250.

Martin, Kathryn. "The Relationship of Theatre of Revolution and Theology of Revolution to the Black Experience," *Today's Speech*, 19 (Spring, 1971), 35-41.

McEdwards, Mary G. "Agitative Rhetoric: Its Nature and Effect," *Western Speech*, 32 (Winter, 1968), 36-43.

McGaffey, Ruth. "Group Libel Revised," *Quarterly Journal of Speech*, 65 (April, 1979), 157-170.

McGee, Michael C. "In Search of 'The People': A Rhetorical Alternative," *Quarterly Journal of Speech*, 61 (October, 1975), 235-249.

——. "'Social Movement': Phenomenon or Meaning," *Central States Speech Journal*, 31 (Winter, 1980), 233-244.

——. "Social Movement as Meaning," *Central States Speech Journal*, 34 (Spring, 1983), 74-77.

McGuire, Michael. "Mythic Rhetoric in *Mein Kampf*: A Structuralist Critique," *Quarterly Journal of Speech*, 63 (February, 1977), 1-13.

McPherson, Louise. "Communication Techniques of the Women's Liberation Front," *Today's Speech*, 21 (Spring, 1973), 33-38.

Medhurst, Martin J. "The First Amendment vs. Human Rights: A Case Study in Human Sentiment and Argument from Definition," *Western Journal of Speech Communication*, 46 (Winter, 1982), 1-19.

——. "The Sword of Division: A Reply to Brummett and Warnick," *Western Journal of Speech Communication*, 46 (Fall, 1982), 383-390.

——. "Resistance, Conservatism, and Theory Building," *Western Journal of Speech Communication*, 49 (Spring, 1985), 103-115.

Mele, Joseph C. "Edward Douglas White's Influence on the Louisiana Anti-Lottery Movement," *Southern Speech Journal*, 28 (Fall, 1962), 36-43.

Merriam, Allen H. "Symbolic Action in India: Gandhi's Nonverbal Persuasion," *Quarterly Journal of Speech*, 61 (October, 1975), 290-306.

Mixon, Harold D. "Boston's Artillery Election Sermons and the American Revolution," *Speech Monographs*, 34 (March, 1967), 43-50.

Monsma, John W., Jr. "John Brown: The TwoEdged Sword of Abolition," *Central States Speech Journal*, 13 (Autumn, 1961), 22-29.

Newman, Robert P. "Under the Veneer: Nixon's Vietnam Speech of November 3, 1969," *Quarterly Journal of Speech*, 56 (April, 1970), 168-178.

Newsom, Lionel and William Gorden. "A Stormy Rally in Atlanta," *Today's Speech*, 11 (April, 1963), 18-21.

Norton, Robert. "The Propaganda of Bodies," *Today's Speech*, 18 (Spring, 1970), 39-41.

O'Brien, Harold J. "Slavery Sentiments that Led to War," *Today's Speech*, 9 (November, 1961), 5-7.

Orban, Donald K. "Billy James Hargis: Auctioneer of Political Evangelism," *Central States Speech Journal*, 20 (Summer, 1969), 83-91.

Patton, John H. "Rhetoric at Catonsville: Daniel Berrigan, Conscience and Image Alteration," *Today's Speech*, 23 (Winter, 1975), 3-12.

Pearce, W. Barnett, Stephen W. Littlejohn, and Alison Alexander. "The New Christian Right and the Humanist Response: Reciprocated Diatribe," *Communication Quarterly*, 35 (Spring, 1987), 171-192.

Phifer, Elizabeth F. and Dencil R. Taylor. "Carmichael in Tallahassee," *Southern Speech Journal*, 33 (Winter, 1967), 88-92.

Pollock, Arthur. "Stokely Carmichael's New Black Rhetoric," *Southern Speech Journal*, 37 (Fall, 1971), 92-94.

Powers, Lloyd D. "Chicago Rhetoric: Some Basic Concepts," *Southern Speech Journal*, 38 (Summer, 1973), 340-346.

Railsback, Celeste Condit. "The Contemporary American Abortion Controversy: Stages in the Argument," *Quarterly Journal of Speech*, 70 (November, 1984), 410-424.

Reed, Robert Michael. "The Case of Missionary Smith: A Crucial Incident in the Rhetoric of the British Anti-Slavery Movement," *Central States Speech Journal*, 29 (Spring, 1978), 61-71.

Reid, Ronald F. "Varying Historical Interpretations of the American Revolution: Some Rhetorical Perspectives," *Today's Speech*, 23 (Spring, 1975), 5-15.

Reynolds, Beatrice K. "Mao Tse-Tung: Rhetoric of a Revolutionary," *Central States Speech Journal*, 27 (Fall, 1976), 212-217.

Riach, W.A.D. "'Telling It Like It Is': An Examination of Black Theatre as Rhetoric," *Quarterly Journal of Speech*, 56 (April, 1970), 179-186.

Rice, George P., Jr. "Freedom of Speech and the 'New Left,'" *Central States Speech Journal*, 21 (Fall, 1970), 139-145.

Richardson, Larry S. "Stokely Carmichael: Jazz Artist," *Western Speech*, 34 (Summer, 1970), 212-218.

Riches, Suzanne V. and Malcolm O. Sillars. "The Status of Movement Criticism," *Western Journal of Speech Communication*, 44 (Fall, 1980), 275-287.

Ritchie, Gladys. "The Sit-In: A Rhetoric of Human Action," *Today's Speech*, 18 (Winter, 1970), 22-25.

Ritter, Ellen M. "Elizabeth Morgan: Pioneer Female Labor Agitator," *Central States Speech Journal*, 22 (Winter, 1971), 242-251.

Ritter, Kurt W. "Confrontation as Moral Drama: The Boston Massacre in Rhetorical Perspective," *Southern Speech Communication Journal*, 42 (Winter, 1977), 114-136.

Robinson, John P., Robert Pilskaln, and Paul Hirsh. "Protest Rock and Drugs," *Journal of Communication*, 26 (Autumn, 1976), 125-136.

Rogers, Richard A. "The Rhetoric of Militant Deism," *Quarterly Journal of Speech*, 54 (October, 1968), 247-251.

Rollins, J. "Part of the Whole: The Interdependence of the Civil Rights Movement and Other Social Movements," *Phylon*, 47 (March, 1986), 61-70.

Rosenfeld, Lawrence B. "The Confrontation Politics of S.I. Hayakawa: A Case Study in Coercive Semantics," *Today's Speech*, 18 (Spring, 1970), 18-22.

Rosenthal, N.B., et al. "Social Movements and Network Analysis: A Case Study of Nineteenth-Century Women's Reform in New York State," *American Journal of Sociology*, 90 (March, 1985), 1022-1054.

Rosenwasser, Marie J. "Rhetoric and the Progress of the Women's Liberation Movement," *Today's Speech*, 20 (Summer, 1972), 45-56.

Rossiter, Charles M. and Ruth McGaffey. "Freedom of Speech and the 'New Left': A Response," *Central States Speech Journal*, 22 (Spring, 1971), 5-10.

Rothman, Richard. "On the Speaking of John L. Lewis," *Central States Speech Journal*, 14 (August, 1963), 177-185.

Rothwell, J. Dan. "Verbal Obscenity: Time for Second Thoughts," *Western Speech*, 35 (Fall, 1971), 231-242.

Rude, Leslie G. "The Rhetoric of Farmer Labor Agitators," *Central States Speech Journal*, 20 (Winter, 1969), 280-285.

Scott, F. Eugene. "The Political Preaching Tradition in Ulster: Prelude to Paisley," *Western Speech*, 40 (Fall, 1976), 249-259.

Scott, Robert L. "The Conservative Voice in Radical Rhetoric: A Common Response to Division," *Speech Monographs*, 40 (June, 1973), 123-135.

——. "Justifying Violence—The Rhetoric of Militant Black Power," *Central States Speech Journal*, 19 (Summer, 1968), 96-104.

Scott, Robert L. and Donald K. Smith. "The Rhetoric of Confrontation," *Quarterly Journal of Speech*, 55 (February, 1969), 1-8.

Seibold, David. "Jewish Defense League: The Rhetoric of Resistance," *Today's Speech*, 21 (Fall, 1973), 39-48.

Shafer, George. "The Dramaturgy of Fact: The Treatment of History in Two Anti-War Plays," *Central States Speech Journal*, 29 (Spring, 1978), 25-35.

Sillars, Malcolm O. "The Rhetoric of the Petition in Boots," *Speech Monographs*, 39 (June, 1972), 92-104.

——. "Defining Movement Rhetorically: Casting the Widest Net," *Southern Speech Communication Journal*, 46 (Fall, 1980), 17-32.

Silvestri, Vito N. "Emma Goldman, Enduring Voice of Anarchism," *Today's Speech*, 17 (September, 1969), 20-25.

Simons, Herbert W. "Requirements, Problems, and Strategies: A Theory of Persuasion for Social Movements," *Quarterly Journal of Speech*, 56 (February, 1970), 1-11.

——. "Patterns of Persuasion in the Civil Rights Movement," *Today's Speech*, 15 (February, 1967), 25-27.

——. "Confrontation as a Pattern of Persuasion in University Settings," *Central States Speech Journal*, 20 (Fall, 1969), 163-169.

——. "Persuasion in Social Conflicts: A Critique of Prevailing Conceptions and a Framework for Future Research," *Speech Monographs*, 39 (November, 1972), 227-247.

——. "On Terms, Definitions and Theoretical Distinctiveness: Comments on Papers by McGee and Zarefsky," *Central States Speech Journal*, 31 (Winter, 1980), 306-315.

——. "Changing Notions about Social Movements," *Quarterly Journal of Speech*, 62 (December, 1976), 425-430.

——. "Genres, Rules, and Collective Rhetorics: Applying the Requirements-Problems-Strategies Approach," *Communication Quarterly*, 30 (Summer, 1982), 181-188.

Simons, Herbert W., James W. Chesebro, and C. Jack Orr, "A Movement Perspective on the 1972 Presidential Campaign," *Quarterly Journal of Speech*, 59 (April, 1973), 168-179.

Smiley, Sam. "Peace on Earth: Four Anti-War Dramas of the Thirties," *Central States Speech Journal*, 21 (Spring, 1970), 30-39.

Smith, Arthur L. "Henry Highland Garnet: Black Revolutionary in Sheep's Vestments," *Central States Speech Journal*, 21 (Summer, 1970), 93-98.

Smith, Craig Allen. "The Hofstadter Hypothesis Revisited: The Nature of Evidence in Politically 'Paranoid' Discourse," *Southern Speech Communication Journal*, 42 (Spring, 1977), 274-289.

____. "An Organic Systems Analysis of Persuasion and Social Movement: The John Birch Society, 1958-1966," *Southern Speech Communication Journal*, 59 (Winter, 1984), 155-176.

____. "Television News as Rhetoric," *Western Speech*, 41 (Summer, 1977), 147-159.

Smith, Donald H. "Martin Luther King, Jr.: In the Beginning at Montgomery," *Southern Speech Journal*, 34 (Fall, 1968), 8-17.

____. "Social Protest. . .and the Oratory of Human Rights," *Today's Speech*, 15 (September, 1967), 2-8.

Smith, Ralph R. "The Historical Criticism of Social Movements," *Central States Speech Journal*, 31 (Winter, 1980), 290-297.

Smith, Ralph R. and Russell R. Windes. "Collective Action and the Single Text," *Southern Speech Communication Journal*, 43 (Winter, 1978), 110-128.

____. "The Innovational Movement: A Rhetorical Theory," *Quarterly Journal of Speech*, 61 (April, 1975), 140-153.

____. "The Rhetoric of Mobilization: Implications for the Study of Movements," *Southern Speech Communication Journal*, 42 (Fall, 1976), 1-19.

Snow, Malinda. "Martin Luther King's 'Letter from Birmingham Jail' as Pauline Epistle," *Quarterly Journal of Speech*, 71 (August, 1985), 318-334.

Solomon, Martha. "The Rhetoric of STOP ERA: Fatalistic Reaffirmation," *Southern Speech Communication Journal*, 44 (Fall, 1978), 42-59.

____. "Stopping ERA: A Pyrrhic Victory," *Communication Quarterly*, 31 (Spring, 1983), 109-117.

____. "Ideology as Rhetorical Constraint: The Anarchist Agitation of 'Red Emma' Goldman," *Quarterly Journal of Speech*, 74 (May, 1988), 184-200.

Sproule, J. Michael. "An Emerging Rationale for Revolution: Argument from Circumstance and Definition in Polemics Against the Stamp Act, 1765-1766," *Today's Speech*, 23 (Spring, 1975), 17-23.

Stewart, Charles J. "A Functional Approach to the Rhetoric of Social Movements," *Central States Speech Journal*, 31 (Winter, 1980), 298-305.

____. "A Functional Perspective on the Study of Social Movements," *Central States Speech Journal*, 34 (Spring, 1983), 77-80.

Stitzel, James A. "Inflammatory Speaking in the Victor, Colorado, Mass Meeting, June 6, 1904," *Western Speech*, 32 (Winter, 1968), 11-18.

Strother, David B. "Polemics and the Reversal of the 'Separate but Equal' Doctrine," *Quarterly Journal of Speech*, 49 (February, 1963), 50-56.

Talmon, Yonina. "Pursuit of the Millennium: The Relation between Religious and Social Change," *The European Journal of Sociology*, 2 (1962), 140-141.

Tedesco, John L. "The White Character in Black Drama, 1955-1970: Description and Rhetorical Function," *Communication Monographs*, 45 (March, 1978), 64-74.

Thomas, Cheryl Irwin. "'Look What They've Done to My Song, Ma': The Persuasiveness of Song," *Southern Speech Communication Journal*, 39 (Spring, 1974), 260-268.

Thomas, Gordon L. "John Brown's Courtroom Speech," *Quarterly Journal of Speech*, 48 (October, 1962), 291-296.

Thurber, John H. and John L. Petelle. "The Negro Pulpit and Civil Rights," *Central States Speech Journal*, 19 (Winter, 1968), 273-278.

Veenstra, Charles. "The House Un-American Activities Committee's Restriction of Free Speech," *Today's Speech*, 22 (Winter, 1974), 15-22.

Veninga, Robert. "The Functions of Symbols in Legend Construction. . .Some Exploratory Comments," *Central States Speech Journal*, 22 (Fall, 1971), 161-170.

Wagner, Gerard A. "Sojourner Truth: God's Appointed Apostle of Reform," *Southern Speech Journal*, 28 (Winter, 1962), 123-130.

Wander, Philip C. "Salvation Through Separation: The Image of the Negro in the American Colonization Society," *Quarterly Journal of Speech*, 57 (February, 1971), 57-67.

———. "The Savage Child: The Image of the Negro in the Pro-Slavery Movement," *Southern Speech Communication Journal*, 37 (Summer, 1972), 335,360.

———. "The John Birch and Martin Luther King Symbols in the Radical Right," *Western Speech*, 35 (Winter, 1971), 4-14.

Ware, B.L. and Wil A. Linkugel. "The Rhetorical *Persona*: Marcus Garvey as Black Moses," *Communication Monographs*, (March, 1982), 50-62.

Warnick, Barbara. "The Rhetoric of Conservative Resistance," *Southern Speech Communication Journal*, 42 (Spring, 1977), 256-273.

———. "Conservative Resistance Revisited," *Western Journal of Speech Communication*, 46 (Fall, 1982), 373-378.

Weatherly, Michael. "Propaganda and the Rhetoric of the American Revolution," *Southern Speech Journal*, 36 (Summer, 1971), 352-363.

Weaver, Richard L., II. "The Negro Issue: Agitation in the Michigan Lyceum," *Central States Speech Journal*, 22 (Fall, 1971), 196-201.

Weisman, Martha. "Ambivalence Toward War in AntiWar Plays," *Today's Speech*, 17 (September, 1969), 9-14.

Weithoff, William E. "Rhetorical Strategy in the Birmingham Political Union, 1830-1832," *Central States Speech Journal*, 29 (Spring, 1978), 53-60.

Whitfield, George, "Frederick Douglass: Negro Abolitionist," *Today's Speech*, 11 (February, 1963), 6-8, 24.

Wilkie, Richard W. "The Self-Taught Agitator: Hitler 1907-1920," *Quarterly Journal of Speech*, 52 (December, 1966), 371-377.

———. "The Marxian Rhetoric of Angelica Balabanoff," *Quarterly Journal of Speech*, 60 (December, 1974), 450-458.

Wilkinson, Charles A. "A Rhetorical Definition of Movements," *Central States Speech Journal*, 27 (Summer, 1976), 88-94.

Williams, Donald E. "Protest Under the Cross: The Ku Klux Klan Presents Its Case to the People," *Southern Speech Journal*, 27 (Fall, 1961), 43-55.

Wimmer, E. "Ideology of 'New Social Movements,' " *World Marx Review*, (July, 1985), 36-44.

Windt, Theodore O. "The Diatribe: Last Resort for Protest," *Quarterly Journal of Speech*, 58 (February, 1972), 1-14.

———. "Administrative Rhetoric: An Undemocratic Response to Protest," *Communication Quarterly*, 30 (Summer, 1982), 245-250.

Woodward, Gary C. "Mystifications in the Rhetoric of Cultural Dominance and Colonial Control," *Central States Speech Journal*, 26 (Winter, 1975), 298-303.

Wurthman, Leonard B. "The Militant-Moderate Agitator: Daniel O'Connell and Catholic Emancipation in Ireland," *Communication Quarterly*, 30 (Summer, 1982), 225-231.

Wuthnow, R. "The Growth of Religious Reform Movements," *Annals of the American Academy of Political and Social Sciences*, 480 (July, 1985), 106-116.

Yoder, Jess. "The Protest of the American Clergy in Opposition to the War in Vietnam," *Today's Speech*, 17 (September, 1969), 51-59.

____. "Communication Between Catholics and Protestants in Northern Ireland," *Religious Communication Today*, 4 (September, 1981), 15-20.

Zacharis, John C. "Emmeline Pankhurst: An English Suffragette Influences America," *Speech Monographs*, 38 (August, 1971), 198-206.

Zarefsky, David. "President Johnson's War on Poverty: The Rhetoric of Three 'Establishment' Movements," *Communication Monographs*, 44 (November, 1977), 352-373.

____. "A Skeptical View of Movement Studies," *Central States Speech Journal*, 31 (Winter, 1980), 245-254.

Book Chapters

Blumer, Herbert. "Social Movements," *Principles of Sociology*, ed. A.M. Lee. New York: Barnes and Noble, 1951.

Boettinger, L.A. "Organic Theory of Social Reform Movements," *Analyzing Social Problems*, ed. John Nordskog, *et al*. New York: Dryden, 1950.

Griffin, Leland M. "The Rhetorical Structure of the Antimasonic Movement," *The Rhetorical Idiom*, ed. Donald Bryant. Ithaca, NY: Cornell University Press, 1958.

____. "A Dramatistic Theory of the Rhetoric of Movements," *Critical Responses to Kenneth Burke*, ed. William Rueckert. Minneapolis: University of Minnesota Press, 1969.

Gronbeck, Bruce E. "The Rhetoric of Social-Institutional Change: Black Action at Michigan," *Explorations in Rhetorical Criticism*, ed. Gerald Mohrmann, Charles Stewart, Donovan Ochs. University Park, PA: Pennsylvania State University Press, 1973.

Hughes, Everett C. "Institutions Defined," *Principles of Sociology*, ed. A.M. Lee. New York: Barnes and Noble, 1951.

Killian, Lewis M. "Social Movements," *Handbook of Modern Sociology*, ed. R.E. Faris. Chicago: Rand McNally, 1964.

Leathers, Dale G. "Belief-Disbelief Systems: The Communicative Vacuum of the Radical Right," *Explorations in Rhetorical Criticism*, eds. Gerald Mohrmann, Charles Stewart, Donovan Ochs. University Park, PA: Pennsylvania State University Press, 1973.

Simons, Herbert W. and Elizabeth W. Mechling. "The Rhetoric of Political Movements," *Handbook of Political Communication*, eds. Dan Nimmo and Keith Sanders. Beverly Hills, CA: Sage, 1981.

Simons, Herbert W., Elizabeth Mechling and Howard Schreier. "Functions of Communication in Mobilizing for Action from the Bottom Up: The Rhetoric of Social Movements," *Handbook on Rhetorical and Communication Theory*, eds. Carroll C. Arnold and John W. Bowers. Boston: Allyn and Bacon, 1984.

Stewart, Charles J. "Labor Agitation in America: 1865-1915," *America in Controversy: History of American Public Address*, ed. DeWitte T. Holland. Dubuque, IA: W. C. Brown, 1973.

Van Graber, Marilyn. "Functional Criticism: A Rhetoric of Black Power," *Explorations in Rhetorical Criticism*, eds. Gerald Mohrmann, Charles Stewart, and Donovan Ochs. University Park, PA: Pennsylvania State University Press, 1973.

Books

Alinsky, Saul D. *Rules for Radicals: A Practical Primer for Realistic Radicals*. New York: Vintage, 1972.
____. *Reveille for Radicals*. New York: Vintage, 1969.
Amter, Joseph A. *Vietnam Verdict: A Citizen's History*. New York: Contimum, 1982.
Apter, David, ed. *Ideology and Discontent*. London: Collier-Macmillan, 1964.
Arendt, Hannah. *On Revolution*. New York, Viking, 1965.
____. *The Origins of Totalitarianism*. New York: World, 1958.
Arlen, Michael J. *Living-Room War*. New York: Penguin Books, 1969.
Armstrong, Gregory. *Protest: Man Against Society*. New York: Bantam Books, 1969.
Auer, J. Jeffrey, ed. *Antislavery and Disunion: 1858-1861*. New York: Harper and Row, 1963.
____, ed. *The Rhetoric of Our Times*. New York: Appleton-Century-Crofts, 1969.
Baechler, Jean. *Revolution*, trans. Joan Vickers. New York: Harper and Row, 1975.
Barbrook, Alee and Christine Bolt. *Power and Protest in American Life*. New York: St. Martin's Press, 1980.
Barkan, Steven E. *Protestors on Trial: Criminal Justice in the Southern Civil Rights and Vietnam Antiwar Movements*. New Brunswick, NJ: Rutgers University Press, 1986.
Bell, Daniel, ed. *The Radical Right*. New York: Doubleday Anchor, 1964.
Bell, J. Bowyer. *A Time of Terror*. Cambridge: Cambridge University Press, 1982.
____. *Transnational Terror*. Washington, DC: Hoover, 1975.
Blaustein, Albert P. and Robert Zangrando, eds. *Civil Rights and the American Negro*. New York: Trident Press, 1968.
Blocker, Jack S. *"Give to the Minds Thy Fears": The Women's Temperance Crusade, 1873-1874*. Westport, CT: 1985.
Boase, Paul H. *The Rhetoric of Christian Socialism*. New York: Random House, 1969.
____, ed. *The Rhetoric of Protest and Reform: 1878-1898*. Athens, OH: Ohio University Press, 1980.
Booth, Wayne, *Modern Dogma and the Rhetoric of Assent*. Chicago: University of Chicago Press, 1974.
Bosmajian, Haig A., ed. *Dissent: Symbolic Behavior and Rhetorical Strategies*. Boston: Allyn and Bacon, 1972.
Bosmajian, Haig A. and Hamida Bosmajian. *The Rhetoric of the Civil Rights Movement*. New York: Random House, 1969.
Bowers, John W. and Donovan J. Ochs. *The Rhetoric of Agitation and Control*. Reading, MA: Addison-Wesley, 1971.
Brandes, Paul D. *The Rhetoric of Revolt*. Englewood Cliffs, NJ: Prentice-Hall, 1971.
Brinkley, Alan. *Voices of Protest: Huey Long, Father Coughlin, and the Great Depression*. New York: Random House, 1983.
Brinton, Crane. *The Anatomy of Revolution*. New York: Prentice-Hall, 1952.
Brockriede, Wayne C. and Robert L. Scott. *Moments in the Rhetoric of the Cold War*. New York: Random House, 1970.
Brooks, Thomas R. *Walls Came Tumbling Down: A History of the Civil Rights Movement*. Englewood Cliffs, NJ: Prentice-Hall, 1974.
Button, James. *Black Violence*. Princeton: Princeton University Press, 1978.

Bytwerk, Randall L. *Julius Streicher: The Man Who Persuaded a Nation to Hate Jews*. Briarcliff Manor, NY: Stein and Day, 1982.

Cameron, William B. *Modern Social Movements: A Sociological Outline*. New York: Random House, 1966.

Campbell, Karlyn Kohrs. *Critiques of Contemporary Rhetoric*. Belmont, CA: Wadsworth, 1972.

Cantril, Hadley. *The Psychology of Social Movements*. New York: Wiley and Sons, 1963.

Carter, April. *Direct Action and Liberal Democracy*. New York: Harper and Row, 1973.

Chesebro, James W., ed. *Gayspeak: Gay Male and Lesbian Communication*. New York: Pilgrim Press, 1981.

Crawford, Alan. *Thunder on the Right*. New York: Pantheon, 1980.

Curry, Richard O. and Thomas M. Brown, eds. *Conspiracy: The Fear of Subversion in American History*. New York: Holt, Rinehart and Winston, 1972.

Davis, Jerome. *Contemporary Social Movements*. New York: Century, 1930.

Dawson, Carol A. and Warner E. Gettys. *Introduction to Sociology*. New York: Ronald, 1935.

DeBenedetti, Charles. *The Peace Reform in American History*. Bloomington, IN: Indiana University Press, 1980.

Deckard, Barbara. *The Women's Movement*. New York: Harper and Row, 1983.

Denisoff, R. Serge. *Sing a Song of Social Significance*. Bowling Green, OH: Bowling Green University Popular Press, 1972.

____. *Great Day Coming: Folk Music and the American Left*. Urbana, IL: University of Illinois Press, 1972.

Denisoff, R. Serge and Richard A. Peterson. *The Sounds of Social Change*. Chicago: Rand McNally, 1972.

Duffy, Bernard K. and Halford Ryan, eds. *American Orators Before 1900: Critical Studies and Sources*. Westport, CT: Greenwood Press, 1987.

Duffy, Bernard K. and Halford Ryan, eds. *American Orators of the Twentieth Century: Critical Studies and Sources*. Westport, CT: Greenwood Press, 1987.

Edelman, Murray. *Constructing the Political Spectacle*. Chicago: University of Chicago Press, 1988.

____. *Politics as Symbolic Action: Mass Arousal and Quiescence*. San Diego, CA: Academic Press, 1971.

____. *The Symbolic Uses of Politics*. Urbana, IL: University of Illinois Press, 1985.

Edwards, Lyford P. *The Natural History of Revolution*. Chicago: University of Chicago Press, 1927.

Fairclough, Adam. *To Redeem the Soul of America: The Southern Christian Leadership Conference and Martin Luther King, Jr.* Athens, GA: University of Georgia Press, 1987.

Fisher, Randall M. *Rhetoric and American Democracy: Black Protest Through Vietnam Dissent*. Lanham, MD: University Press of America, 1985.

Fortas, Abe. *Concerning Dissent and Civil Disobedience*. New York: American Library, 1968.

Gamson, William A. *The Strategy of Social Protest*. Homewood, IL: Dorsey Press, 1975.

____. *Power and Discontent*. Homewood, IL: Dorsey Press, 1969.

Garner, Roberta Ash. *Social Movements in America*. Chicago: Markham, 1977.

Graber, Doris Appel. *Mass Media and American Politics*. Washington, DC: Congressional Quarterly, 1984.

Griffith, Robert. *The Politics of Fear*. Lexington, KY: University of Kentucky Press, 1977.

Gurr, Ted Robert. *Why Men Rebel*. Princeton, NJ: Princeton University Press, 1970.

Gusfield, Joseph R., ed. *Protest, Reform, and Revolt: A Reader in Social Movements*. New York: John Wiley, 1970.

Haiman, Franklyn S. *Freedom of Speech: Issues and Cases*. New York: Random House, 1965.

Hampton, Wayne. *Guerrilla Minstrels: John Lennon, Joe Hill, Woody Guthrie, and Bob Dylan*. Knoxville, TN: University of Tennessee Press, 1986.

Hart, B.H. Liddell. *Strategy*. New York: Praeger, 1960.

Heberle, Rudolf. *Social Movements: An Introduction to Political Sociology*. New York: Appleton-Century-Crofts, 1951.

Hoffer, Eric. *The True Believer*. New York: Mentor, 1951.

———. *The Ordeal of Change*. New York: Harper and Row, 1963.

Holland, DeWitte T., ed. *Preaching in American History*. Nashville, TN: Abingdon Press, 1969.

———, ed. *American in Controversy: A History of American Public Address*. Dubuque, IA: W. C. Brown, 1973.

Horton, Paul B. and Chester L. Hunt. *Sociology*. New York: McGraw-Hill, 1964.

Hribar, Paul A. *The Social Fasts of Cesar Chavez: Critical Study of Nonverbal Communication, Nonviolence, and Public Opinion*. Los Angeles: University of Southern California, 1978.

Huey, Gary. *Rebel with a Cause: P.D. East, Southern Liberalism, and the Civil Rights Movement, 1953-1971*. Wilmington, DE: Scholarly Resources, 1985.

Hughes, Langston. *Fight for Freedom: The Story of the NAACP*. New York: W.W. Norton, 1962.

Jaggar, Alison and Paula Rothenberg. *Feminist Frameworks*. New York: McGraw-Hill, 1984.

Jameson, J. Franklin. *The American Revolution Considered as a Social Movement*. Boston: Beacon, 1956.

Jeffreys-Jones, Rhodri. *Violence and Reform in American History*. New York: New Viewpoints, 1978.

Johnson, Chalmers. *Revolutionary Change*. Boston: Little, Brown, 1966.

Katope, Christopher George and Paul Zolbrod. *The Rhetoric of Revolution*. New York: Macmillan, 1970.

Kendrick, Alexander. *The Wound Within: America in the Vietnam Years, 1945-1974*. Boston: Little, Brown, 1974.

King, Wendell C. *Social Movements in the United States*. New York: Random House, 1956.

Kriesberg, Louis. *The Sociology of Social Conflicts*. Englewood Cliffs, NJ: Prentice-Hall, 1973.

———. *Social Conflicts*. Englewood Cliffs, NJ: Prentice-Hall, 1982.

Lang, Kurt and Gladys E. Lang. *Collective Dynamics*. New York: Crowell, 1961.

Lens, Sidney. *Radicalism in America*. New York: Crowell, 1966.

Lipset, Seymour and Sheldon S. Wolin, eds. *The Berkeley Student Revolt: Facts and Interpretations*. Garden City, NY: Anchor Books, 1965.

Lomas, Charles W. *The Agitator in American Society.* Englewood Cliffs, NJ: Prentice-Hall, 1968.

Lowenthal, Leo and Norbert Guterman. *Prophets of Deceit.* New York: Harper and Row, 1949.

Maclear, Michael. *The Ten Thousand Day War: Vietnam, 1945-1975.* New York: Dodd, Mead, 1975.

Marable, Manning. *Black American Politics from the Washington Marches to Jesse Jackson.* London: Verso, 1985.

McAdam, Doug. *Political Process and the Development of Black Insurgency.* Chicago: University of Chicago Press, 1982.

McLaughlin, Barry, ed. *Studies in Social Movements.* New York: Free Press, 1969.

Meier, August, Elliot Rudwick, and Francis L. Broderick, eds. *Black Protest Thought in the Twentieth Century.* Indianapolis: Bobbs-Merrill, 1971.

Mendlovitz, Saul H. and R.B.J. Walker, eds. *Toward a Just World Peace: Perspectives from Social Movements.* London: Butterworth, 1987.

Michener, James. *Kent State: What Happened and Why.* New York: Random House, 1971.

Miller, Gerald R. and Herbert W. Simons, eds. *Perspectives on Communication in Social Conflicts.* Englewood Cliffs, NJ: Prentice-Hall, 1974.

Nordskog, John Eric, ed. *Contemporary Social Reform Movements.* New York: Scribner's, 1954.

Oates, Stephen B. *Let the Trumpet Sound: The Life of Martin Luther King, Jr.* Bergenfield, NJ: New American Library, 1982.

Oberschall, Anthony. *Social Conflict and Social Movements.* Englewood Cliffs, NJ: Prentice-Hall, 1973.

Olasky, Marvin. *The Press and Abortion, 1838-1988.* Hillsdale, NJ: Lawrence Erlbaum, 1988.

Oliver, Robert T. *History of Public Speaking in America.* Boston: Allyn and Bacon, 1965.

Oppenheimer, Martin and George Lakey. *A Manual for Direct Action.* Chicago: Quadrangle, 1965.

Payne, Gregory. *Mayday: Kent State.* Dubuque, IA: Kendall/Hunt, 1981.

Phillips, Donald E. *Student Protest, 1960-1970: An Analysis of the Speeches and Issues.* Lanham, MD: University Press of America, 1985.

Poloma, Margaret M. *The Charismatic Movement: Is There a New Pentecost?* Boston: Twayne, 1982.

Powers, Thomas. *The War at Home: Vietnam and the American People, 1964-1968.* New York: Grossman, 1973.

Price, Jerome B. *The Antinuclear Movement.* Boston: Twayne, 1982.

Raboy, Marc. *Movements and Messages: Media and Radical Politics in Quebec.* Trans. by David Homel. Bridgewater, NJ: Baker and Taylor, 1984.

Reid, Loren, ed. *American Public Address: Studies in Honor of Albert Craig Baird.* Columbia, MO: University of Missouri Press, 1961.

Roberts, Ron E. and Robert M. Kloss. *Social Movements: Between the Balcony and the Barricade.* St. Louis: C.V. Mosby, 1974.

Rush, Gary B. and R. Serge Denisoff. *Social and Political Movements.* New York: Appleton-Century-Crofts, 1971.

Sale, Kirkparteick. *SDS.* New York: Vintage, 1974.

Schandler, Herbert. *The Unmaking of the President: Lyndon Johnson and Vietnam*. Princeton: Princeton University Press, 1977.

Schmid, Alex and Janny de Graaf. *Violence as Communication: Insurgent Terrorism and the Western News Media*. Beverly Hills: Sage, 1982.

Scott, Robert L. and Wayne E. Brockriede. *The Rhetoric of Black Power*. New York: Harper and Row, 1969.

Shelling, Thomas G. *The Strategy of Conflict*. Cambridge: Harvard University Press, 1960.

Shupe, Anson D. and David G. Bromley. *The New Vigilantes: Deprogrammers, Anti-Cultists, and the New Religions*. Beverly Hills, CA: Sage, 1980.

Skolnick, Jerome H. *The Politics of Protest*. New York: Ballantine, 1969.

Smelser, Neil J. *Theory of Collective Behavior*. New York: Free Press of Glencoe, 1963.

Smith, Arthur L. *Rhetoric of Black Revolution*. Boston: Allyn and Bacon, 1969.

_____. *Language, Communication, and Rhetoric in Black America*. New York: Harper and Row, 1972.

Stohl, Michael, ed. *The Politics of Terrorism*. New York: Dekker, 1983.

Stohl, Michael and George Lopez, eds. *The State as Terrorist: The Dynamics of Governmental Violence and Repression*. Westport, CT: Greenwood, 1984.

Taylor, Michael and Charles Lomas. *The Rhetoric of the British Peace Movement*. New York: Random House, 1976.

Toch, Hans. *The Social Psychology of Social Movements*. New York: Bobbs-Merrill, 1965.

Tompkins, Phillip K. *Communication in Action*. Belmont, CA: Wadsworth, 1982.

Touraine, Alain. *The Voice and the Eye: An Analysis of Social Movements*, trans. Alan Duff. Cambridge: Cambridge University Press, 1981.

Turner, Kathleen J. *Lyndon Johnson's Dual War: Vietnam and the Press*. Chicago: University of Chicago Press, 1985.

Turner, Ralph and Lewis M. Killian. *Collective Behavior*. Englewood Cliffs, NJ: Prentice-Hall, 1957.

Turner, Victor. *The Ritual Process*. Chicago: Aldine, 1969.

_____. *Dramas, Fields, and Metaphors*. Ithaca, NY: Cornell University Press, 1974.

Unger, Irwin. *The Movement: A History of the American New Left, 1959-1972*. New York: Dodd, Mead, 1975.

Viorst, Milton. *Fire in the Streets: America in the 1960s*. New York: Simon and Schuster, 1979.

Walker, Daniel. *Rights in Conflict: The Walker Report to the National Commission on the Causes and Prevention of Violence*. New York: Bantam, 1968.

Waller, Douglas. *Congress and Nuclear Freeze: An Inside Look at the Politics of a Mass Movement*. Amherst, MA: University of Massachusetts Press, 1987.

Wardlaw, Grant. *Political Terrorism*. Cambridge: Cambridge University Press, 1982.

Waskow, Arthur. *From Race Riot to Sit-in*. Garden City, NY: Doubleday, 1966.

Watters, Pat. *Down to Now: Reflections on the Southern Civil Rights Movement*. New York: Pantheon Books, 1971.

Westin, Alan. *Freedom Now*. New York: Basic Books, 1964.

Wilkinson, Paul. *Social Movements*. New York: Praeger, 1971.

_____. *Terrorism and the Liberal State*. London: Macmillan, 1977.

Wilson, John. *Introduction to Social Movements*. New York: Basic Books, 1973.

Vood, James L. and Maurice Jackson. *Social Movements: Development, Participation and Dynamics*. Belmont, CA: Wadsworth, 1982.

Vright, Sam. *Crowds and Riots: A Study in Social Organization*. Beverly Hills: Sage, 1978.

'oung, Richard, ed. *Roots of Rebellion*. New York: Harper and Row, 1970.

aretsky, Irving I. and Mark P. Leone, eds. *Religious Movements in Contemporary America*. Princeton, NJ: Princeton University Press, 1974.

Sources of the Persuasive Efforts of Social Movements

Albert, Judith and Stewart Albert. *The Sixties Papers: Documents of a Rebellious Decade*. New York: Praeger, 1984.

Baird, A. Craig. *American Public Addresses: 1740-1952*. New York: McGraw-Hill, 1956.

Bormann, Ernest G. *Forerunners of Black Power: The Rhetoric of Abolition*. Englewood Cliffs, NJ: Prentice-Hall, 1971.

Brandes, Paul D. *The Rhetoric of Revolt*. Englewood Cliffs, NJ: Prentice-Hall, 1971.

Brandt, Carl G. and Edward M. Shafter, Jr. *Selected American Speeches on Basic Issues: 1850-1950*. Boston: Houghton Mifflin, 1960.

Breitman, George. *Malcolm X Speaks*. New York: Grove, 1966.

Burns, W. Haywood. *The Voices of Negro Protest in America*. New York: Oxford Press, 1963.

Capp, Glenn R. *Famous Speeches in American History*. Indianapolis: Bobbs-Merrill, 1963.

Carawan, Guy and Candie Carawan. *We Shall Overcome*. New York: Oak, 1963.

Carmichael, Stokely and Charles V. Hamilton. *Black Power: The Politics of Liberation in America*. New York: Random House, 1967.

Cleaver, Eldridge. *Post-Prison Writings and Speeches*, ed. Robert Scheer. New York: Random House, 1969.

____. *Soul on Ice*. New York: Dell, 1968.

Copeland, Lewis and Lawrence Lamm. *The World's Great Speeches*. New York: Dover, 1958.

Fabrizio, Ray, Edith Karas and Ruth Menmuir. *The Rhetoric of NO*. New York: Holt, Rinehart and Winston, 1970.

Foner, Philip S. *American Labor Songs of the Nineteenth Century*. Urbana, IL: University of Illinois Press, 1975.

Glazer, Tom. *Songs of Peace, Freedom and Protest*. Philadelphia: University of Pennsylvania Press, 1953.

Hill, Roy L. *The Rhetoric of Radical Revolt*. Denver, Bell Press, 1964.

Hille, Waldemar. *The People's Song Book*. New York: Sing Out, 1960.

Hoffman, Abbie. *Revolution for the Hell of It*. New York: Dial, 1968.

Holland, DeWitte T., ed. *Sermons in American History*. Nashville, TN: Abingdon Press, 1971.

Johnston, Kenneth R. *Rhetoric of Conflict*. New York: Bobbs-Merrill, 1969.

Linkugel, Wil A., R.R. Allen, and Richard L. Johannesen. *Contemporary Speeches*. Belmont, CA: Wadsworth, 1965, 1969, 1972.

Malcolm X. *The Autobiography of Malcolm X*. New York: Grove, 1966.

Matson, Floyd D. *Voices of Crisis: Vital Speeches on Contemporary Issues*. New York: Odyssey, 1967.

Oliver, Robert T. and Eugene E. White, eds. *Selected Speeches from American History.* Boston: Allyn and Bacon, 1966.

O.M. Collective. *The Organizer's Manual*. New York: Bantam, 1971.

Rinzer, Alan. *Manifesto: Addressed to the President of the United States from the Youth of America*. New York: Collier Books, 1970.

Rosen, David M. *Protest Songs in America*. Westlake Village, CA: Aware Press, 1972.

Salisbury, Harrison E. *The Eloquence of Protest: Voices of the 70s*. Boston: Houghton Mifflin, 1972.

Seeger, Pete. *American Favorite Ballads*. New York: Oak Publications, 1961.

Smith, Arthur and Stephen Robb. *The Voice of Black Rhetoric*. Boston: Allyn and Bacon, 1971.

Wrage, Ernest J. and Barnet Baskerville. *American Forum: Speeches on Historic Issues, 1788-1900.* New York: Harper and Row, 1960.

——. *Contemporary Forum: American Speeches on Twentieth-Century Issues*. New York: Harper and Row, 1962.

Index

Abernathy, Ralph, 45
Act
  in dramatistic pentad, 146, 147
Action
  called for, by slogans, 246-247
  called for, in songs, 225-226
  contrasted with motion, 138
  dramatism as a means for analyzing, 140
  importance of, 149
  mobilizing for, 129-131, 225-227
  prescribed by narrative, 194
  slogans as symbolic justification for, 235
  social movements created and sustained by, 140
  what, who, and how for, 127-129
  what, who, and how for, in slogans, 244-246
  what, who, and how for, in songs, 222-225
Adaptive behavior
  influence as, 106
Adaptive strategies, 114
Adjustment tactics, 92-93
  cooperation, 92
  incorporation, 92
  risks of, 92-93
  sacrificing personnel, 92
  symbolic, 92
Administrative rhetoric, 87
  principles of, 87
Advertising slogans, 238
Agencies
  used to counter social movements, 12
Agency
  in dramatistic pentad, 146, 148
Agent
  in dramatistic pentad, 146, 148
Agents
  used to counter social movements, 12
Agitational rhetoric, 258
Agitators, 24, 26, 29
Agnew, Spiro, 85
Alinsky, Saul, 111
Allen, Gary, 62
Ambiguities and contradictions
  closed mind intolerant of, 161
Ambiguity of language, 234
  allowing transformations of meanings, 259
American Federation of Labor (AFL), 26, 42, 43, 101, 128
American Indian Movement (A.I.M.), 5, 8
American Nazi Party, 123
American Opinion, 42, 160, 161, 170
American Orators, 111
American Railway Union, 102
The Anatomy of Swearing, 254
Anthony, Susan B., 40

Anti-slavery movement, 122
Anti-Vietnam War movement, 23, 45, 77, 85, 101, 123, 141-142, 268
  obscenity used by, 260
Arrest, 91
Assassination, 91
Assimilation effects, 55
Authoritarian character
  basis for judging people, 162-163
  contrasted with democratic character, 162-164
  intolerant of diversity, 162
  John Birch Society meeting psychological needs of, 164
  judgements of superiority made by, 162-163
  judging by externals, 162-163
  sado-masochistic tendency of, 163
  seeing life as threatening, 161-162
  submission to leader important to, 163, 168-169, 170
  superior-inferior relationships, 162, 163, 169
  world view of, 162, 164, 170
Authoritarianism
  characteristics of, 161-164
  leader-follower relationship in, 163
  protector-protected relationship, 162
  satisfaction impossible under, 164
  superiority and inferiority in, 163-164
  view of people, 163
Authority
  concepts of, 167
The Autobiography of Malcolm X, 47
Avoidance tactics, 88-90
  dealing with individuals rather than messages, 89-90
  denial of means, 89
  direct counter-persuasion, 88
  evasion, 89
  generation of fear, 89
  labelling and name-calling, 88-89, 125, 219
  postponement, 89
  ridicule, 89, 125, 219, 241
Back to Africa movement, 9
Bargaining
  attempted by social movements, 14-15
Barnett, Ross, 108
Belief-disbelief systems, 160-161
Beliefs
  about authority, 160, 161. *See also* Authoritarianism
  derived from authority, 160
Beneficiaries
  used to counter social movements, 12
Bio-physical metabolism, 105
Black
  adoption of, to replace negro, 126-127
Black panther party, 31, 91
"Black Power," 144
Black power concept, 127
  interpretations of, 234-235
  interpreted for different audiences, 144-145
  as a slogan, 243, 248
Black Power Movement, 123, 126
Black United Front, 44
Blasphemy
  See also Obscenity
  defined, 255
Blessitt, Arthur, 144
The Blue Book of the John Birch Society, 41, 164, 167, 168, 170
Brown, H. Rapp, 126, 263-264
Burkean analysis of social movements, 148-154
  nature of society in, 148-149
  social control in, 149-150
  social movements in, 150-153
  sociodramas in, 153
Burkean approach to social movement persuasion, 137-155
  analysis of social movements, 148-154
  dramatistic pentad in, 146-148
  identification a key concept in, 143-146
  key concepts in, 143-148
  philosophy of human communication, 137-139
  theory of dramatism, 139-143

The Call, 237-238
Campaigns
compared with social movements, 9
confused with social movements, 5, 6
Capitulation, 93
Carmichael, Stokely, 44, 127, 144-145, 247, 248
Carter, Jimmy, 198, 199, 200, 200-208
Charisma
characteristic of social movement leaders, 39-40
insufficient alone, 44
Charismatic leaders, 39-40
examples of, 40
maintaining unity within movement, 40
Christian Crusade, 123
The Christmas Carol, 194
Civil rights movement, 25, 38, 44, 45, 85, 102
Cleaver, Eldridge, 31-32, 261, 263, 266-267
Closed belief systems, 161
Closed mind
intolerant of ambiguities or contradictions, 161
John Birch Society illustrating, 160-161
Closed systems, 102-103
equilibrium in, 102
Coactive strategies, 74-76
to attain legitimacy, 74-76
attracting legitimizers, 75
conforming with rules, 75
emphasizing traditions, 75
essential for social movements seeking legitimacy, 76
limitations of, 76
strategy of transcendence, 75-76. *See also* Rhetoric of transcendence
Coercion
consequences of, 15
inseparable from persuasion, 15-16
threat of, 16
used by social movements, 14, 15-16
Coercive acts
Supreme Court ruling on, 15
as symbolic speech, 15
Coercive persuasion
attribution errors following, 73
justification for use of, 73
Coherence
importance of, for narrative, 195
Cohesiveness
enhanced by obscenity, 266-267
Communication
as a means of social control, 149
Burke's philosophy of human communication, 137-139
communication breakdown concept challenged, 104
essential to social order, 150
fallacy of linearity, 104
fallacy of mechanism, 104
fallacy of noncommunication, 104
fallacy of reification, 104
fallacy of success, 104
mechanical systems model of, 103-104, 116-117
recent failures of, 116
role in developing cohesion within groups, 100
social systems model of, 105-110, 116-117
Communication breakdown, 104
Communication channels
See also Media
limited access to, 130
use of, by social movements, 130-131
Communist Party, 31
Compromising
as a function of social movements, 120
Conflict
between rights, 180-181
conceptions of human conflict, 107-108, 116
followed by victimage, 140, 142
in group relationships, 21
as opportunity, 107-108, 116
over narratives, 195
relationship with obscenity, 254

Confrontation, 256-257
  value of, 175
Confrontational rhetoric
  obscenity as, 256-257
Confrontational strategies, 74, 76-78
  attacking institutional powers, 78
  to attain legitimacy, 76-78
  byproducts of, 77
  drawbacks of, 78
  militant, 77
  nonviolent, 77
  provoking overreaction, 77
Congress of Industrial Organizations (CIO), 30, 101
Congress of Racial Equality (CORE), 38
Consciousness-raising, 100, 127
Conservatism
  in Rossiter's political spectrum, 54, 56
Conservatism in America, 54
Content adaptation
  for identification, 145
Contrast effects, 55
Control power, 73
Cooperation with protestors, 92
Counter-culture movement, 256
Counter-persuasion, 88
Covert harassment, 90
Crane, Philip, 199, 200-208
Cranston, Alan, 200
Cursing
  See also Obscenity
  defined, 254

Debs, Eugene V., 39, 57-58, 85, 110, 123
Decision makers
  leaders as, 37-38
Declaration of Independence
  modified by First Womans' Rights Convention, 24
  modified by National Labor Union, 24
  seeds of independence predating, 23
Defining
  as a function of social movements, 120
Democracy
  and freedom of expression, 85-86
  problems inherent in, 86-87
  and resistance to social movements, 85-87
Democratic character
  contrasted with authoritarian character, 162-164
  judging on functional characteristics, 163
  judging people on basis of performance, 163
  seeing personal differences as horizontal, 162
  view of people, 163
  world view of, 162
Democratic National Convention riots, 261-262, 269
Denial of means, 89
Depiction, 151-152
  as a process, 151
  functions of, 151
Despair
  rhetoric of, 124
Devils
  attacked using obscenity, 261
  identifying, 24, 125
  portrayal of, 125-126
  in slogans, 240-241
  in songs, 217-218
Disciples of Christ Movement, 9
Division
  as counterpart of identification, 143-144
Dolan, Terry, 199
Domino theory, 124
Douglass, Frederick, 40, 145
Dramatism, Burke's theory of, 139-143
  as a communication theory of human behavior, 143
  action at the heart of, 140
  elements of, 146
  Kent State demonstrations illustrative of, 141-143
Dramatistic pentad, 146-148
  act in, 146, 147
  agency in, 146, 148
  agents in, 146, 148
  applied to social movements, 147
  applied to society, 147

applied to specific events, 147
and discussion of human motivation, 147-148
purpose in, 146, 148
ratios between elements considered, 147-148
scene in, 146, 147-148

Edwards, Mickey, 199
Ego-involvement, 55
and distortion of comparative judgements, 55
Elliott, Roland, 197
Ely, Ezra Styles, 13
Enthusiastic mobilization stage of social movements, 25-28
creation of counter movements, 26
dealing with competition, 27
effects of confronting opposition, 26
expanding ideology, 27
gradualism becoming a problem, 28
persistent crises for leaders, 26-27
prompting efforts to counter, 26
united front essential for survival, 27
violent acts risking loss of support, 27
we-they distinctions emphasized, 27-28
Entropy, 102
Established institutions
accused of ignoring problems, 36
control power of, 73
faith in, 35-36
identification power of, 73
ignoring symbolic acts, 30
goaded by obscenity, 261-262
moral suasion power of, 74
power a weapon of, 72-74, 84
relationship with social movements, 130-131, 279
reward power of, 73, 84
terministic control power of, 73-74
using pejorative labels for social movements, 36
Euphemistic swearing
See also Obscenity
defined, 255
Evasion, 89
Events
dramatistic pentad applied to, 147
Expert power, 84
Expulsion, 91

Fantasy, 195-196, 206, 208
Fantasy-chaining, 195-196
Fantasy theme analysis, 195-196
Farber, Jerry, 260, 261
The Feminine Mystique, 23
Fidelity
importance of, for narrative, 195
First Woman's Rights Convention, 24
Fisher, George, 88
Flood, Daniel, 196
Ford, Gerald, 197, 198, 199
Ford, Henry, 59
Free speech
abuses of, 86
appropriate level of, 85-86
attempts to restrict, 85
challenges to restrictions, 85
reactions to, 86
Frustration
leading to disaffection, 25
Fulbright, J. William, 208
Function
structures developed to assure performance of, 101
Functional approach to social movement persuasion, 119-132
cautions for use of, 121-122
as a scheme for studying persuasion, 120-122
Functions
compromising, 120
defining, 120
in-gathering, 120
legitimizing, 120. *See also* Legitimacy
mobilizing for action, 129-131
persuasion as agency for, 119
prescribing courses of action, 127-129
pressuring, 120
satisfying, 120
sustaining the movement, 131-132

Labelling and name-calling, 88-89, 125, 219
Language
 adapting to audience, 144-145
 producing hierarchies, 152
 as symbols, 146
Laxalt, Paul, 199
Leaders. *See* Social movement leaders
Leadership in social movements
 See also Social movement leaders
 attainment of, 39-43
 maintenance of, 43-48
 nature of, 37-39
Legitimacy
 bases for conferring, 71
 and control power, 73
 and identification power, 73
 needed by social movements, 278
 notion of, 71-72
 and moral suasion power, 74
 powers conferred by, 72-74
 and power to reward, 73
 retaining, 71-72
 and terministic control power, 73-74
 through coactive strategies, 74-76
 through confrontational strategies, 74, 76-78
Legitimate authority
 emotional consequences of disobeying, 74
Legitimizing
 as a function of social movement leadership, 120
Lewis, John L., 39
Liberalism
 in Rossiter's political spectrum, 54, 56
"Liberty Amendment," 64-65
Life cycle of social movements, 21-33, 114-115
 enthusiastic mobilization stage, 25-28
 evolutionary shifts, 114-115
 genesis stage, 22-24
 maintenance stage, 28-30
 role of early leaders, 22-23
 role of triggering events, 23, 25, 30
 social unrest stage, 24-25
 termination stage, 30-32
Linearity
 fallacy of, 104

McCarthy, Eugene, 200
McDonald, Larry, 199
McFarlane, Robert, 198
McGovern, Eugene, 200
Maintenance stage, 28-30
 appeal of single issue goals, 30
 decline in membership and commitment, 29-30
 need for triggering events, 30
 visibility decreasing, 29-30
Malcolm X, 16, 47, 57, 61, 110
Manifesto, 24
 functions of, 24
The Marxist Minstrels: A Handbook on Communistic Subversion of Music, 213
Material resource base for power, 84
Mechanical systems
 compared with social systems, 103-105
 impact of conflict on, 107
 influence in, 106
Mechanical systems model of communication, 103-104, 116-117
 and human conflict, 108-109
 and human influence, 108
 and human relationships, 108-109
 implications of, 109
 weaknesses of, 106, 107, 108, 109
Mechanism
 fallacy of, 104
Media
 See also Communication channels
 as channels for persuasion, 141
 as sources and mediators of information, 141
 transformation of role of, 141
 used by social movements, 130-131
Meredith, James, 247
Metaphor
 obscenity as, 259
Moral suasion power, 74
Most, Johann, 66

Mobilizing for action, 129-131, 225-227, 246-250
Motion
contrasted with action, 138
Motive, 139
Motives in human communication, 152-153
Movement cohesiveness
enhanced by obscenity, 266-267
Music
See also Protest music
persuasive aspects of, 214
as persuasive message, 214

Name-calling, 88-89, 125
in songs, 219
Naming and renaming, 123
See also Terministic control power
Narrative
See also Stories
coherence as a basis for judging, 195
conflicting, 195
fidelity as a basis for judging, 195
future projected by, 194
good reasons as a basis for judging, 195
past structured by, 194
positioned by narrator's perspective, 194
prescribing action, 194
time experienced through, 193
reader-narrator identification central to, 194
values for judging, 195
Narrative coherence, 195
Narrative fidelity, 195
Narrative rationality, 195
applied to Panama Canal treaty narratives, 206-208
illustrated by conflicting narratives about Panama Canal treaties, 206-207
Narrative vision
See also Panama Canal treaty narratives
groups coalescing around, 208-209
and social movements, 209
National Association for the Advancement of Colored People
(NAACP), 26, 38
National Farmers Organization (NFO), 35
National Labor Union, 24
National Organization for Reform of Marijuana Laws (NORML), 5
National Organization for Women (NOW), 5, 10, 29
National Right to Life Committee, Inc., 178, 183, 185, 186
New Right movement
using Panama Canal Treaty issue, 199-200, 206, 208
Newton, Huey P., 236
Nixon, Richard M., 85, 142, 145, 196-197
Noncommunication
fallacy of, 104
Nonpartisan League, 23
Nonsummativity
characteristic of systems, 99-100

Obscenity
action prescribed by, 263-264
adverse effects of, 267-269
allowing control of media, 265
as a safety valve, 267
benefits of, 269
as confrontational rhetoric, 256-257
consequences of use of, 270
context essential to power of, 258
defined, 255
demonstrating user's "liberation," 263
describing the opposition, 261-262
development impossible from, 268
distracting effect of, 267
enhancing credibility of movement leaders, 266
enhancing self-concept, 262-263
expressing contempt for standards of society, 264
forcing established institutions to prepare to react, 265-266
gaining media attention, 264-265

as imagery, 259
implications carried by, 259
increase in use of, 253
as metaphor, 259
movement cohesiveness enhanced by, 266-267
persuasive functions of, 259-267
polarizing effect of, 261
producing violent responses, 262, 268-269
provoking confrontation, 265
reasons for use of, 269-270
reflecting frustration and separateness, 257
relationship with conflict, 254
repugnance for, restricting use of, 268
as rhetoric, 255-256
rhetorical characteristics of, 257-259
short-lived attention gained by, 267-268
as symbolic aggression, 265
as symbolic violence, 254
transforming perceptions of history, 260
transforming perceptions of society, 260-261
used to goad established institutions, 261-262
use justified by Vietnam war protestors, 256
violating social norms, 259
O'Connell, Terry, 198
Odets, Clifford, 58
Openness of systems, 102-103
Open systems, 102-103
Opposition
pressuring, 129
in slogans, 240-242
in songs, 217-220
transforming perceptions of, 125-126
Oppression
perception of, 126
Organizational/syntactic base for power, 84
Overt harassment, 90-91
Panama Canal Treaties
becoming a political issue, 199-200
contrasting narrative visions about. *See* Panama Canal treaty narratives
controversy avoided under Ford, 197, 207
disagreements on sovereignty issue, 199, 201-202
lack of concern about, 198
narrative rationality of Crane and Carter's positions, 206-207
politics of renegotiation, 196-203
rationale withheld by Ford administration, 197-198
used by New Right movement, 199-200, 206
Panama Canal treaty narratives, 200-208
appropriateness of, 207
and audience beliefs, 206-207
audience involvement in, 206
conflicting futures envisioned by, 206
consequences of ratification presented by, 205-206
consistency of, 207
depictions of Panama in, 203, 204, 205
divergent histories presented by, 202-203
divergent values demonstrated by, 205
future in, 205-206
narrative rationality criteria applied to, 206-208
and Panamanian economic interest, 204
past in, 200-203
present in, 203-205
"promising" aspect of, 207
sovereignty issue in, 201-202, 204
views of Pan-American relations in, 203-204
Parks, Rosa, 25
Parsons, Albert, 66-67
Past
altering perceptions of, 123
in Panama Canal treaty narratives, 200-203
in slogans, 238-239
in songs, 216
structured by narratives, 194

Pawley, William Douglas, 197
Persuasion
  and bargaining, 15
  Burkean approach to, 137-155
  during enthusiastic mobilization stage, 27, 28
  essential to social movements, 13-16
  expectations of, 25
  functional approach to, 119-132. *See also* Functional approach to social movement persuasion
  functional scheme for studying, 120-122
  inseparable from coercion, 15-16
  interpreting events, 16
  during maintenance stage, 28-30
  narrative rationality important to, 195, 206-207
  slogans as tools of, 235-237
  social systems approach to, 99-117. *See also* Social systems; Systems theory
  and symbolic behavior, 139
  to transform perceptions of history, 122-125
Persuasion-coercion dichotomy, 15
Phillips, Howard, 199
Postponement, 89
Powderly, Terence, 46-47
Power, 7
  as a weapon of establishments, 84
  bases of, 84
  conferred by legitimacy, 72-74
  controlled by establishment, 83-84
  expert, 84
  held by established institutions, 7, 72-74
  referent, 84
Power of control, 73
Power of identification, 73
Power of moral suasion, 74
Power of terministic control, 73-74
Power to reward, 73, 84
Pragmatism
  needed by social movement leaders, 42-43
Present
  altering perceptions of, 123
  in Panama Canal treaty narratives, 203-205
  in slogans, 239-240
  in songs, 216
Pressuring
  as a function of social movement leadership, 120
Procedures, powers and financial support
  as advantages of institutionalized groups, 6-7
Pro-choice groups, 178
  attitude to pro-life supporters, 178-179
  charges made against pro-life position, 179
Profanity
  See also Obscenity
  defined, 254
Progressive argument, 60-61
  offering systematic approach, 60
  referring to insurgent threat, 61
Pro-life movement, 123
  challenges to leadership of, 185
  and church and state argument, 183-185
  comparing abortion to war, 182-183
  expanding ideology, 183
  explaining and defending position, 181-187
  fetus as a human argument basic to, 179-180
  implying transcendence, 188
  justifications for violence based on transcendence, 186
  militancy defended by, 185-187
  non-religious support for, 183
  not seen as a threat, 10-11
  position criticized by pro-choice groups, 178-179
  reaction to single issue charge, 182-183
  relying on rhetoric of transcendence, 187-189
  terministic control used by, 188
  transcending Roman Catholic church, 184-185
  value of rhetoric of transcendence to, 188-189
Prophecy

used by social movement leaders, 41-42
"Prophets," 22-23
becoming agitators, 24
source of legitimacy for, 41
Protector-protected relationship, 162
Protest music, 213-214
characteristics of, 214
exaggerated danger of, 214
Protest songs
as in-group activities, 226-227
Psycho-social base for power, 84
Purpose
in dramatistic pentad, 146, 148

Quality
transcendence based on, 176, 186
Quantity
transcendence based on, 176, 183, 184-185

Radicalism
in Rossiter's political spectrum, 54, 56
Reaction
in Rossiter's political spectrum, 54, 56
Reagan, Ronald, 62, 167, 198
Reality
constant redefinition of, 138-139
defined by Burke, 140
The Rebel Worker, 238
Recollections, 194-195
Redemption
following victimage, 153
Referent power, 84
Reification
fallacy of, 104
Relational patterns, 113-114
importance of, 114
Relationships in groups
communication stages in, 21
interaction stages in, 21-22
Relative deprivation, 112-113
"The Report of the Committee on the Advancement and Refinement of Rhetorical Criticism," 223
The Republic, 213
Resistance social movements, 9, 22
view of history, 124
Resistance to social movements, 83-93
administrative rhetoric, 87
and democracy, 85-87
establishments and social order, 83-85
strategy of adjustment, 92-93
strategy of avoidance, 88-90
strategy of capitulation, 93
strategy of suppression, 90-91
Restorative argument, 64-65
immoderate nature of, 65
Restrictive legislation and policies, 91
Retentions, 194-195
Retentive argument, 61-63
ominous tone of, 62
presenting unattractive picture of adversaries, 62-63
Reversive argument, 63-64
immoderate nature of, 64
reasons for failure, 64
seeing danger in current direction of society, 63-64
Revivalistic social movements, 9, 22
view of history, 124
Revolutionary argument, 65-67
advocates of, 66-67
confrontational nature of, 66
justifying violence, 65, 66
Revolutionary reaction
in Rossiter's political spectrum, 54, 56
Revolutionary radicalism
in Rossiter's political spectrum, 54, 56
Reward power, 73, 84
Rhatican, William, 199
Rhetoric
defined, 255
Rhetorical events
to maintain visibility, 132
Rhetorical requirements for movement leadership, 120
"The Rhetorical Situation," 113
Rhetorical vision, 196
connection with narrative vision, 196
Rhetoric of despair, 124

"The Rhetoric of Historical Movements," 119
Rhetoric of hope, 123-124
A Rhetoric of Motives, 143
"The Rhetoric of Social-Institutional Change: Black Action at Michigan," 120
Rhetoric of transcendence, 175-189
  transcendence based on hierarchy, 176-177, 180-181, 186
  transcendence based on quality, 176, 186
  transcendence based on quantity, 176, 183, 184-185
  transcendence based on value, 176, 180-181, 182, 187
Riddle, Sam, 32
Ridicule, 89, 125
  in slogans, 241
  in songs, 219
Rights
  conflict between, 180-181
Right to Life movement, 63
Rockefeller, Nelson, 64
Roe V. Wade decision, 177-178
Rossiter's political spectrum, 54-56
  conservatism in, 54, 56
  liberalism in, 54, 56
  radicalism in, 54, 56
  reaction in, 54, 56
  revised, 55-56
  revolutionary radicalism in, 54, 56
  revolutionary reaction in, 54, 56
  rhetorical implications of, 54-55
  shortcomings of, 55
  standpattism in, 54, 56
Rubin, Jerry, 45-46
Rules for Radicals, 77, 267
Rusher, William, 63

Sacrificing personnel, 92
Sado-masochism
  of authoritarian character, 163
  of John Birch Society, 167-169
Sanctioned slogans, 237-238
Satisfying
  as a function of social movement leadership, 120
Satrom, LeRoy, 142
Satyagraha, 41
Scapegoats, 153
Scene
  in dramatistic pentad, 146, 147-148
Scheidler, Joseph, 179
Schlafly, Phyllis, 11, 89
Scott, Bill, 199
Self
  transforming perceptions of, 126-127
Self-concept
  enhanced by obscenity, 262-263
  in slogans, 242-244
  in songs, 220-222
Separation of church and state, 188
  and pro-life movement, 183-185
Shuttlesworth, Fred, 45
"The Silent Scream," 123, 179
The Silent Spring, 23
Single issue goals, 30
Slavery
  perceptions of, 122
Slogans, 24
  action called for by, 246-247
  action prescribed by, 244-246
  advertising, 238
  appealing beyond the movement, 247-248
  appeals to power and strength in, 243
  attempting to activate audiences, 244
  attributes enhancing persuasiveness of, 236
  audiences for, 247, 249
  "blindering" effect of, 236
  definitions of, 234
  devil appeals unusual in, 240-241
  early use of, 234
  future presented in, 240
  ideal for advertising, 236
  identifiable with specific movements, 236
  interpretations of, 234-235
  issues simplified by, 245

language usually mild, 241-242
memorable and inimitable, 236
movement sustained by, 250
nature of, 233-235
opposition in, 240-242
opposition pressured by, 248-249
past not dwelt on, 238-239
persuasive functions of, 238-251
persuasive nature of, 237
present portrayed in, 239-240
redefining reality, 240
ridicule rare in, 241
sanctioned, 237-238
self in, 242-244
as social symbols, 234, 250
specific targets for, 242
spontaneous, 237
as symbolic justification, 235, 250
as tools of persuasion, 235-237
transforming perceptions of history, 238-240
transforming perceptions of society, 240-244
types of, 237-238
unifying power of, 144, 248
used to release emotions, 236

Small group development
phases in, 21

Social control, 149-150
communication as a means of, 149

Social movement leaders, 278
See also Leadership in social movements
ability to change important to, 45, 47
adaptability essential for, 45-47
agitators, 24, 26, 29
characteristics of, 37
charisma important for, 39-40
charisma insufficient for, 44
compromising as a function of, 120
contact with movement essential for, 47-48
conversion experiences of, 32
credibility enhanced by obscenity, 266
as decision makers, 37-38
defining as a function of, 120
difficulties faced by, 38
discrediting, 89
external persuasive crises faced by, 27
facing new challenges during termination stage, 31
functions of, 120
identified with movement by public, 39
impact of loss of, 28
incorrect assumptions about, 36-37
in-gathering as a function of, 120
internal persuasive crises faced by, 27-28
legitimizing as a function of, 120
named in slogans, 246
named in songs, 223-224
need for information about, 110-111
operating environment for, 37, 38
pragmatism needed by, 42-43
pressuring as a function of, 120
problems following transformation of movement, 31
problems with handling diverse roles, 44-45
prophecy used by, 41-42
"prophets," 22-23, 24
requiring a mix of attributes, 43-44
responding to movement changes, 45-46
rhetorical dilemmas of, 6
rhetorical requirements for, 120
rhetorical-social situation faced by, 37
satisfying as a function of, 120
seeking to suffer for the cause, 26
as symbols, 38-39
unable to satisfy members, 28
visibility of, 5

Social movement members
altering self-perceptions of, 126-127
need for information about, 111
perceptions of environment, 112-113
self-images of, 111-112

Social movement organizations
confused with social movements, 5-6

Social movement persuasion, 280
See also Persuasion

Social movements. *See also* Analysis of social movements; Social systems
action creating and sustaining, 140
adaptive strategies used by, 114
adjustment as a response to, 92-93
administrative rhetoric in response to, 87
adopted into system, 31
agencies used to counter, 12
agents used to counter, 12
altering self-perceptions of supporters, 126-127
attacking opposition, 125-126
avoidance tactics in response to, 88-90
bargaining attempted by, 14-15
beneficiaries used to counter, 12
Burkean analysis of, 148-154
capitulation as a response to, 93
and change, 9-11
coercion used by, 14, 15-16
collective action definitions of, 4
compared with campaigns, 9
compared with institutionalized groups, 6-8
confrontational form identifying, 255
confused with campaigns, 5, 6
confused with social movement organizations, 5-6
constraints placed on, 121
crushed by system, 31
distribution of slogans among, 239
distribution of songs among, 215
dramatistic pentad applied to, 147
efforts to counter, 26
efforts to type, 9-11
environments for, 112-113
established order opposing, 12-13
frustrated by cooperation, 92
frustration energizing, 277-278
gaining sympathy of legitimizers, 130-131
growth speeded by presence of other movements, 23
impact of loss of leader on, 28
importance of relational patterns when studying, 113-114
incorporation of members into establishment, 92
innovative, 9, 10-11, 13, 124
interpreting and using events, 16
involvement in increasing tolerance, 144
justifying setbacks, 131
labels and definitions for, 3-4
lacking procedures, powers and financial support, 6-7
large scope necessary to, 8-9
legitimacy needed by, 278
legitimacy of not recognized, 71
life cycle of. *See* Life cycle of social movements
losing public support, 27
maintaining viability, 131
maintaining visibility, 132
minimal organization essential to, 5-6
mobilizing for action, 129-131, 225-227, 246-250
moral arguments needed by, 278
moral tone of rhetoric characteristic of, 11
and narrative vision, 209
nature of ideologies, 10
nature of resistance to, 83-93. *See also* Resistance to social movements
new movements overshadowing old, 26
not connected with established order, 6-8
organization in, 5-6
organizing and uniting the discontented, 129
perceived as illegitimate, 7
perceived as radical or moderate, 10
persuasion essential to, 13-16
persuasion permeating, 13-16
phases in growth of, 150
polarization within, 27-28, 29
prescribing action, 127-129
pressuring opposition, 129
as a process of transformation, 150
reaction to opposition, 26
reasons for joining, 10
redefined, 277-278
reform or revolutionary, 9-10

relationship with established institutions, 130-131, 279
resistance, 9, 22, 124
revivalistic, 9, 22, 124
rhetorical definitions of, 4
rhetorical situation of, 72-74
social psychological definitions of, 4
strategies and arguments used by, 10. *See also* Typology of political argument
suppression as a response to, 90-91
sustaining, 131-132
tactics available to, 129
triggering events for growth of, 22, 23, 25, 30
typology of, 278-279
value of confrontation to, 175
valuistic or normative, 9
Social order
communication essential to, 150
hierarchy an expression of, 84, 149
legitimized through symbols, 150
Social symbols
slogans as, 234, 250
Social systems
compared with mechanical systems, 103-105
and criticism, 110-115
influence in, 106-107
maturation of, 108-109
reacting to conflict as opportunity, 107-108, 116
response to conflict, 108, 116
Social systems approach to social movements persuasion, 99-117. *See also* Social systems; Systems theory
Social systems model of communication, 105-110, 116-117
human conflict in, 107-108, 116
human influence in, 106-107
human relationships in, 108-109
value of, 110
Social unrest stage of social movements, 24-25
development of ideology, 24
framing of manifesto, 24
we-they distinctions emphasized in, 25
Society
dramatistic pentad applied to, 147
importance of social interaction, 148-149
nature of, 148-149
psychological approach to, 148
sociological approach to, 148
transforming perceptions of, 125-127, 217-222, 240-244
Society for Cutting Up Men (SCUM), 29
Sociodramas, 153
Songs, 23
action prescribed by, 222-227
advocating change, 225
advocating violence, 224-225
appealing beyond the movement, 226-227
appeals to self-concept in, 220-221
calls to action in, 225-226
conspiracy appeals rare in, 218-219
dealing with self, 220-222
demands in, 222, 223
devils identified in, 217, 218
expressing commitment to movement, 228
focusing on the present, 216
functions not performed by, 231
future portrayed positively by, 217
heroes or martyrs unusual in, 229
invective unusual in, 219
looking to the future, 217
opposition pictured in, 217-220
past portrayed as negative by, 216
persuasive functions of, 214
predicting victory, 227, 228-229
present portrayed as negative in, 216
referring to the past, 216
ridicule unusual in, 219
satire and parody rare in, 219-220
social movements addressed by, 215
solutions rare in, 222-223
sustaining movements, 228-229
threats in, 227

transforming perceptions of history, 216-217
transforming perceptions of society, 217-222
variations in persuasive content of, 230-231
"we-they" distinctions lacking in, 222
outhern Christian Leadership Conference (SCLC), 26, 38
overeign, James R., 47
pontaneous slogans, 237
tandpattism
in Rossiter's political spectrum, 54, 56
tories
See also Narrative
groups coalescing around, 194
psychological functions of, 193
retentions and recollections, 194-195
social relationships organized around, 195
social relationships organized through, 194
trategic pictures, 151
trategy of transcendence, 75-76, 177
See also Rhetoric of transcendence
tructures
developed to insure performance of functions, 101
The Student as Nigger," 260
tudent Nonviolent Coordinating Committee (SNCC), 38
tudents for a Democratic Society, 10
uccess
fallacy of, 104
unday school movement, 13
uperiority
authoritarian judgements of, 162-163
democratic judgements of, 162, 163
generalized from external characteristics, 162-163, 166
rhetoric of transcendence stressing, 189
as seen by John Birch Society, 166-167
Suppression tactics, 90-91
advantages for establishment, 91
arrest, 91
covert harassment, 90
expulsion and assassination, 91
indirect and opportunistic, 91
overt harassment, 90-91
restrictive legislation and policies, 91
using counter-demonstrators, 90
Swearing
See also Obscenity
culturally learned behavior, 253
defined, 254
definitions and forms of, 254-255
euphemistic, 255
research on, 254
used by nonliterate peoples, 253
Swinton, John, 57
Symbolic acts, 27
choice of, 129
events at Kent State as, 141-143
ignored by institutions, 30
perceptions of, 16
Symbolic aggression
obscenity as, 265
Symbolic behavior, 138-139
extending leader's influence, 40
persuasive nature of, 139
Symbolic bridgecrossing, 234-235
Symbolic gestures of adjustment, 92
Symbolic speech
coercive acts as, 15
Symbolic violence
obscenity as, 254
Symbols, 132, 255-256
ambiguity of, 234, 259
to express identification, 145
language as, 146
leaders as, 38-39
transcending differences, 151
Symbol systems, 138-139
Systems theory
characteristics of systems, 99-103
and communication, 99-103
consequences of interdependence among

components, 99-101
evolution of systems, 101
explaining interdependent relationships, 101
hierarchical organization of systems, 101-102
principle of nonsummativity, 99-100
principle of openness, 102-103
role of structure, function, and evolution, 101

Taboo language, 258
See also Obscenity
Termination stage, 30-32
adaptation possible, 30-31
conversion experiences of leaders, 32
problems for leaders following change, 31
reasons for shrinkage and death, 31
Terministic control
used by pro-life movement, 188
Terministic control power, 73-74
See also Naming and renaming
Three Mile Island, 25
Time
experienced through narratives, 193
Torrijos, Omar, 203, 204
Transcendence. *See* Rhetoric of transcendence
Transformation
identification as an instrument of, 144-145
Triggering events, 23, 25, 30
The True Believer, 36
Typology of political argument, 53-67
innovative argument, 58-60
insurgent argument, 57-58
progressive argument, 60-61
restorative argument, 64-65
retentive argument, 61-63
reversive argument, 63-64
revolutionary argument, 65-67
Rossiter's political spectrum, 54-56

The United States v. Husband, 202

Value
transcendence based on, 176, 180-18 182, 187
Values
and identification, 145
Verbal taboo, 258
See also Obscenity
Vernardos, Lane, 141
Viability
maintaining, 131
Victimage
and concept of purification, 153
followed by redemption, 153
following conflict, 140, 142
homicidal, 152-153
relieving guilt, 152-153
suicidal, 152
Viguerie, Richard, 199, 200
Violence
advocated in songs, 224-225
condoned by insurgent argument, 57-5
innovative argument averse to, 59
justified by revolutionary argument, 6 66
justifications based on transcendence 186
obscenity as, 254
Visibility
maintaining, 132
Visual symbols
to express identification, 145
Vulgarity
defined, 255

Wallace, George C., 36
Wassaji, 238
Weathermen, 10, 31
Welch, Robert H. W., 41-42, 65, 110, 124 159, 164, 165, 166, 167, 168, 169
"We-they" distinction, 24, 25, 27-28, 12
lacking in songs, 222
need to create, 125
within movements, 128
Weyrich, Paul, 199
Wilkins, Roy, 45
Wilson v. Shaw, 202

Women's Christian Temperance Union (WCTU), 47-48
Women's International Terrorist Conspiracy from Hell (WITCH), 10, 29
Women's liberation movement, 23, 29, 40, 88-89, 122, 126, 127
World as jungle
  for authoritarian character, 161-162
  for John Birch Society, 164-165

Young, Andrew, 45